The Music Producer's U Guide to FL Studio 21

Second Edition

From beginner to pro: compose, mix, and master music

Joshua Au-Yeung

<packt>

BIRMINGHAM—MUMBAI

The Music Producer's Ultimate Guide to FL Studio 21
Second Edition

Copyright © 2023 Packt Publishing

All rights reserved. No part of this book may be reproduced, stored in a retrieval system, or transmitted in any form or by any means, without the prior written permission of the publisher, except in the case of brief quotations embedded in critical articles or reviews.

Every effort has been made in the preparation of this book to ensure the accuracy of the information presented. However, the information contained in this book is sold without warranty, either express or implied. Neither the author, nor Packt Publishing or its dealers and distributors, will be held liable for any damages caused or alleged to have been caused directly or indirectly by this book.

Packt Publishing has endeavored to provide trademark information about all of the companies and products mentioned in this book by the appropriate use of capitals. However, Packt Publishing cannot guarantee the accuracy of this information.

Senior Publishing Product Manager: Manish Nainani

Acquisition Editor – Peer Reviews: Tejas Mhasvekar

Project Editor: Amisha Vathare

Content Development Editor: Matthew Davies

Copy Editor: Safis Editing

Technical Editor: Karan Sonawane

Proofreader: Safis Editing

Indexer: Pratik Shirodkar

Presentation Designer: Ganesh Bhadwalkar

Developer Relations Marketing Executive: Sohini Ghosh

First published: February 2021
Second edition: June 2023

Production reference: 1200623

Published by Packt Publishing Ltd.
Livery Place
35 Livery Street
Birmingham
B3 2PB, UK.

ISBN 978-1-83763-165-0

www.packt.com

To my parents – my mother for her devotion, love, and care, and my father for his boundless curiosity, support, and determination.

To my friends – Sasha, for her encouragement, dedication, and kindness. To Jagdeep, Ryan, Pavel, and Tomo for making me laugh.

Contributors

About the author

Joshua Au-Yeung (professionally known as Chester Sky) is a music producer, composer, director, and software developer. He's published eleven music albums, directed and composed for short films, created board games, and hosted two podcasts. He's an instructor for several online courses, including bestselling courses on music production and composing for films and creating art using artificial intelligence. Joshua has also written two other books with Packt Publishing, titled *The Music Producer's Ultimate Guide to FL Studio 20* and *Music for Film and Game Soundtracks with FL Studio*.

About the reviewers

Alad Joseph Solomon is a music producer with a unique background that helped shape his career. Coming from an area of India where music education opportunities are limited, he is a self-taught musician who has worked hard to hone his skills in music production.

Since completing an audio engineering course, he has worked on a variety of projects, including regional films, creating songs for various albums, and designing sounds for a range of applications. Alad is particularly passionate about developing plugins that can create unique and captivating soundscapes.

Through his work as a music producer, Alad has established a reputation for creating music that experiments with different sounds and genres, continually pushing the boundaries of what is possible in music production. He is excited to continue exploring new sounds and techniques, and to create music that inspires and moves others.

Gilde Flores is an award-winning and Grammy-nominated music producer and composer with over 25 years of experience as a professional in the entertainment industry. Flores contributes his music to countless TV shows, films, video games, advertisements, and trailer campaigns, including the scoring of an HBO Max series. Flores has also collaborated with legendary producer Timothy "Timbaland" Mosley on numerous projects.

In addition to his work as a producer and composer, Flores is also committed to giving back to the industry he loves. He currently serves on two committees for the Recording Academy, the Education Committee and the Songwriters and Composers Committee, where he works to help support and advance the careers of fellow music professionals. He also serves as a mentor for the Recording Academy's "Grammy U" program, inspiring and guiding the next generation of music creators.

Table of Contents

Preface — xvii

Section I: Getting Up and Running with FL Studio

Chapter 1: Getting Started with FL Studio — 1

Technical requirements — 2
Exploring the music production landscape — 2
The musician's career path — 3
Steps of composing a song — 4
What is FL Studio? — 5
Exploring the FL Studio workspace — 7
Making your first song — 9
- Creating a drum beat with the channel rack • 9
- Adding an instrument to the channel rack • 11
- Creating a melody with the piano roll • 15
- Routing channels to the mixer • 17
- Exporting the song • 19
  - *Song exporting options • 23*

Summary — 24

Chapter 2: Exploring the Browser, Playlist, and Channel Rack — 25

Introducing the FL Studio workbench 26

Using the browser 30

    Locating a sample's file location • 34

    Searching in the browser • 36

    Getting the most out of your samples • 38

    Adding your own samples to the browser • 40

    Swapping samples • 42

Using the channel rack 42

    Channel rack options • 44

        Piano roll • 45

        Graph editor • 45

    The Rename, color and icon option • 47

    Instrument options • 50

    Detaching windows • 53

    Installing new instruments • 55

    Using channel rack layers • 57

Using the playlist 59

    The playlist toolbar • 61

    Element pattern options • 62

Using the main header toolbar features 63

    Version control • 64

    Revert to last backup • 64

    Audio Stream Input/Output (ASIO) • 65

    Purge unused audio clips • 66

    Undo and redo • 66

    Viewing project info • 66

Summary 68

Table of Contents ix

Chapter 3: Composing with the Piano Roll — 69

Using the piano roll 69

Choosing an instrument • 70

Adding notes in the piano roll • 72

Selecting multiple notes • 72

Deleting notes • 73

Muting and unmuting notes • 73

Slicing notes • 74

Sliding notes • 74

Using the stamp tool to get assistance with scales • 79

Composing great chord progressions 81

Recording into the piano roll with MIDI instruments 90

The snap-to-grid (magnet) tool • 91

Quantizing notes • 93

Editing note articulations with the event editor • 94

Using piano roll velocity • 95

Comparing instrument melodies with ghost notes • 96

Exporting sheet music 97

Using and exporting MIDI scores 98

Summary 99

Chapter 4: Routing to the Mixer and Applying Automation — 101

What is mixing? 102

Routing audio to the mixer 102

Navigating the mixer console 108

Understanding the insert mixer track • 110

Understanding the master channel • 111

Understanding the effects rack • 111

Applying an effect • 113

Applying automation 114

Editing automation clips 118
Applying automation to external third-party plugins 124
    Using MultiLink to controllers to add automation • 124
    Creating an editor thumbnail to add automation • 128
Freezing audio clips 132
Summary 139

Section II: Music Production Fundamentals

Chapter 5: Sound Design and Audio Envelopes   143

What is sound? 143
What causes a note's pitch? 145
How do we hear things? 146
How do instruments create sound with different pitches? 147
Why do different instruments playing the same pitch sound different? 151
Modifying sound envelopes 151
Using Mod X and Mod Y for automation 154
    What's the point of Mod X and Mod Y? • 160
Summary 161

Chapter 6: Compression, Sidechaining, Limiting, and Equalization   163

Understanding compression 164
    Applying compression with Fruity Limiter • 165
        Understanding parallel compression • 170
Applying gates and expanders 170
    When to use gating • 172
Applying sidechaining 172
Using limiters 179
Applying equalization 181
    EQ best practices • 184
    EQ general rules • 185

Table of Contents   xi

Summary 187

Chapter 7: Stereo Width (Panning, Reverb, Delay, Chorus, and Flangers) and Distortion   189

Panning audio 190
   Panning best practices • 192

Using reverb 192
   Applying digital reverb with Fruity Reeverb 2 • 193
   Applying convolution reverb with Fruity Convolver • 195

Using LuxeVerb 197

Using delay effects 202
   Applying delay effects with Fruity Delay 3 • 203
   Delay effect best practices • 205

Using chorus effects 206
   Using Fruity Chorus • 206
   Chorus effect best practices • 207

Using Vintage Chorus 207

Using flanger effects 210

Using phaser effects 212

Using Vintage Phaser 213

Understanding distortion effects 217
   Using Distructor • 217
   Distortion best practices • 225

Understanding mix buses 225
   Mix bus best practices • 228

Summary 229

Chapter 8: Recording Live Audio and Vocal Processing   231

Technical requirements 231

Understanding microphones 232
   Dynamic microphones • 232

Condenser microphones • 233

Ribbon microphones • 233

USB microphones • 233

Setting up your recording environment **234**

Recording instruments • 234

Recording drum kits • 235

Preparing to record vocals • 236

Using pop filters • 237

Recording audio into FL Studio **237**

Recording with Edison • 240

Loop recording with Edison • 242

Using pitch correction with Newtone **243**

Pitch correction best practices • 246

Retiming audio samples with Newtime **247**

Vocals effect processing best practices **254**

Backing vocals effects best practices • 256

Summary **256**

Chapter 9: Vocoders and Vocal Chops — 259

Understanding vocoders **259**

Understanding MIDI **260**

Using vocoders **261**

Harmonizing vocals with Pitcher • 261

Using Vocodex **269**

Vocoder best practices • 273

Creating vocal chops **274**

Using Slicex to create vocal chops • 275

Vocal chopping considerations • 285

Summary **285**

Table of Contents   xiii

Chapter 10: Creating Your Own Instruments and Effects   287

Understanding glitch effects 287

Creating glitch effects with Gross Beat 288

    Gross Beat presets • 292

    Mapping time and volume effects to a sample • 294

    Gross Beat sequencer • 296

Creating instruments with DirectWave 297

Creating effects with Patcher 301

    Creating custom dashboards in Patcher • 304

Send any instrument to Patcher 308

Exploring Patcher presets 310

Using VFX Sequencer 318

Summary 327

Chapter 11: Intermediate Mixing Topics and Sound Design Plugin Effects   329

Using Pitch Shifter 330

    Controlling Pitch Shifter effects with a controller • 333

Using Frequency Shifter 338

Creating granular synthesis with Fruity Granulizer 341

Creating delay effects with Multiband Delay 347

Multiband processing with Frequency Splitter 349

    Using Frequency Splitter for mastering • 353

Summary 355

Section III: Postproduction and Publishing Your Music

Chapter 12: Mastering Fundamentals   359

What is mastering? 359

    Can you master music yourself? • 360

    When should you master your music? • 360

How do I get good at mastering? • 360

What equipment do I use to master music? • 361

Equalization in mastering 361

Diagnosing frequency problems • 363

Understanding spectrograms • 363

Adjusting dynamics • 365

Using multiband compressors 366

Applying multiband compression with Maximus • 366

I've compressed my sound, now what? • 372

Using reference tracks • 373

What are saturators/harmonic exciters? 374

Understanding limiters 374

Understanding stereo imaging with vectorscopes 376

Stereo imaging best practices • 377

Listening to your audio in different environments • 378

Exporting audio for third-party mixing and mastering 380

Summary 382

Chapter 13: Marketing, Content Creation, Getting Fans, and Going Viral   383

Marketing essentials 383

Creating a brand 384

Choosing your artist name • 384

Creating a website • 385

Making the most of your live performances 385

Booking your first gigs • 386

Filming your shows • 387

Streaming performances online • 387

Collaborating with others to promote yourself 387

Getting more views on YouTube • 389

What about YouTube video titles and thumbnails? • 390

TikTok for musicians • 390

    Creating album artwork using AI art generators (Stable Diffusion) • 391

Creating music visuals with ZGameEditor Visualizer 394

Summary 401

Chapter 14: Publishing and Selling Music Online   403

Registering your music 403

Tagging your music in preparation for distribution 406

Selling music on online stores and streaming services 408

    Get signed to labels using LabelRadar • 408

    Selling music as an independent artist • 409

        DistroKid walk-through • 410

Claiming revenue from songs on YouTube using AdRev 413

    What are ISRC, ISWC, and UPC codes? • 415

Summary 416

Share your music 416

Conclusion 417

More from the author 417

Further reading 419

Other Books You May Enjoy   423

Index   427

Preface

FL Studio is a cutting-edge software music production environment. It's an extremely powerful and easy-to-use tool for creating music. This book will cover everything you need to know to produce music with FL Studio at a professional level.

You'll begin by exploring FL Studio's vast array of tools and discover best practices, tips, and tricks for creating music. You'll learn how to set up your studio environment, create a beat, compose a melody and chord progression, mix sounds with effects, and export songs. You'll learn how to use tools such as the piano roll, the mixer console, audio envelopes, types of compression, equalizers, vocoders, vocal chops, and tools for increasing stereo width.

The book introduces you to mixing best practices and how to mix and master your songs. Along the way, you'll explore glitch effects and create your own instruments and custom-designed effect chains and sound design. We'll also cover ZGameEditor Visualizer, a tool for creating reactive visuals for your songs. Finally, you'll learn how to register, sell, and promote your music.

By the end of this FL Studio book, you'll be able to utilize cutting-edge tools to fuel your creative ideas, mix and master music effectively, and publish your songs.

Who this book is for

This book is for musicians, music producers, composers, songwriters, DJs, and audio engineers interested in creating their own music, improving their music production skills, mixing and mastering music, and selling songs online. To get started with this book, all you need is a computer and FL Studio.

What's new in the second edition

In this second edition of the book I include topics on FL Studio's newly added plugins. I've added topics on Luxeverb, Vintage Chorus, Vintage Phaser, Distructor, Fruity Newtime, VFX Sequencer, Pitch Shifter, Frequency Shifter, Fruity Granulizer, Multiband Delay, and Frequency Splitter.

I have also updated existing topics to ensure you're using the latest and greatest FL Studio features.

How to use this book

This book is organized in a logical order assuming you know nothing at the start and gradually builds up skills and techniques as you progress. I've tried to compartmentalize topics so you can jump into any chapter and learn the topic without having to rely too much on other chapters. My goal is for this book to act as an easy-to-use reference guide regardless of whether you're new to music production or on your way to becoming a pro and just want to learn the ins and outs of a specific FL Studio feature.

What this book covers

Section I: Getting Up and Running with FL Studio

Chapter 1, Getting Started with FL Studio, introduces you to FL Studio. Here we'll discuss a brief history of music production, the musician career path, and overall process of song creation you'll discover throughout this book. You'll end the chapter by creating your first song and learning how to export music out of FL Studio.

Chapter 2, Exploring the Browser, Playlist, and Channel Rack, helps you learn about the main features in the browser, playlist, and channel rack. These, along with the piano roll and mixer, are the core tools of FL Studio.

Chapter 3, Composing with the Piano Roll, helps you understand how the piano roll adds melody notes, arranges them, adjusts the inflection of notes, and easily moves notes between instruments. You'll learn tips for creating excellent chord progressions from scratch. Once you know how to use the piano roll, you'll be able to compose melodies for any instrument.

Chapter 4, Routing to the Mixer and Applying Automation, gets you familiar with the process of how audio is passed around the mixer in order to apply effects to your music. We'll explore methods of automating effects and how to freeze audio.

Section II: Music Production Fundamentals

Chapter 5, Sound Design and Audio Envelopes, lays the foundation of how sound works. We'll learn what it is, how it's manipulated, and how instruments create sounds. We'll learn how to use Mod X and Mod Y as another method of applying automation.

Chapter 6, Compression, Sidechaining, Limiting, and Equalization, teaches you mixing techniques with compressors and equalizers. We'll explore the Fruity Limiter and Fruity Parametric EQ 2 plugins.

Preface | xix

Chapter 7, *Stereo Width (Panning, Reverb, Delay, Chorus, and Flangers) and Distortion*, explores tools to increase stereo width. We'll explore the Reeverb 2, Fruity Convolver, Luxeverb, Fruity Delay 3, Fruity Chorus, Vintage Chorus and Fruity Flanger, Fruity Phaser, Vintage Phaser, and Distructor plugins.

Chapter 8, *Recording Live Audio and Vocal Processing*, discusses the setup and preparation you need before recording. We'll learn how to record into FL Studio, how to mix your vocals, and best practices for applying effects to vocals. We'll explore microphones, record audio with Edison and pitch correct with the Newtone plugin. We'll learn how to retime audio samples with the Newtime plugin.

Chapter 9, *Vocoders and Vocal Chops*, teaches you about special effects that can be used on vocals. We'll discuss how to create vocal harmonies and how to use vocoders to modulate your vocals with an instrument. We'll explore the Pitcher, Vocodex, and Slicex plugins.

Chapter 10, *Creating Your Own Instruments and Effects*, teaches you how to create glitch effects with sounds, transform samples into playable instruments, and create custom instruments and effect chains that can be reused in any project. We'll explore the Gross Beat, DirectWave, and Patcher plugins. We'll learn how to use the advanced arpeggiator called VFX Sequencer inside Patcher.

Chapter 11, *Intermediate Mixing Topics and Sound Design Plugin Effects*, introduces you to FL Studio's sound design plugins. We'll explore Pitch Shifter, adjusting frequencies with Frequency Shifter, stretching audio waves with Fruity Granulizer, and delay effects with Multiband Delay. We'll learn multiband processing with Frequency splitter.

Section III: Postproduction and Publishing Your Music

Chapter 12, *Mastering Fundamentals*, helps you understand the mastering process. This will help your music get to production-level quality and be ready for distribution. We'll explore using the Maximus plugin to master your music.

Chapter 13, *Marketing, Content Creation, Getting Fans, and Going Viral*, will help you learn about developing your brand, marketing/promoting yourself, getting booked for music gigs, developing a show, suggestions for musicians using YouTube and TikTok, and tips for creating visuals for your music. We'll explore using the ZGameEditor Visualizer plugin to create reactive visuals.

Chapter 14, *Publishing and Selling Music Online*, helps you understand how you can release your music online to the world and collect royalty revenue.

Download the color images

We also provide a PDF file that has color images of the screenshots and diagrams used in this book. You can download it here: https://packt.link/zyMHh.

Conventions used

There are a number of text conventions used throughout this book.

`Code in text`: Indicates code words in text, database table names, folder names, filenames, file extensions, pathnames, dummy URLs, user input, and Twitter handles. Here is an example: "Mount the downloaded `WebStorm-10*.dmg` disk image file as another disk in your system."

Bold: Indicates a new term, an important word, or words that you see onscreen. For example, words in menus or dialog boxes appear in the text like this: "Select **System info** from the **Administration** panel."

> Tips and tricks appear like this.

> Warnings or important notes appear like this.

Get in touch

Feedback from our readers is always welcome.

General feedback: Email feedback@packtpub.com and mention the book's title in the subject of your message. If you have questions about any aspect of this book, please email us at questions@packtpub.com.

Errata: Although we have taken every care to ensure the accuracy of our content, mistakes do happen. If you have found a mistake in this book, we would be grateful if you reported this to us. Please visit http://www.packtpub.com/submit-errata, click **Submit Errata**, and fill in the form.

Piracy: If you come across any illegal copies of our works in any form on the internet, we would be grateful if you would provide us with the location address or website name. Please contact us at copyright@packtpub.com with a link to the material.

If you are interested in becoming an author: If there is a topic that you have expertise in and you are interested in either writing or contributing to a book, please visit http://authors.packtpub.com.

Share your thoughts

Once you've read *The Music Producer's Ultimate Guide to FL Studio 21, Second Edition*, we'd love to hear your thoughts! Scan the QR code below to go straight to the Amazon review page for this book and share your feedback.

https://packt.link/r/1837631654

Your review is important to us and the tech community and will help us make sure we're delivering excellent quality content.

Download a free PDF copy of this book

Thanks for purchasing this book!

Do you like to read on the go but are unable to carry your print books everywhere?

Is your eBook purchase not compatible with the device of your choice?

Don't worry, now with every Packt book you get a DRM-free PDF version of that book at no cost.

Read anywhere, any place, on any device. Search, copy, and paste code from your favorite technical books directly into your application.

The perks don't stop there, you can get exclusive access to discounts, newsletters, and great free content in your inbox daily

Follow these simple steps to get the benefits:

1. Scan the QR code or visit the link below

https://packt.link/free-ebook/9781837631650

2. Submit your proof of purchase
3. That's it! We'll send your free PDF and other benefits to your email directly

Section I

Getting Up and Running with FL Studio

In this section, we will get up and running with FL Studio. We will learn how to navigate the FL Studio workspace and learn core tools such as the piano roll and mixer console. We will learn essential skills for anyone working with music: composing melodies and routing tracks to the mixer.

We will cover the following chapters in this section:

- *Chapter 1, Getting Started with FL Studio*
- *Chapter 2, Exploring the Browser, Playlist, and Channel Rack*
- *Chapter 3, Composing with the Piano Roll*
- *Chapter 4, Routing to the Mixer and Applying Automation*

1

Getting Started with FL Studio

Think about your favorite songs. What makes you like them? Is it the melody, the chords, the catchy rhythm? Maybe a combination of a whole bunch of things that fit together perfectly. Perhaps you've tried making songs at home and realized there's a big difference between the sound you're making and the level of professionalism you hear from your favorite musicians.

In the pages ahead, you'll learn the ins and outs of music production and be well on your way to making music similar to your favorite songs. You'll learn about tools used for composing, mixing, mastering, and publishing your music. By the time you've finished reading this book, you'll have all the tools you need to create music at a professional level.

In this chapter, you'll be introduced to music production and FL Studio. Here, you'll create your first song and export it out of FL Studio.

This chapter comprises the following topics:

- Exploring the music production landscape
- A musician's career path
- Steps of composing a song
- What is FL Studio?
- Making your first song
- Exporting music from FL Studio

We'll start with a general overview of what FL Studio is and what it can do for you.

Technical requirements

In this chapter, we'll be using FL Studio. You can download a free trial version or a paid version of FL Studio from `https://www.image-line.com/`. So if you're hesitant about paying, you can download and try out all of FL Studio's features before buying. The difference is you won't be able to open saved projects until you obtain a paid version, but you can still try out all the plugins.

Exploring the music production landscape

Music production has changed significantly in the last two decades. Before, a musician required the assistance of a music producer. You'd go to a studio to meet with a series of technicians who'd play around with mixing equipment that cost as much as your car or house. Then, you'd sign a deal locking you into a music contract for the foreseeable future. The studio would control how your album got released and what royalties you got paid. You had very little negotiating power.

Digital Audio Workstations (known as **DAWs**) changed everything. Software came out that revolutionized the music playing field. It became possible to be a music producer in your bedroom using just your computer. Nowadays, most music producers create music on their own long before they venture into a recording studio (if they do at all).

Studios started to decrease their investment in developing artists from scratch. They preferred artists that already had success and popularity with fans before considering them. ITunes appeared, along with iPods and smartphones that could hold an entire music catalog in your pocket. Consumers wanted to get their music online instead of from physical stores so that they could download music directly onto their phones. Independent artists gained the ability to sell their music online on their own. Artists could now release their own music and collect their own royalties.

Music streaming platforms such as Spotify, Apple Music, Amazon Music, and YouTube became mainstream. Why buy individual songs when you can access all of them, all the time, anywhere you go? Consumers now have their own personalized playlist recommendations, filled with songs that suit their own personal taste. New artists can find their way onto a playlist by accident, subject to the whims of mystical algorithms behind the scenes.

All of this poses a powerful opportunity for the independent artist. You can promote yourself using tools equivalent to what record companies use. You can produce a song on your own, get your music into households around the world, and market your own brand. That's what this book is about. It's a handbook to show you the ins and outs of music production and jump-start your musical career. By the end of this book, you will know how to compose, record vocals, mix, master, market your music, and sell it online. This can all be done from home on a minimal budget.

The DAW we'll use in this book is FL Studio. FL Studio is a music software suite that contains all the tools you'll need to produce music. It's one of the, if not *the*, leading music production workstation software currently on the market and is used by professional musicians all around the world.

The musician's career path

Many of you reading this book will be looking for guidance on how to begin your music career. You've come to the right place. Whether you are a musician, DJ, composer, or music producer, this book will provide you with a how-to guide to making music.

Let's briefly look at your career path ahead. First, you'll spend some time getting familiar with your DAW. You'll come up with song ideas, record, and learn mixing techniques. You might invest in music plugins, synthesizers, hardware, and samples to play with.

At a certain point, you'll feel comfortable with your tools. It's here you'll realize that knowing how to use your tools is only one part of coming up with music. You need to develop a unique sound for yourself. To do this, you'll go out and listen to lots of music you like. You'll watch successful musicians and learn how to create similar sounds. You'll experiment with genres to find one or a combination that resonates with you. You'll begin to come up with ideas of your own that combine many influences.

You'll share your music with friends and colleagues. Likely, you'll want feedback from people who have some experience in the music business. You'll reach out to local musician groups in your community and attend their meetings. If you stay on course, this cycle of inventing and feedback will shift your music from amateurish to something that other people will enjoy listening to.

You'll get a few songs under your belt, and perhaps have an album ready to go. You'll post your music online and come to the realization that even though your music is amazing, you don't have many fans yet. How come? People don't know about you yet. You'll need to cultivate a brand identity that fans can relate to and get excited about. You'll need to spend time thinking about the type of brand persona that you want to be recognized for. You'll look into artwork and visuals. You might make them yourself or outsource the art creation to a third party. You'll spend time on social media and websites, researching what other musicians are doing, and trying out their marketing techniques yourself.

You'll have to figure out what kind of equipment you need to perform live. You'll also need to come up with something visually impressive to entertain audiences. This could include costumes or some sort of game or gimmick that can be repeated with different crowds.

You'll spend time thinking about banter and jokes that you can use to tie the gap between your songs while performing. Once again, you'll research what other musicians have done on stage and try out their techniques yourself. You'll discover that in order to have success getting booked at venues, it helps to have associated acts with you. You'll team up with other bands to create a whole packaged performance that you can present to a venue. Congratulations, you now have a show that you can take on the road! You're now a working musician. We've seen the big picture. It might seem like a lot now, but the good news is that most of the steps along the way are small and easy to do.

Steps of composing a song

Here's a roadmap that you can keep in the back of your mind as you journey through making your songs. Rest assured, it's easier than it sounds and is actually a lot of fun.

First, decide the **parameters** of the song. What mood, genre, and emotion do you want? Once your criteria are decided, come up with a melody and accompanying chords. Usually, the melody is experimented on with an instrument such as a keyboard or a guitar. You will likely go through a few iterations and drafts until you find a combination you like.

Now we have a melody and some accompanying chords. The melody notes are fed into a DAW as **MIDI notes**. From there, we select an **instrument plugin** to play the notes. This usually involves experimenting with different instrument plugins and possibly some sound design.

We add accompanying melodies and additional verses. We layer our instruments to thicken the sound. We add drums and percussion instruments to complement our melody. We add **sound effects**. This is a mix of single sound samples that could include percussion, rising and falling sounds, glitch effects, impacts, and drum fills.

If the song requires it, we record **vocals**. A vocalist is sought out and the song instrumental is sent to the singer to work on. Lyrics are written, and several vocal melody combinations are experimented with. The vocalist records the vocals. The singer and the music producer make adjustments to the song and go back and forth a few times, providing feedback to each other. The vocals are processed, usually separately from the instrumental at first, before adding the finished vocals back into the mix. Effects are applied to enhance the vocals.

We have our melodies, instruments, percussion, sound effects, and vocals. Now it's time to begin mixing. **Mixing** is a process you take to polish your music and give it a professional feel. It requires understanding how instruments and sounds complement each other in a song and knowing how effects can enhance them.

This part gets very technical. This book will give you lots of tips and tricks to help you with mixing.

Our song is exported and shared with all parties involved. We give feedback to and collect feedback from each other and make adjustments.

Now it's time for mastering. **Mastering** is what you do after you have a song that has been mixed. The goal is to make the song sound consistent regardless of what device you use to play the song. A song benefits from mastering in several aspects. It allows you to form a second opinion when listening to your song. It forces you to take a step back and re-evaluate your music from a distance from an audience's perspective. Instead of tweaking individual notes and instruments, you're now forced to think about how the song sounds as a whole package. What is the overall effect of the song on a listener? One way to think about mastering is that you're thinking from a sales perspective. What will make this song have the widest appeal to listeners? This book will give you mastering tips and techniques.

Congratulations, you have a production-ready song! You register your music with the necessary organizations for your territory to prove your copyright ownership and that any rights and royalties belong to you.

You create music videos and cover art to give your audience something to look at while listening. Often, a song's success is made or broken by the choice of visuals used.

You upload your music to an online distributor to sell your music on online stores and streaming platforms such as Spotify, Amazon, and so on. You upload your music videos to YouTube.

You leverage your social media and the existing fanbase you've curated ahead of time (hopefully). You self-promote your upcoming music release, tell everyone you know, and reach out to local outlets to play your music. Congratulations, you've published a song!

Composing a full song may seem like a lot of steps and quite technical, but rest assured, by the time you've finished this book, you'll have a solid grasp of how to execute each of these steps. Hopefully, after going through this process, you'll find it intuitive, fulfilling, and profitable.

So far, we've learned about music production from a high-level perspective. Now it's time to get our hands dirty and start making music with FL Studio.

What is FL Studio?

FL Studio is a music production software. It's a DAW consisting of tools, effects, and synthesizers designed to compose, mix, and master music.

It's a software application used to record, edit, and produce audio with a collection of software plugins that can handle all your audio production needs, whether you are a musician, a film/video game composer, or a music producer. It has been designed to be quick to pick up and provides enough features to satisfy sound designers. Once you get comfortable with the main workflow, you'll find it intuitive and easy to use. Most importantly, in my opinion, using FL Studio is fun and a delight to play with. I frequently find myself losing track of time while having fun with it.

You can download a free trial version of FL Studio, which allows you to try out all the features of the software; however, it won't let you reopen your saved projects until you purchase a paid version.

FL Studio comes with several paid, tiered versions with more features for the higher tiers. A user can upgrade from a cheaper tier to a higher tier to unlock more features at any time. If you are unsure of what version you need, you can start with the cheapest tier and upgrade later to a higher tier. There is a $10 additional charge for upgrading. Here are the different editions:

- The **Fruity Edition** is the cheapest. It includes all the basic features, such as access to the playlist, channel rack, and piano roll. It includes the **Autogun**, **BassDrum**, **BeepMap**, **Drumpad**, **FLEX**, **Fruity Kick**, **Fruity DX10**, **Groove Machine Synth**, **VFX Sequencer**, **Fruity Granulizer**, **Frequency Splitter**, **Distructor**, and **MiniSynth** plugins. It does not include audio recording.
- The **Producer Edition** includes all features in the Fruity Edition plus audio recording and post-production tools. It includes the **Edison**, **Slicex** (loop slicer and re-arranger), **Sytrus**, **Maximus**, **Vocodex**, **Frequency Shifter**, **Multiband Delay**, **Newtime**, and **SynthMaker** plugins. In this book, we include an introduction to the **Edison**, **Slicex**, **Maximus**, and **Vocodex** plugins.
- The **Signature Bundle** includes everything in the Producer Edition plus **Fruity Video Player**, the **DirectWave** sampler, **Harmless**, **NewTone**, **Pitcher**, **Gross Beat**, **Vintage Chorus**, **Vintage Phaser**, **Pitch Shifter**, and the **Hardcore** guitar effects suite. **Fruity Video Player** allows you to see videos in sync with your music, which is handy for film composers. In this book, we include an introduction to the **DirectWave**, **NewTone**, **Pitcher**, and **Gross Beat** plugins.

Chapter 1   7

- The **All Plugins Bundle** includes all possible plugins and features, including a large selection of synthesizers.

To see a full comparison chart of the features offered in the different tiers, visit https://www.image-line.com/fl-studio/compare-editions/.

Exploring the FL Studio workspace

FL Studio is a software work environment. It comes equipped with tons of tools to assist you with your music creation. In order to create a song, you need to understand the basic workflow. When you first open FL Studio, you will be greeted with a workspace similar to the following screenshot:

Figure 1.1 - FL Studio workspace

It's possible that you may see a slightly different landing screen depending on what version of FL Studio you are using. To ensure that we are all seeing the exact same workspace, open a new template using **Basic with limiter**, as shown in the following screenshot. The reason we're using this template is to create a nice simple introductory setup with a few drum samples preloaded into our project.

This will help you follow the simple examples in this chapter.

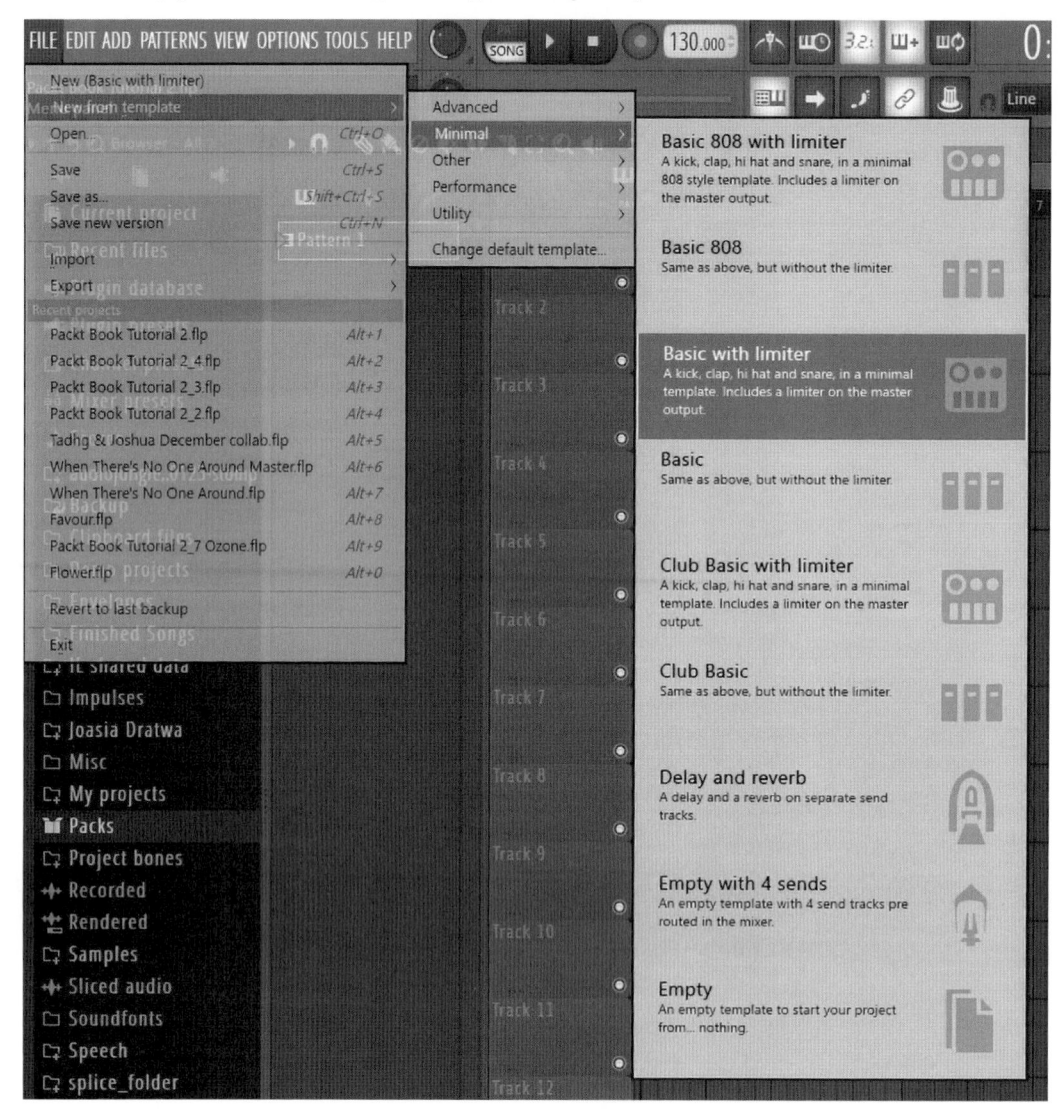

Figure 1.2 - Basic with limiter

You'll notice that there are lots of other templates to get you up and running quickly. I encourage you to explore the other available templates as well if you're curious. Each template offers an initial starting setup with preloaded plugins to save you some time. The template is just a suggestion to begin with though; you can always add the plugins yourself regardless of whether you use a template or not.

Chapter 1

The FL Studio workbench is divided up into five panel sections:

Figure 1.3 - Workbench

These panels can be opened or hidden by left-clicking the icons in the toolbar. The first five buttons on the toolbar open up the main sections of FL Studio. They can be opened or hidden by clicking on the tool symbol.

Here are the buttons in the order they appear from left to right:

- **Playlist**: Used to arrange your song compositions.
- **Piano roll**: Used to compose melodies. Here is where you will add and edit MIDI notes. We'll discuss this in detail in *Chapter 3, Composing with the Piano Roll*.
- **Channel rack**: Used to load your instruments and compose percussive rhythms.
- **Mixer**: Used to connect our instruments together and apply effects for mixing and mastering.
- **Browser**: Contains all your files. It's an organizer used to navigate through your samples.

The playlist, piano roll, channel rack, mixer, and browser are the foundational building blocks of FL Studio. Using these five tools, you'll be able to create, organize, and apply effects to your music.

Making your first song

FL Studio is a tool and the best way to learn it is to just jump in and make something with it. Some topics, such as composing melodies, are more complex and better left for later chapters. For now, let's work on something basic. To make our first song, we'll do the following:

1. Create a drum beat with the channel rack.
2. Add an accompanying instrument.
3. Route the drum beat and instrument to the mixer.
4. Export the song.

Let's get started.

Creating a drum beat with the channel rack

One of the key features of the channel rack is that it allows you to create percussive patterns with ease.

To create a drum pattern in the channel rack, you need drum sound samples and notes to indicate when to play the sound samples. To do this, perform the following steps:

1. Open the channel rack by selecting the channel rack icon:

Figure 1.4 - Toolbar, including the channel rack

2. Here, you'll see the following window. Since we used a template, we already have four sound samples preloaded into the channel rack for us:

Figure 1.5 - Channel rack opened

3. Extend the window by clicking the right edge of it to make it longer.
4. The channel rack allows you to view and load up all of your instruments and samples. Here, we can see that four instruments have been preloaded for us. In this case, they are single percussive sound samples.
5. Add notes by left-clicking on any of the gray and reddish buttons to the right of the instrument, so your channel rack looks like the following screenshot. If at any point you want to delete notes, you can right-click on the notes you want to remove:

Chapter 1 11

Figure 1.6 - Channel rack

6. Select **PAT** (short for **pattern**) and press play (the triangle symbol) or hit the *spacebar* so that you can listen to your drum beat:

Figure 1.7 - Player menu

So far, we have created a drum beat by adding notes for our percussion samples to play. In a real-life scenario, you'll want to swap out the samples used (for example, **Kick**, **Clap**, **Hat**, or **Snare**) with other samples. A drum beat on its own is pretty boring though, so let's look into adding an accompanying instrument.

Adding an instrument to the channel rack

We've created our first drum beat pattern. A drum beat isn't very interesting on its own. Music in general always needs a melody to give the song a sense of progression. To create a melody, we need an instrument that can play notes of different pitches. FL Studio has lots of instruments available. Let's add a simple bass guitar instrument to our composition:

1. To create a new pattern, left-click on the plus icon next to the words **Pattern 1** in the top toolbar:

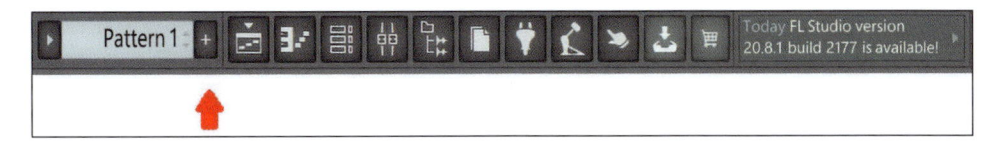

Figure 1.8 - New pattern

2. A **pattern** is the name that FL Studio uses to refer to a sequence of notes. Give it a name such as Bass melody and press *Enter*.

3. Back in the channel rack, hover your cursor over one of the instruments (**Kick, Clap, Hat,** or **Snare**) and right-click, or select the plus symbol at the bottom of the channel rack. A list of instruments will open up. Insert the one called **BooBass**. The reason we're using BooBass is just because it's simple. We don't want to overload you with features all at once.

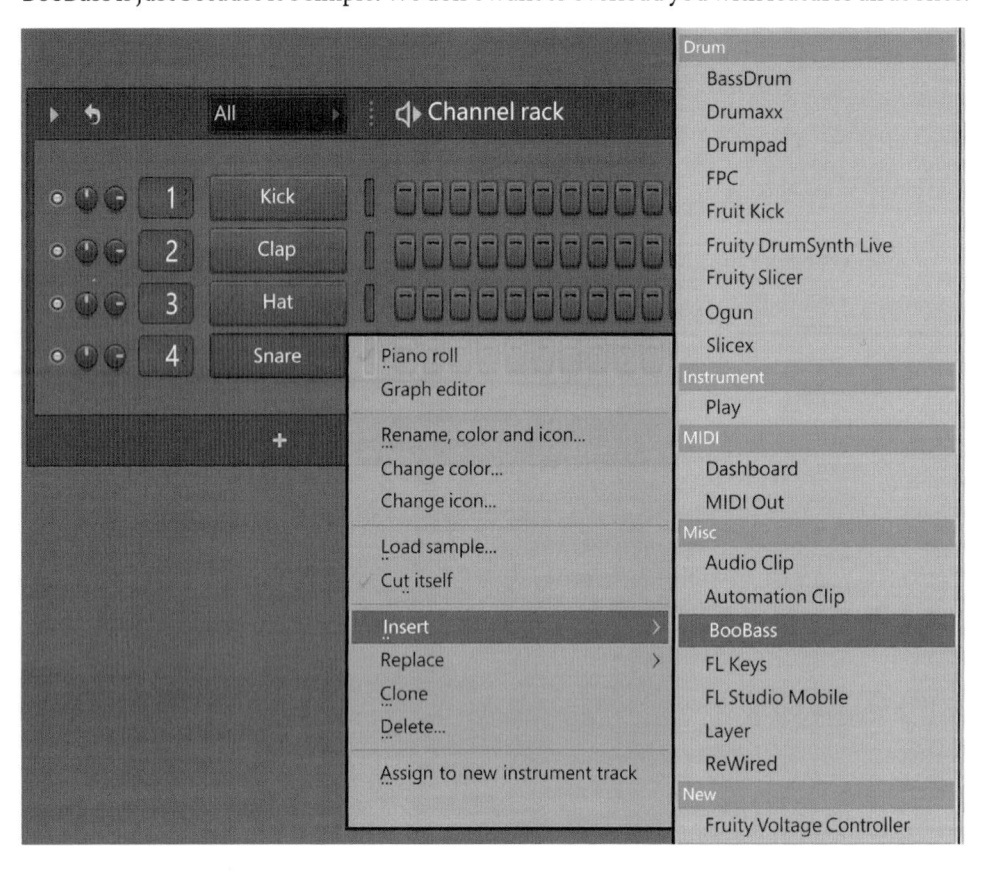

Figure 1.9 - Inserting an instrument

Chapter 1

4. The **BooBass** instrument will load up and you'll see the following:

Figure 1.10 - BooBass

5. Let's add some notes for our **BooBass** instrument to play. Right-click on **BooBass** and select **Piano roll**:

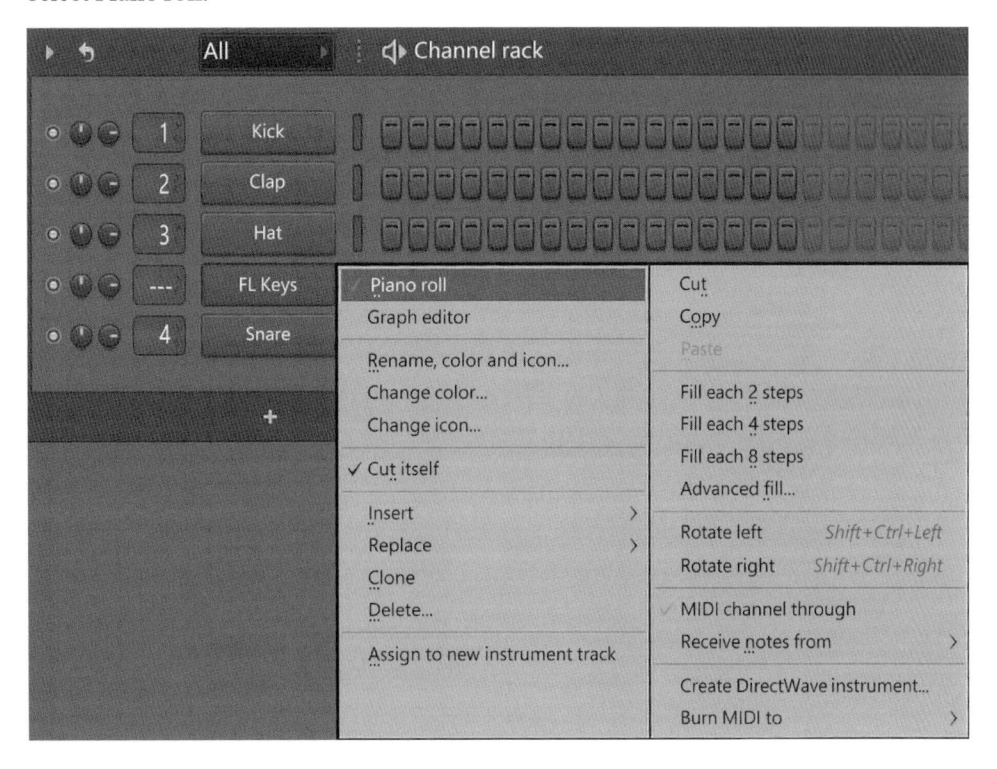

Figure 1.11 - Opening the piano roll

6. The piano roll will open, and you'll see the following window:

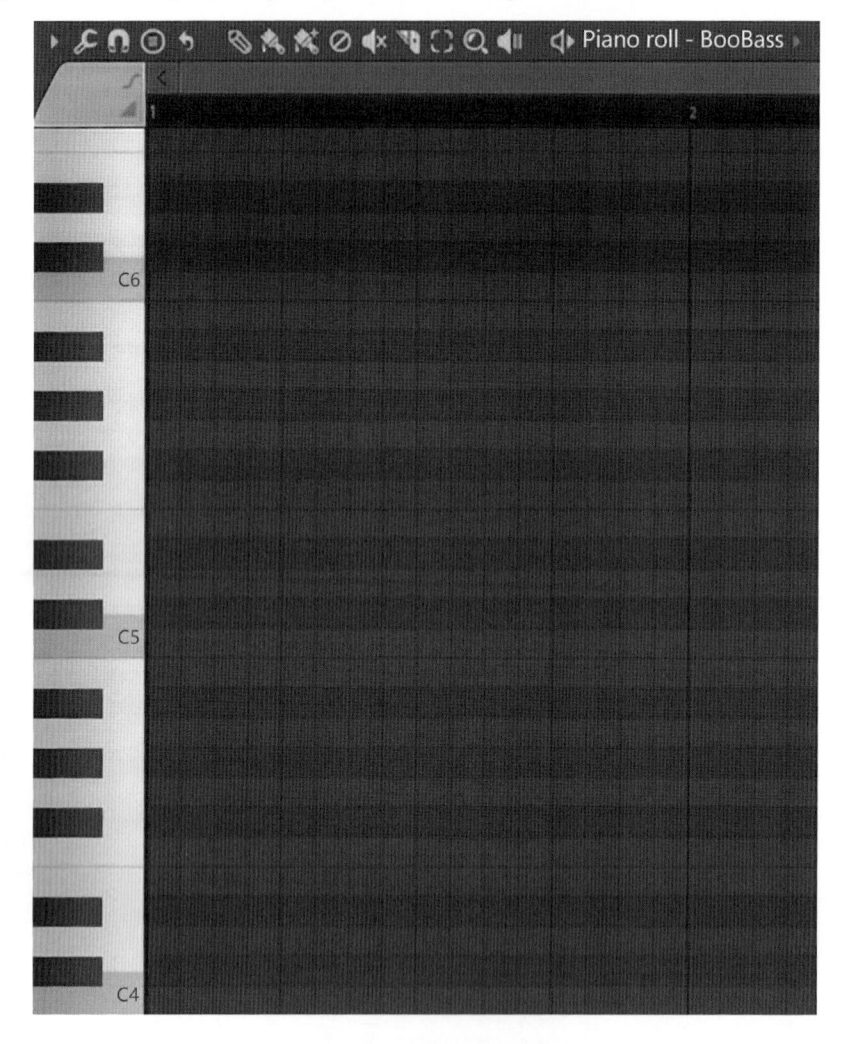

Figure 1.12 - Empty piano roll

The piano roll is designed to combine a piano with a timeline from left to right. On the left, you'll see black and white rectangular boxes to represent piano keys. If you know how to play the piano, this will feel very intuitive to you. To the right of it, you'll see a series of blue boxes in what resembles a spreadsheet table. These boxes indicate a position in time. By adding notes, you are telling the instrument to play a certain pitch at a certain time.

You'll notice that at the top of the piano roll in the preceding screenshot, there is a little pencil icon near the top left. Make sure that this is selected. It will allow you to add and delete notes, which will be important in the following pages.

Creating a melody with the piano roll

So far, we've loaded up an instrument. It's time to give the instrument some notes to play.

1. You can add notes by left-clicking in the blue boxes. Add notes to the piano roll to create a melody similar to the following:

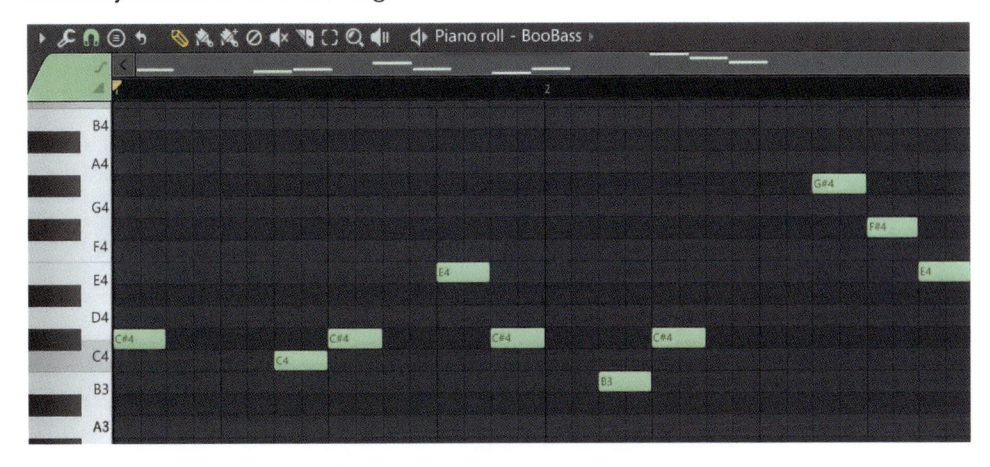

Figure 1.13 - Added notes to the piano roll instrument

2. Great, we've now created a simple bass melody.
3. Let's add the drum beat and our bass melody to our playlist. The playlist is where you can arrange the timing of your music patterns. Open the playlist (usually in the top center of FL Studio) by selecting the playlist icon:

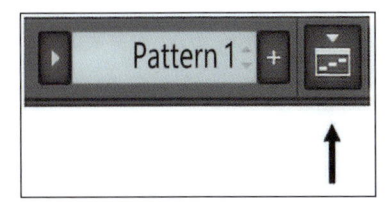

Figure 1.14 - Playlist icon

4. The playlist will now open and you'll see a window similar to the following:

Figure 1.15 - Playlist

5. On the left side, you'll see **Pattern 1** and **Bass Melody**. **Pattern 1** is our drum beat. **Bass Melody** is the melody that we just created. You can add the patterns to the playlist by left-clicking the patterns on the left and dragging them onto the blue grid on the right. Once done, it will look like the following:

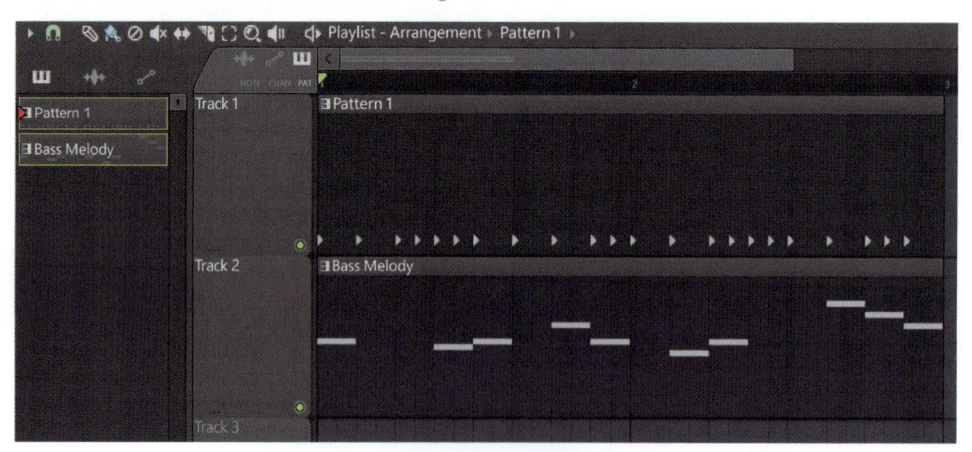

Figure 1.16 - Added patterns to the playlist

6. Let's play our entire arrangement and see how the patterns sound when played at the same time. Ensure that the setting is set to **SONG** instead of **PAT** and press the play symbol (triangle symbol) at the top of the screen. You will now be able to hear both of your music patterns being played at the same time:

Chapter 1

Figure 1.17 - Player menu

So far, we have created a drum pattern, added an accompanying instrument, and added both patterns to the playlist. Now we need to route these instruments to the mixer.

Routing channels to the mixer

It's time to think about **mixing** our music. Mixing is where we can add effects to our music to enhance it. We need to send our sounds to the mixer in order to apply effects to them. This is known as *routing* to the mixer. We will go into lots of detail about what is and how to do mixing throughout this book.

Let's route our instruments and samples to the mixer:

1. Open up the channel rack:

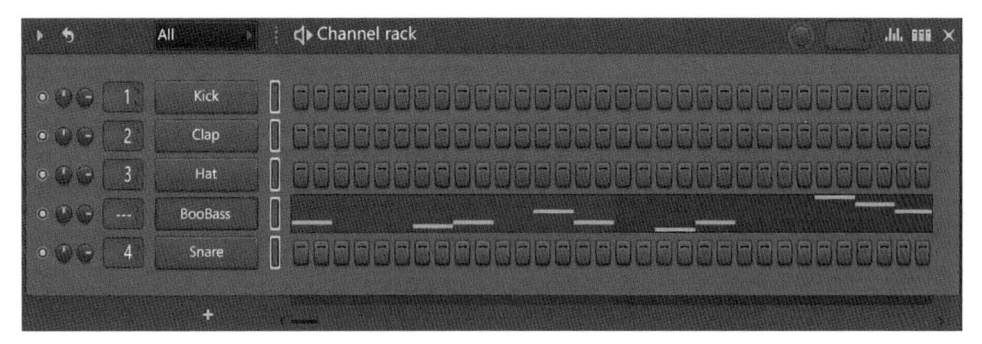

Figure 1.18 - Selecting channels in the channel rack

2. In the preceding screenshot, we can see that **Kick** has the number **1** beside it by default. This means that it is currently routed to mixer track channel 1. **Clap** is routed to track **2** and **Hat** is routed to track **3**.

3. Our **BooBass** instrument has no mixer channel number assigned. Let's route it to the mixer. Double-left-click the rectangle buttons directly to the right of the instruments. This will highlight all of the available instruments with a green outline, as in the preceding screenshot. This indicates that they are selected.

4. Next, press *Ctrl + L*. This will automatically assign BooBass and all other selected instruments to the mixer, as well as any color properties given to them. Alternatively, you can manually change the mixer number by clicking on the number and dragging it up or down to increase or decrease the value. You'll see that **BooBass** now has the number **5** assigned to it. This means it has been assigned to mixer track **5**:

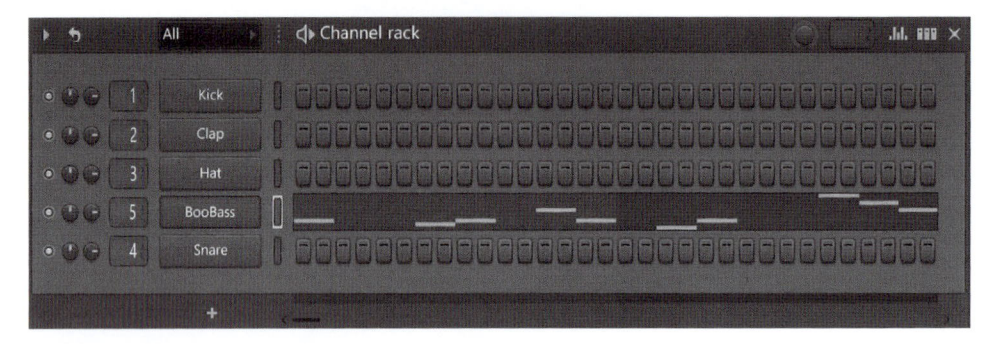

Figure 1.19 - Routing BooBass to the mixer

5. Let's see our routed instrument in the mixer. Select the mixer icon from the toolbar to open up the mixer:

Figure 1.20 - Mixer icon in the toolbar

In the mixer, we can now see that our instruments from the channel rack have been assigned channels in the mixer. Notice how the numbers on the channel rack correspond to the numbers on the mixer. The mixer channel track numbers can also be changed by selecting a mixer channel, holding down *Shift*, and scrolling with your mouse wheel:

Chapter 1

Figure 1.21 - Mixer

We have routed our instruments to the mixer. In future chapters, we'll learn how to apply effects to our instruments. Next, let's learn how to export our song out of FL Studio.

Exporting the song

Let's export our song out of FL Studio so that we can listen to it anywhere. Songs, when played on your phone or streamed online, are stored in the format of an MP3 or WAV file, so we need to convert it in to one of those. To do this, follow these instructions:

1. First, check that the **SONG** setting is selected so we export our entire composition, rather than just a single pattern. The **SONG** button is at the top of FL Studio, as shown in the following screenshot:

Figure 1.22 - Player menu

2. Next, go to **FILE | Export | MP3 file...**, as seen in the following screenshot:

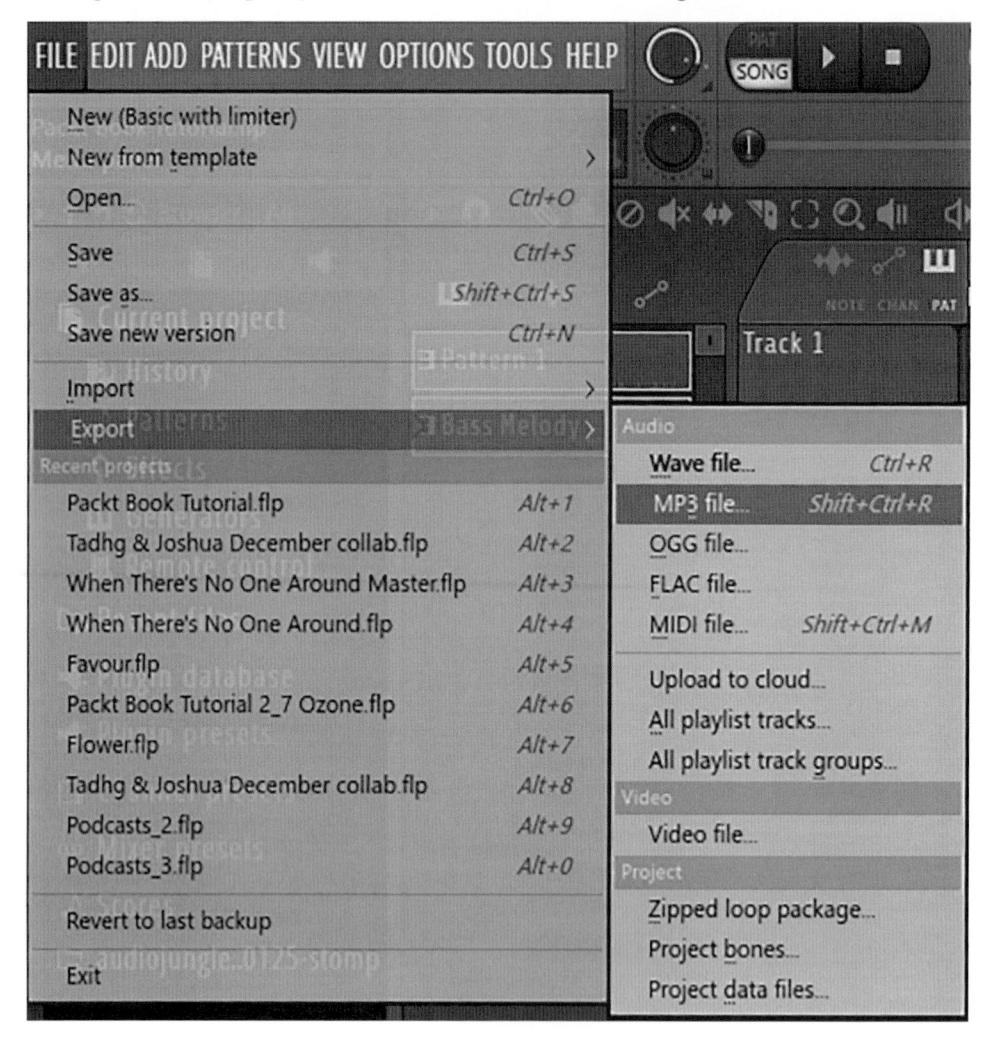

Figure 1.23 - Exporting the song

3. Choose a location on your computer (somewhere easy to find) to save your song:

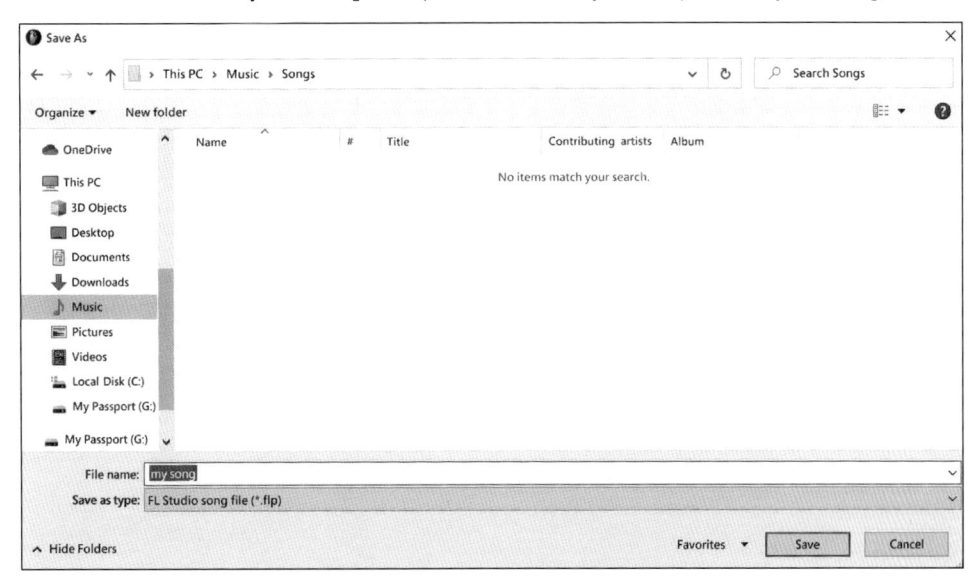

Figure 1.24 - Saving the song

4. Once you select **Save**, a window will pop up with information on rendering. This window gives you options on how to export your song. If you want to export quickly with the default settings, you can choose **WAV** or **MP3** and select **Start** to export your song.

We'll discuss the difference between **WAV** and **MP3** in the next section.

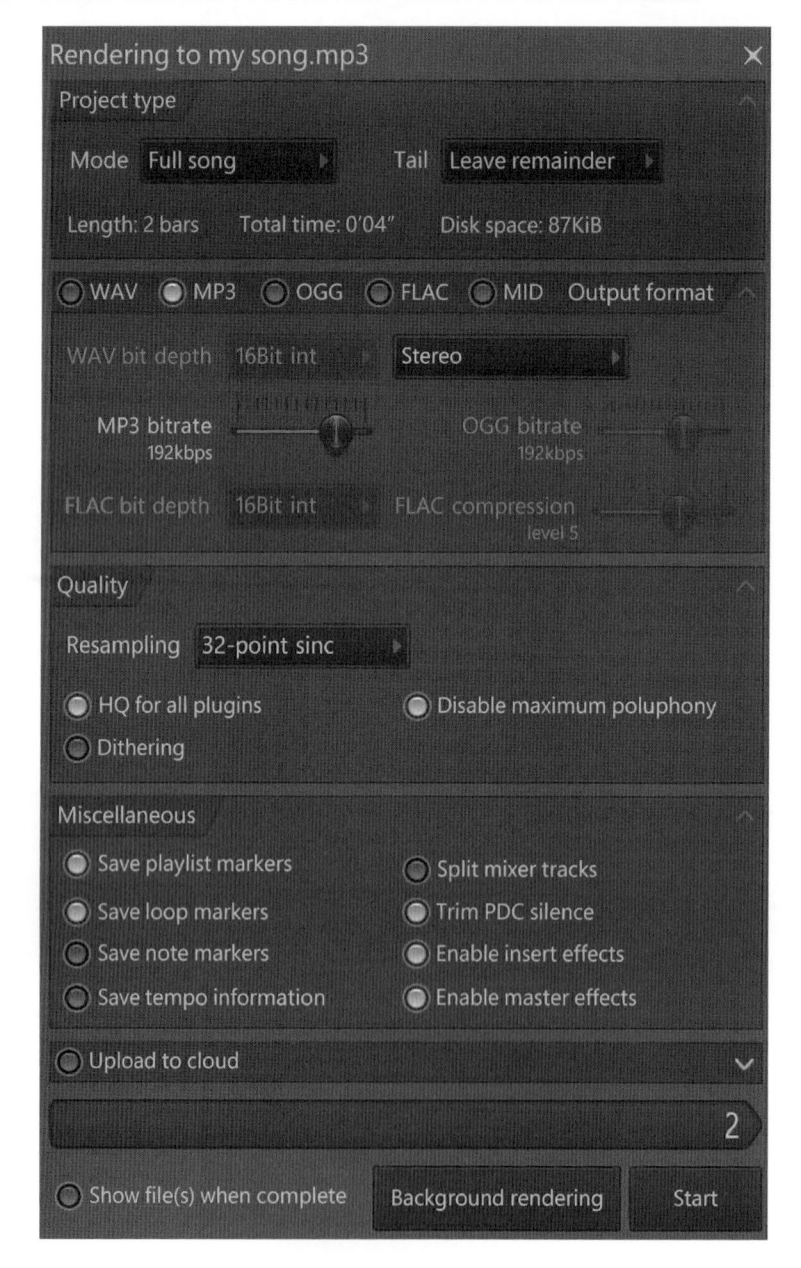

Figure 1.25 - Song render

Congratulations, you have successfully created your first song!

Song exporting options

If you're curious about the exporting features, here's a breakdown of the export settings. In the **Project type** options, you can choose to export your full song or just a single pattern.

The **Tail** option has three choices to pick from:

- **Cut remainder** abruptly ends the song the moment the sound and samples stop playing.
- **Leave remainder** allows synthesizers to naturally decay to silence at the end of your song. This is usually the choice you'll want in most scenarios.
- **Wrap remainder** takes any decay that would appear at the end of your song and places it at the start of your song. This is useful in circumstances where you are creating a loop and want the sound to repeat.

Underneath, you can see the song length in bars, the total elapsed time of the song, and the size of the file the exported song will create.

You can choose between several outputted format types. You can choose to export as **WAV** or **FLAC**, which are lossless formats, which means you will not lose any audio quality. Bit depth is the resolution you can choose to output. The options available are as follows:

- **16Bit**, the standard for CD quality
- **24Bit**, recommended for streaming
- **32Bit**, for sound archive size

You can usually select **16Bit** as you likely won't be able to tell the difference in most cases.

FLAC uses data compression to reduce the file size; however, the sound will be identical to a **WAV** file. You can then increase the FLAC compression, which will make the file size smaller, but it still won't affect the sound quality; it will just take a little longer to export.

MP3 and **OGG** are formats that will lose audio quality when exporting. They throw away data while maintaining audio sound. **MP3 bitrate** determines the audio quality. A higher bitrate allows a higher-quality sound.

The **MID** format allows you to export your project as MIDI data, assuming that you created MIDI data in your project.

You also have the option of selecting to output in **Stereo** or **Mono**. This refers to whether you allow different sounds to come out of the left versus the right speaker. You'll usually want to leave this as **Stereo**.

We'll discuss mono and stereo in detail in *Chapter 7, Stereo Width (Panning, Reverb, Delay, Chorus, and Flangers) and Distortion*.

The **Quality** section refers to dithering, which is a highly technical topic, but as a general rule, leave it on as it improves audio quality.

Under **Miscellaneous**, you'll want to make sure that the **Enable insert effects** and **Enable master effects** options are selected so that your mixer effects are applied. Leave **Trim PDC silence** on. This adds any necessary silence at the beginning of your track to ensure that the sounds are in sync. **Split mixer tracks** is what you'll use if you want to export a different sound file for each mixer track. You do this if you want to send your song to a third party for mixing or mastering.

Congratulations, you've just created your first song in FL Studio! That was quick and easy, wasn't it? In just a few minutes, you were able to create a drum beat, add an accompanying instrument, compose a melody, and export your music.

Summary

You've had a glimpse of the journey ahead on your way to producing your own music. In this chapter, we created our first song in FL Studio. We made a simple drum pattern, added an accompanying instrument and melody, routed the instruments to the playlist and the mixer, and exported the song. All songs you make will use these steps.

In the next chapter, we will explore some key FL Studio workbench tools in detail, including the browser, channel rack, and playlist.

2

Exploring the Browser, Playlist, and Channel Rack

It would take a very long time to create a song if you had to learn how to play every single instrument in a band from scratch. Thankfully, FL Studio has some tools you can reuse in every song you make regardless what genre or style.

In the following pages, we will learn about the main features of the **browser**, **channel rack**, and **playlist**. These, along with the piano roll and mixer, are the core tools of FL Studio. These are the fundamental key components of using FL Studio and you will use them continually from now onward in your journey through FL Studio. We will be reusing these tools throughout the book. Learning about these tools is a continual learning process and you'll find yourself discovering new features and techniques years into using FL Studio.

In this chapter, we will cover the following topics:

- Introducing the FL Studio workbench
- Getting the most out of your samples
- Using the browser
- Using the channel rack
- Using the playlist
- Using the main header toolbar features

Introducing the FL Studio workbench

In the pages ahead, we'll explore the browser, channel rack, and playlist and highlight the most useful features. If you are new to FL Studio, this may seem like a lot of information to process all at once. Don't fear, you don't need to know everything about these tools. You can just have a quick skim through this chapter to get the basics. Once you've got a few songs under your belt, you can come back and examine these tools in greater detail.

Let's start off with some theme customization to make FL Studio visually interesting for you and then we'll dive into the core controls. Let's select a color theme for your FL Studio interface. The theme will color the tools you use in FL Studio. It won't change how the tools work, but it can make your FL Studio experience more enjoyable. Sometimes, you need inspiration, and a different color theme may be all you need to get your creative juices flowing.

You can choose a theme by selecting **OPTIONS | Theme settings** as shown in the following screenshot.

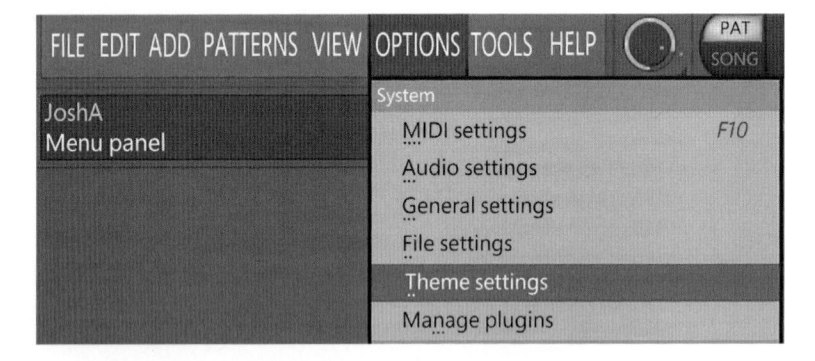

Figure 2.1 – Theme settings

Chapter 2

A list of themes will appear as shown in the following screenshot.

Figure 2.2 – Theme | Options

You can select a color theme for FL Studio. There is an **Adjustments** section for further control if you want to change the color of specific elements. If you mess up, you can always go back to the **(Default)** theme preset. You now know how to choose a color theme for FL Studio.

Before diving into the tools, there is a handy feature that tells you the name of everything your mouse cursor hovers over. At the top left, under **FILE**, you'll see some description text:

Figure 2.3 – Description text

For everything in FL Studio, if you hover over an item with your cursor, a description of the tool will appear here. For brevity's sake, we will just describe essential features that are not self-explanatory by reading the description when you hover over them.

To the right of the description text, you will see the player. This lets you play your compositions:

Figure 2.4 – The player

The player allows you to switch between playing a pattern or the whole song. It can play, pause, stop, and record input. You can control the global volume, the pitch, and the number of music beats that are played per minute (known as the BPM). This is the speed/tempo of your song. Feel free to adjust the BPM of your song to a higher value (for a faster song) or a lower value (for a slower song).

Directly to the right of the BPM number value, you'll see the metronome icon:

Figure 2.5 – Metronome

If selected, a click track will play, giving a click sound in time with the beat when a song or pattern is playing. To turn it off, simply click it again.

What if you're not sure what BPM number to use but intuitively you know how fast the song is when you sing the tune? **The tempo tapper** is a useful feature to use to quickly get the desired tempo for the song:

Figure 2.6 – The tempo tapper button

The icon opens up the tempo tapper plugin:

Figure 2.7 – Tempo tapper

By left-clicking on the tempo tapper, the BPM of the composition will adjust to the tempo of your tapping. As you tap faster or slower, you'll notice that the BPM adjusts to the speed of the tapping. I find this very useful if I'm playing a live instrument and want FL Studio to match the timing I'm playing at.

So far, we've seen how to play our song and adjust the timing of it. Next, we'll talk about how to use the browser.

Using the browser

The **browser** organizes your samples and instruments and provides convenient access to easily insert and swap them in and out of your project. Using the browser, you can easily swap out instruments and samples, add MIDI notes to instruments, load presets, and add effects. It's an excellent way to explore the different sounds available to you. Simply by swapping items with the browser, you can stumble across new sounds you wouldn't expect.

In this chapter, we'll keep things simple and focus just on how to use the browser to swap samples. But you can use the same technique to swap elements in the browser using a similar approach.

Let's explore the browser features:

1. Open the browser by selecting the browser icon:

Figure 2.8 – Browser button

The browser window will open up with a list of folder names. You can see a list of various samples, instruments, and effects organized by folder name. You can think of these just like any other folders on your computer. They are simply there to provide you with convenient shortcuts to your files:

Chapter 2

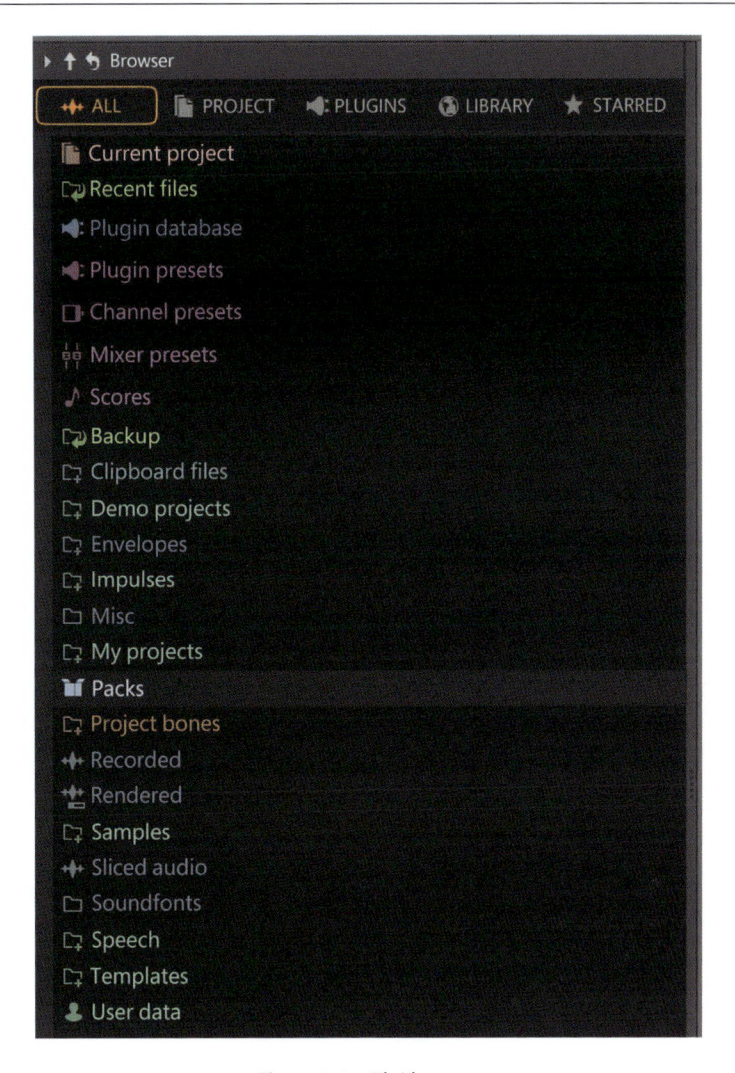

Figure 2.9 – The browser

You can navigate the folders using the arrow keys on your keyboard. The right arrow key will open up the selected folder, while the left arrow key will close the folder and move to the level above it.

2. Let's take a look at the samples inside some of the folders. Click the icon that says **Packs**:

Figure 2.10 – Packs

Within the **Packs** folder, we can see a list of folders with instruments and samples.

3. Select one of the folders, such as **Vocals**:

Figure 2.11 – Vocals

A list of vocal sound samples becomes viewable. You can listen to any sample preview by left-clicking on it.

4. Let's bring a sample into the playlist. You'll need to have the playlist open to do this, which can be done by selecting the view playlist icon:

Figure 2.12 – Toolbar

By selecting the playlist icon, the playlist window will open up. The browser and the playlist are now both viewable, side by side.

5. Let's bring a sample into the playlist. Left-click on a sample in the browser and drag it into your playlist, into an empty area of the blue grid:

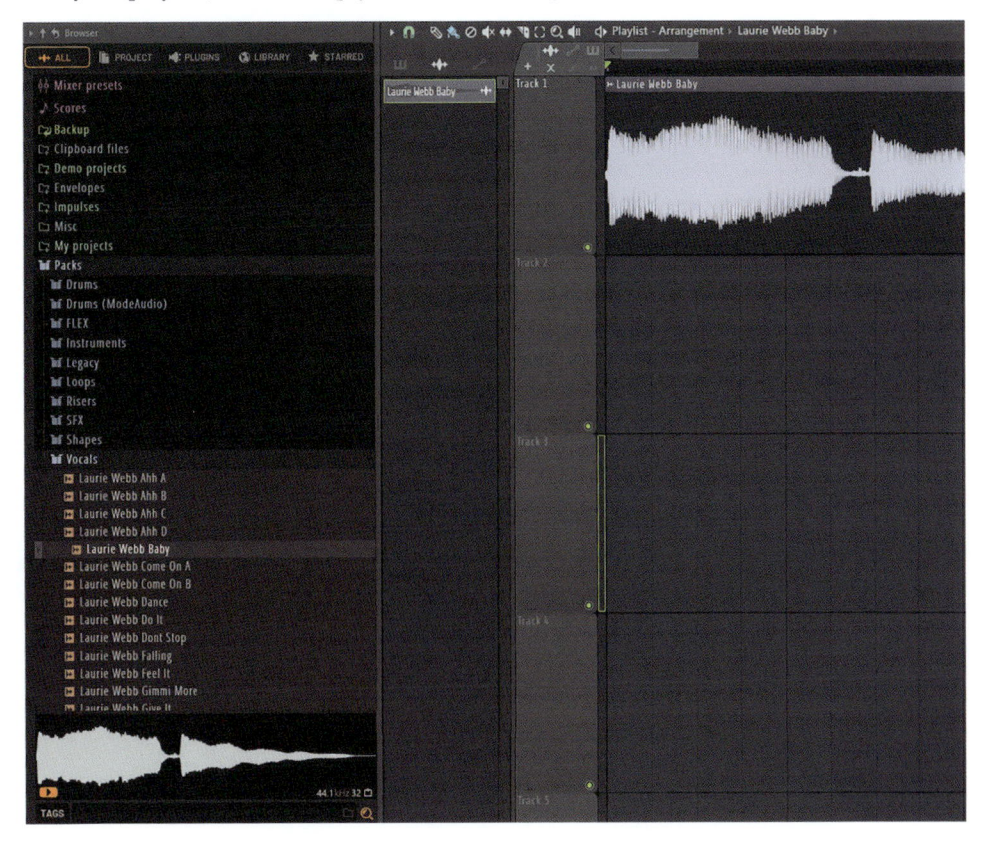

Figure 2.13 – Adding a sample to the playlist

You can drag multiple clips from the browser into the playlist at the same time.

We have successfully brought a sample from the browser into the playlist. You can now play the song and hear the sample play in time with your music patterns.

Locating a sample's file location

At some point, you'll have a song with a bunch of samples, and you'll want to find where the samples came from to find similar sounds. FL Studio makes it easy to find the folder that samples were taken from:

1. First, double left-click on the sample in your playlist. A window will pop up that looks like the following:

Figure 2.14 – Sample

Chapter 2

Here, we can see a list of controls over the sample. We will explore these controls in detail later in *Chapter 5, Sound Design and Audio Envelopes*.

2. Click on the *locate sample in browser* icon as shown in the following screenshot:

Figure 2.15 – The locate sample in browser icon

This will navigate to the location of the sample in the browser:

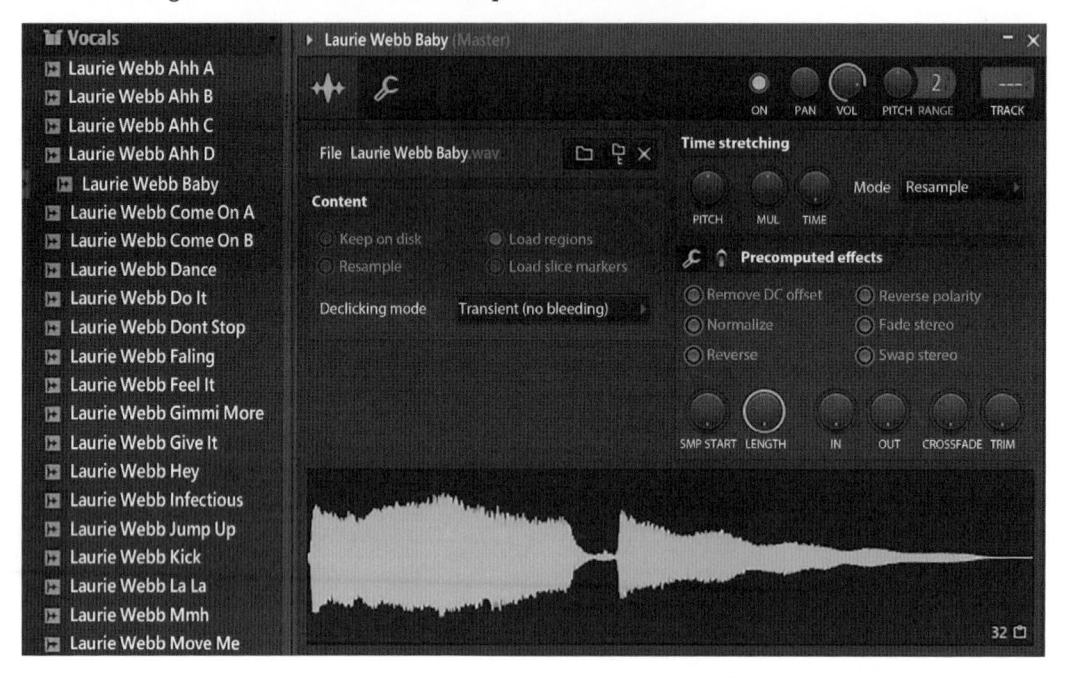

Figure 2.16 – Navigating to the sample location

We can now see the sample location in the browser and any other samples in the same folder. This process makes it very easy to find similar samples.

Next, let's look at how to search for samples by name.

Searching in the browser

At the bottom of the browser, you'll find the browser search bar. You can type into the search bar, press *Enter*, and the browser will bring up any samples or instruments that have the included search text in the name. If you want to find only results that have the exact name, surround your text with quotations. For example, `"808 Kick"`.

Figure 2.17 – Search bar

Chapter 2

You can press the **TAGS** button at the bottom left of the search bar to reveal the additional search filter options, as shown in the preceding screenshot. You'll notice the following filters: Star, Plugin, VST, and VST3. **VST** stands for **Virtual Studio Technology**; it's how software synthesizers can connect to digital audio workstations. These are filters to narrow your search results.

If you want to add a specific sample, plugin, VST, or VST3 to your favorites tag list, right-click on the item in the browser and select the option **Favorite** as shown in the following screenshot:

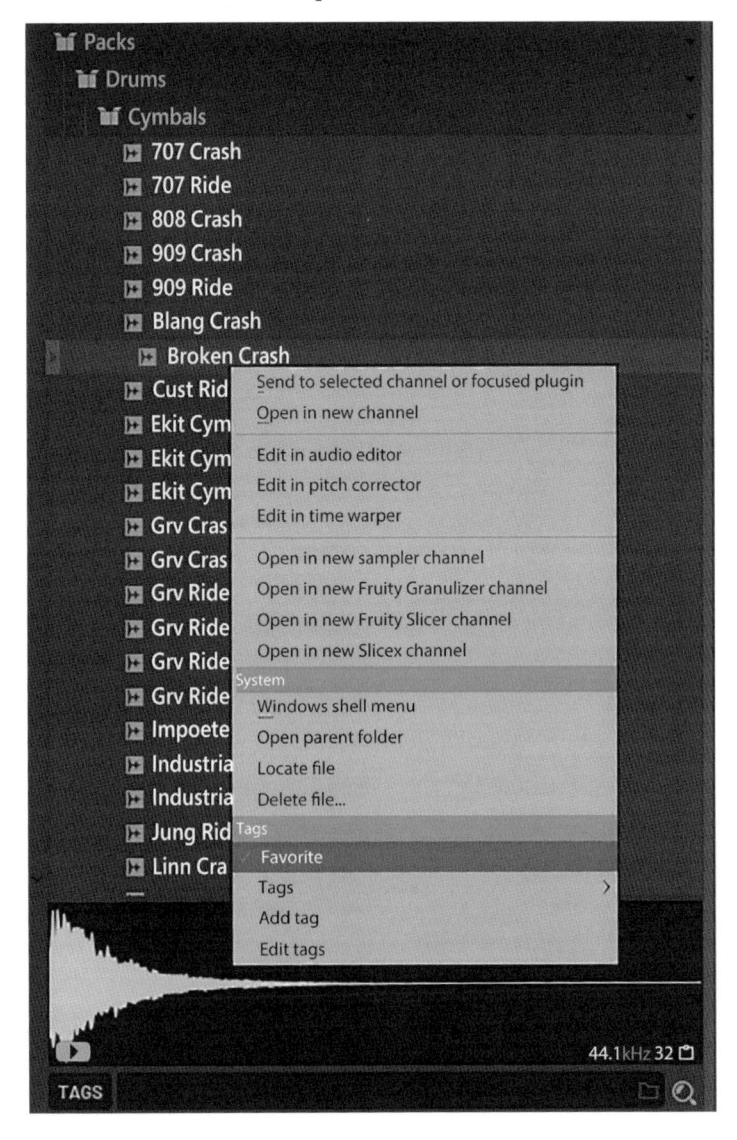

Figure 2.18 – Favorite tag

This will favorite the item. You can then quickly access it in the **STARRED** favorites section of the browser. Alternatively, you can simply hover over the sample in the browser and left-click on the star symbol that appears to the right of it.

Figure 2.19 – Starred

You now know how to navigate the FL Studio browser.

Now that you've found the sample, you can left-click on it to play a preview of it. If this isn't the sample that you're looking for and you want to see the next result, you can press *F3* to skip to the next search result. You can press *F2* to go to the previous result. You now know how to find samples in the browser.

Getting the most out of your samples

Sample packs are audio files that have been created for use in music production. There are many sample packs that are available for free online that you can easily find with a quick Google search. There are also premium paid samples for purchase.

When you're producing music, samples can be a useful tool to have. They can provide you with inspiration to get started. A sample pack may give you a head start in learning how to make sounds in a specific genre of music. For example, if you like house-style dance music, an **Electronic Dance Music (EDM)** sample pack can give you sounds that are commonly used in EDM, such as EDM-style percussive kicks, FX impacts, and riser sounds. I personally have a collection of percussion and FX one-shot samples that I frequently use in my songs.

However, buying sample packs is an easy way to get sucked into spending a lot of money on products that you'll never use. In particular, I recommend avoiding buying sample packs that use the name *construction kit* that say they contain an entire completed song. A construction kit contains a fully created song that is fully finished, straight out of the box. I find these to be a waste of money. What you want to be doing is creating your own music, rather than copying what someone else has already made.

Sample packs may include MIDI note examples. These are note arrangements that can be loaded into your instrument plugin. These can then be tweaked to your liking afterward. I personally prefer using MIDI notes as opposed to samples when composing melodies as it's easy for me to change the note keys to fit my song.

Some samples can be easily adjusted to fit into a new key. If the sample is a one-shot sample (a single note), you can use an FL Studio plugin called **DirectWave** to analyze the sample and simulate a full instrument. We will cover DirectWave in *Chapter 10, Creating Your Own Instruments and Effects*.

There are many sites out there that offer free and paid royalty-free audio samples available for your compositions. Royalty-free means that the sample is legally allowed to be used without copyright infringement. The Image Line website contains sample packs for purchase. Other recommended sites with samples for purchase include `www.pluginboutique.com` and `loopmasters.com`.

A word of caution on samples: if you think that you need to buy samples to become good at music producing, you're headed in the wrong direction. I personally made this mistake when I started out and spent a lot of money on samples before realizing that I wouldn't use them most of the time. Samples are most useful once you're already comfortable with producing music. If you're starting out and new to music producing, it's a much better investment of your time and money to master your instrument plugins and effects and create sounds yourself, rather than going out and buying samples. You want to be able to make original sounds yourself from scratch so that you develop your own signature style.

Next, let's learn how to add new samples to the browser.

Adding your own samples to the browser

If you have acquired additional samples online, you can add them as a new folder in the browser. To add a new folder of samples, take the following steps:

1. Go to the drop down arrow in the top-left corner of the browser and select **Configure extra folders**:

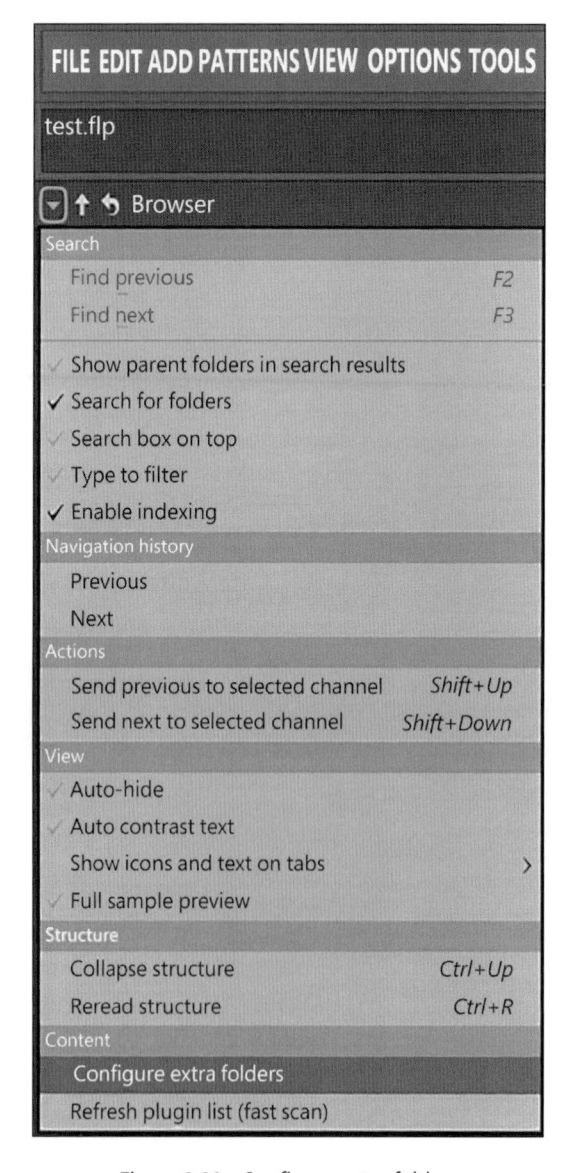

Figure 2.20 – Configure extra folders

Chapter 2

2. This will open the **Settings - Files & folders** window:

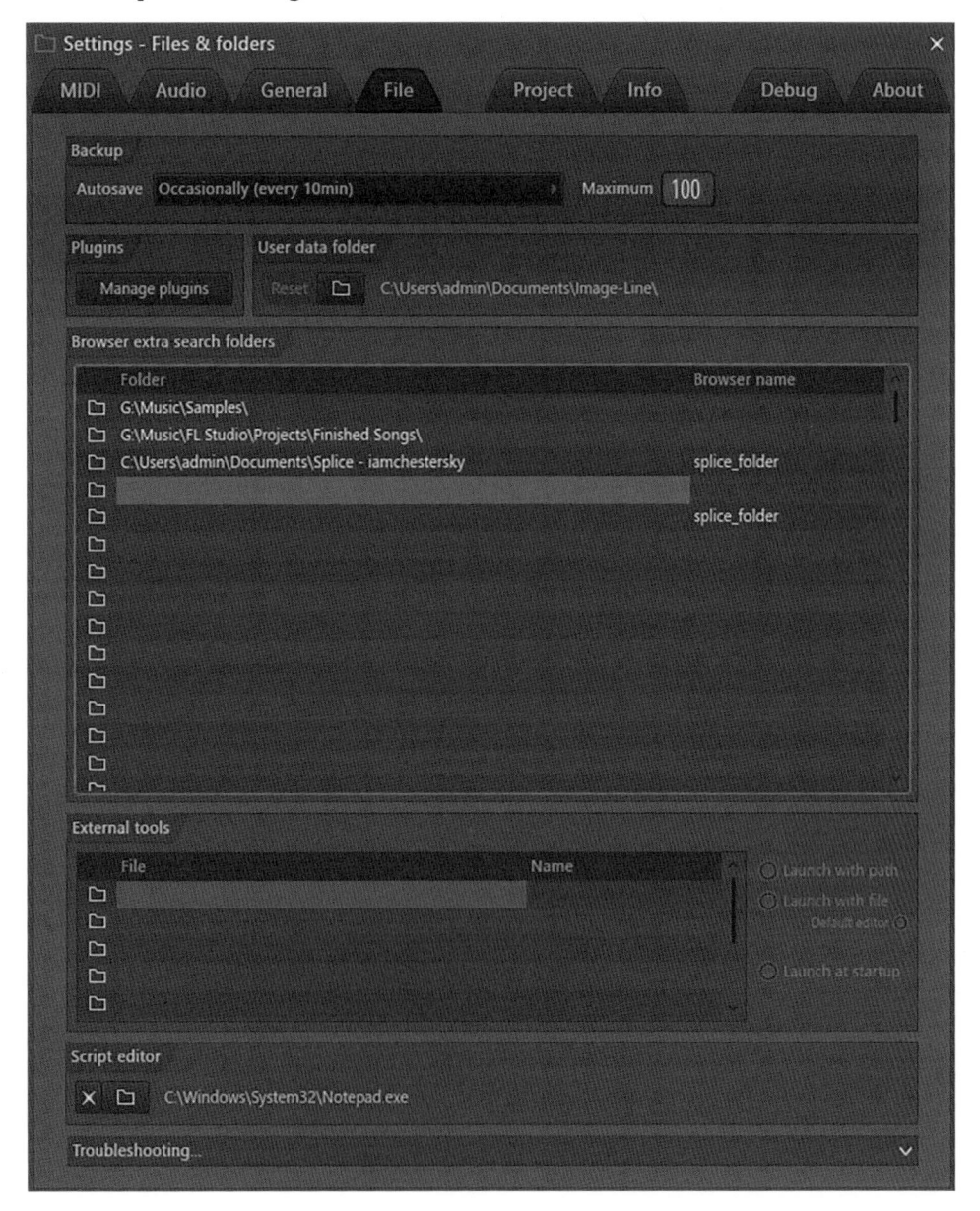

Figure 2.21 – Settings - Files & folders

Here, you can click on any folder icon under **Browser extra search folders** and navigate to the folder containing the new samples you want to add to the browser library. This will add your new folder to the browser.

You can now go back to your browser, and you'll see the new folder with your samples.

You now know how to add samples to the browser. Next, let's learn how to swap samples in and out of the playlist from your browser.

Swapping samples

Frequently, you'll insert a sample into your playlist and realize it's not a sound you like, but you like the timing position of the sample in the playlist. FL Studio makes it easy to swap one sample with another while retaining the timing position and mixer track routing.

You can easily swap out one sample with another sample. To swap samples, left-click on a sample in the playlist that you want to replace, then using the scroll wheel of your mouse, click on the sample with which you want to replace it in the browser. This will swap the sample in the playlist with the sample in the browser.

So far, we've looked at how the browser can be used to bring in samples for use in our compositions. Next, let's look at how to load up instruments in the channel rack.

Using the channel rack

The **channel rack** contains the instruments and samples you are currently using in a music pattern. It's here in the channel rack that you'll add and remove instruments, create percussive rhythms, and flip between music patterns. A music pattern is a group of notes that are played by instruments on the channel rack. Multiple instruments can play notes at the same time in a single pattern. Audio from each channel on the channel rack is then routed to the mixer.

Open up the channel rack by selecting the channel rack icon on the main toolbar:

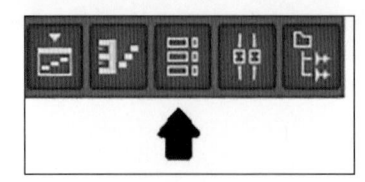

Figure 2.22 – Channel rack in the toolbar

The channel rack will open up and show the currently selected music pattern. The following screenshot shows the channel rack:

Figure 2.23 – Channel rack pattern

Moving from left to right on the channel rack, first, you see a green light to indicate whether the instrument is on or muted (deactivated). Instruments can be turned on or off by left-clicking on the light. If you want to only listen to a single instrument to focus on it, you can play it on its own (known as **soloing it**). To solo the instrument, hold down *Ctrl* and then left-click on the light of the desired instrument. All other instruments will become muted except for your solo-ed instrument (the lights will turn off). To unmute everything, hold down *Ctrl* and click the light again. The lights of all other instruments will become active again. This same process works exactly the same in the playlist and in the mixer.

Next are the panning knobs, which control whether audio comes out of your left or right speaker. By default, audio is set to the middle. This means audio plays out of the left and right speakers equally. The panning can be changed by left-clicking on the panning knob and dragging up or down. This is further discussed in *Chapter 7, Stereo Width (Panning, Reverb, Delay, Chorus, and Flangers) and Distortion*.

To the right of the panning knobs, you can see the volume control knobs. Volume can be changed by left-clicking on the volume knob and dragging up or down.

The mute setting, panning knobs, and volume knobs can all have automation assigned to them. I recommend when you're using automation that you only make volume changes *for instruments* in the channel rack. It's better to set the *global level* of volume in the mixer, rather than the channel rack. This will benefit you later on in mixing. For example, you may want to have the volume of an instrument gradually fade in; you could do this with automation using the channel rack volume knob. This way, later on, while mixing, you can still ensure that the volume of the instrument balances well with other instruments without having to fiddle with automation a second time. We will discuss the mixer and automation in *Chapter 4, Routing to the Mixer and Applying Automation*.

To the right of the volume knobs, you can see a number, representing the mixer channel that the instrument is currently assigned to.

We assign each instrument to individual mixer tracks so that we can apply effects to each instrument separately. The mixer channel the instrument is routed to can be changed by hovering over the number and scrolling with your mouse.

To the right of the mixer channel numbers are the samples and instruments that are currently loaded. To the right of the instrument are the MIDI notes that are actively being played by the instrument. This is a simplified layout of the piano roll focusing on a single-note pitch. It's done this way to allow you to focus on rhythm instead of note pitch.

You can shift instrument notes left or right in the channel rack. Select the instrument with notes by left-clicking on the rectangular button directly to the right of the instrument, and then pressing *Ctrl* + *Shift* + the left arrow key or *Ctrl* + *Shift* + the right arrow key. This will move the notes in the piano roll.

So far, we've seen the components that make up the channel rack. Next, let's look at the options that the channel rack has to offer.

Channel rack options

By right-clicking on one of the instruments, you can see a list of channel rack menu options. In the upcoming pages, we will work our way through the menu options as shown in the following screenshot:

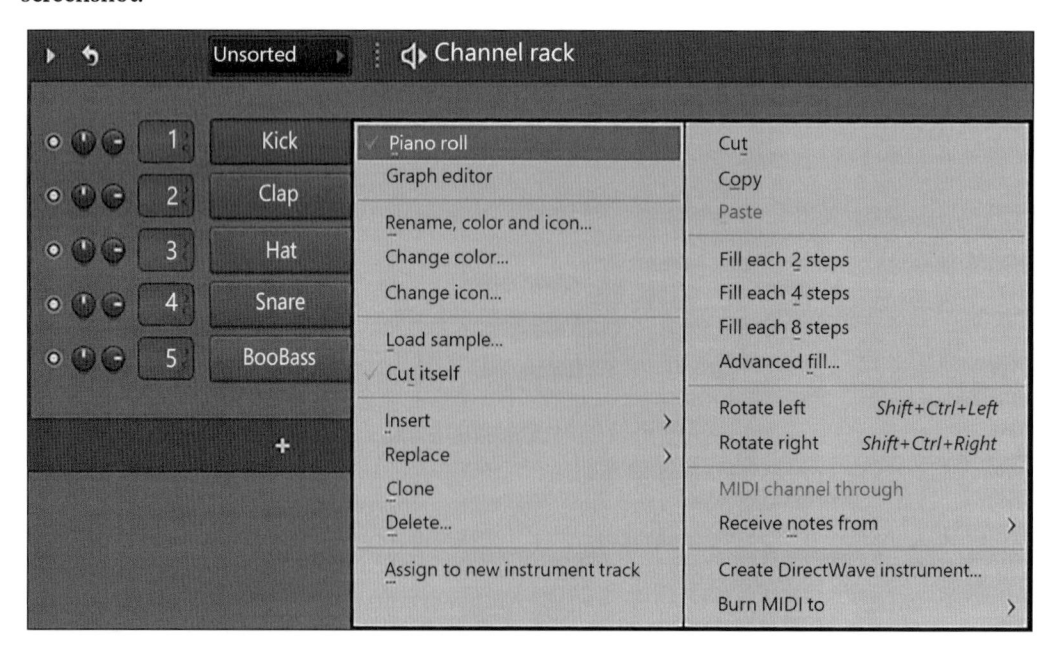

Figure 2.24 – Piano roll option

Chapter 2

Let's take a look at the channel rack options.

Piano roll

The **Piano roll** option opens up the selected instrument in the piano roll:

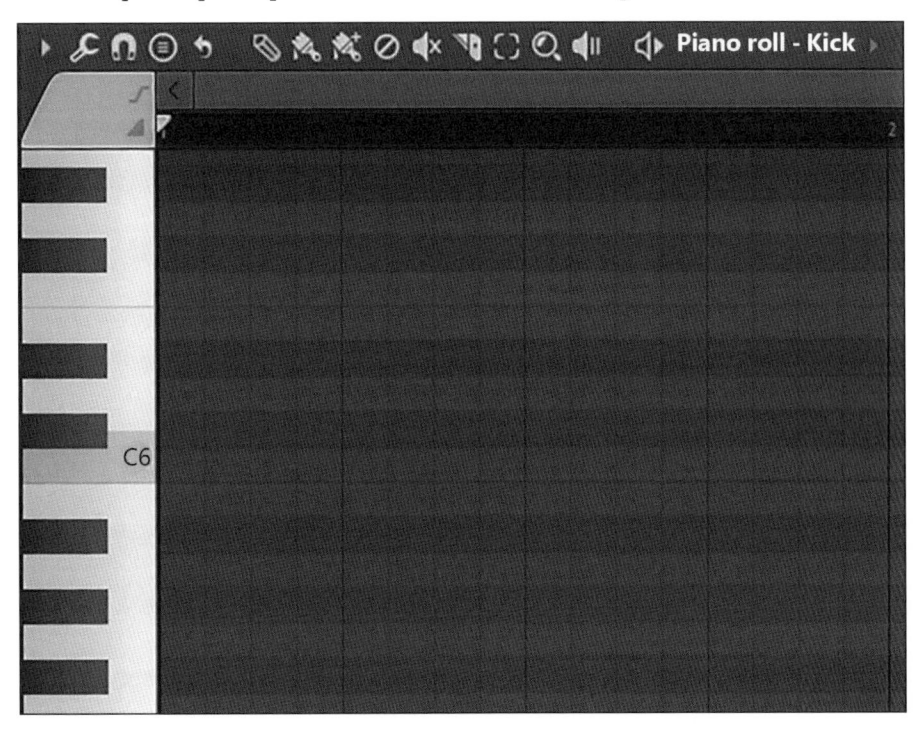

Figure 2.25 – Piano roll

The piano roll allows you to add notes to a selected instrument. The piano roll is where you can compose all the melodies for your song. It's where all the creative magic happens. We will explore the piano roll in detail in *Chapter 3, Composing with the Piano Roll*.

Graph editor

Once you've created notes in the channel rack, you can adjust the properties of the notes. Under the **Piano roll** option, you can find the **Graph editor** option.

The graph editor opens up a list of controls to edit the individual notes in the pattern. In the following screenshot, you can see the notes that are currently enabled for the piano roll and the controls underneath for editing them:

Figure 2.26 – The graph editor

Here's a brief summary of the controls in the graph editor:

- **Note pitch** is what note is being hit.
- **Velocity** is similar to how hard the note is hit. This will only be noticeable for instruments that have percussive volume control built into them. Drum samples tend to have more explosive sounds at higher velocities.
- **Release velocity** is how quickly the sample volume fades away.
- **Fine pitch** allows you to shift the pitch of a sound up or down. It's intended for if you want to detune a note slightly higher or lower.

- **Mod X** controls the cutoff of a filter.
- **Mod Y** controls the cutoff of a resonance.
- **Shift** controls the note start time offset. This allows you to have a note come in slightly after the normal timing position.

Next in the channel rack option menu list is the **Rename, color and icon** option. The menu options appear when you right-click on an item in the channel rack.

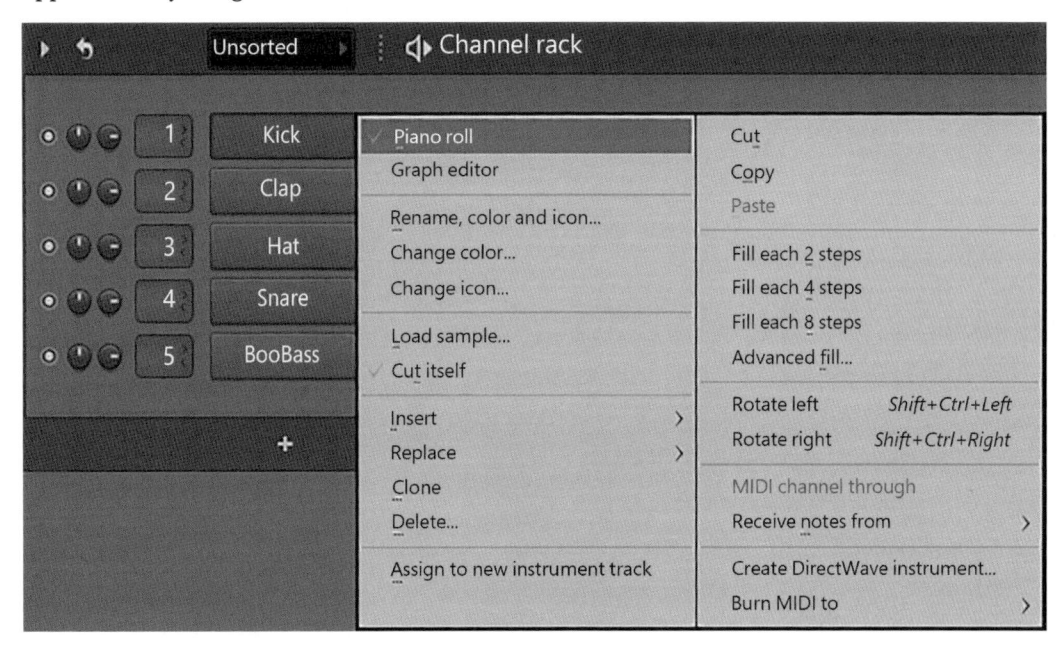

Figure 2.27 – Rename, color and icon option

The Rename, color and icon option

When you have multiple instruments playing, organization becomes more and more important to keep track of all your sounds, or else it can become a disorganized mess. Visual aids make organization much easier.

You can give a custom name and color to your instruments by selecting the **Rename, color and icon** option, which will open up the following window:

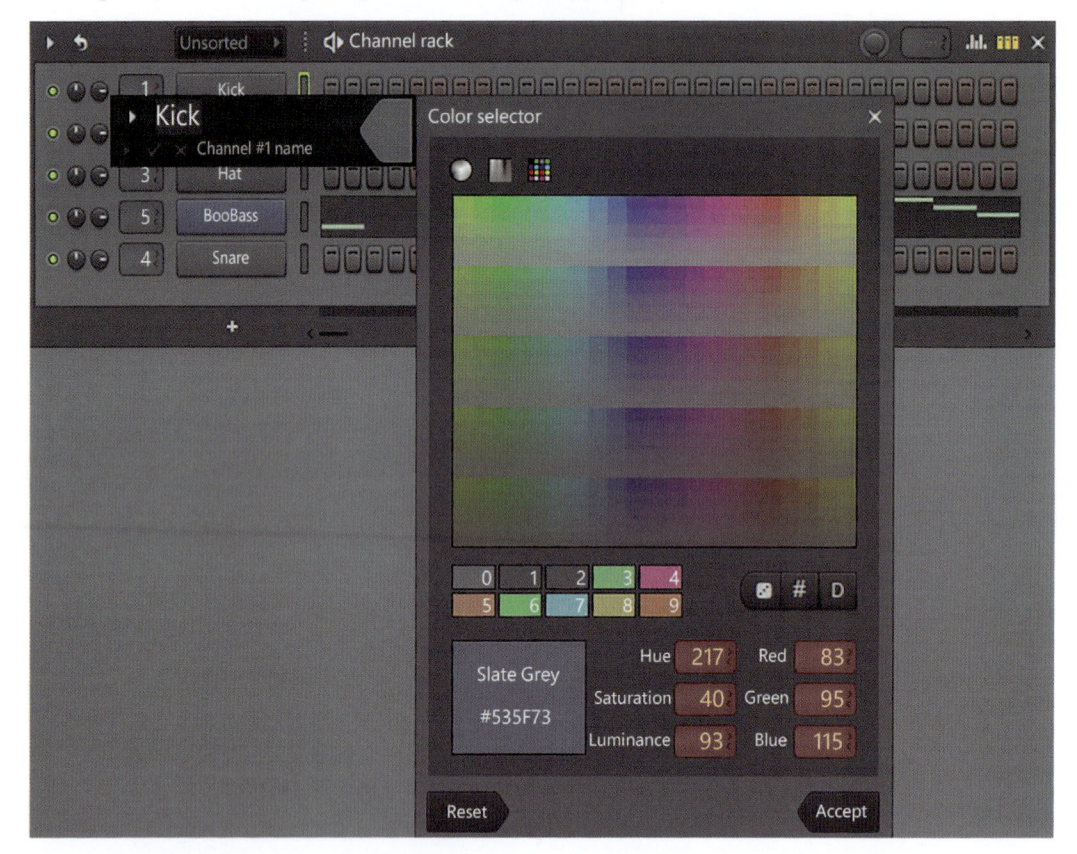

Figure 2.28 – Color selector

Here, you can click on a color to assign it to the instrument.

Chapter 2

There is an easy way to quickly color all of your instruments at once, rather than manually choosing a color each time. Under the channel rack drop down arrow, there's a feature that lets you color all selected instruments at once using either a gradient or a color chosen randomly:

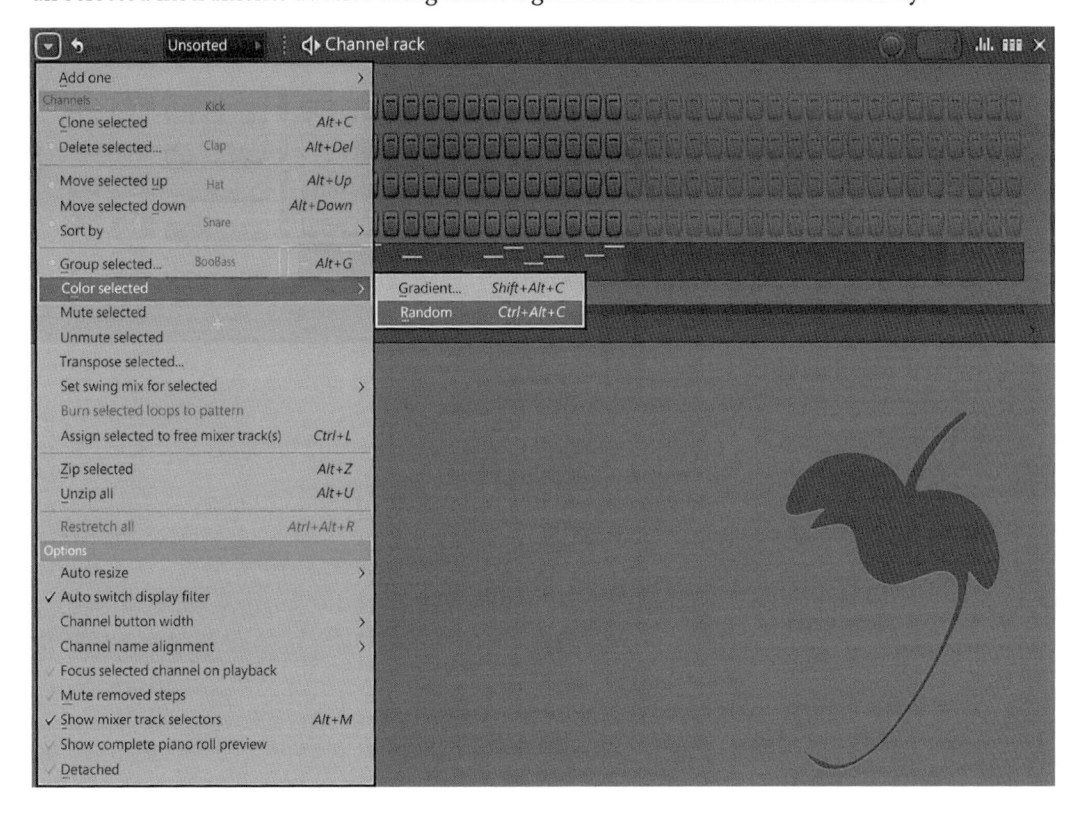

Figure 2.29 – Random color selector

Using **Random** or selecting a gradient is my recommended approach to giving all of your selected instruments a color.

Instrument options

Let's return to the drop down menu that appears after right-clicking an instrument or sample. In the following screenshot, we can see the list of available options:

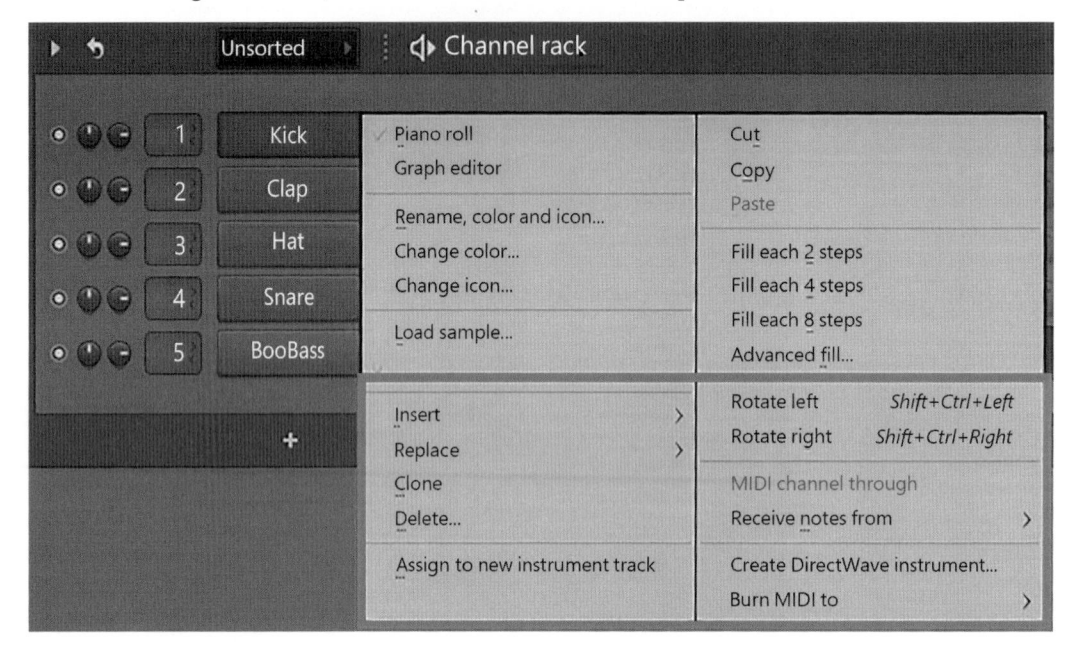

Figure 2.30 – Instrument options

Here's a brief summary of the options:

- **Insert** allows you to insert a new instrument.
- **Replace** works the same way as **Insert** for loading up instruments. It allows you to swap out your current instrument for another.
- **Clone** allows you to copy the instrument, audio, or automation currently in the channel rack. This only copies the instrument, not the notes played by the instrument.
- **Delete...** allows you to remove the selected track. Alternatively, you can select multiple tracks in the channel rack at once and press left *Alt + Delete* on your keyboard to delete them.

To move notes from one instrument to another, select a single instrument/sample that contains notes and press *Ctrl + C* or the copy option (or, alternatively, cut with *Ctrl + X*). Then, select a different instrument/sample and press *Ctrl + V*. This will paste the notes into the new instrument. You can paste notes into different patterns by switching to a different pattern first and then pasting.

Advanced fill... opens up a tool that generates a sequence of notes. Here, you can add notes by left-clicking on the circles around the dial or rotating the dial to move the notes left or right in the pattern. Selecting the die symbol will generate a completely random pattern of notes:

Figure 2.31 – Advanced fill

Create DirectWave instrument... takes a single sample sound and creates a simulated instrument out of it using the DirectWave plugin. We will explore DirectWave in *Chapter 10, Creating Your Own Instruments and Effects*.

Burn MIDI to... Current pattern or **Burn MIDI to... New pattern** allows you to convert plugin arpeggio sequence sounds into MIDI notes and output them in the piano roll:

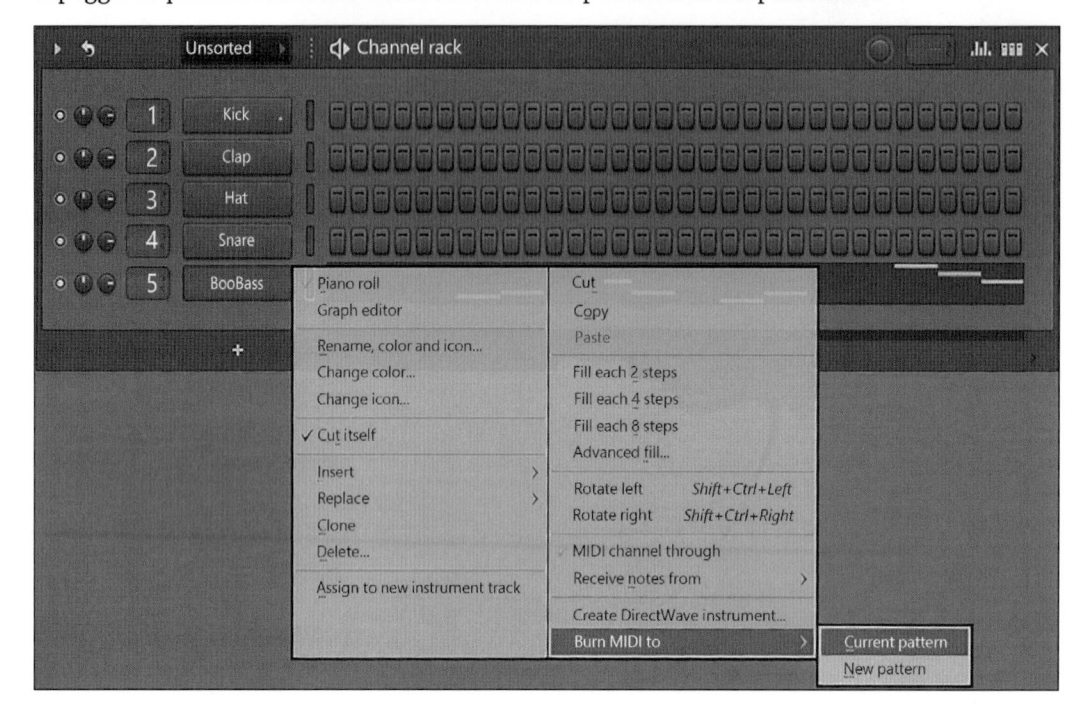

Figure 2.32 – Burning to MIDI

We need a little background to explain what this feature does. **MIDI** notes refer to the timing and pitches of notes. **Arpeggios** are chords that are broken down into a sequence of notes. What the **Burn MIDI to...** feature does is analyze a synthesizer making an arpeggio sound and figure out what notes and pitches are being played. It then outputs the notes of the sequence in the piano roll.

By burning to MIDI, you can get the MIDI notes that were used in an arpeggiator plugin. This won't do anything with the BooBass instrument though as the BooBass does not create an arpeggio. If you want to use this feature, you need to load up a synthesizer that does arpeggiation.

If you're burning MIDI using a plugin that isn't native to FL Studio, you need to set an output port to a number other than blank before MIDI burning, as seen in the following screenshot:

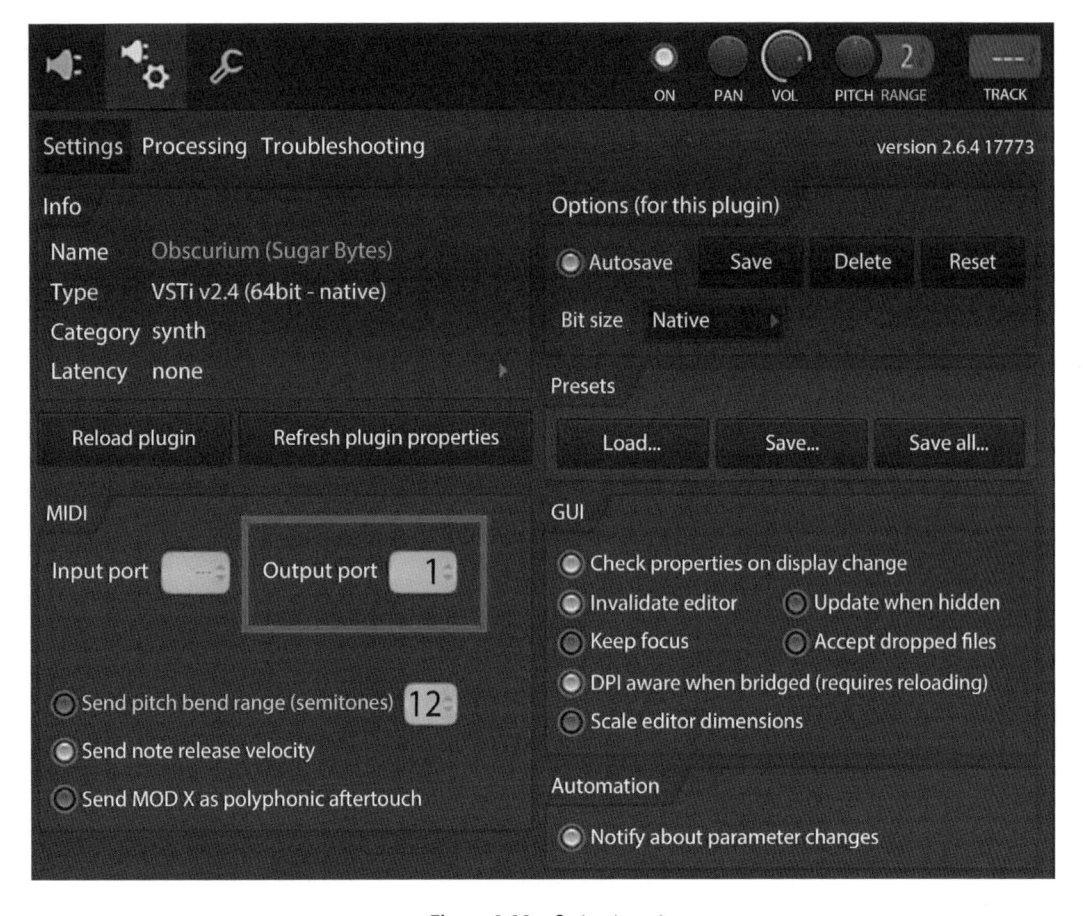

Figure 2.33 – Output port

For the preceding screenshot, you can see I've set **Output port** to **1**. This will now allow a non-native FL Studio arpeggiator synthesizer to burn audio to MIDI.

Detaching windows

For all instruments and plugins, you can make the window of the plugin detach so that when you click away from the window, it remains open. I use the **Detached** feature constantly when working as I need to have multiple windows open at once to move stuff between them.

To detach any window, simply go to the drop down arrow at the top left of the plugin and select the **Detached** option:

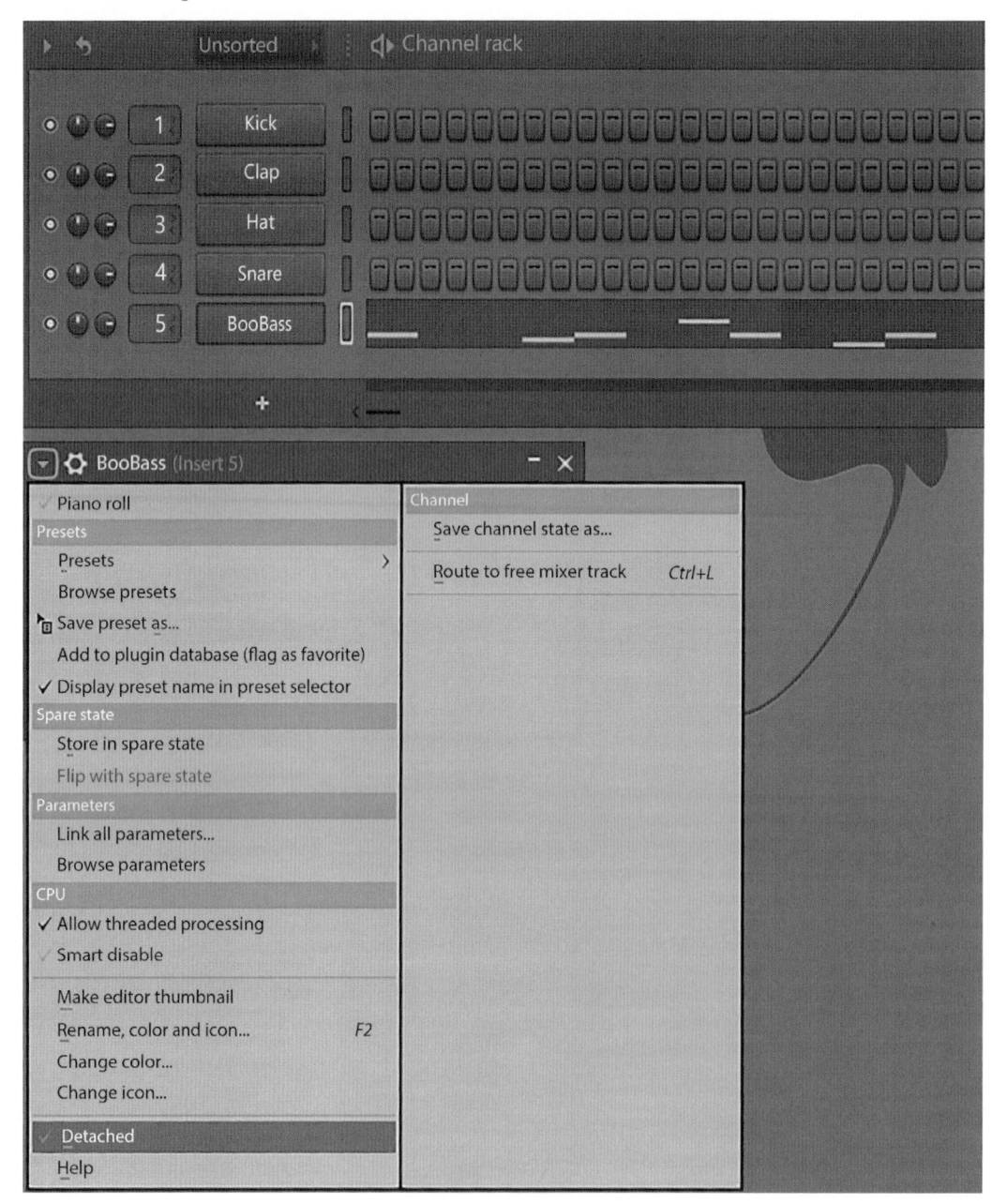

Figure 2.34 – Detached

Detached also applies to effect plugins in the mixer.

Installing new instruments

There are many instruments and effects that you can get online and import into FL Studio. Many of them are free, and if you do a Google search, you'll find thousands of synthesizers and effects. If you are looking for premium paid plugins, a few of the best market-leading plugins are those created by the following:

- **Native Instruments, for synthesizers, effects, and MIDI hardware**: https://www.native-instruments.com
- **Izotope, for effect plugins**: https://www.izotope.com/

When you want to import an external VST instrument, right-click on any instrument in the channel rack, then select **More plugins...** | **Manage plugins**:

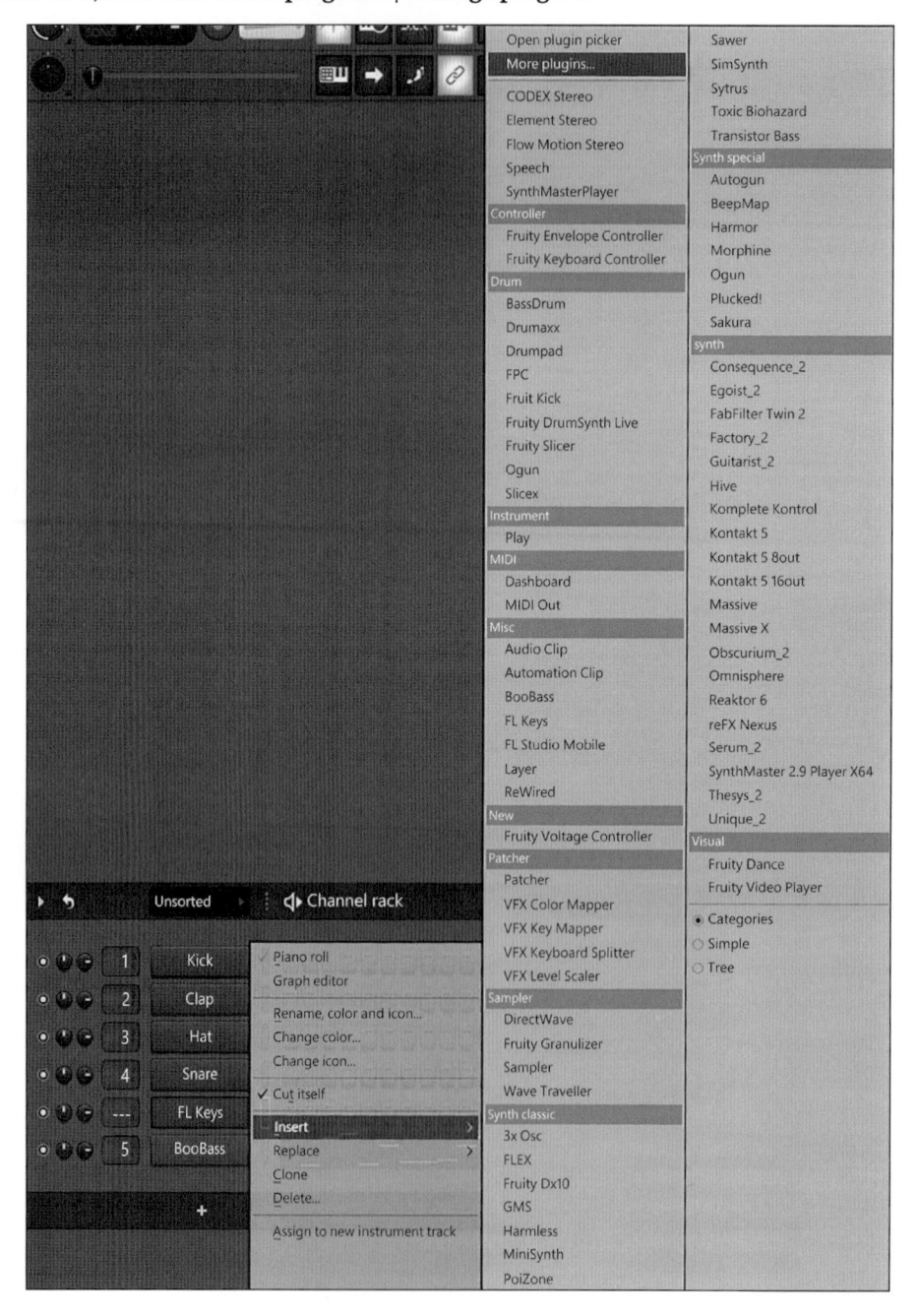

Figure 2.35 – Inserting more plugins

Chapter 2   57

A window will pop up that shows all the plugins that FL Studio currently knows about. You can click **Find more plugins** to scan for any newly installed plugins. There's also an option to add a custom search path to a folder to search for your plugin:

Figure 2.36 – Fl Studio Plugin Manager

Every time you install an external instrument or effect plugin, you will need to add the instrument using this process.

Using channel rack layers

Layers allow you to play several instrument tracks at once. When a layer encounters the notes in the piano roll, all instruments belonging to the layer will play the same notes. If you are stacking several instrument sounds together, this is an efficient way of having all the instruments play identical notes, rather than copying the same notes to all the instruments.

To insert a layer, right-click on an instrument, then select **Insert | Layer**:

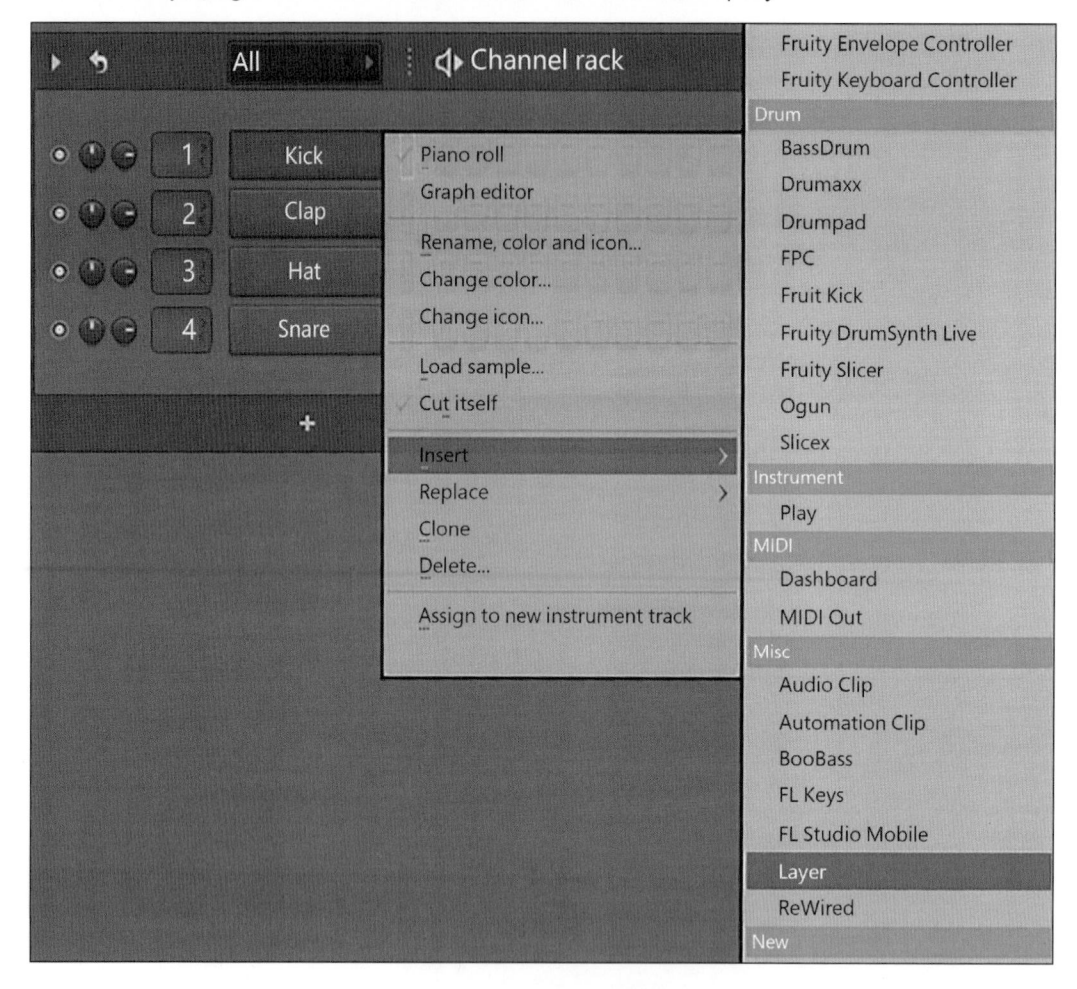

Figure 2.37 – Inserting a layer

A layer will now be created. If you left-click on the layer to open it, a window will pop up. Here, you'll see a button called **Set children**. This allows you to choose which instruments you want to belong in the layer.

To use **Set children**, first, select/highlight the instruments in the channel rack. To select several at the same time, you will need to hold down *Shift* while left-clicking. Once you have your channels selected, return to the layer window and left-click **Set children**. This will assign the instruments to the layer.

From here on, all instruments in the layer will play any MIDI notes that the layer receives:

Figure 2.38 – FL Studio Plugin Manager

If you want to see all instruments currently belonging to the layer, the **Show children** button will highlight the related instruments. If you later need to change which instruments belong to the layer, simply reselect the instruments you want, and press **Set children** again. You now know how to use layers to play multiple instruments at the same time.

You now have an overview of the main features offered by the channel rack. Next, let's take a look at the playlist to organize our music patterns.

Using the playlist

The **playlist** is where you arrange the timing of all elements for your song. It's what you'll spend most of your time looking at from a high-level perspective. This is where you'll sit back and watch your song when it's playing. It holds patterns, audio clips, and the automation of effects. You can open the playlist by selecting the playlist icon:

Figure 2.39 – Playlist icon in the toolbar

The playlist will open up and you will see a window similar to the following:

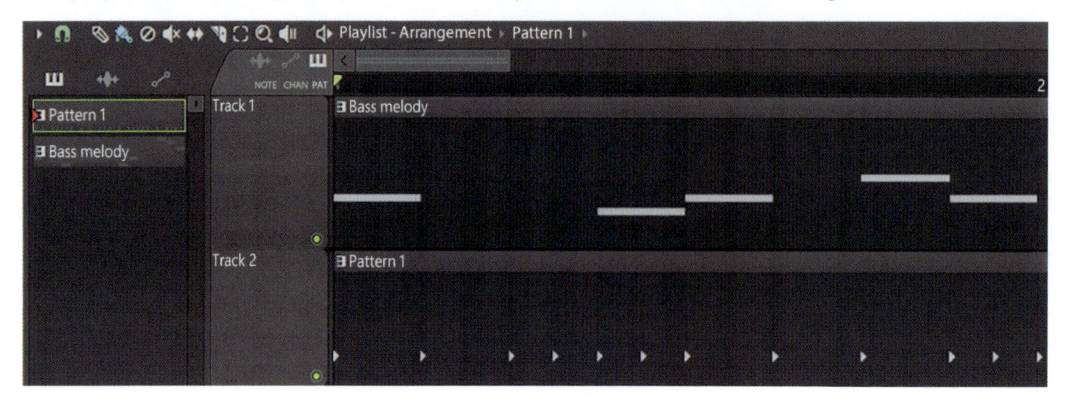

Figure 2.40 – Playlist

On the left-hand side, you can see the pattern, audio, or automation that is currently selected. In the preceding screenshot, we can see that **Pattern 1** is currently selected. We can left-click on patterns and drag them into the playlist.

To the right of the patterns, you can see the name **Track 1** and a light to indicate that the track is active (not muted). You can mute the track by left-clicking on the light. You can customize the name and color of the track by right-clicking on it and selecting **Rename and Color**. In the following screenshot, we can see that we have left-clicked on **Bass melody** in the playlist to select it:

Figure 2.41 – Bass melody

You can also right-click and rename the track as well if you like.

There are several ways to switch between active music patterns. You either left-click on a pattern to the left of the playlist, as seen in the preceding screenshot, or choose a different pattern from the pattern selector at the top of the screen, as seen in the following screenshot:

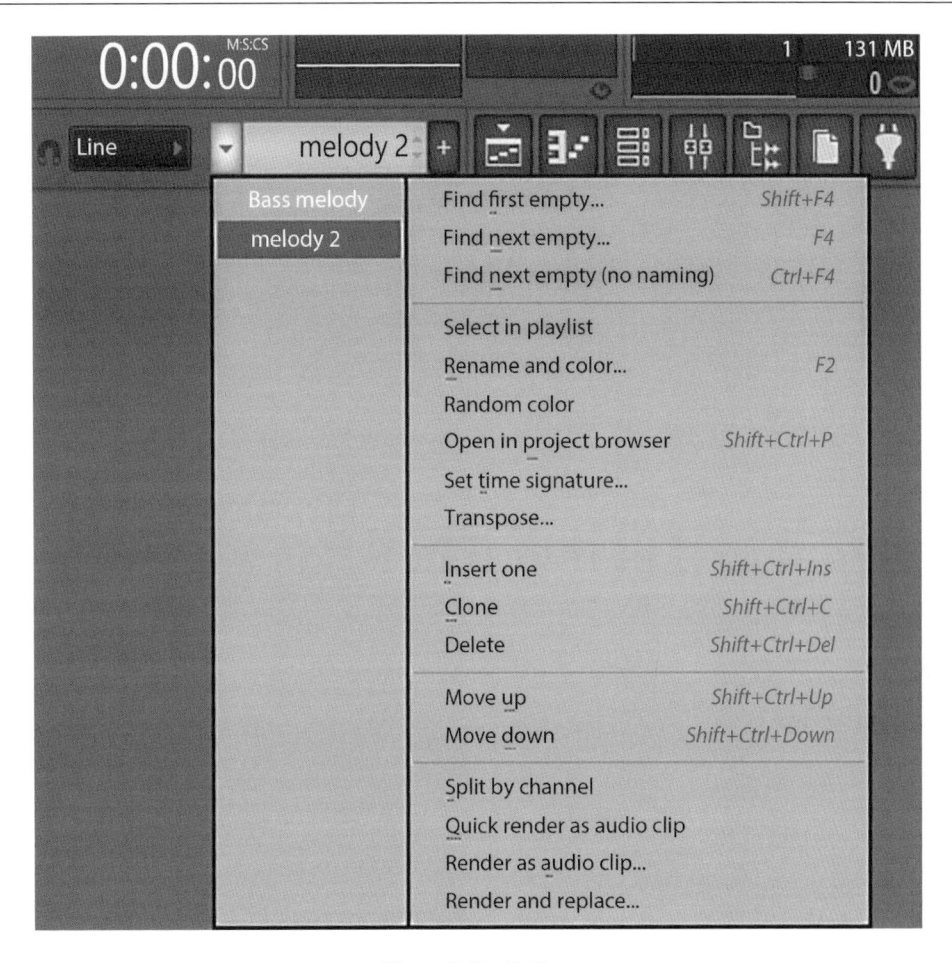

Figure 2.42 – Pattern

So far, we've looked at the components of the playlist. Now, let's take a look at the tools it offers.

The playlist toolbar

Let's look at the tools available in the playlist toolbar:

Figure 2.43 – Playlist toolbar

In the playlist toolbar, you can see a series of tool icons. Let's go through the tools from left to right, starting with the draw tool (we'll come back to the magnet tool in the next chapter when we look into the piano roll in detail):

- **Draw:** At the top left, you'll see a symbol that looks like a pencil. Selecting this allows you to add the currently selected pattern, sample, or automation to the playlist. Once the draw tool is active, you can left-click anywhere in the playlist to place a selected element. While the draw tool is selected, you can also left-click on any element in the playlist and move it around freely. You'll want the draw tool active by default most of the time.
- **Paint:** The paint tool is similar to the draw tool except that it continues to add notes as long as you hold down your left click (as opposed to the draw tool, which adds a single note per click).
- **Delete:** The delete tool deletes anything you left-click on while active. You can also delete an element by right-clicking on any element in the playlist while the draw tool is selected.
- **Mute:** The mute tool mutes (deactivates) any element that is clicked while active. If a pattern is muted, all instruments in that pattern are muted.
- **Slip:** This allows you to shift the position of notes in any pattern left or right. To do so, click on any pattern with active notes and drag left or right. The notes will shift accordingly.
- **Slice:** This allows you to split an element into pieces at the position clicked.
- **Select:** This allows you to select a group of elements. Another way to select elements is to hold *Ctrl* + left-click and drag over the elements that you want to select.
- **Zoom:** This allows you to zoom in and out of any element on the playlist. Another way to zoom is to hold down *Ctrl* and scroll with your mouse scroll button. This will zoom in or out on your patterns horizontally. To resize the playlist to fit your screen, press *Ctrl* + right-click while hovering your cursor in the playlist. To zoom into or out of your patterns vertically, hold down *Alt* + mouse scroll.
- **Playback:** This plays the song, starting at the position that is clicked in the playlist.

These tools are not something you need to memorize. You'll gradually learn how to use these tools over time through practice.

Element pattern options

On patterns, audio, or automation, you'll see a little symbol that looks like a piano:

Figure 2.44 – Bass melody

By left-clicking on the symbol, you'll see a list of options available.

Of importance is the **Make unique** option. This allows you to create a unique copy of your selected element. This is useful in a variety of situations. For example, say you had a pattern where an instrument played several notes. You now want to use the same pattern elsewhere in your song but have it play a few different notes. If you make changes to the original, the pattern will be changed everywhere in your song. By selecting **Make unique**, it allows you to create a unique copy of the pattern, which you can then adjust without affecting the original.

So far, we've seen that the playlist allows you to arrange patterns and samples. It gives you a bird's-eye view of your entire project, as well as the ability to zoom in and see and edit precise details. Next, let's take a look at the features contained in the top toolbar.

Using the main header toolbar features

Now that we understand some of the main workbench tools, let's take a look at some of the features offered in the main toolbar at the top of the screen:

Figure 2.45 – The main toolbar

There are lots of features available in the main toolbar. Let's discuss some of the most important ones, such as version control.

Version control

As when coding, it's a good idea to create your project in stages so that you can go back to an earlier stage if you need. It's good practice to save your project often. FL Studio has an option that will do this for you under **FILE | Save new version**:

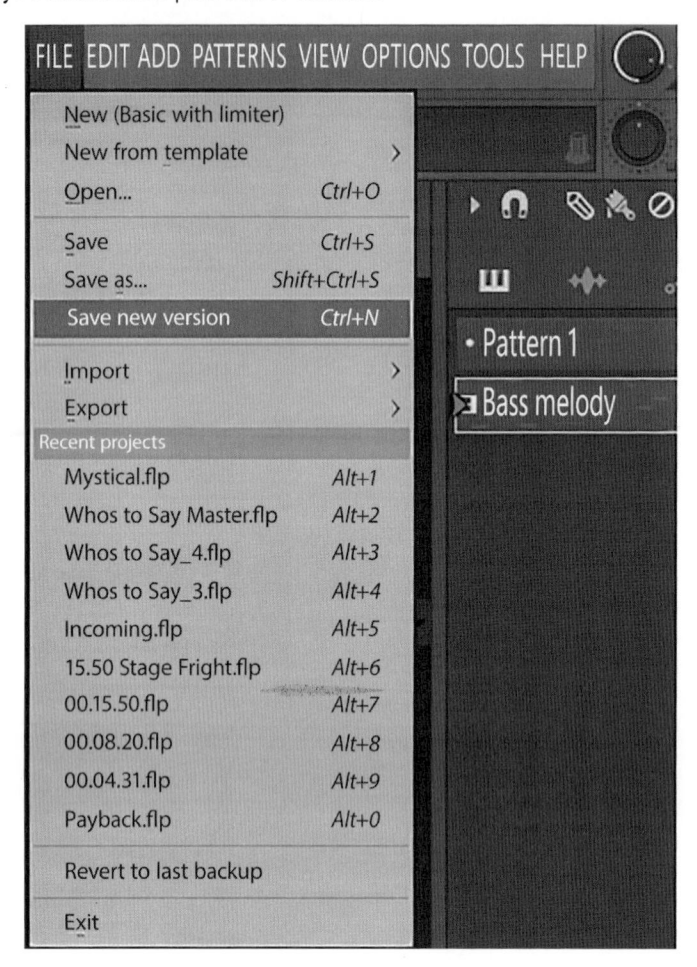

Figure 2.46 – Save new version

This will save your file as a new copy of the project. If you even need to go back, you can simply open up the original project.

Revert to last backup

Sometimes, your computer might crash while you are working. In these cases, there is a way to go to the last autosaved version by navigating to **FILE | Revert to last backup**.

Audio Stream Input/Output (ASIO)

This will load up the project's last autosave. Remember to save your project before closing every time as well.

Audio Stream Input/Output (ASIO) is a sound card driver for computer audio. ASIO drivers allow a lower CPU overhead and buffering than your standard sound driver and will make your project run faster. Under the **Options** | **Audio** settings, you can find some configuration settings. You'll see an option to change the device to **ASIO4ALL v2**:

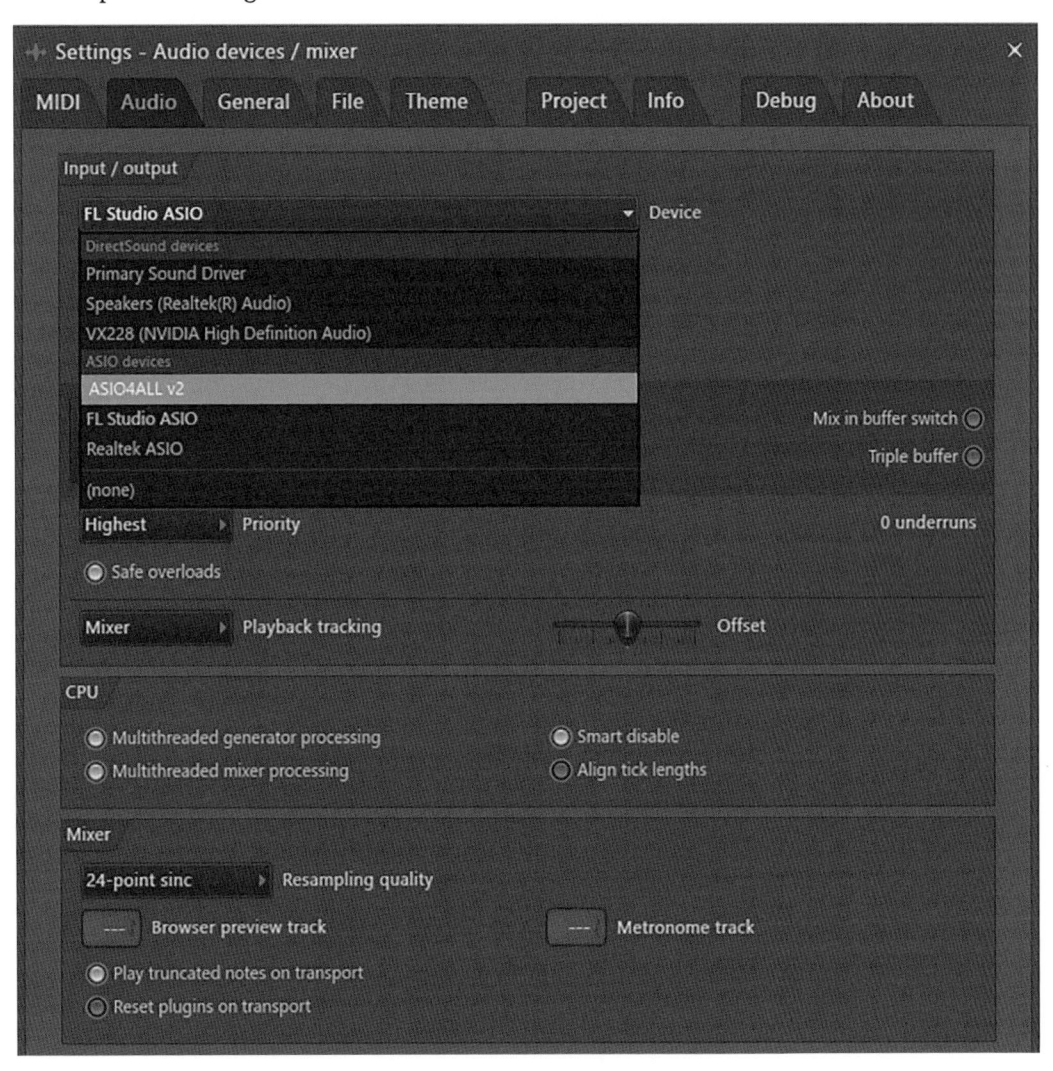

Figure 2.47 – FL Studio ASIO

This is a newer version of the sound card driver, which tends to work better with FL Studio. If you find FL Studio to be lagging, you may want to turn on **ASIO4ALL v2**.

However, turning on **ASIO4ALL v2** means that any other program you are running on your computer will likely no longer play audio and will possibly crash (YouTube, Netflix, and so on), so you'll need to turn this option back off when you want to have another program play sound. Many times, I'll find that my other programs that are running aren't playing sound and I can't figure out what's causing the problem until I realized that **ASIO4ALL v2** was turned on.

Purge unused audio clips

Sometimes, you'll find your channel rack getting messy with many samples and you'll want to clean it up. **Purge unused audio clips** looks at all the samples that you currently have loaded into your channel rack and playlist. Any samples that are not being used in the playlist are discarded. This is handy when you have a large selection of samples loaded up and you want to clean up but aren't sure whether a sample has been used or not. You can find this option by clicking **Tools | Macros | Purge unused audio clips**.

Undo and redo

When you make a mistake, it's easy to go back and fix it by undoing your last few actions. The undo and redo keyboard shortcuts allow you to go back and forward through the changes you've made:

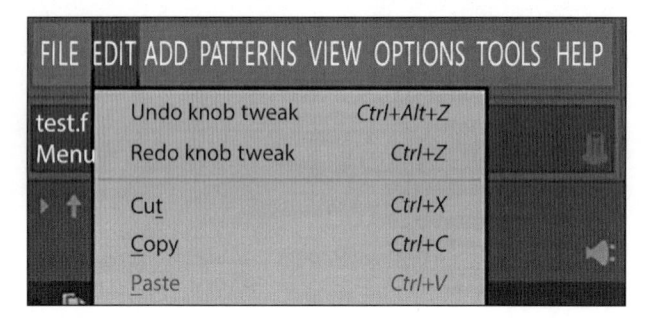

Figure 2.48 – Copy and undo

Viewing project info

If you want to keep notes about your project, there is a text record available for every song:

Figure 2.49 – Project info

For example, I know some producers who like to use these note records to list the key of a song, or links to YouTube or SoundCloud songs that they have used for inspiration.

Summary

In this chapter, you learned how to use the **browser, channel rack,** and **playlist.** You will use these tools again and again with every song you make. The browser allows you to navigate through your samples and swap them in and out of your playlist with ease. The channel rack lets you load up your instruments, navigate through them, and create percussive rhythms. The playlist allows you to arrange the timing of your music patterns, samples, and automation.

In the next chapter, we'll look at the **piano roll** tool so that you can compose melodies for your instruments.

3
Composing with the Piano Roll

When you want to make a melody for your song, you need a tool to help you compose it. The FL Studio piano roll is arguably the best piano roll in the market for composing melodies. The piano roll allows you to add melody notes, arrange them, adjust the inflection of notes, and easily move notes between instruments. Once you know how to use the piano roll, you'll be able to compose melodies for any instrument.

In this chapter, we will cover the following topics:

- Using the piano roll
- Composing great chord progressions
- Recording MIDI notes with MIDI instruments
- Exporting sheet music
- Using and exporting MIDI scores

Using the piano roll

The piano roll is the tool for composing melodies. The piano roll is essentially a piano with a timeline. On the y axis, note pitches are shown, and on the x axis, time is divided into a grid of beats and smaller increments of beats. Notes are displayed as horizontal bars, as shown in the following screenshot:

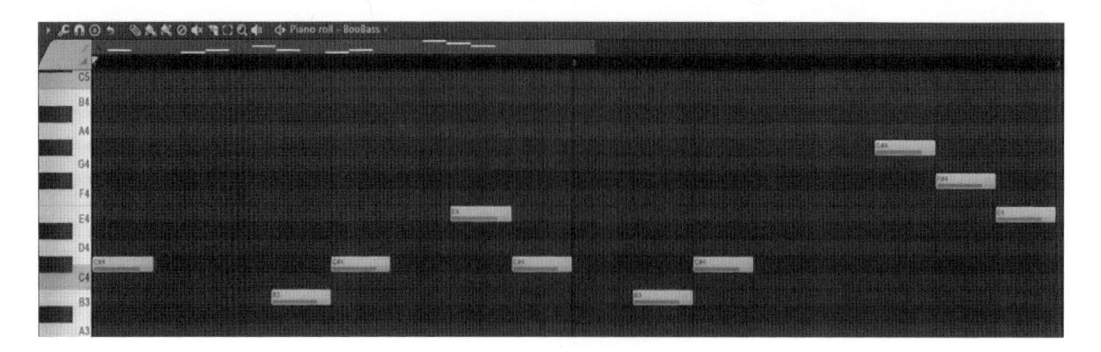

Figure 3.1 – Piano roll

Let's talk about what the piano roll is great at. The piano roll is really good at taking a melody and mapping out the exact timing. It's easy to generate chords and experiment with notes that complement your melody. It's also good at comparing the timing of notes to other instruments playing in the same pattern and jumping between instruments. We'll explore these in detail throughout the chapter.

If you need help with coming up with melody ideas, here are a few quick suggestions. I like to have a physical instrument nearby that I can use to experiment with chords or a melody. I play around with the instrument until I have a few chords that I like and then think about recording the notes into the piano roll. I have a MIDI keyboard so that when I play my instrument, FL Studio records the MIDI notes directly into the piano roll. Alternatively, I'll listen to a sound sample or another song for inspiration to get ideas or import **Musical Instrument Digital Interface (MIDI)** notes to experiment with (discussed later in this chapter). Once I have a basic melody, the piano roll gives me the freedom to expand upon my idea.

The piano roll offers a large set of useful tools for composing melodies. The piano roll toolbar tools are the same as the toolbar in the playlist. So, once you learn the piano roll tools, you'll know how to use them in both places. If you need a recap on the playlist, we covered it in *Chapter 2, Exploring the Browser, Playlist, and Channel Rack*. Okay, let's learn how to use the piano roll.

Choosing an instrument

Before composing a melody, we first need to choose an instrument to use in the piano roll. You can choose the instrument you want to use by clicking on the channel rack drop down menu in the piano roll, as seen in the following screenshot:

Chapter 3

Figure 3.2 – Choosing instruments

Alternatively, you can open the channel rack, right-click on the instrument you want to edit in the piano roll, and select the **Piano roll** option:

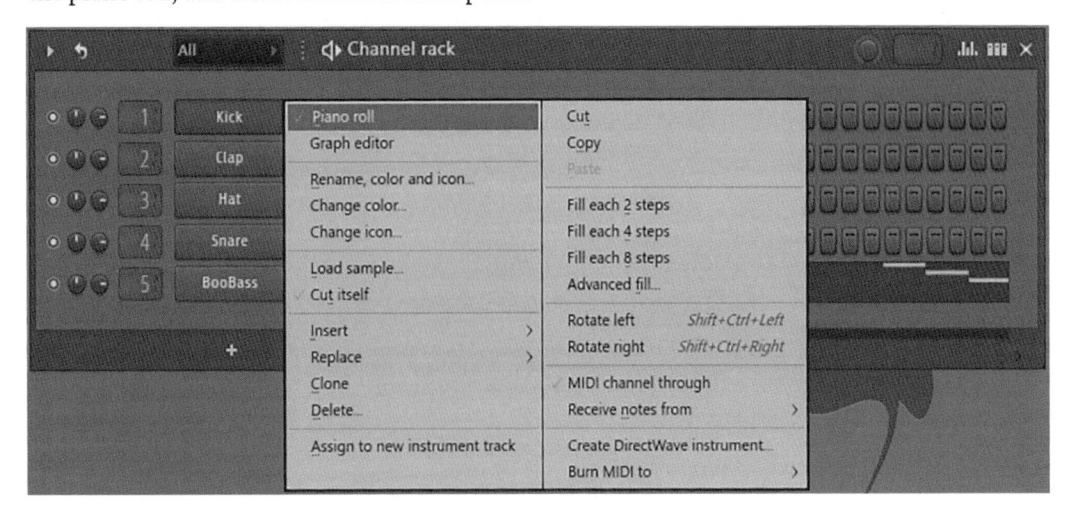

Figure 3.3 – Choosing instruments

Now that you have chosen your instrument for composing a melody, we can begin adding notes. Note that you don't have to get too fixated on any particular instrument early on in the composing process. You can easily swap instruments with FL Studio in the channel rack and have the new instrument play the same notes.

Adding notes in the piano roll

To add notes, first, make sure that the draw symbol is selected:

Figure 3.4 – Draw tool

Then, left-click in the blue grid section of the piano roll to add notes.

It helps if you are playing the music pattern at the same time that you're adding notes so that you can hear the melody being played and get the timings correct. To do so, make sure **PAT** is selected for the desired music pattern, and then press play:

Figure 3.5 – Player

When **PAT** is selected, only instruments within the current pattern will play. However, if **SONG** is selected, all patterns in the playlist and anything they contain will play.

Selecting multiple notes

Sometimes, you'll want to select multiple notes at a time and move them all at once or copy them to another instrument. You can select multiple notes by pressing *Ctrl + Shift*, then left-clicking and dragging over the notes.

Alternatively, you can use the select tool:

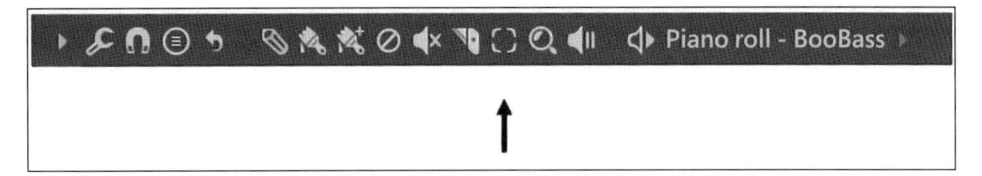

Figure 3.6 – Select tool

You'll also want to select multiple notes when you're making changes in the event editor, such as velocity adjustments. We discuss the event editor and velocity in the pages ahead.

Deleting notes

What if you make a mistake and need to remove a note? There are multiple ways to do this:

- The easiest way to delete notes is by right-clicking on the note you want to remove.
- You can select multiple notes at the same time and press *Delete* on your keyboard.
- Select the delete tool (shown in the following screenshot) and then left-click on the notes you want to remove:

Figure 3.7 – Delete

If you delete more notes than you meant to, the undo (*Ctrl* + *Z*) and redo (*Ctrl* + *Shift* + *Z*) keyboard shortcuts are always there to help you.

Muting and unmuting notes

There's a way to use note placeholders to keep a reference of note positions without actively playing them. This is useful if you want to try out an alternative melody but don't want to lose the original notes. You can mute notes without deleting them by double-right-clicking on an empty space next to a note and dragging over the note. To unmute, do the exact same steps.

Alternatively, you can select notes and then press *Alt + M*, or you can select the mute tool and then click on the notes:

Figure 3.8 – Mute notes

You'll find muted notes very useful when you clone a music pattern and want to change some of the notes but still want to remember the position of the original notes.

Slicing notes

From time to time, you'll want to chop up notes into several smaller notes. My preferred way to slice notes is to use right *Alt* + right *Shift* and then click on the notes that you want to slice. Alternatively, you can use the slice tool:

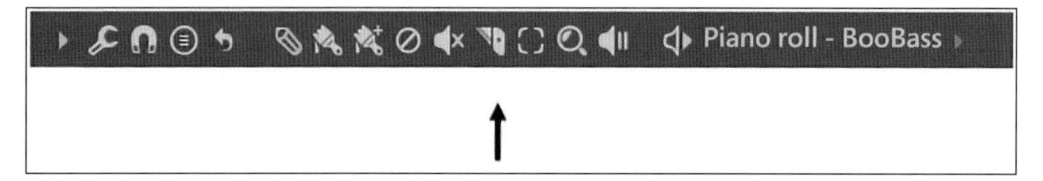

Figure 3.9 – Slice tool

The slice tool is most useful when you want to chop up several notes at once rather than changing the length of an individual note.

Sliding notes

Sliding notes are where the pitch of one note transforms into a new pitch. Sliding notes are very commonly used with sub-bass instruments. You can use the piano roll to add notes that slide from one pitch to another. Only native FL Studio plugins are guaranteed to be able to use the sliding note feature in the piano roll. External plugins often are unable to use this feature. To use sliding notes, we need to load up a plugin that allows sliding notes. To do so, execute the following steps:

1. Create a new pattern.

Chapter 3   75

2. In the channel rack, insert the **3x Osc** (short for oscillator) synthesizer:

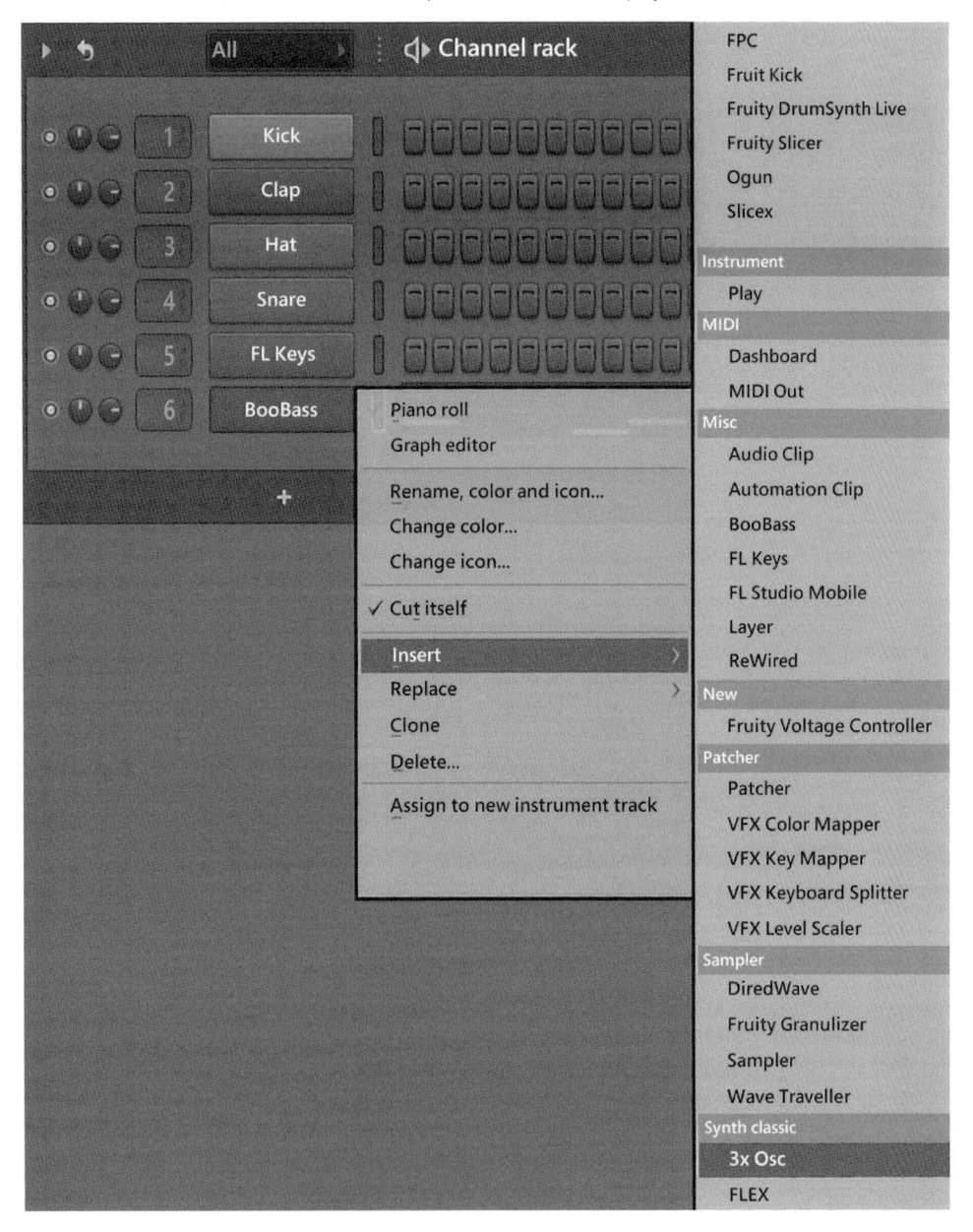

Figure 3.10 – Inserting the 3x Osc synthesizer

3. Using **3x Osc**, we can create sliding notes. Open up the **3x Osc** instrument in the piano roll:

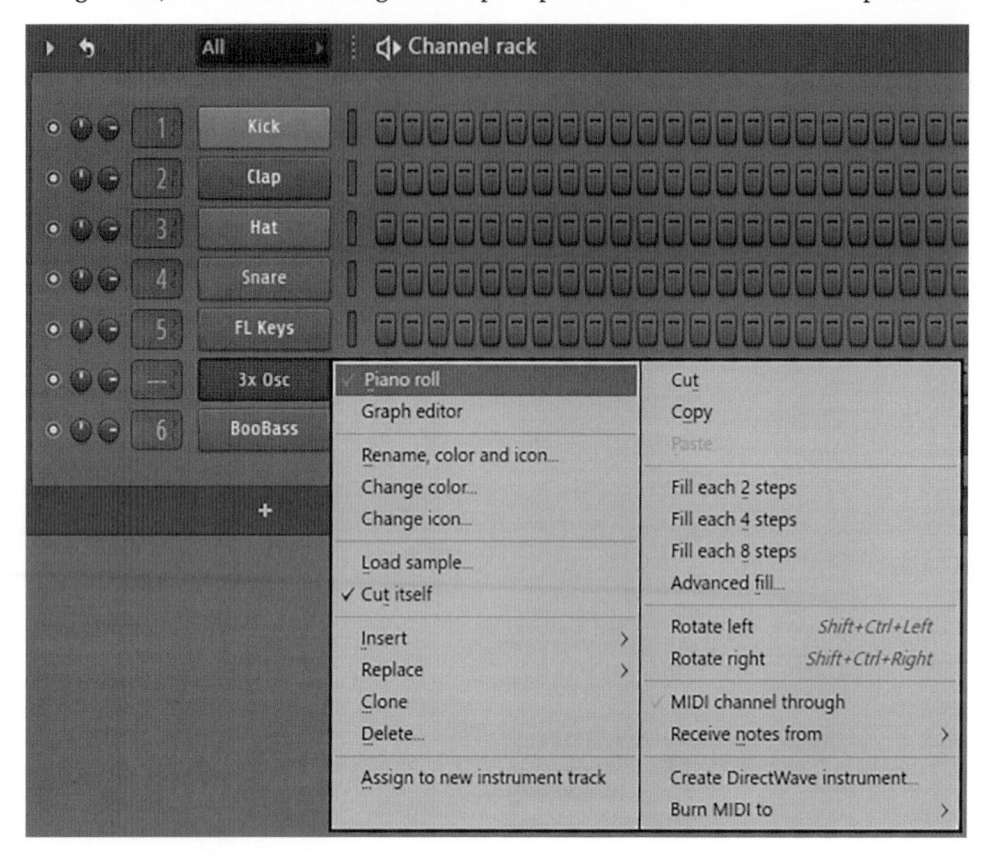

Figure 3.11 – The 3x Osc synthesizer in the piano roll

4. Once in the piano roll, left-click to add notes so that you have the following pattern:

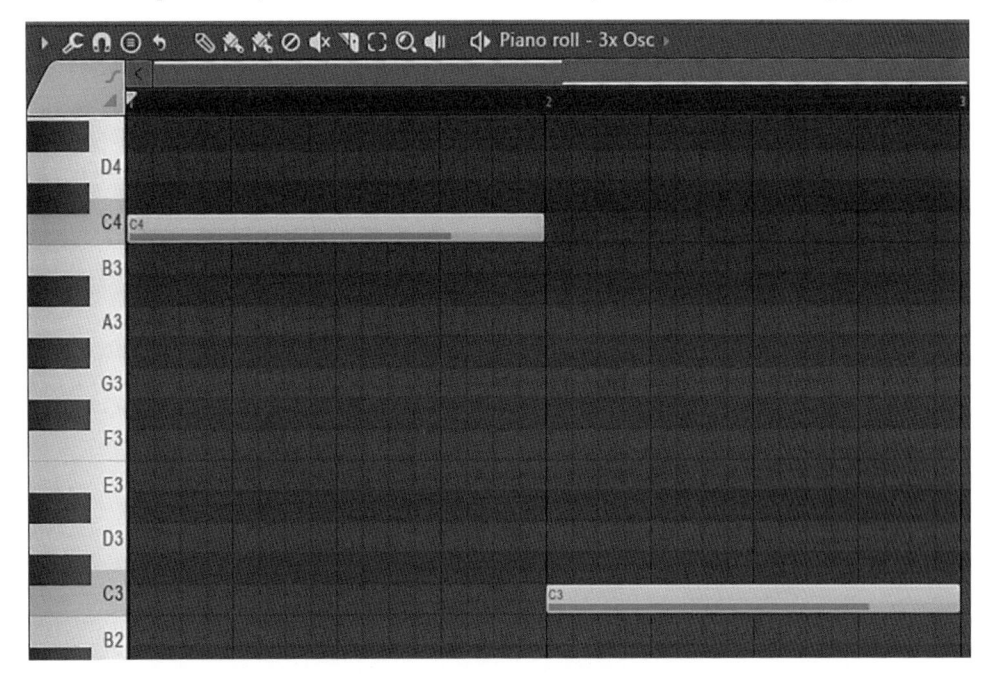

Figure 3.12 – Adding notes to the piano roll

Here, we've added two notes to **C4** and **C3**. What we want to happen is for the pitch to slide from the first note into the second note.

5. To add a sliding pitch, select the slide tool from the top-left corner of the piano roll:

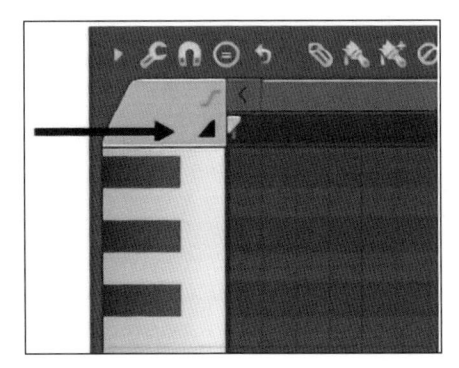

Figure 3.13 – Slide tool

6. When the slide tool is selected, it will add notes that slide from the current pitch into the new slide pitch. Add the **C3** note as shown in the following screenshot. You can tell that a note is a slide note by the slide symbol on the right of the note (the triangle icon):

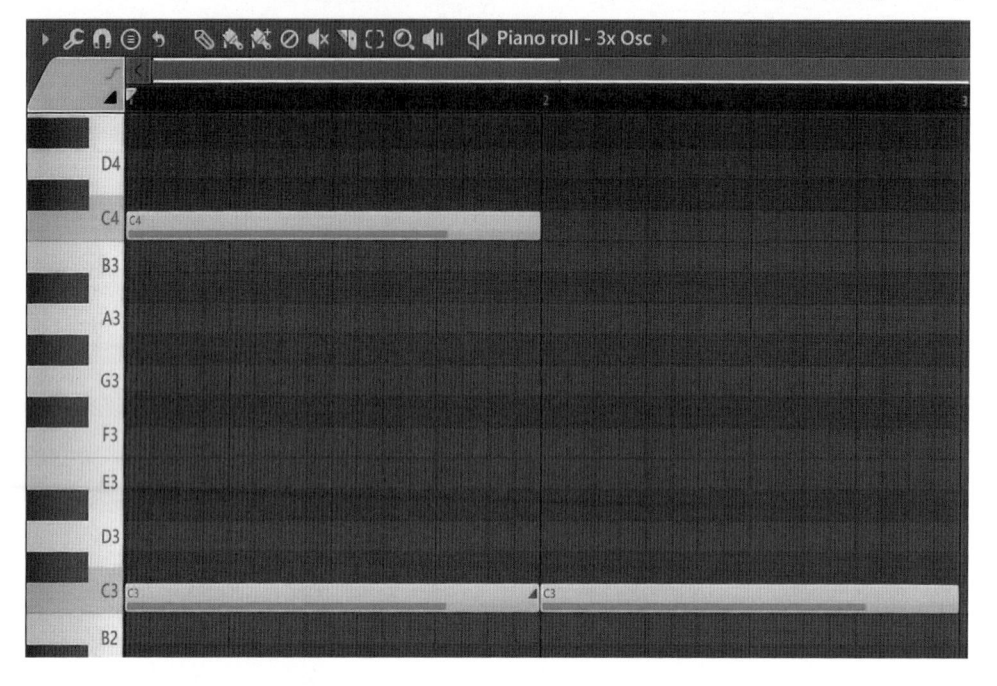

Figure 3.14 – Added sliding note

When you play the pattern, you'll hear the note with pitch **C4** sliding downward until it hits pitch **C3**. This technique can be used for sliding multiple notes at once.

Remember to click the slide tool again to turn it off when you're done, or else all notes you add going forward will be slide notes.

This technique can be used for samples as well as instruments. To do so, you can use samples in the **DirectWave** plugin (which we will explore in *Chapter 10, Creating Your Own Instruments and Effects*). You can then use the pitch slide effect on DirectWave. This is a big deal because you can turn any sound into a sample, even sounds from external VST instruments. In other words, with a little creativity, any sound can be turned into a slide note.

So far, we've learned how to add notes manually. Next, let's learn how to compose chord melodies.

Using the stamp tool to get assistance with scales

There are many music scales. The most commonly known ones are major and minor, but these are only two scales out of many possible ones. Notes that fit within a given scale sound good together and consistent as long as you use notes that stay within the scale. Depending on the scale you pick, your music will have a different emotional feel and sound happier, sadder, lighter, darker, and so on.

> To learn more about scales, check out Classic FM's guide to modes with examples (https://www.classicfm.com/discover-music/latest/guide-to-musical-modes/) and this guide to piano scales: https://pianoscales.org/jazz.html.

When starting to compose a new piece of music, I find it helpful to force myself to use only notes that fit within a chosen scale. This reduces the choice of possible notes I can add and makes it easier to pick notes and chords that complement each other. The piano roll provides several tools to assist you with choosing notes that fit within a scale.

The stamp tool lists a series of chords, scales, and percussion rhythm examples to aid you in coming up with melodies.

Choosing one of these will give you example notes. To use this tool, do the following:

1. Open up the stamp tool, as shown in the following screenshot, and choose any one of the presets:

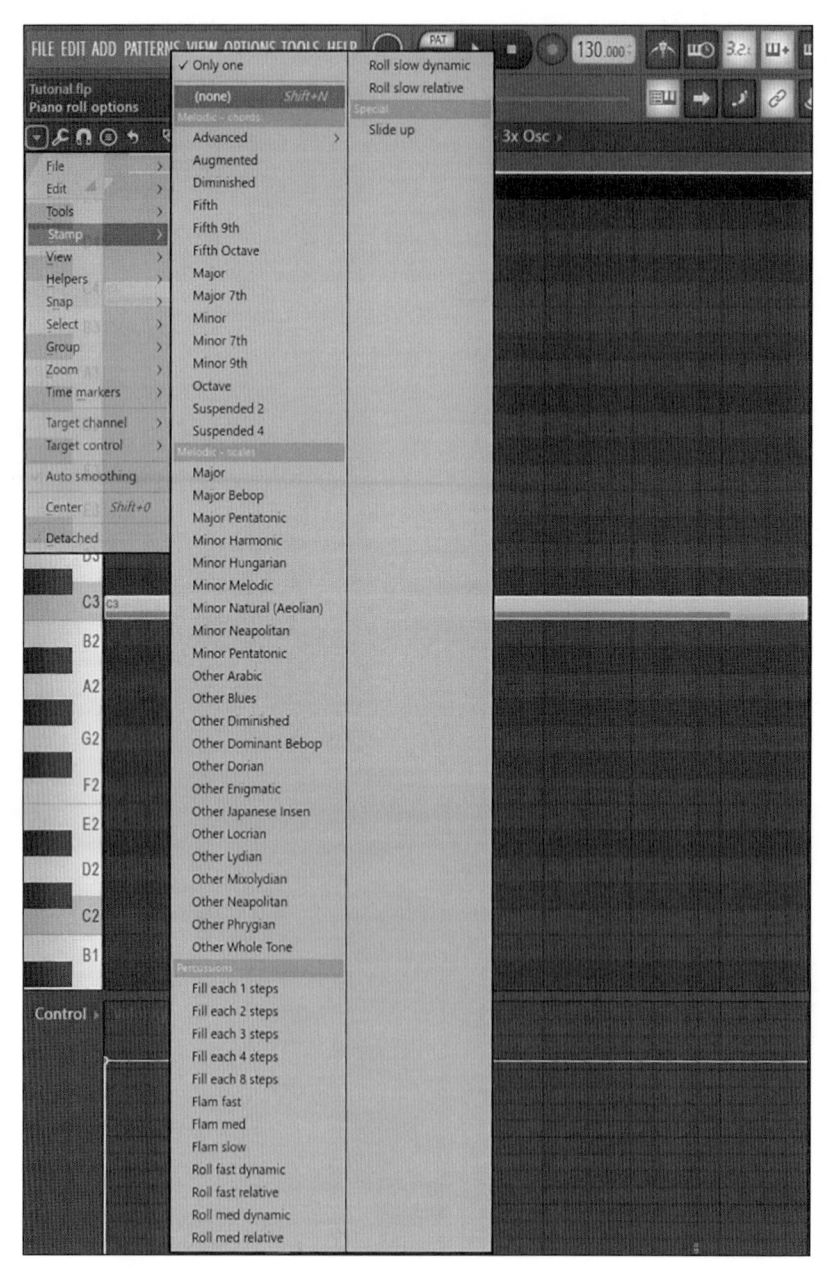

Figure 3.15 – Stamp tool

2. Next, left-click inside the piano roll, and the example notes will be inserted.

Using the stamp tool is a quick way to determine what notes are available in a scale. Let's say I was composing a piece of music for a film and needed a sound that was dark and emotional. I'd look up some example songs that were dark and emotional and figure out what scale they were using. If, for example, I found out that the scale used in a song was a phrygian scale and I wanted a similar sound, I could use the stamp tool to identify which notes are in the phrygian scale by selecting the **Other Phrygian** stamp preset. I could then insert the example notes from the stamp tool into the piano roll and use that as my guide. The notes inserted would be my visual aid to knowing what note pitches are used in my scale.

If you want to see a list of available scales, consider checking out the website pianoscales.org: `https://www.pianoscales.org/major.html`

We've learned about the tools the piano roll offers. Next, let's learn how to compose a chord progression.

Composing great chord progressions

A **chord** is when three or more notes are played simultaneously. A **chord progression** is a sequence of chords that sound good together and have a sense of movement throughout.

Understanding how to build a strong chord progression from scratch is one of the most valuable skills a composer can develop. It's the foundational building block of songs. It's usually the first thing that gets created, and it sets the rules for all instruments and vocals that follow. If you hear a song whose melody isn't very interesting, usually a subpar chord progression is the culprit.

Let's compose a chord progression:

1. Create a new music pattern.
2. Load up an instrument that can play multiple notes at once, such as the **FL Keys** instrument.

3. Add notes in the piano roll by left-clicking in the blue grid and creating a pattern such as the one shown in the following screenshot:

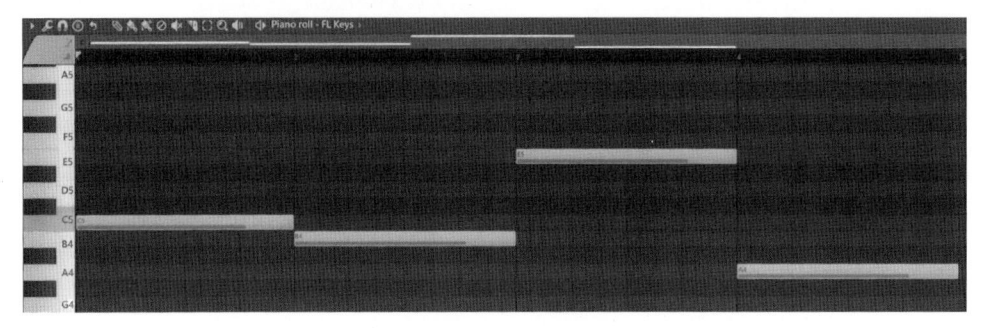

Figure 3.16 – Adding notes

I've chosen the A minor scale, so notes that we pick from here on will be within this scale. What we have so far is a baseline for our notes: C, B, E, and A. This is a starting point on which we'll build. The exact four notes that we pick aren't that important as long as they're within the same scale.

Our arrangement doesn't sound very interesting yet. One tool to add interest is to have the notes play a rhythm. At the top of the piano roll, you'll see the numbers 1, 2, 3, 4…, and so on. This represents the number of music bars. **Music bars** are a measurement of relative time in music used to keep track of the beat. In pop music, baselines tend to be 4 or 8 bars long for a given song's verse or chorus. Right now, our notes are playing one note for four beats in each bar. This is boring to listen to. Let's break up the notes into a rhythmic pattern so that we can hear variations within the bar.

4. Break up the notes until they look like the following pattern:

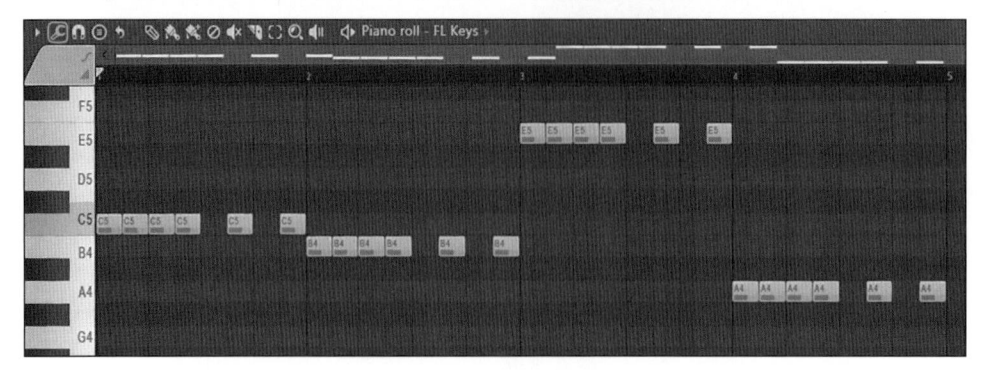

Figure 3.17 – Added rhythm

What we've done is create a percussive pattern. Note the empty space between some notes. Deciding where to place silence is just as important as deciding where to place notes.

We're repeating the same general rhythmic pattern throughout each bar. This will make it clear to the listener that there is a cohesive theme that is easy to follow.

Let's form our chords. Remember that **chords** are a combination of three or more notes played simultaneously. Playing multiple notes at once gives the sound some texture, which makes it more interesting. I want to add notes that will complement my baseline melody. For any baseline, complementing notes include notes that are a third or a fifth higher or lower than the root (original) note. In music theory, a **third** means three scale degrees of difference from the root note; in other words, three pitches away. A **fifth** is five pitches away. Let's add some thirds and fifths to our root notes.

5. Add notes as shown in the following screenshot. As long as we add notes that are within our scale (A minor), notes that are a third or a fifth will sound good in combination with the root note:

Figure 3.18 – Added thirds and fifths

We've added notes to complement our baseline. I've colored the new notes with a different color for visual convenience. Our arrangement is already sounding better. We're aiming for chords, though, which means we need to add another unique note to play at the same time. When I say unique note, I mean that we are playing a unique pitch. For example, if I play the note **A4** when I add a unique note, the note I add will be a pitch other than an A pitch.

What notes could we add to finish our chords? This time, we need to use our ears and experiment until we find a sound that complements our existing two notes. There isn't an exact rule but rather a series of attempts at trying out different notes until we find one that we like.

6. Add notes as shown in the following screenshot:

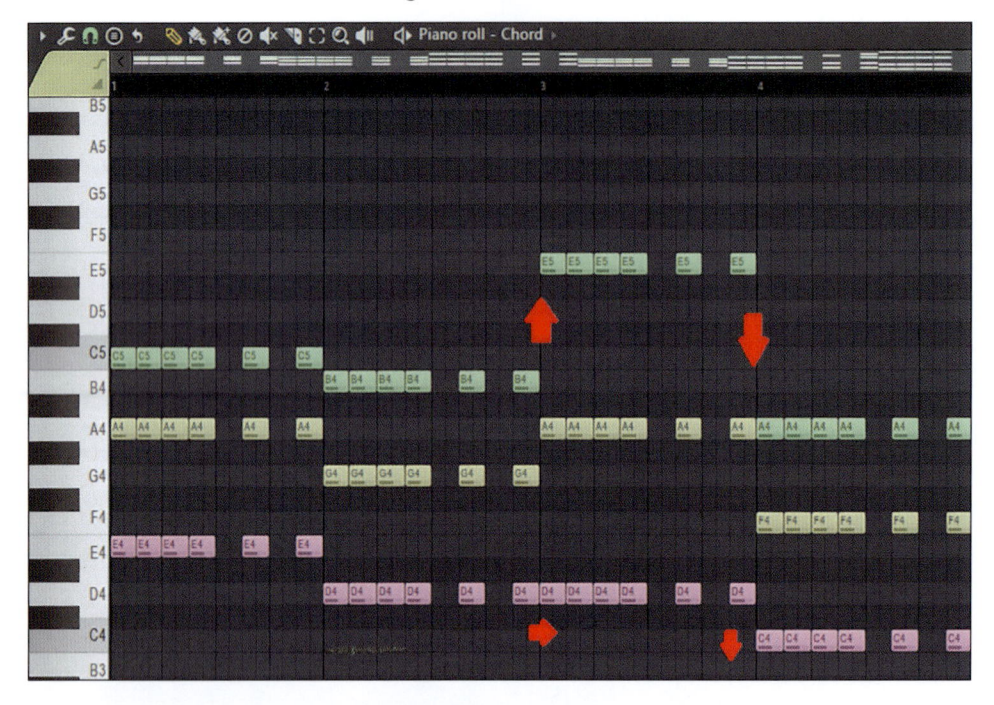

Figure 3.19 – Created chords

Here, we can see that all of our notes have now been turned into chords. It helps to think of the notes in a chord progression as separate melodies that interact with each other.

In our example, our original root notes are the highest-pitch notes. They start out moving in a descending direction, moving from C to B in bars 1 and 2. In bar 3, they change direction and move upward to E before descending to A in bar 4.

The last chord notes I added are the lowest pitch in the chord. The lowest melody moves in a downward direction descending from E to D and then to C. In bar 3, the highest melody and the lowest melody diverge in the pitch direction. The high-pitch melody is moving upward, and the low-pitch melody is not.

They then reunite in bar 4, moving in the same direction again.

Chord melodies diverging in upward and downward pitch directions are interesting to your ears. If your chord melody sounds boring, consider making your high and low melodies diverge in the pitch direction.

Bar 4 sounds a little bland and predictable. Let's give it some variation to distinguish it from the other chords. Specifically, I want to change the last two notes in bar 4 so that they aren't playing at the exact same pitch for the entire bar. I want the notes to feel like they're leading back to the beginning chord of the first bar.

7. Replace the last bar with notes, as shown in the following screenshot:

Figure 3.20 – Adding variation to bar 4

In the last bar on the right, we can see two single notes not yet in a chord. Let's build chords around them.

We can repeat the steps that we did earlier to flesh out these individual notes into chords. Add a second note, using a third or fifth higher or lower in the scale. Then, experiment to find a third chord note that complements this.

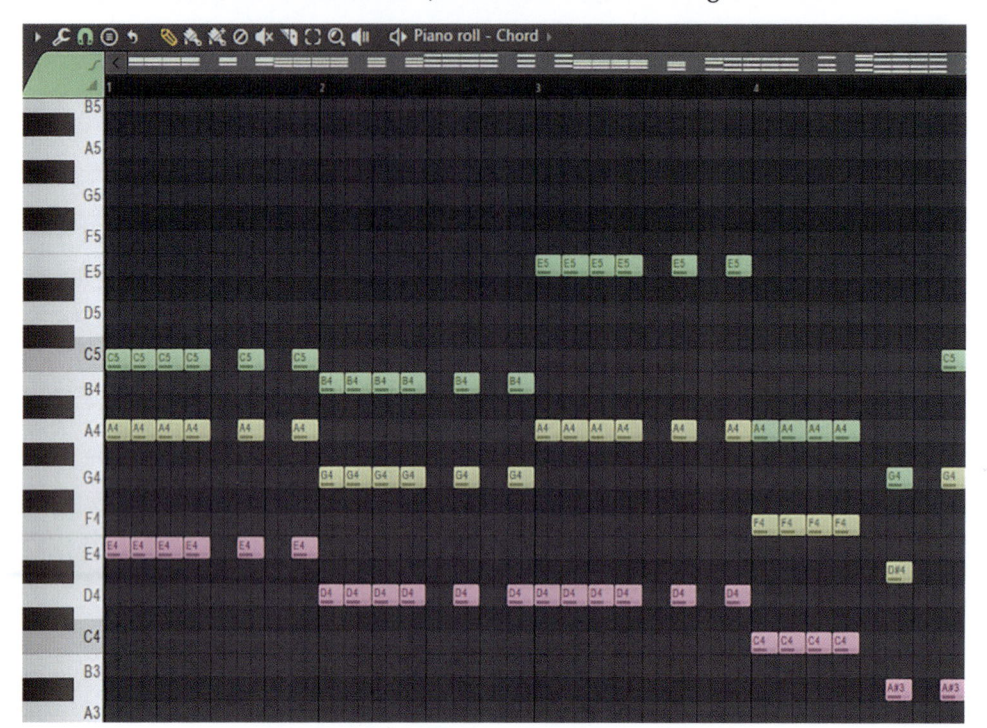

8. Add notes to fill out the chord in bar 4, as shown in the following screenshot:

Figure 3.21 – Filling in the chord

Our chord progression is coming along now. It's time to polish our chords. One way to give our chords some more texture is to add another unique note to the scale to make a four-note chord. The more notes, the more textured and nuanced our chords will sound.

However, adding unique notes is something that needs to be done sparingly. Converting all three chords into four-note chords is not always a good idea. Creating all four-note chords will likely result in losing out on the overall melody of the chord progression. We only want to add additional notes if it doesn't detract from the overall melody. Deciding when to add more notes is something that needs to be done through experimentation. You tinker and play around to see whether it enhances or detracts. You add and take away notes until the chord sounds better.

9. After playing around and experimenting, I've decided that bar 4 could be enhanced by adding a fourth unique note to the chords. Add notes to bar 4, as shown in the following screenshot:

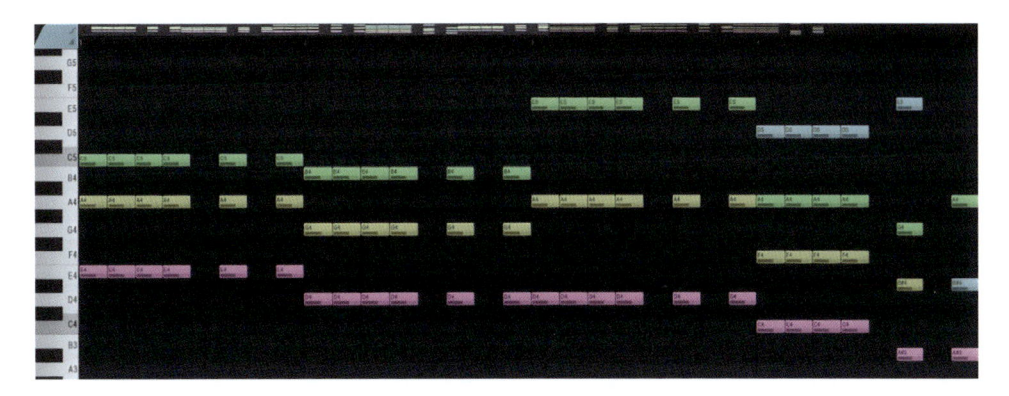

Figure 3.22 – Creating four-note chords in bar 4

We have the first four bars of our chord progression. It has a sense of momentum where each chord sounds like it logically flows into the next chord. There is one problem, though: when this progression is played, it feels too short. When you listen to it, your ears want it to repeat again and reach some sort of conclusion. Right now, it resembles a cliffhanger in a book that is unresolved. Your ears want the chord progression to resolve itself. Let's resolve the chord progression by expanding it from a four-bar to an eight-bar chord progression.

10. Copy the notes from the first four bars and paste them directly after so that your piano roll looks as in the following screenshot. You can quickly copy and paste notes by selecting notes and then pressing *Ctrl + B*:

Figure 3.23 – Copied notes

We now have the same chord progression playing twice, back to back. In the second iteration, we will make a melody variation and resolve the chord progression.

We're going to make some changes to the melody in bars 5-9. Our ears naturally gravitate toward the highest-pitch notes and pay the most attention to them, so they will form our main melody. As such, we want to manipulate the highest-pitch notes in our chord progression.

What to move, add, or take away is once again a series of trial and error. You experiment with adding and moving notes and see whether the melody is improved. A guideline is that the notes should fit within notes of our chosen scale (in our case, A minor).

11. Add notes in bars 5-9 so that the piano roll looks as in the following screenshot:

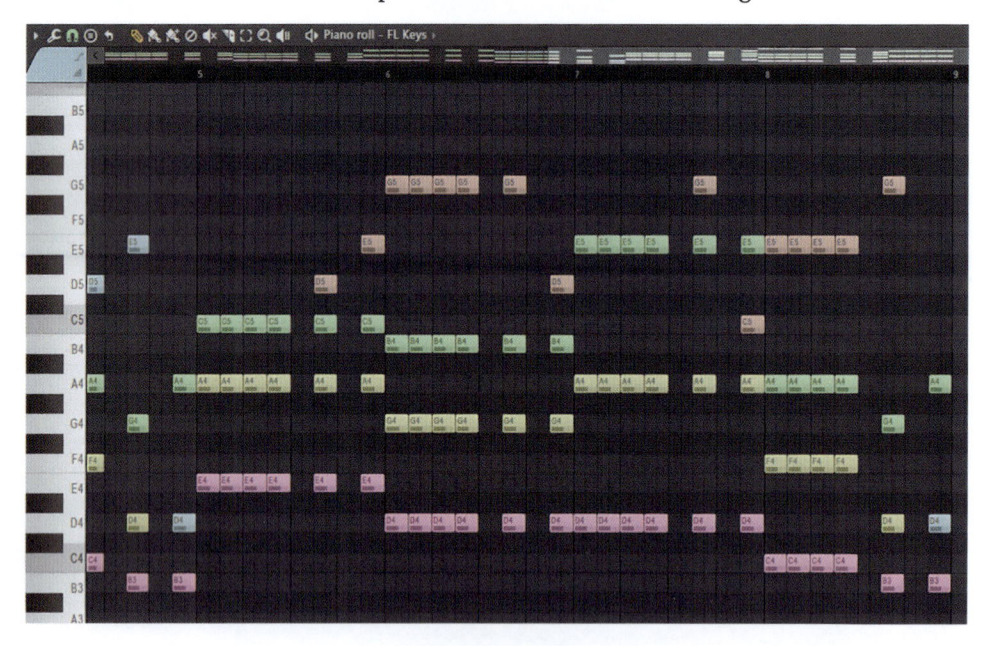

Figure 3.24 – Bars 5–9

In the preceding screenshot, we gave the second iteration of our chord progression variation by adding notes in bars 5-9. Specifically, we focused on the highest-pitch notes.

In bar 8, we adjusted our four-note chord. We moved the highest-pitch note from **D5** to **E5**. By making this change, our chord has a slightly different texture from the chord in bar 4.

In bar 6, we added one of the same notes in our chord (**G4**) to an octave higher on the pitch of **G5**. An **octave** means a note of double the pitch, eight tones higher, but that still sounds like the *same note*. When you have a chord, you can add notes that are the same as existing notes in the chord an octave higher or lower, and it won't change the chord. It will still sound good.

Knowing that you can add notes that are octaves higher or lower is another tool. We can **transpose** any existing notes in our chord progression to octaves higher or lower, and the chord progression will still work. When I say transposing, I mean moving a note pitch up or down an octave. By spreading out our chords across several octaves, we can unclutter our chords and give our chords a sense of space to make the sound feel larger.

12. Take existing notes and experiment with transposing them an octave higher or lower. You can quickly transpose notes to a high or low octave by selecting notes and then using *Ctrl* + the up arrow or *Ctrl* + the down arrow:

Figure 3.25 – Transposing notes

In the preceding screenshot, we can see that I've taken chord notes in bars 1, 2, 4, 5, 6, and 8 and transposed them down an octave until they formed the lowest-pitch notes of the chords. Specifically, I transposed notes that were in the middle of the chords. The notes in the middle are generally the most cluttered sounds and benefit the most from transposing. By transposing these notes from the middle of the chords and spreading them down an octave, I've uncluttered our chords and given them a sense of space.

Our chord progression is now finished. Whew, sounded like a lot of work. The good news is that the steps are easy to replicate for a variety of scenarios and can be broken down into a simple checklist. Let's summarize the steps we took:

1. Create a simple baseline melody with unique note pitches.
2. Add some rhythm by breaking up the notes and adding breaks between some of them.
3. Add note harmonies by adding a complementing note, such as a third or fifth pitch higher or lower than the root note.
4. Add another note to complete the chord by experimenting with pitches until you find one that fits.

5. Polish your chord progression. Experiment with adding additional unique note pitches to your chords to form 4 or more note chords.

6. When repeating your chord progression a second time, give the second playthrough some variation from the first to distinguish it. The main melody is generally your highest-pitch notes. Your ears will look for this as your main melody, so the highest-pitch notes are usually the notes that you want to adjust.

7. Experiment with transposing notes in your chord progressions an octave higher or lower. Usually, the notes in the middle need to be transposed as they will sound cluttered in the middle. This will add a sense of space and unclutter your chords.

You now have a solid base for building your song. Once you have a chord progression, the rest of the song is easy. It's just a matter of taking notes from your chord progression and assigning and layering various instruments to play them. For the lowest notes, choose a bass instrument. For the higher notes, pick instruments or vocals.

Another bonus is that coming up with vocal melodies becomes much simpler. Just by listening to the chord progression, your mind will naturally want to hum along to the chords and improvise melodies over it.

We've finished learning how to create a chord progression. Next, let's look at how to record MIDI instruments into the piano roll.

Recording into the piano roll with MIDI instruments

MIDI is a way for software and electronic devices to pass music information from one device to another so that the new device knows what notes to play.

If you already know how to play live instruments, you may want to look into acquiring a MIDI instrument. If you have MIDI instrument hardware, such as a MIDI keyboard, MIDI guitar, or another MIDI controller, you can play notes on the hardware instrument live, and FL Studio can record the notes directly into the piano roll. This is a very efficient method of recording melodies and gives you the benefit of being able to go back and correct any mistakes you make.

To record notes with your MIDI instrument hardware, take the following steps. If you don't have a MIDI keyboard, you can play notes by pressing keys on your computer keyboard as well, but this is less convenient than a designated MIDI device:

1. Create a new pattern and select the instrument from the channel rack that you want to play.
2. Select the record button and select the **Notes and automation** option:

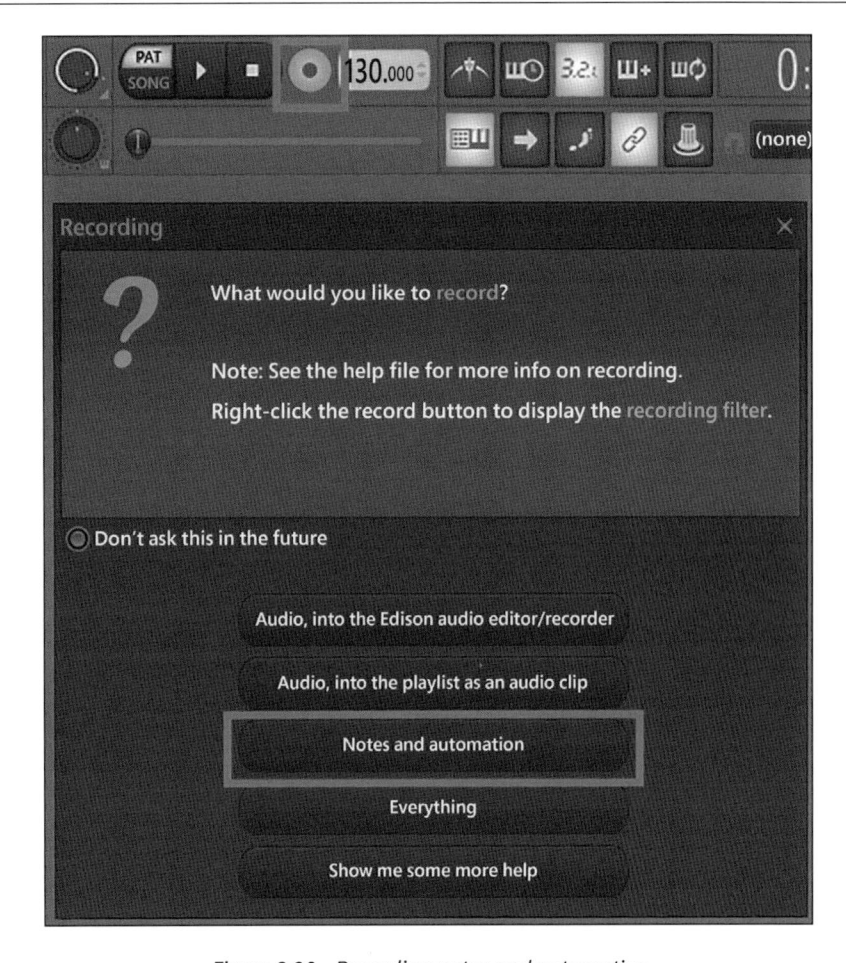

Figure 3.26 – Recording notes and automation

Once you press play, any notes that you play into the MIDI instrument will be inserted into the piano roll as the pattern progresses.

Once your music is recorded into the piano roll, you'll need to adjust the timing of the notes to make it fit with the rest of your arrangement. Next, we'll learn how to fine-tune your note timing.

The snap-to-grid (magnet) tool

The snap-to-grid tool assists with making notes fit in the song tempo. The piano roll segments notes in the piano roll by beats. A **beat** is a basic unit of time and is the click you'll hear when you turn on the metronome.

The number that you see at the top of the screen is known as **BPM** (or **Beats Per Minute**); this is how fast your music is playing.

Using snap-to-grid, you can control what increments of a beat you want the piano roll to divide into. By left-clicking on the snap-to-grid tool in the top-left corner of the piano roll, you can see the timing options:

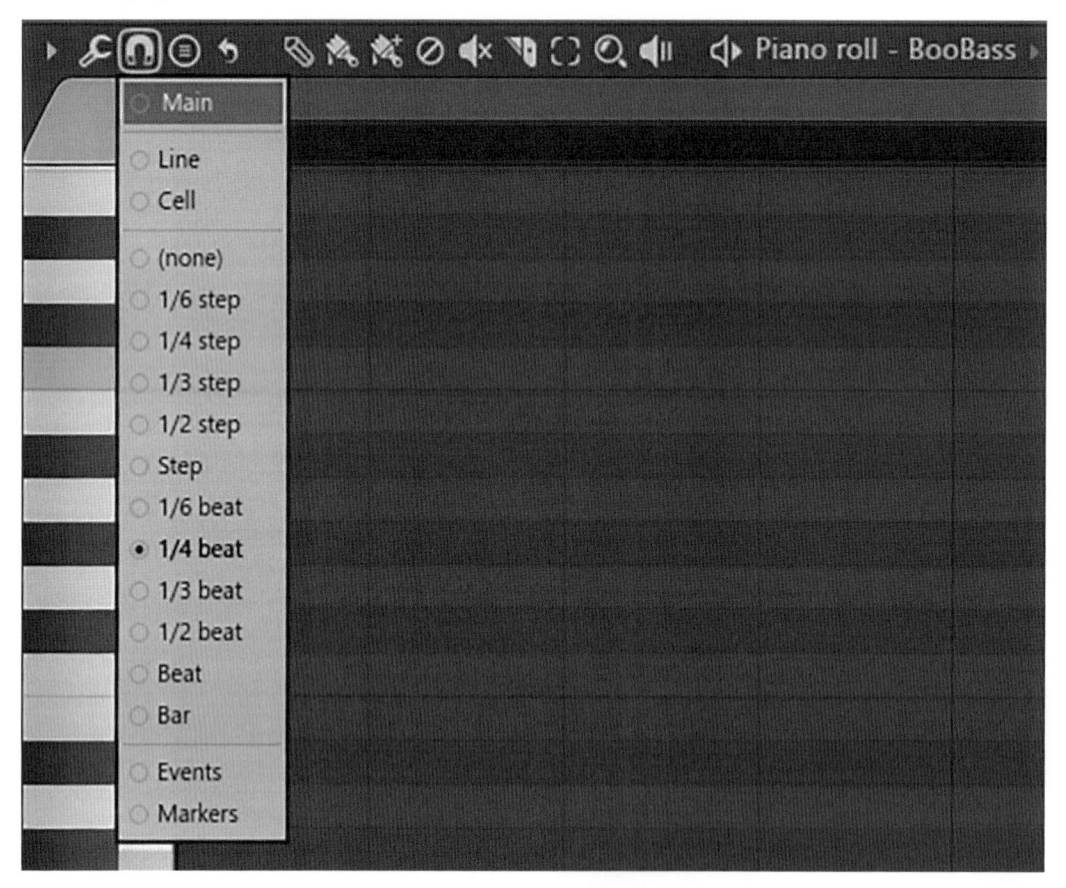

Figure 3.27 – Magnet tool

As you can see in the preceding screenshot, you can divide the piano roll grid into increments of **Bar, Beat, 1/2 beat,** and so on. Once you've selected an option, you'll notice that the number of increments in the piano roll grid will increase or decrease depending on your selection. The snap-to-grid tool works the same way in the playlist as it does in the piano roll.

Quantizing notes

If you record notes directly into the piano roll with a MIDI instrument, you might notice your notes are out of sync with the timing of your song. You can fix this with a tool known as quantizing. **Quantizing** means you're making your notes sync up with the piano roll grid. The tool will adjust the start and end times of your notes to fit in time with the grid.

Whether to quantize your music or not is partly due to personal preference. Quantizing will make your music perfectly in time. If you are composing for EDM, you may want all your music to hit exactly on the beat, and quantizing is an easy way to make this happen. The more instruments you have playing at the same time, the more likely you will want all your instruments to sync up with each other. If you're trying to create a solo acoustic performance, you may want to encourage a little imperfection and find that quantizing makes your music too robotic.

You can quantize everything in the piano roll or just the start times of your selected notes, as seen in the following screenshot:

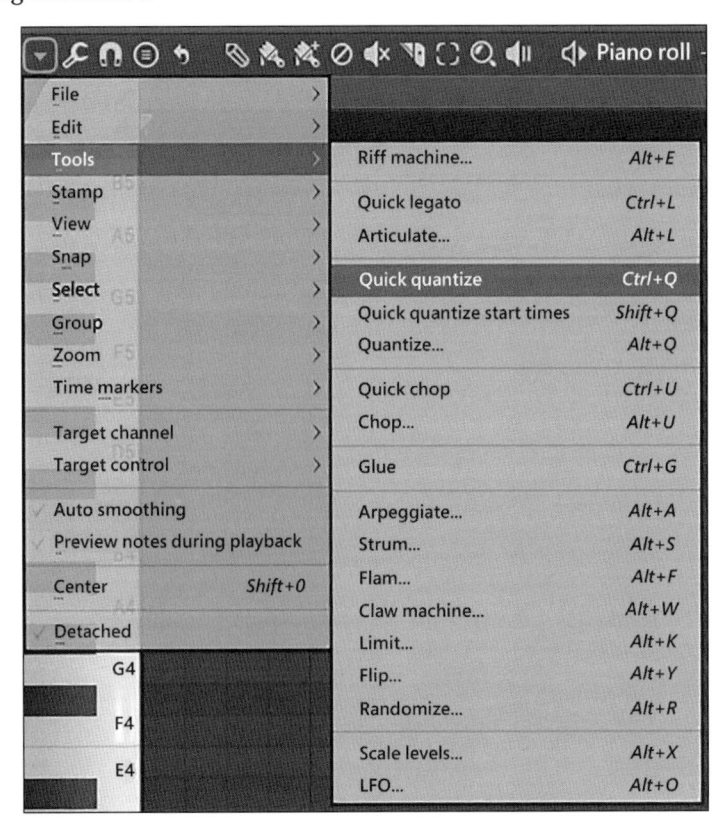

Figure 3.28 – Quantizing

If your notes are already in sync, you won't see any difference because your notes are already quantized. In addition to quantizing, there are a series of other tools available that I encourage you to try out:

- **Chop**: Slices your notes into smaller chunks based on the grid set by the grid magnets.
- **Glue**: Combines two adjacent notes into a single note.
- **Arpeggiate**: Takes your notes, breaks them down into smaller pieces, and spreads the notes across several octaves.
- **Strum**: Shifts the timing and velocity of notes to give the impression of strumming the way a guitar is strummed.
- **Flam**: Allows you to play two notes very close together, blurring the sounds. This is a term mostly used with percussive instruments.
- **Claw Machine**: Removes notes, adds notes, and shifts the timing of notes to create new rhythms. This is good when used in combination with samples already sliced with the **Slicex** plugin, which is discussed in *Chapter 9, Vocoders and Vocal Chops*.
- **Limit**: Allows you to choose a limit of pitches to which the piano roll is confined. Any notes outside of the pitch range are transposed until they fit within the set range. For example, if you set a limit to notes within C1 to C2, any notes lower than C1 or higher than C2 will be transposed up or down in pitch until they fit inside the range.
- **Flip**: Inverts selected notes horizontally or vertically in the piano roll.
- **Randomize**: Creates random notes. This can be confined within a set key.
- **Scale Levels**: Manipulates the velocity level of selected notes. Allows you to adjust the overall volume of all your notes rather than individually for each note.
- **LFO**: Controls the **Low Frequency Oscillator** (**LFO**). This means adjusting the parameter of a control based on a soundwave.

So far, we've covered inputting notes into the piano roll. Next, let's look at the bottom of the piano roll in the event editor to learn how to fine-tune note inflection.

Editing note articulations with the event editor

The event editor gives you fine control over the inflection of notes in the piano roll. At the bottom of the piano roll, you'll find the event editor. Here, you can control a variety of parameters by clicking on the word **Control** in the bottom-left corner of the piano roll:

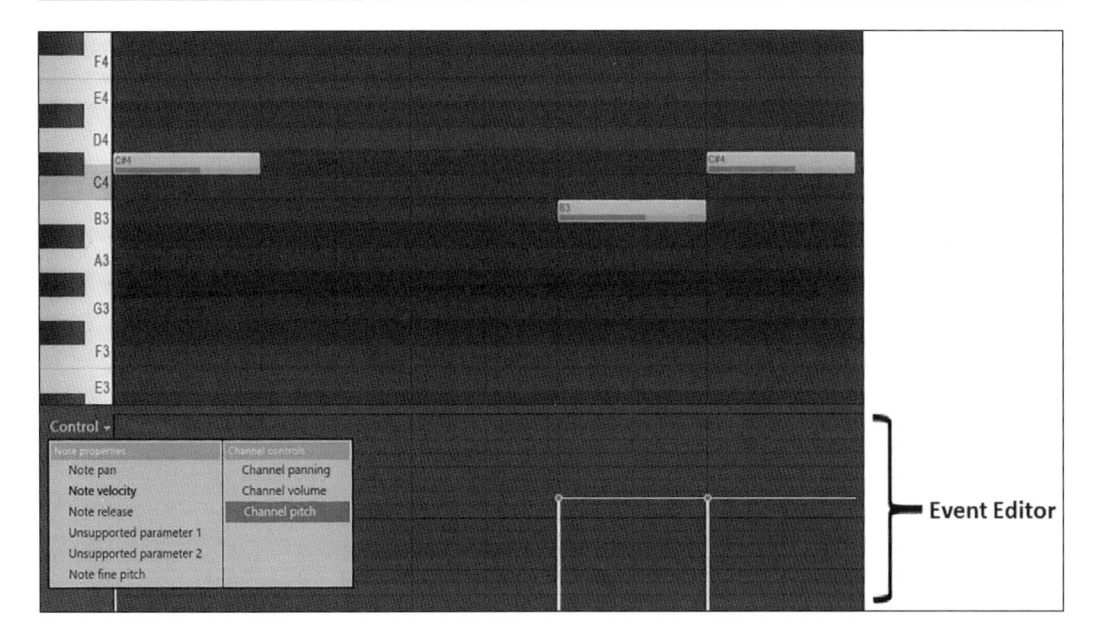

Figure 3.29 – Event editor

Under the **Control** menu options, you can see controls for adjusting note inflections:

- **Note pan**: Determines whether you want the sound to come out of the left or right speaker. By default, it comes out of both equally.
- **Note velocity**: How forcefully a key is struck.
- **Note release**: The rate at which the sound of a note drops to no sound once a note finishes playing.
- **Note fine pitch**: The pitch of a given note. This can be changed on a note-to-note basis.
- **Channel panning**, **Channel volume**, and **Channel pitch**: These are the same as the note panning, volume, and pitch options, except that they affect the whole channel in the active pattern instead of the individual instrument selected. Any changes will affect all instruments in the pattern.

Using piano roll velocity

In the event editor, velocity is selected by default. **Velocity** is how forcefully a note is struck. For every note, you'll see a corresponding vertical line in the event editor. You can have a different velocity for every note.

My preferred way to adjust velocity is to hover over the note, press *Alt*, and scroll with the computer mouse. You can also adjust the velocity by left-clicking in the event editor in the grid section.

Here's a tip on how to use velocity. A real piano player wants to emphasize the melody. The main melody is usually high-pitch notes, and the lower notes are usually the accompaniment. To emphasize the main melody, the emphasized notes are played louder than the accompaniment.

In the piano roll, you can mimic a real instrument player by giving a higher velocity to notes of the melody you want to emphasize. Usually, these are the notes with the highest pitch. When moving between chords, transition notes may have less velocity than the chords in focus. By playing around with velocity, you can add realism to synthesizer instruments.

Comparing instrument melodies with ghost notes

If you have another instrument playing notes in the same pattern, these will show up as faded-out notes, known as ghost notes. You can double-right-click on the grayed-out notes to switch to the instrument playing the notes:

Figure 3.30 – Ghost notes

In the preceding screenshot, the **BooBass** instrument is currently selected, and we are seeing the BooBass notes in the piano roll. In the channel rack, we can also see that **FL Keys** has several notes. In the piano roll, these show up as faded-out notes (**D5** and **A5**). What this means is that even though we have the BooBass instrument selected, we can still see the notes being played by FL Keys in the pattern.

If we wanted to change from the BooBass instrument to the FL Keys instrument, we could easily do this by double-right-clicking on the grayed-out notes.

We've learned how to easily switch between instruments. Next, let's learn how to create sheet music.

Exporting sheet music

Traditionally, when learning to play music, musicians learn to read sheet music. Sheet music allows musicians to transfer a musical idea to another musician so that they understand how to play the song. To read sheet music, they'd need to learn a large vocabulary of symbols and syntax so that they could understand what the other musician is saying.

If you want to export your music in the form of sheet music so that a live musician can play it, select the **FILE | Export as score sheet** option. This will provide you with controls over the sheet music, such as the time signature and scale, as seen in the following screenshot:

Figure 3.31 – Export as score sheet

After clicking **Start**, a PDF will be created with the sheet music, such as the one in the following screenshot:

Figure 3.32 – Sheet music

For a trained musician, this sheet music may not provide enough syntax notation. If this is the case, you'll need to look into a more powerful music notation-creating tool. I recommend the open source music notation software MuseScore: https://musescore.org/en.

With MuseScore, you can copy your MIDI file and create any kind of sheet music notation you desire.

Using and exporting MIDI scores

The piano roll opens up the playing field for creating music for people who have not studied music theory. Reading music is now completely optional and not mandatory in order to make music.

If you wanted to copy music into FL Studio, do you need to manually write each note? No, there is a much easier method. You can copy MIDI notes directly into the piano roll just by importing them. Doing so will require MIDI notes to copy. You can get MIDI notes for almost any song just by Google searching the name of the song followed by the words *MIDI notes*. Once you've found and downloaded the MIDI notes, you need to bring the MIDI notes into the piano roll. You can do this either by dragging the file from anywhere on your computer into the piano roll or by locating the MIDI note file in the FL Studio browser and then dragging it into the piano roll or channel rack instrument. Once you've done this, the piano roll will populate with notes from the MIDI file.

There are MIDI notes for songs for free and for sale online, and these can be useful for getting song inspiration. An example of a website that sells MIDI note packs is loopmasters.com.

What if you wanted to export your music in a format that another musician can use? It's easy to export your MIDI notes or sheet music. To export your piano roll melody as a MIDI file that another musician can then copy into their digital audio workstation, select the **Export as MIDI file...** option:

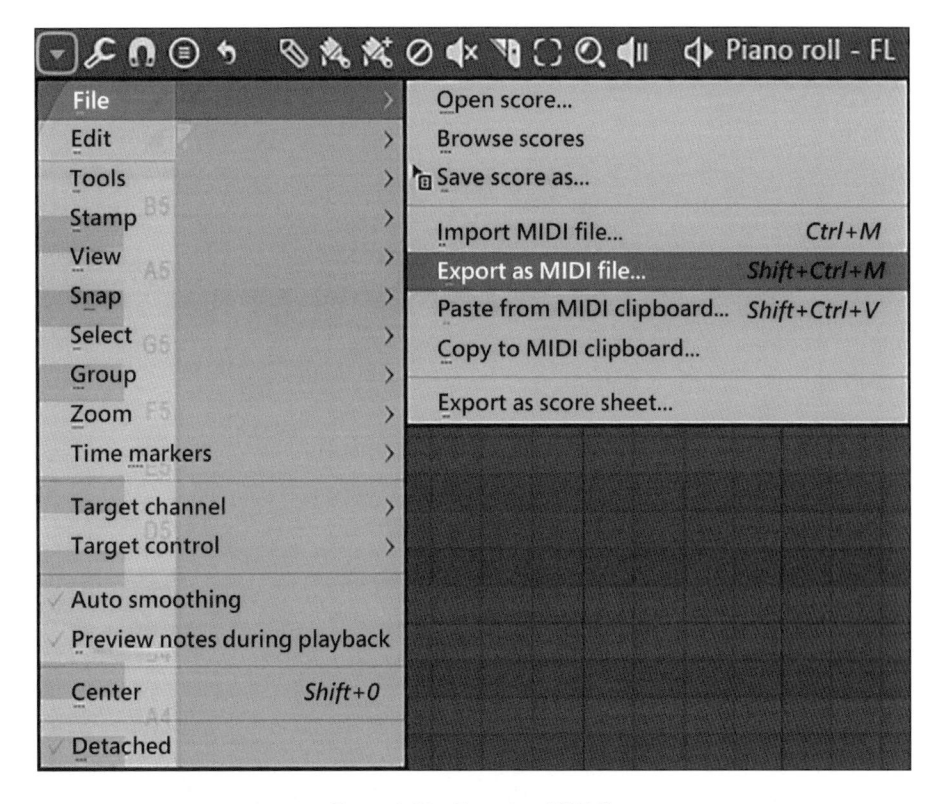

Figure 3.33 – Export as MIDI file

Exporting as a MIDI file will allow another music producer to copy the file into their digital audio workstation (regardless of whether they use FL Studio or another digital audio workstation) and receive the notes that you used in the piano roll. We now know how to export music from the piano roll.

Summary

In this chapter, we learned that the piano roll is used to compose melodies. We learned the steps to follow to create chord progressions from scratch.

The piano roll makes it easy to compare melodies played by accompanying instruments and to copy notes from one instrument to another. The piano roll also allows you to import and export MIDI notes and sheet music.

If you can learn to play the piano roll, it means you can play any plugin that plays MIDI notes. This is a big deal as it allows you to compose melodies for any instrument.

The piano roll will mean different things to you depending on the stage you are at in your music career. In the beginning, it will be a challenge figuring out how to use the tools. Once you understand the tools, you'll compose simple melodies. At some point, you'll realize that your melodies are bland and look to other people's music and tutorials to figure out how to make your composition more interesting. You may copy existing song MIDI notes onto the piano roll and analyze chord progressions and structures. You'll experiment with piano roll techniques and become efficient at pounding out melodies.

Once you've understood how other songs were composed, you'll take the influences and combine them in your own work. You'll reach the stage where you'll want to come up with your own signature style. The piano roll now becomes the way that you record the ideas you dream up in your mind.

In the next chapter, we'll explore the mixer and learn how to apply automation to controls.

4

Routing to the Mixer and Applying Automation

Once you've arranged melodies for your song, you can begin mixing. **Mixing** is the process where you combine instrument sounds and strategically blend them together. You need to be familiar with how audio is passed around the mixer (known as **routing**) in order to mix music efficiently, and in this chapter, we will learn how.

In order to use effects, we need to understand how instruments' signals get passed around. This chapter is intended to show you how to configure your setup for any mixing need. The goal of this chapter is to give you a general foundation understanding of the mixer. In future chapters, we will apply our understanding of the mixer by adding effects to our sounds, such as compression and stereo-width effects.

In this chapter, we'll cover the following topics:

- What is mixing?
- Routing audio to the mixer
- Navigating the mixer console
- Applying automation
- Freezing audio clips (rendering to WAV)

What is mixing?

Mixing is the process where you balance out the sounds of instruments with one another to allow each voice to be heard. You then apply effects to sounds to enhance them. Traditionally, this was done in a hardware device called a **mixer control panel**. These devices were very expensive pieces of equipment, selling for thousands of dollars. In a mixer console, you'd plug your instruments and microphones into the mixer's ports and play sounds. The sound would be recorded on a recording device called a **tape**, which would store the audio information. The tape could then be played back and send the audio signals through the mixer. The mixer had knobs and buttons to finely adjust the volume, panning, and level of the input and output signals. You could then send the audio signals to effect plugins that manipulated the sound before sending the signal back to the mixer.

Digital audio workstations like FL Studio replicate a mixer console in looks and functions. Sounds are routed to the mixer and given their own channel, known as a **mixer track**. The tracks allow you to process instrument sounds and apply effects to the audio. After the effects have been applied, the sounds are combined in a single channel called a **master track**. The master track is what gets exported as the finished song, as an MP3 or WAV file.

From a high-level perspective, mixing is a very simple task: send signals to a mixer, add effects, and export the song. Knowing what effects to apply to make the song sound good is what distinguishes an amateur mixer from a seasoned mixing engineer. Let's discuss how to get your sounds into the FL Studio mixer.

Routing audio to the mixer

Before we can mix our music, we first need to route audio to the mixer. The following is a screenshot showing the **FL Keys** and **BooBass** instruments in our channel rack, which we are going to route to the mixer:

Chapter 4

Figure 4.1 – Channel rack and mixer

In the preceding screenshot, we can see four samples and two instruments in the channel rack. Our mixer has no information mentioning instruments or samples yet. Currently, all sounds are being routed directly to the master channel. When we're done routing, all instruments and samples in the channel rack will have their own assigned channel and will visually show up in the mixer.

There are two ways to route an instrument in FL Studio to the mixer. The first way is using the channel rack, and the second is by using the individual instrument itself.

Let's look at the channel rack method first. This is the shortcut way:

1. In the channel rack, select all instruments by double-left-clicking the rectangular button directly to the right of an instrument:

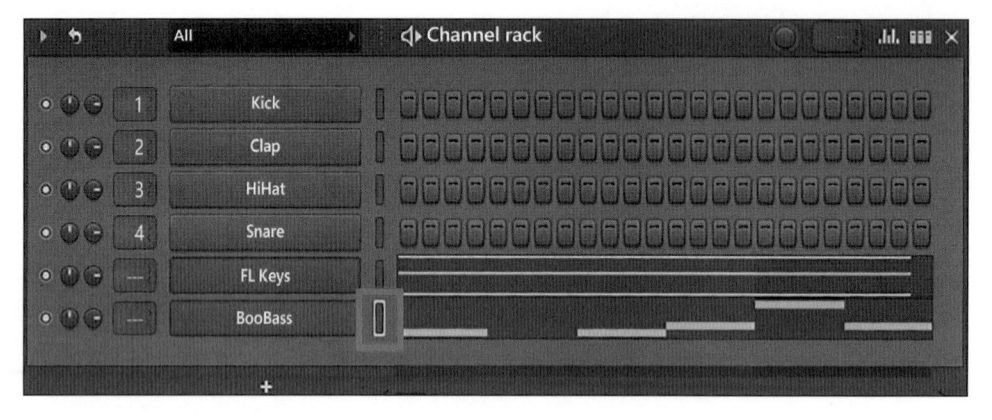

Figure 4.2 – Selecting channel rack instruments

Chapter 4

2. Next, go to the channel rack option menu using the drop-down arrow, and select **Color selected | Random**:

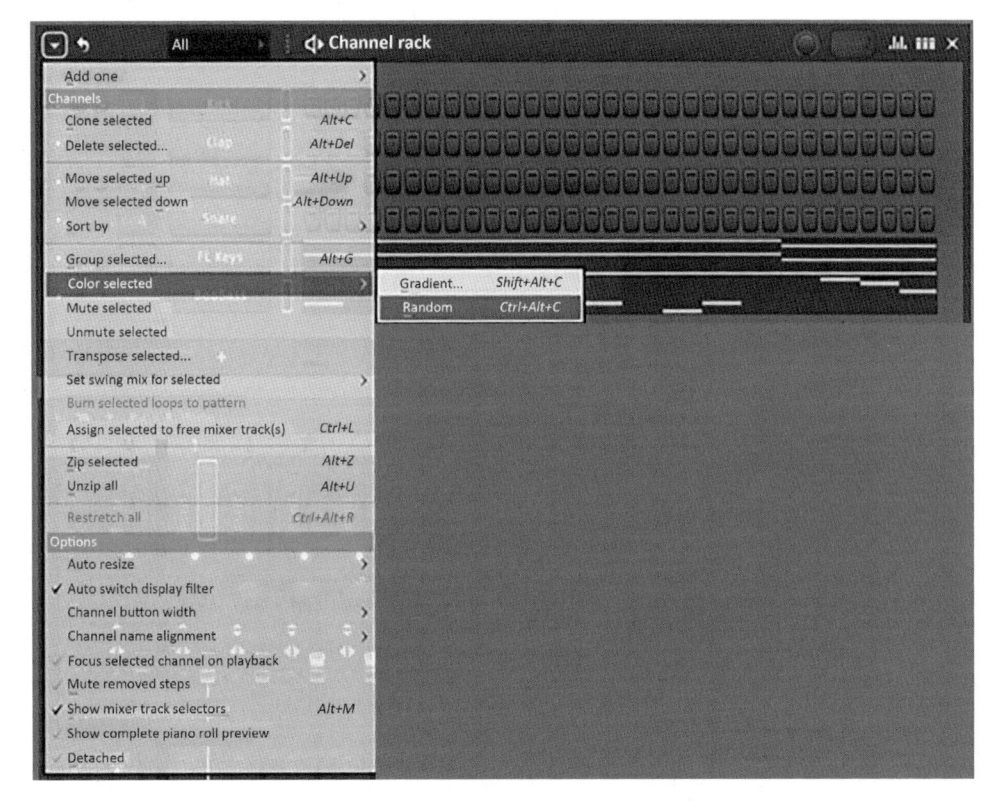

Figure 4.3 – Assigning instruments colors

Once selected, your instruments will be assigned a color at random. This will make it easy to visually distinguish your instruments in the mixer.

3. Next, we assign the instruments to mixer tracks. Select all the instruments in the channel rack that you want to route to the mixer, as shown in the following screenshot. Open up the mixer and left-click on **Insert 1** in the mixer. Then, press *Shift + Ctrl + L*. This is a shortcut method to route the instruments to the mixer track:

Figure 4.4 – Routed instruments to the mixer

Your instruments have been routed to the mixer. You can see that any names and colors in the channel rack were transferred to the mixer. This is the easiest way of routing your tracks to the mixer.

Although I recommend the first approach, there are other methods too. An alternative method is to right-click on a single instrument and select **Assign to new instrument track**:

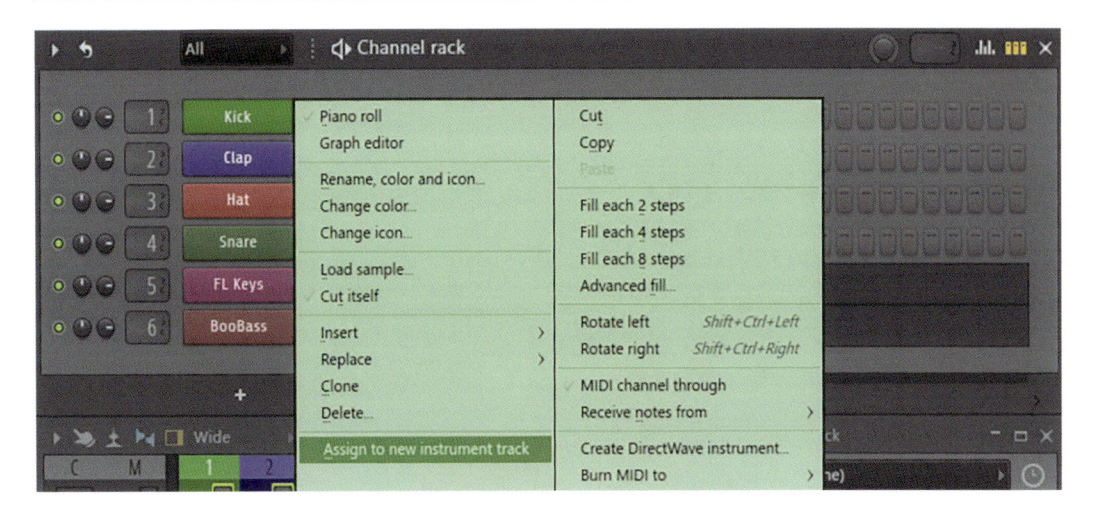

Figure 4.5 – Assign to new instrument track

The **Assign to new instrument track** option will route the instrument to the mixer. However, this second approach will not include the color of the instrument, so I don't recommend this alternative. Another way to route an instrument is to route from the instrument directly, as follows:

1. Left-click on any instrument in the channel rack. I've opened up **BooBass**, as shown in the following screenshot:

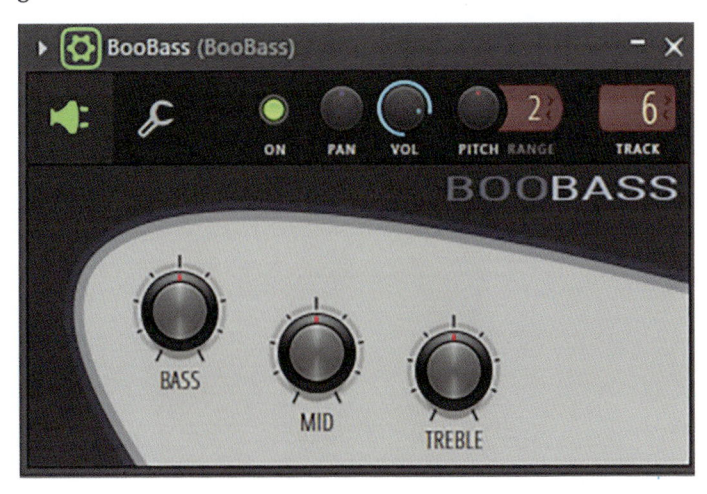

Figure 4.6 – Instrument

The plugin will open up with a series of controls at the top of the plugin. If you don't see these controls, it means that they're hidden. They can be unhidden by left-clicking the gear icon at the top left of the plugin window, as shown in the preceding screenshot.

2. At the top right, you can see the mixer track number that the instrument is currently routed to. If you want to assign it to a brand-new track, you can left-click on the **TRACK** box, as shown in the following screenshot:

Figure 4.7 – Routing to a new track

BooBass will now be routed to a new track on the mixer.

Any of the three methods shown will route instruments to the mixer. Now that we have our instruments routed, let's take a detailed look at the mixer console.

Navigating the mixer console

I like to think of the mixer console in terms of three distinct components:

- **The master channel**: A channel that all other channels eventually route to. Audio exiting this channel is what gets exported as the final song.
- **The insert mixer tracks**: Where audio is routed to from each instrument.
- **The effects rack**: Lists effects that are applied to each mixer insert channel.

Chapter 4

In the following screenshot, we can see the mixer and its components:

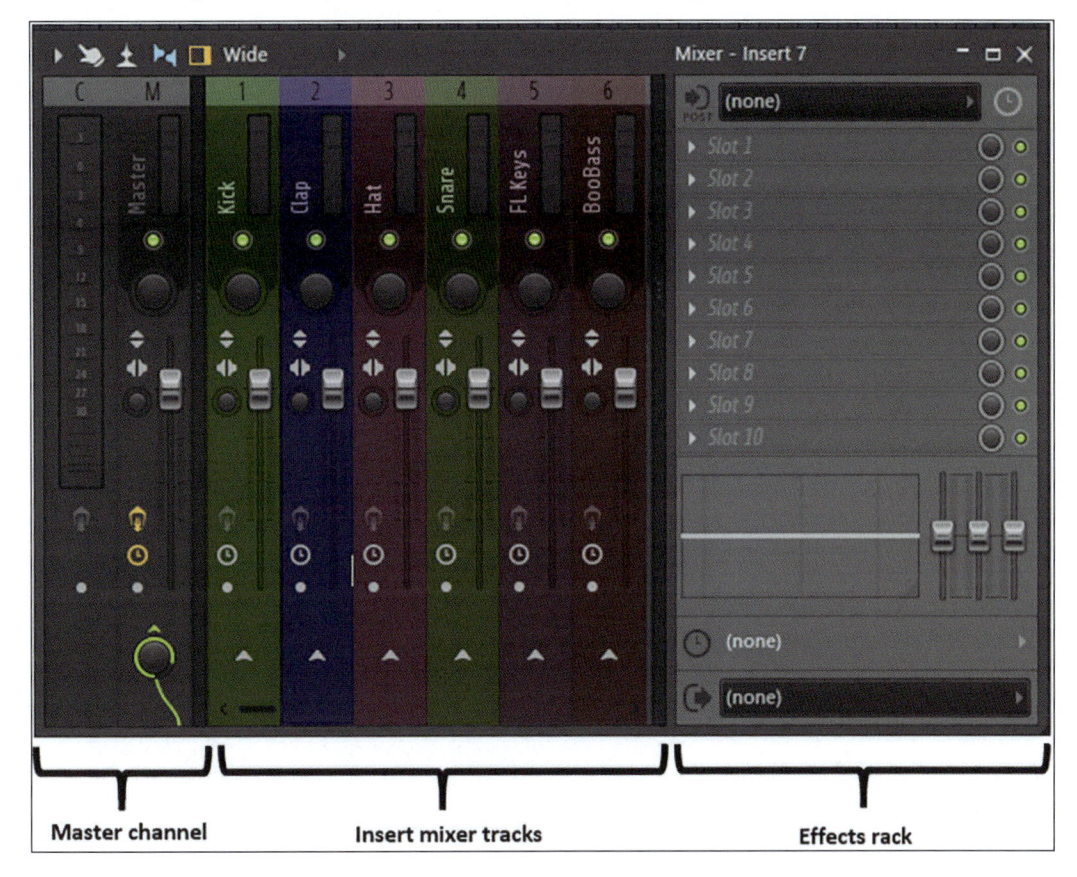

Figure 4.8 – Mixer

Audio signals flow from the channel rack into the insert mixer tracks. For each insert mixer track, effects from the effects rack are applied. Audio then leaves the insert mixer track and is either sent to another insert mixer track or the master channel.

> The words *track* and *channel* can be used interchangeably.

Understanding the insert mixer track

It's called an *insert mixer track* because, in the old days, these used to be individual pieces that you connected like LEGO bricks in the mixer console. You literally *inserted the track* into the mixer. Let's explain the parts of an insert mixer track from the top down:

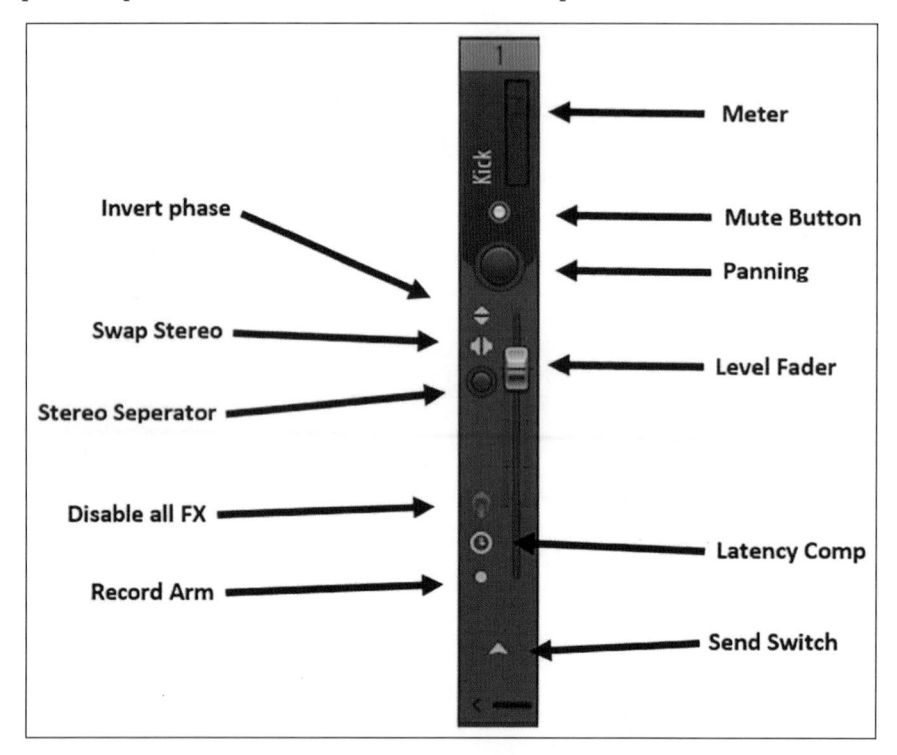

Figure 4.9 – Parts of an insert mixer track

Here's a breakdown of the insert mixer track:

- **Meter:** The volume of the audio signal received.
- **Mute button:** Allows you to stop audio from exiting the mixer track. Useful for soloing individual tracks so that you can hear one sound at a time.

- **Panning**: Allows you to choose whether the audio comes out of the left or the right speaker.
- **Invert phase**: Flips the audio waveform so that positive peaks become negative and vice versa. When playing two sounds simultaneously, sometimes audio waveforms can cancel one another out. If this is the case, you can invert the phase of one of the audio waveforms to remove this issue.
- **Swap stereo**: Swaps any panning effects from the left to the right and vice versa.
- **Stereo separator**: A filter that allows you to increase or reduce any stereo effects. Stereo means that sound comes out of both speakers, which may be different for each one. The alternative is called **mono**, which means that all speakers have the exact same sound coming out of them.
- **Level fader**: Controls how much audio input exits the insert mixer track after effects are applied. This controls the volume of the sound.
- **Disable all FX**: Allows you to turn on and off all effects applied to the track at once.
- **Latency compensation**: Adjusts for latency issues. Latency is when you have an unwanted time delay, commonly known as **lag**.
- **Record arm**: Turn on to receive audio from external microphones or devices.
- **Send switch**: Allows you to choose where you want to send audio signals from this track. By default, it is set to send the audio signal to the master channel.

Understanding the master channel

The **master channel** has all the features of an insert mixer track. The only difference is that all insert mixer tracks eventually route into the master channel. The master channel is what eventually gets exported into the finished song.

Understanding the effects rack

For each insert mixer track, you can apply effects. An example of an effect is **delay**, which creates an echo of your sound.

We will discuss the effects that you can apply throughout the rest of the book. Let's take a look at the effects rack:

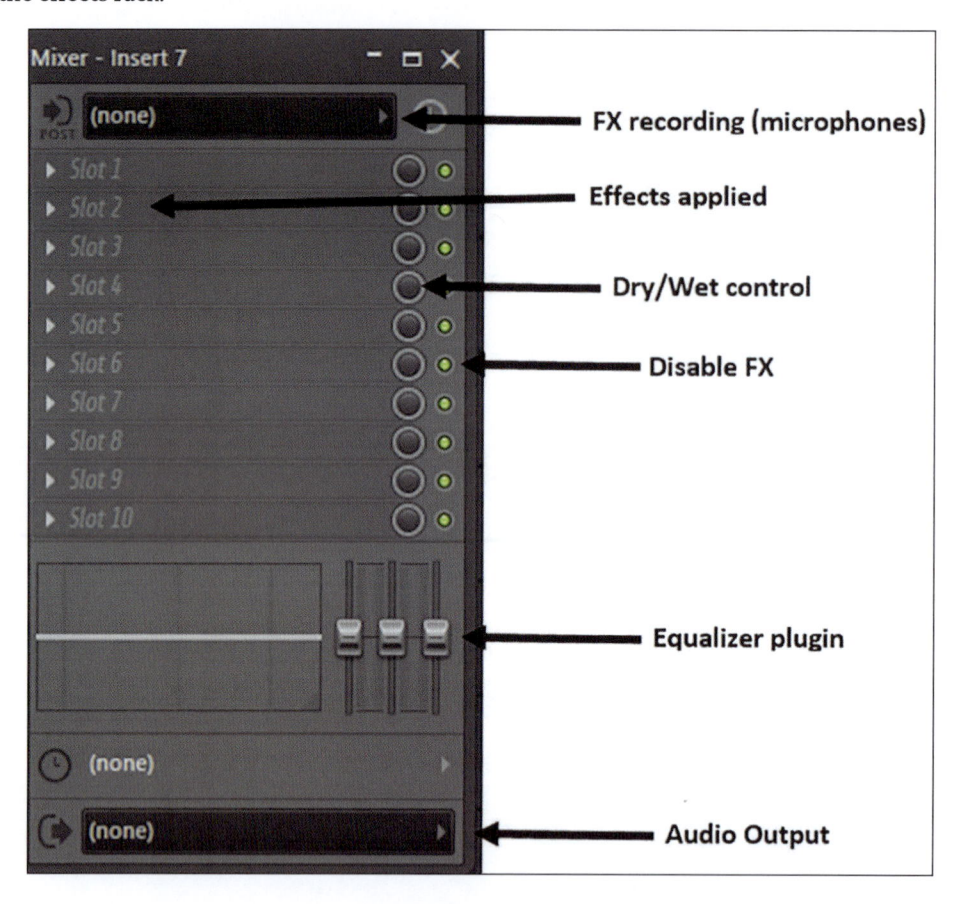

Figure 4.10 – Effects rack

Here's a brief breakdown of the effects rack:

- **FX recording**: Allows you to choose which input device you want to use, such as a microphone.
- **Effects**: This is where you add effects. By left-clicking on an empty slot, you can add effect plugins.
- **Dry/Wet**: Controls how much effect is applied from 0 to 100%. **Dry** means *off*, and **wet** means *on*. If you hear someone talking about playing with the dry/wet of a plugin, it just means how much you turn it on.

Chapter 4

For example, if you had a delay effect on a guitar to create an echo sound, turning the wet up would allow you to hear more of the echo. Dry would mean you'd hear less of the echo.

- **Disable FX**: Turns the effect on or off.
- **Equalizer plugin**: Allows you to apply equalization effects to the audio signal.
- **Audio output**: Allows you to choose to send the audio signal to another audio interface.

Applying an effect

Let's apply an effect to our sounds on a mixer channel:

1. Select the **FL Keys** mixer track by left-clicking on it.
2. In the effects rack, left-click on an empty slot.
3. Select a plugin, such as **Fruity Delay 3**.
4. The following screenshot illustrates adding an effect plugin:

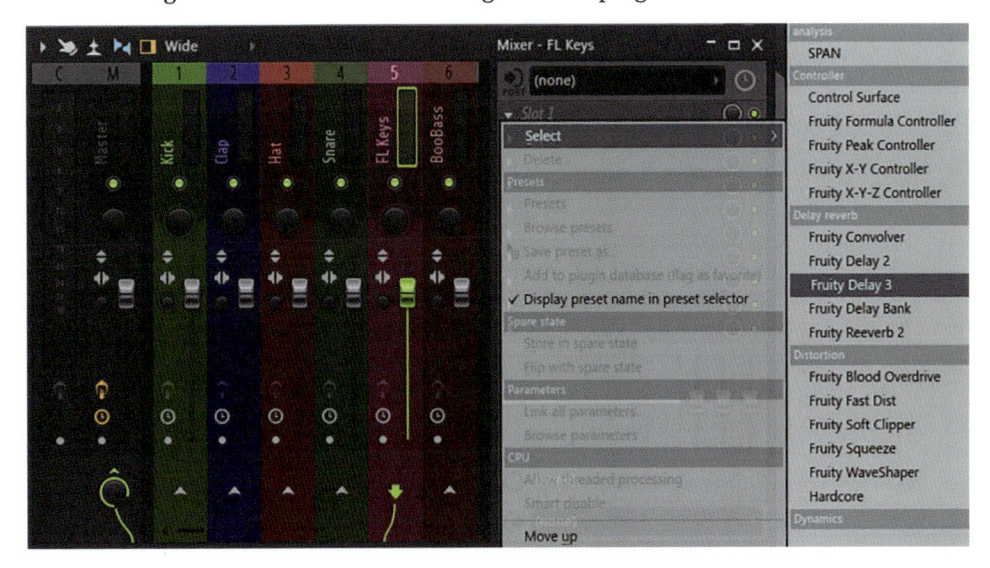

Figure 4.11 – Adding Fruity Delay 3

5. Play your song. You will be able to hear the delay plugin effect applied to your FL Keys sound. You will use this same process to add effects to your song constantly going forward.

So far, we've taken a look at the mixer console. Next, let's look at how to automate controls in the mixer so changes can occur while a song is playing.

Applying automation

You can make effects and controls change over time. This is called **automation**. Automation allows you to have fine control over your instruments and effects. In the following example, we will look at applying automation in the mixer; however, it should be noted that automation can be applied to any effect plugin, the channel rack, the playlist, and any instrument plugin. This is a big deal, as you can have sounds evolving over time throughout a song.

Essentially, any time that you want to have a sound transition from one state to another, you use automation. Here are some examples of automation that you hear in music:

- Sounds gradually getting quieter or louder. Any time a sound fades in or out, it's using automation.
- Any time in a film that you hear footsteps or a car sound appear to move from left to right, you're hearing panning effect automation.
- Rising or falling effects can be created through the use of automation. A riser effect usually involves increasing the pitch of a sound over time, while a falling effect usually decreases a pitch over time. These pitch changes are usually combined with moving a high or low pass filter over time.
- When you want a synth instrument to gradually become more or less intense, you use automation. Progressive house music often involves gradually building up layers of plucks and synth chords over time. Changes in intensity and the fading in of instruments are done through automation.
- Vocal effect automation is used to create dubstep monster growls.
- Pretty much all dubstep bass instruments require automation to create the filtering instrument effects.

Let's illustrate automation through a simple volume change scenario:

1. Right-click on **BooBass** or any other instrument level fader (volume knob) and select **Create automation clip**:

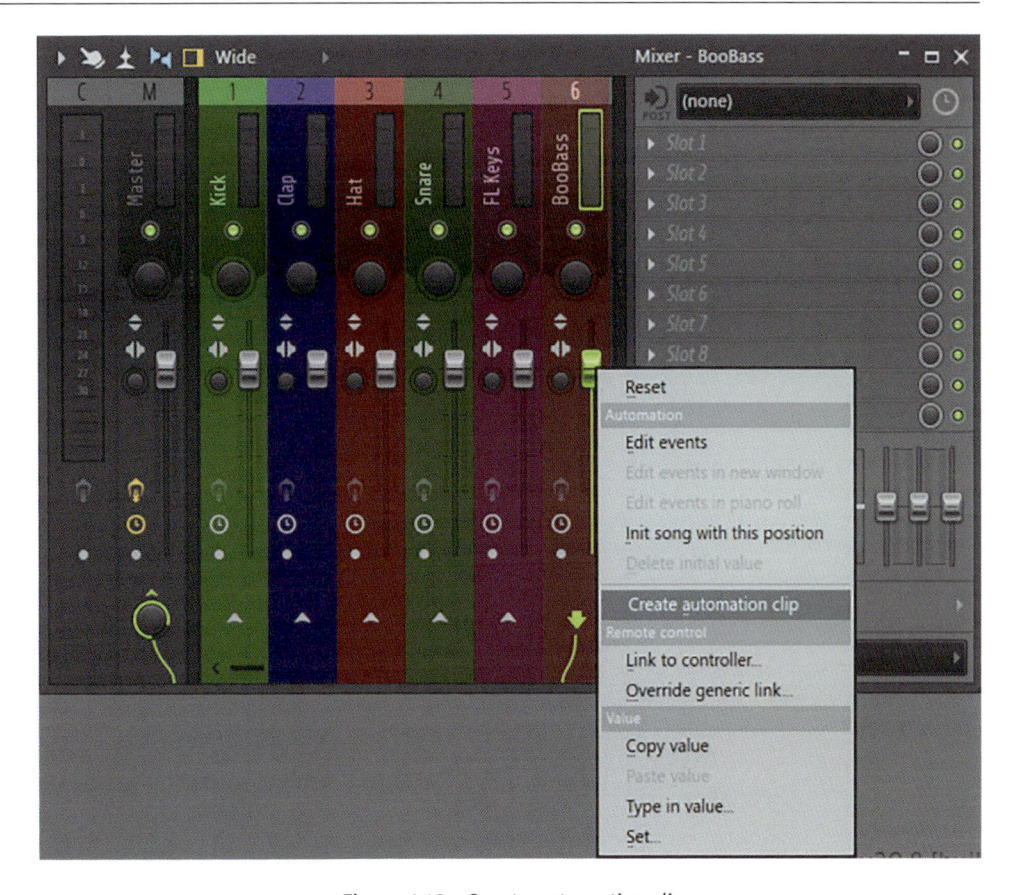

Figure 4.12 – Create automation clip

In the playlist, you'll see an automation clip created for the selected parameter at the top left of the playlist and in the grid section. In this case, the parameter that we are automating is **Volume**. The automation clip in the playlist grid in track 3 consists of a line and a keyframe at the beginning and end.

These indicate the level of volume for the BooBass instrument, set by default to 80%.

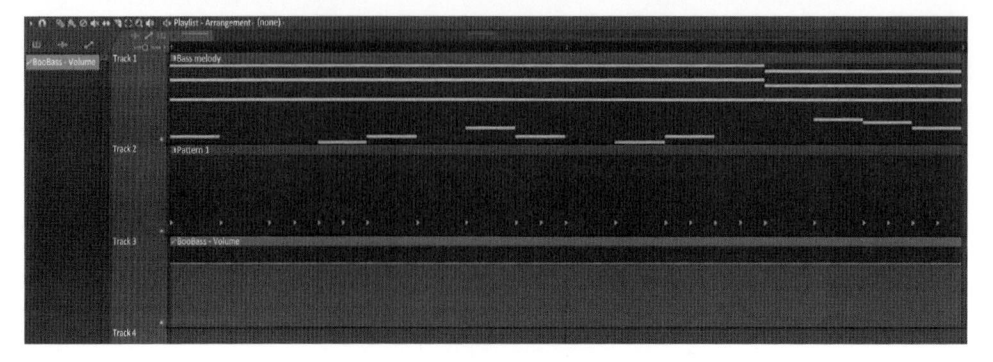

Figure 4.13 – Automation clip created

2. Right-click on the automation clip on the playlist grid – in the following screenshot we have done this in the middle of the clip in track 3. This will add a new keyframe with a volume change:

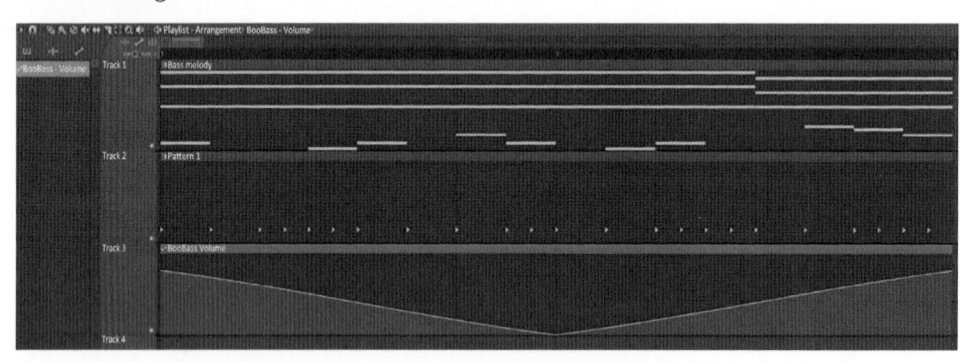

Figure 4.14 – Keyframe created

Chapter 4   117

By adding the keyframe, the level of the volume fader for the BooBass instrument has been set to decrease over time until the middle of the clip, and then increase again toward the end of the clip. Play the song to hear the volume automation.

3. There are several automation presets. Right-click on the keyframe that we created in the automation clip. You'll see a menu of available automation presets:

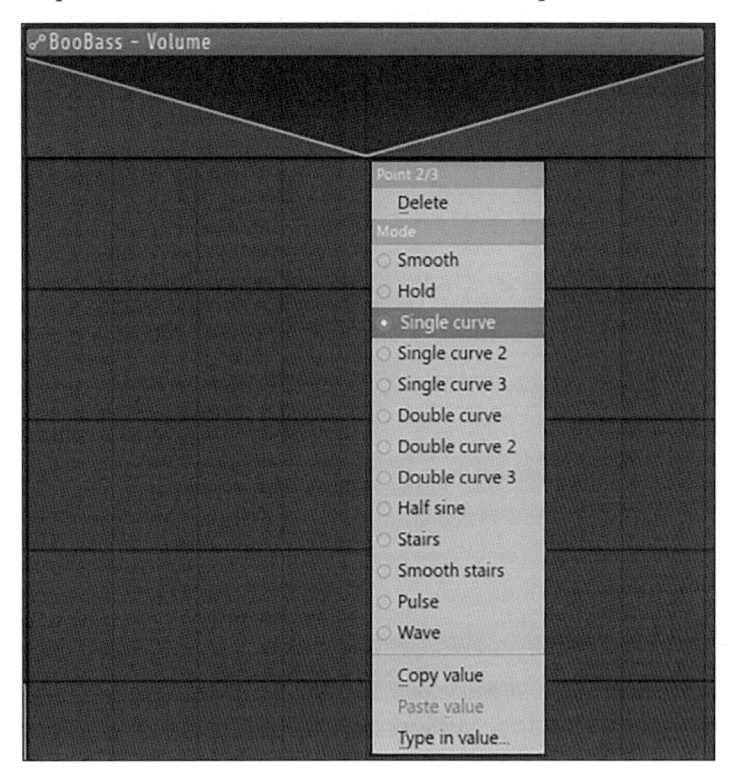

Figure 4.15 – Automation presets

These presets give examples of automation curves to choose from. If you select a curve, you'll see a new kind of automation clip curve. At the bottom of the menu, there is also an option to type in a value to specify the automation point. Feel free to select any one of the presets.

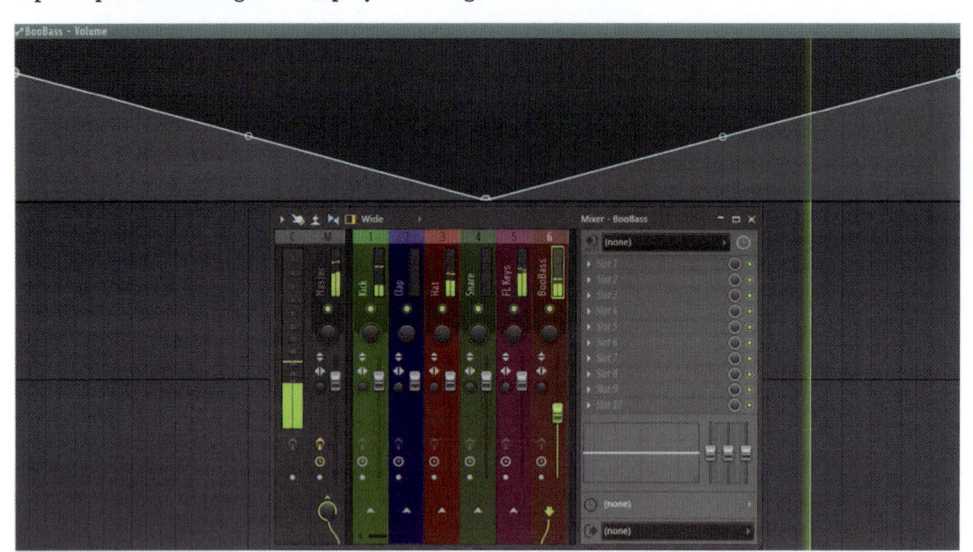

4. Open up the mixer again and play the song:

Figure 4.16 – Volume automated

As you play the song, you'll see the insert mixer volume fader adjust as the automation clip progresses throughout the song.

Automation can be applied to any knob or button in FL Studio and you can change it over time.

Editing automation clips

Once you've created an automation clip, you can edit the automation. Let's see this through an example:

1. Right-click on any automatable control and create an automation clip in the playlist.
2. Double-left-click on the automation clip name in the playlist. The automation editor will appear as shown in the following screenshot.

Chapter 4

Figure 4.17 – Automation editor

In the preceding screenshot, we made a bunch of random selections for the automation. The exact automation isn't important; the goal is just to show you how to navigate to the automation editor.

In the automation editor, you can refine automation curves. You can play your clip in the playlist simultaneously to see how your song is affected by the automation.

In the automation editor, you'll see a grid of points indicating automation. Higher points mean an increase in control value and lower points mean a lower value. The value will depend on the type of control used.

On the right of the window, you'll see the **Step Editing, Snap To Grid,** and **Slide Succeeding Points** controls. A description is as follows:

- **Step Editing (the pencil icon)**: When enabled, this allows you to add automation points by drawing on the grid. Right-clicking and dragging over automation points deletes them. When the step editor is disabled, you can drag points around the grid and can add points by right-clicking on the grid.
- **Snap To Grid (magnet icon)**: Snaps automation points.
- **Slide Succeeding Points/regions (double arrow icon)**: Allows points to slide around the grid when dragged.

At the top of the automation editor, you can enable the LFO button to view a series of LFO controls available for automation. **LFO** stands for **low frequency oscillator**, and just means a waveform. It's simply a pattern that gets repeated over and over.

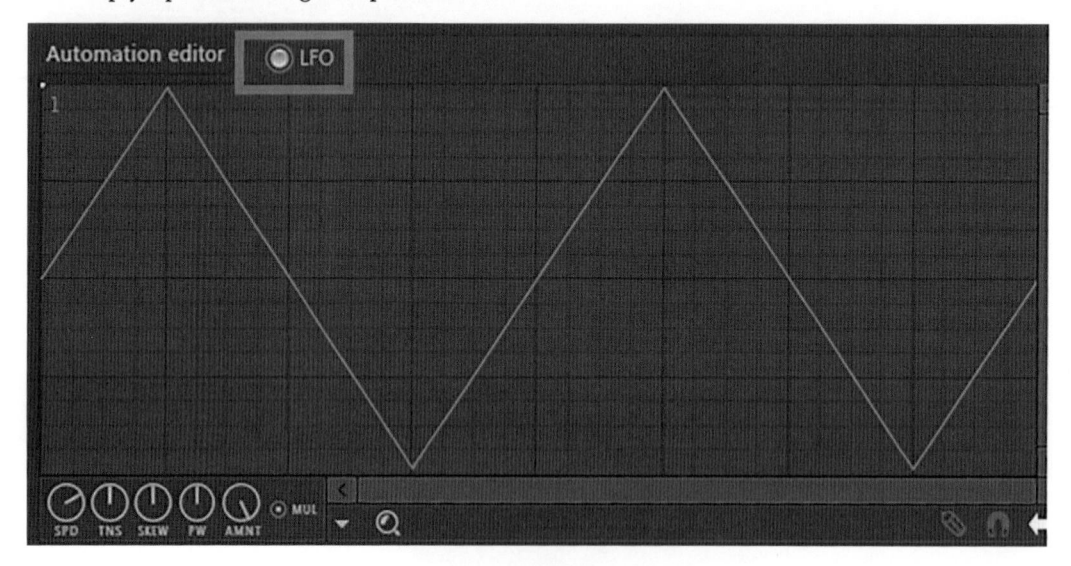

Figure 4.18 – Automation editor LFO

You'll notice that the automation points change into a sine wave. On the left, you'll now see a series of control knobs that can be used to adjust the LFO, such as speed, tension, skew, and pulse width. This is useful if you want to create repeating automation.

Let's un-toggle the LFO again. At the bottom, you'll find the **Target links** controls. The **Target links** section shows us all the controls we apply our automation to in the selected clip. This section allows you to have multiple controls automated simultaneously.

Chapter 4   121

In the following screenshot, we automate the BooBass channel volume. However, you could add additional controls to be automated here.

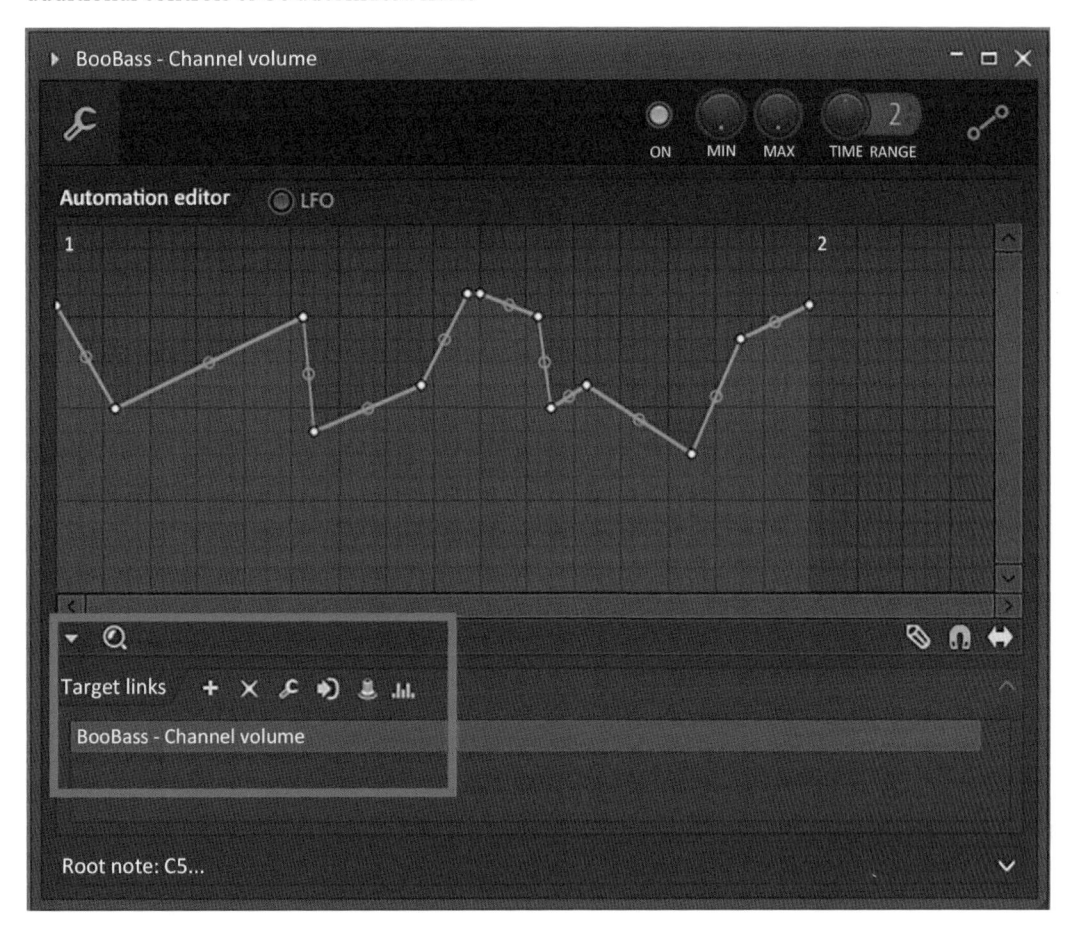

Figure 4.19 – Target links

Here's a description:

- **Add target links**: Allows you to assign controls to follow the automation pattern. After clicking this button, it will prompt you to select controls to be assigned to this automation clip. It will continue to add controls until you click it again. Afterward, all of the controls you selected will have their values affected by this automation. This might sound a little confusing to read, but if you try it out, you'll find it intuitive.
- **Remove target link**: Removes a control from being assigned to the automation.

- **Edit target link:** Opens up a window for additional control options.
- **Locate target link parameter:** Opens up the plugin with the assigned control.
- **Animate target link parameter:** Lights up when **Add target links** is used to indicate that it's waiting for a control to be selected.
- **Convert target to events in the current pattern:** Takes all of the automation points used in the automation editor and copies it into the events editor.

You may be thinking…what's the difference between event automation and automation clips? Event automation is bound to a specific pattern or pattern clip; automation clips are not.

Event automation means you can open up the piano roll and view the event automation in relation to the MIDI notes of the pattern. You can then view event automation in the piano roll by selecting the **Control** drop-down and finding your event automation. The following shows an example in the piano roll:

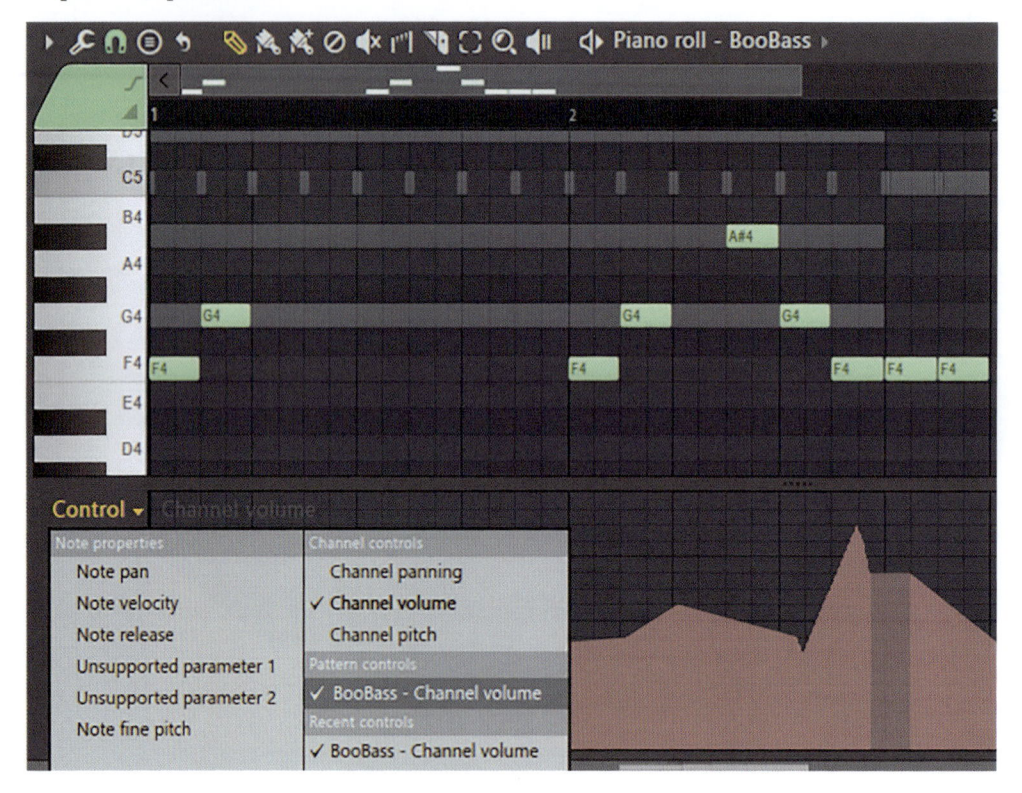

Figure 4.20 – Event automation

In the preceding screenshot, we can see MIDI notes in the piano roll. Below in the red is the event automation. In this example, the channel volume is automated to change throughout the pattern.

Chapter 4

If you want even more control over your automation clips, there are additional options, as shown in the following screenshot:

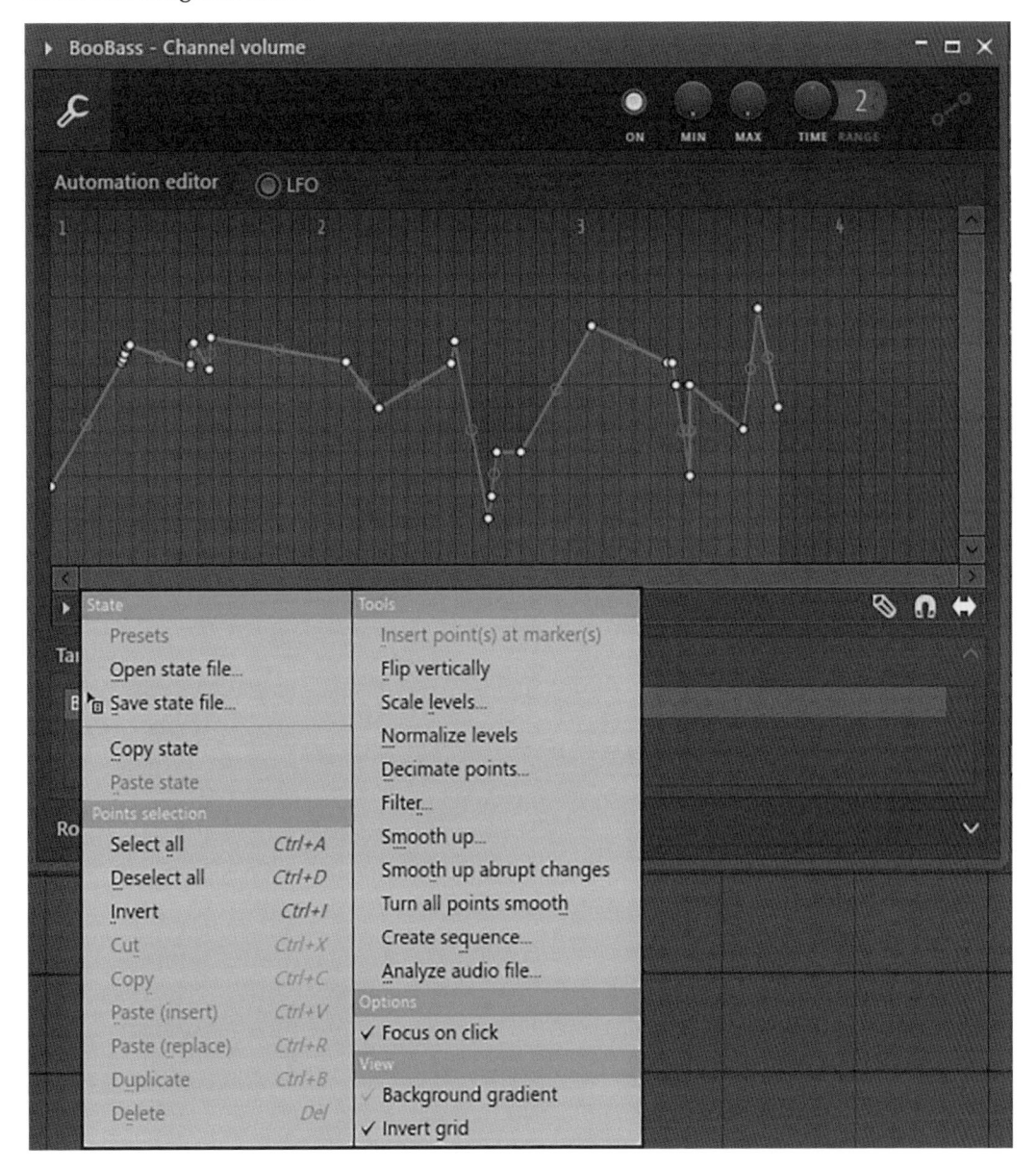

Figure 4.21 – Automation editor options

Here you'll find additional tools to adjust your automation clips: flipping, scaling, normalizing, decimating, filtering, smoothing, and creating an automation sequence.

We've learned how to create automation clips and how to edit them. Next, let's learn how to create automation clips for third-party plugins.

Applying automation to external third-party plugins

If you want to apply automation to an external plugin (not a native FL Studio plugin), you won't be able to right-click to apply automation. In order to apply automation for third-party plugins, you need to use another method.

We're going to explore two techniques to add automation. The first approach, *MultiLink to controllers*, is the easiest and most intuitive. The second approach of *creating an editor thumbnail* is more of a legacy technique but can still be used.

Using MultiLink to controllers to add automation

There's an easy way to add automation clips for any plugin using the **MultiLink to controllers** feature. The plugin doesn't have to be a native FL Studio plugin. It can be an installed **Virtual Studio Technology** (**VST**) instrument or effect. This technique also works for adding automation for hardware controllers' controls.

As a brief overview of how it works, you first enable the **MultiLink to controllers** feature. Once this is enabled, it listens for any control that is touched next. You touch the control of whatever plugin or hardware feature you want to change. The **MultiLink to controllers** feature now remembers the last control touched. This feature will save you a ton of time and make adding automation for plugins easy. Let's explore the **MultiLink to controllers** feature with a simple example:

1. Enable the **MultiLink to controllers** button by left-clicking it. An example is shown in the following screenshot:

Figure 4.22 – MultiLink to controllers

Chapter 4

If you see the **MultiLink to controllers** button lit up, you know that it's enabled and listening for you to adjust a control for automation.

2. In the channel rack, load up any instrument plugin where you want to automate a control. In my example, I'll use the FLEX plugin.

3. Change a control that you want to add automation to. The following screenshot shows an example, where I am changing the pitch. All you need to do is slightly move the control.

Figure 4.23 – FLEX pitch controller

By moving the pitch controller, the **MultiLink to controllers** button will store the changes. You can adjust multiple controls at once. In fact, I encourage you to adjust a few of the controls.

4. Right-click on the **Multilink to controllers** button, and you'll see the ability to add an automation clip:

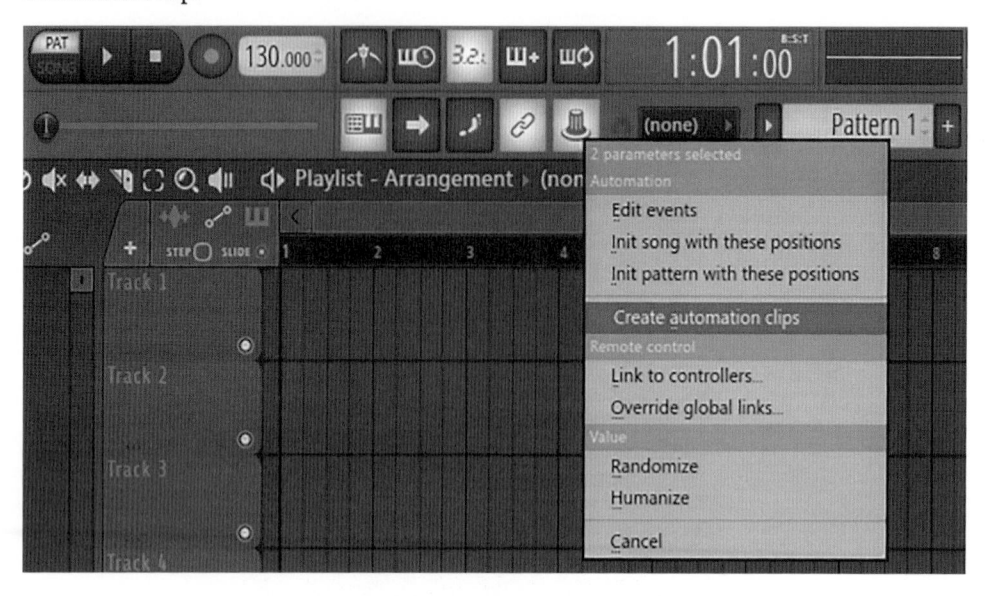

Figure 4.24 – MultiLink to controllers

After selecting the option **Create automation clips**, FL Studio will generate an automation clip of the control that was adjusted. An example is shown in the following screenshot:

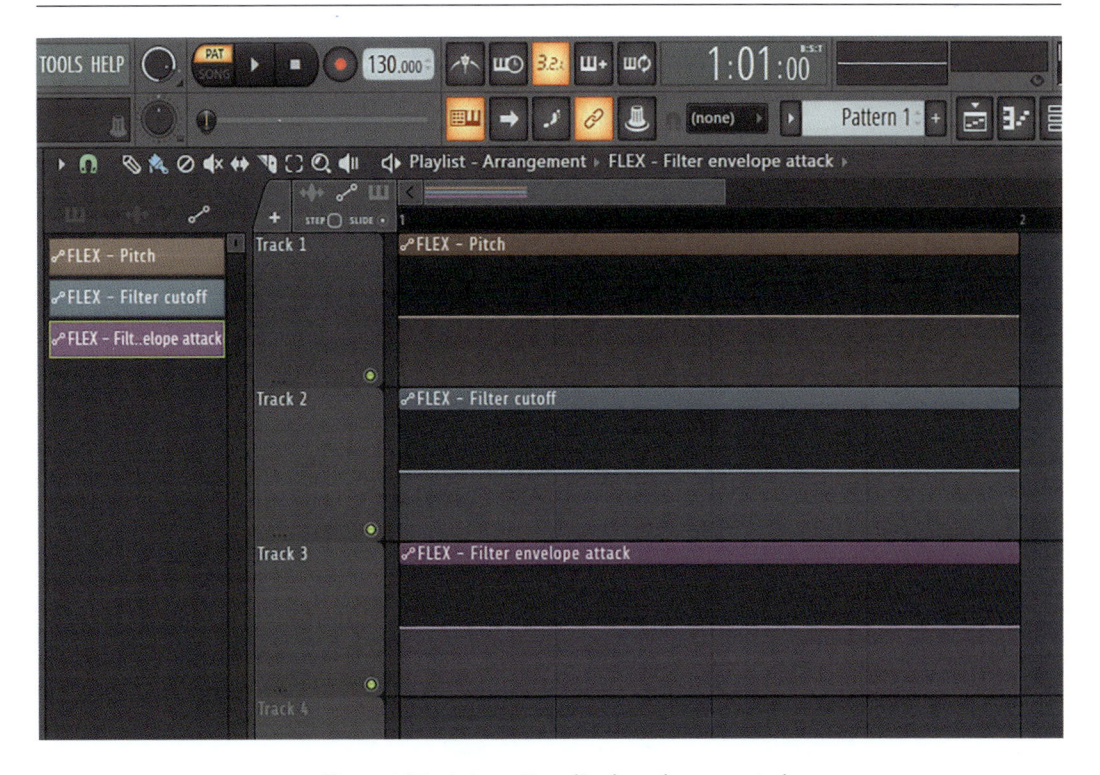

Figure 4.25 – Automation clips have been created

Automation clips have been created for every control that was adjusted. In my example, I adjusted the **Pitch, Filter cutoff**, and **Filter envelope attack**, so it created three automation clips. You can now adjust the values on the automation clips however you see fit.

> This technique works for hardware controllers connected to FL Studio. Simply enable **MultiLink to controllers**, jiggle whatever knobs you want to on your hardware, and then add an automation clip.

You now know how to use **MultiLink to controllers**.

Creating an editor thumbnail to add automation

You can add automation to third-party plugins by creating what is known as an editor thumbnail. This is a legacy technique if you don't want to use the **MultiLink to Controller** method.

When you create an editor thumbnail, you're telling FL Studio to take a look at the plugin and analyze it for controls for use in automation:

1. To create an editor thumbnail, open your external plugin, go to the top-left drop-down arrow menu, and select **Make editor thumbnail**, as shown in the following screenshot:

    You won't have the **Serum** plugin; you'll have to download some third-party external VST plugin in order to do this example. If you're interested in additional music plugins such as the plugin Serum in the following example, you can find lots of plugins at https://splice.com/plugins.

Figure 4.26 – Make editor thumbnail

Chapter 4

2. The browser will open up the instrument plugin. Click on the instrument in the browser:

Figure 4.27 – Clicking on an instrument in the browser

3. A list will appear of all the automatable controls of the plugin, as shown in the following screenshot:

Figure 4.28 – Automation clip for an external plugin

4. Right-click on any of the controls listed below the instrument and add an automation clip for the effect. An automation clip will appear in the playlist, as shown in the following screenshot:

Chapter 4 131

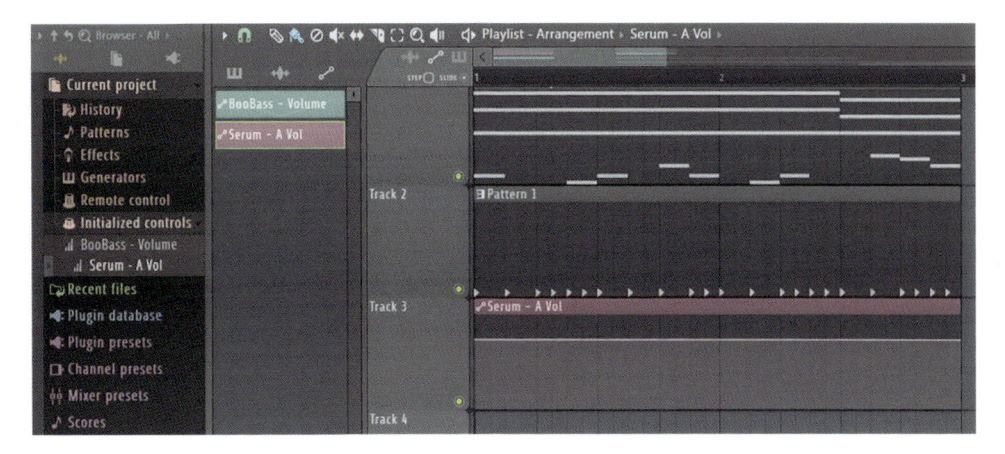

Figure 4.29 – Automation clip in the playlist for an external plugin

5. If you want to automate another control parameter of an external plugin, it's much easier the second time, as you've already taken an editor thumbnail. To automate another control of a plugin where you've already taken an editor thumbnail, go to the browser and select **Generators**. This will list all currently used plugins in your project. Click on the instrument you want to automate. This will display the controls available for automation, as illustrated in the following screenshot:

Figure 4.30 – Automation controls of used plugins available under Generators in the browser

We've learned how to apply automation effects. Next, let's learn how to freeze audio.

Freezing audio clips

You can render any audio into an audio clip. Rendering to audio is more commonly known as **freezing**. Like version control, freezing gives you a version of your sound that will not change. Rendering to audio or freezing means creating an audio clip sample out of any sound that passes through a mixer track. Freezing audio clips into samples has several benefits:

- It allows you to chop up the audio sample and access audio sample controls. You gain all the benefits of using a sample, such as being able to control sample envelope controls and use samples in other plugins, such as in **DirectWave**.
- A sample is less CPU-intensive than an instrument with effects. If you notice your computer lagging due to the usage of lots of plugins, you can speed up your computer by freezing CPU-intensive mixer tracks into audio.

Although you may not use freezing tracks at first, it's something that will become important when you start to have tons of effects and your CPU starts to lag. I mostly find myself freezing tracks when I need to process vocals, as these often require a lot of effect plugins that slow down my computer. Let's look at an example and render our sound to an audio clip:

1. To freeze tracks, select the arm disk recording button on all the mixer tracks that you want to freeze, as shown in the following screenshot. The arm disk recording buttons will appear red after selection:

Figure 4.31 – Arm disk recording

As we can see in the preceding screenshot, the insert mixer tracks **5** and **6** are now ready to record audio input. Arming disk recording for a track tells the mixer to get ready to record any input that comes through the tracks and export it as a new audio file.

134　　　　　　　　　　　　　　　*Routing to the Mixer and Applying Automation*

2. Next, select the drop-down menu from the top left of the mixer and select **Disk recording | Render to wave file(s)...**; alternatively, use the *Alt + R* shortcut. A dialog box will pop up, where you can then select the default option of **Start**:

Figure 4.32 – Render to wave file(s)

Once the rendering is finished, you will see new audio sample clips appear in your playlist. You have successfully rendered your audio to a new audio sample, as shown in **Track 4** and **Track 5** of the following screenshot:

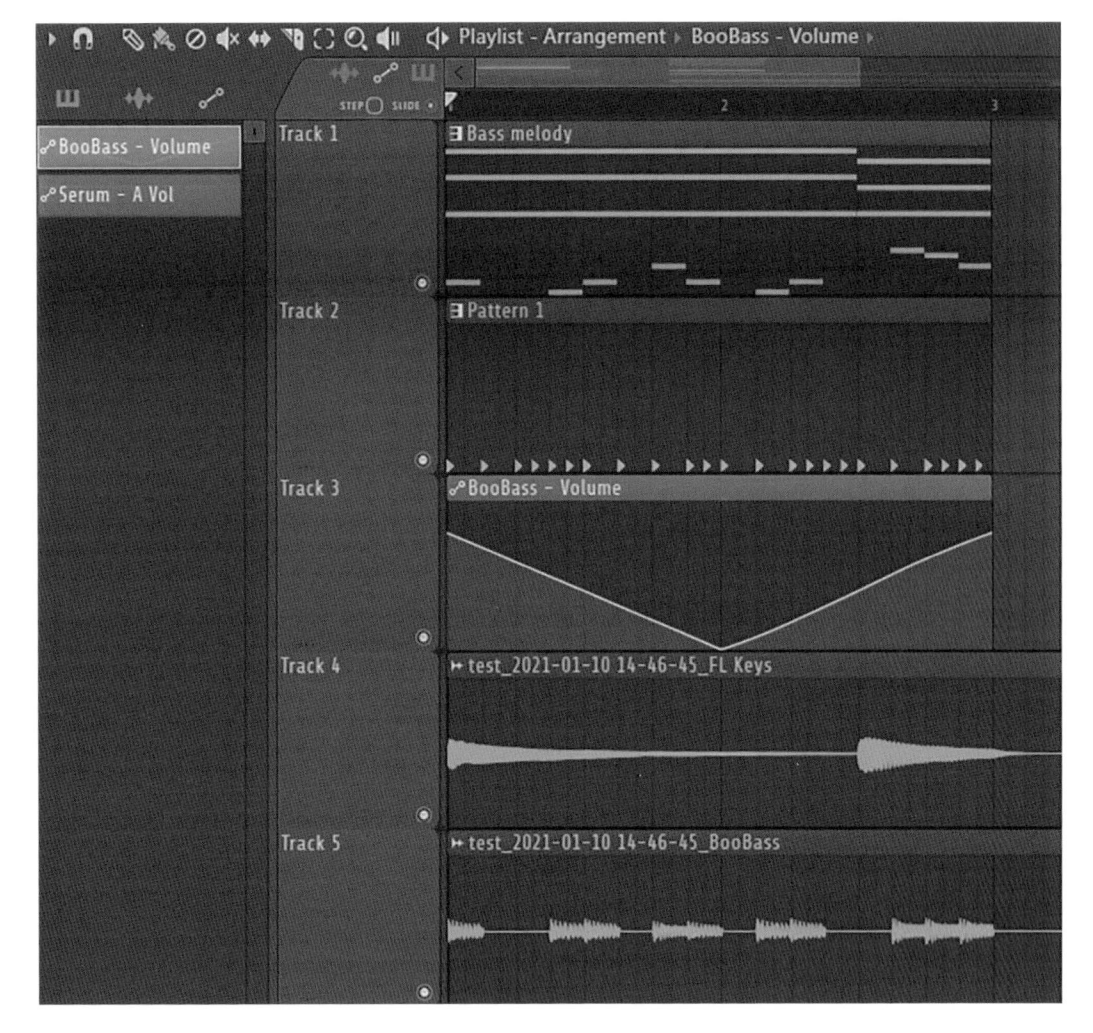

Figure 4.33 – Rendered audio

In this example, the BooBass instrument and the FL Keys instrument mixer tracks have been rendered into audio samples. If you play the song in the playlist, you'll be able to hear the samples playing.

> Once the tracks have been rendered, you can mute the original mixer tracks and disable any plugins that were applied. This will save CPU processing.

There is an alternative, quicker way to render tracks to audio that doesn't involve using the arm disk recording buttons. It's essentially the same technique as the one just described, except that you no longer need to designate a track to be armed.

Simply select multiple tracks on the mixer by holding down *Ctrl* + *Shift* + left-clicking on tracks. You'll know the tracks are selected because they'll be highlighted. Then, select the options drop-down arrow in the top-left corner of the mixer. An example is shown in the following screenshot:

Figure 4.34 – Select tracks

Chapter 4

When clicking the mixer options, a list of options will appear. Select **Disk recording | Render selected tracks to wave file(s)** as shown in the following screenshot. Alternatively, you can just use the shortcut *Shift + Alt + R*. An example is shown in the following screenshot:

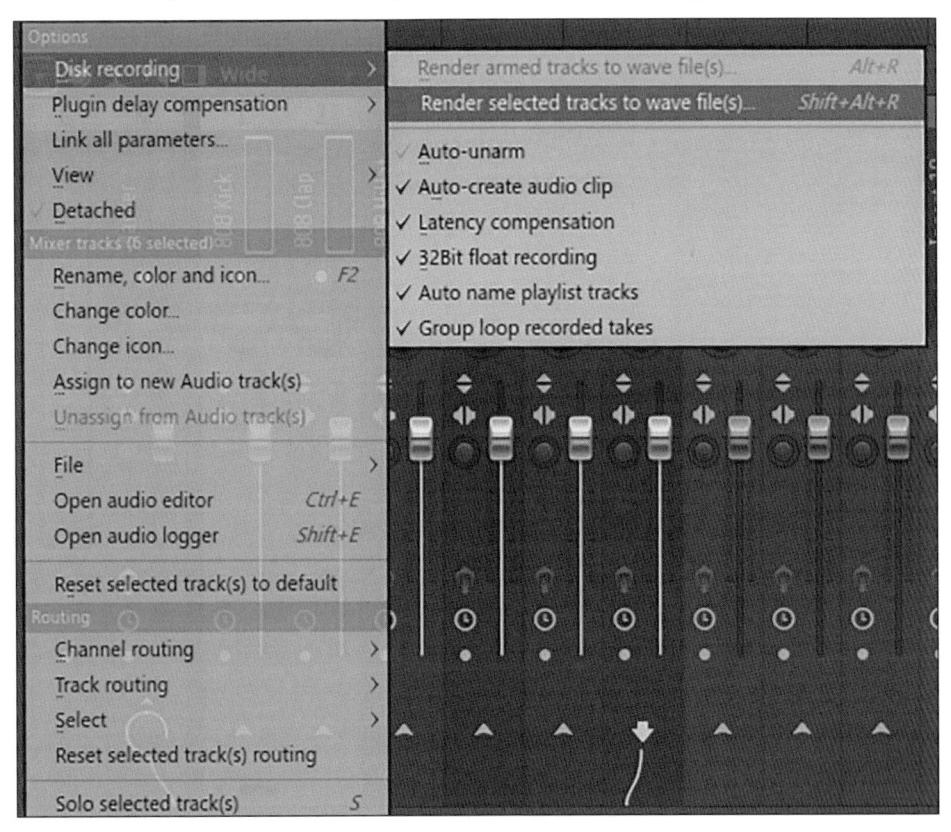

Figure 4.35 – Render selected tracks to wave file(s)

Rendered audio clips will be created. To view the audio clips, navigate to the audio clips tab of the playlist as shown in the following screenshot:

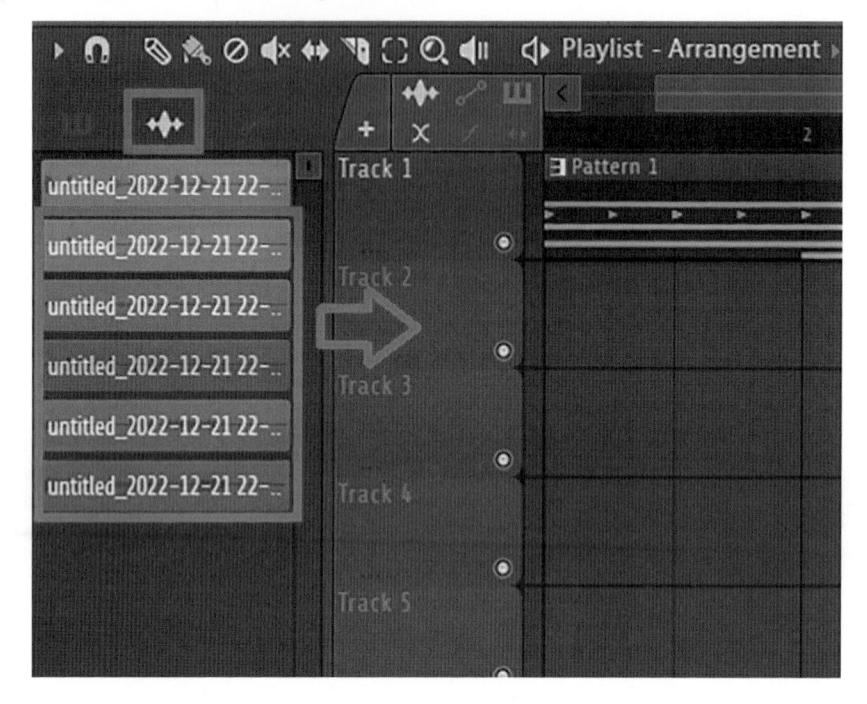

Figure 4.36 – Audio clips

You can then drag the clips onto the playlist. The preceding screenshot shows an example of dragging the audio from the browser into the playlist.

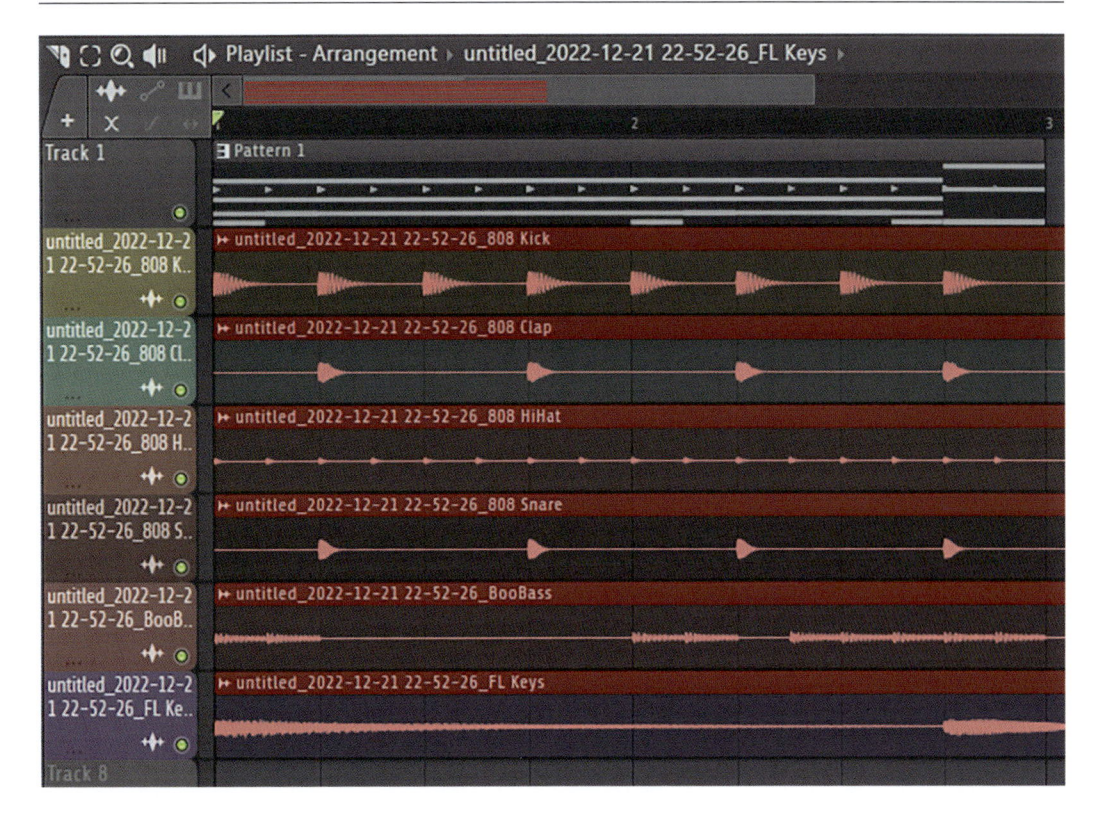

Figure 4.37 – Rendered audio clips

The audio clips will appear in the playlist. You now know how to render any mixer track into an audio clip.

Summary

In this chapter, we learned about the mixer console. The mixer console is where you combine your sounds, balance and blend them together, and apply effects to them. We learned how to route audio and instruments to the mixer. We learned about the components that make up the mixer and what they're used for. We also learned how to apply automation to our plugin controls to change them over time, and how to render audio in the mixer into new audio clips. We've just begun learning about mixing. We will return to the mixer and explore mixing techniques, starting in *Chapter 6, Compression, Sidechaining, Limiting, and Equalization*. In the next chapter, we'll learn about sound design and audio envelopes.

Section II

Music Production Fundamentals

In this section, you will learn how to mix your music like a pro. You'll learn the foundations of sound: the physics principles behind how sound works and its practical applications. You'll explore a wide range of mixing techniques to improve your music including compression, equalization, and stereo width. You'll learn sound design and create your own instruments and effects. You'll learn how to record vocals, process them, create vocal chops, and use vocoders.

We will cover the following chapters in this section:

- *Chapter 5, Sound Design and Audio Envelopes*
- *Chapter 6, Compression, Sidechaining, Limiting, and Equalization*
- *Chapter 7, Stereo Width (Panning, Reverb, Delay, Chorus, and Flangers) and Distortion*
- *Chapter 8, Recording Live Audio and Vocal Processing*
- *Chapter 9, Vocoders and Vocal Chops*
- *Chapter 10, Creating Your Own Instruments and Effects*
- *Chapter 11, Intermediate Mixing Topics and Sound Design Plugin Effects*

5
Sound Design and Audio Envelopes

In this chapter, you'll learn the foundations of how sound works. We'll learn what it is, how it's manipulated, and how instruments create sounds. We'll also discuss how to adjust the audio envelope of any sound sample. Once you understand how sound is created, you'll be able to quickly learn about instrument plugins and have a basic idea of how they work.

In this chapter, we'll explore the following topics:

- What is sound?
- What causes a note pitch?
- How do instruments create sound with different pitches?
- Why do different instruments playing the same pitch sound different?
- Manipulating audio sample envelopes
- Using Mod X and Mod Y for automation (using an automation clip in multiple places)

What is sound?

In the following chapters of this book, we will learn how to use plugins that manipulate sound. But what exactly is sound? When we talk about sound design, what exactly are we designing?

Sound is a form of energy like electricity and light. Sound is made when molecules vibrate and move in a wave pattern, which we call **sound waves**. Air is able to support many sound waves simultaneously. When you clap your hands, your clapping causes energy to move outward into the air.

The air molecules vibrate, bump into neighboring molecules, and transfer energy, causing them to vibrate. This energy gets dispersed outward from the source, around the room, and continues until the molecules' energy is equally dispersed. The energy gets weaker as it gets distributed over a wider area. This is why there's no sound in outer space; there are no air molecules vibrating to support sound waves.

Molecules don't move around the room with sound. Instead, the energy is transferred between molecules. A molecule moves from its original position, transfers energy to a new molecule, and then returns to its resting point. This movement of the molecule is what we call the *vibration* or *oscillation*.

The following figure shows how molecules vibrate in a wave pattern:

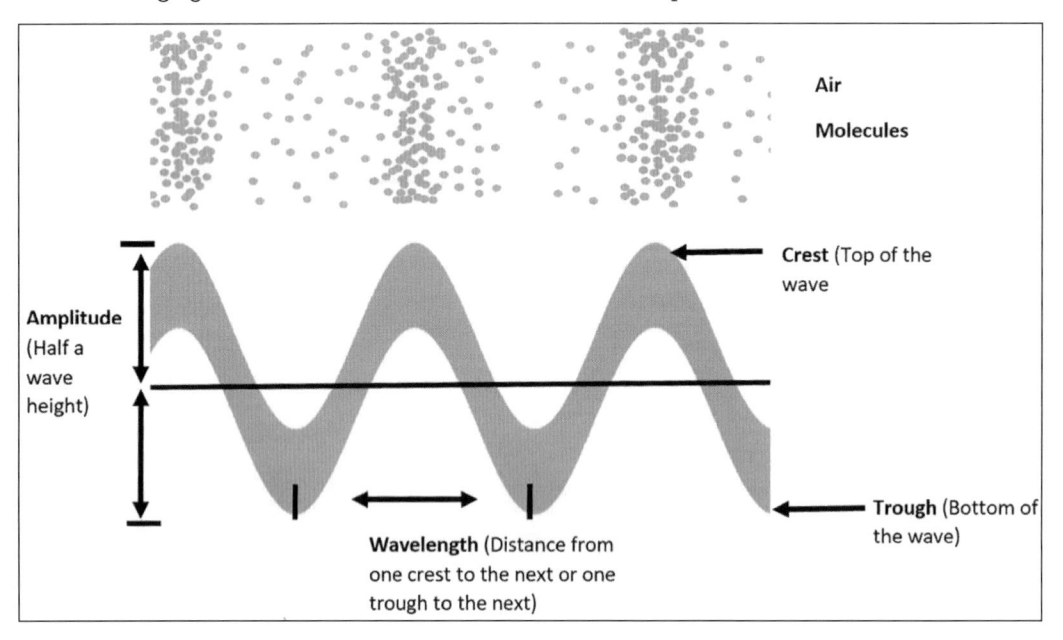

Figure 5.1 – Sound wave

The preceding diagram shows an example of how molecules bunch up together while vibrating. They collect in some places and are less frequent in others. This can be visualized as a wave. The top of the wave indicates that there are more molecules and the bottom of the wave indicates that there are fewer molecules.

One of the factors dictating what the wave sounds like is the amplitude of the wave. The **amplitude** of a wave is the distance from the point of rest (the middle) to the crest (top of the wave).

The amplitude is the same distance from the middle to the trough of the wave. The amplitude is what we think of as volume. The larger the amplitude, the louder the sound.

There are two kinds of waves:

- **Transverse waves** are where the oscillation is perpendicular to the direction that the wave is traveling in. Imagine a water wave moving up and down.
- **Longitudinal waves** are where the oscillations happen in the same direction that the wave travels, similar to what you see when a spring compresses. Imagine a spring moving horizontally back and forth. Sound is a longitudinal wave.

What causes a note's pitch?

When you think of pitch, you think about how high or low a sound feels. The **pitch** of a sound is determined by the frequency of the vibrations. **Frequency** is how many wave cycles pass through a given point per second. The more vibrations per second, the higher the frequency and the higher the pitch. The following figure shows an example of high and low frequency:

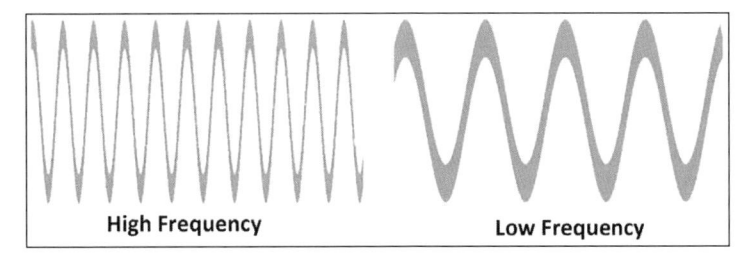

Figure 5.2 – Frequency

The higher frequency will have a higher pitch and the lower frequency will have a lower pitch. An example of a pitch is a middle C note, which has a frequency of 261.6 Hz.

Human ears can pick up frequencies between 20 and 20,000 Hz. **Hertz (Hz)** is the unit to measure how many wave cycles pass per second. As you get older, your ears lose the ability to pick up higher-pitch sounds. Sounds that are higher than this range are called **ultrasonic**. Sounds that are lower are called **infrasonic**. Some animals can hear sounds outside of this frequency range. Dogs hear sounds that are higher, which is why they can hear dog whistles. Elephants and whales can hear sounds that are lower.

We now know that sound has something to do with wavelengths, amplitudes, and frequencies, but how do we hear sounds?

How do we hear things?

Sound causes air to expand and contract. Air expands under low pressure and compresses under high pressure. Changes in air pressure are useful because we can use devices to measure air pressure. Microphones detect changes in air pressure. Microphones are made up of a diaphragm stretched over a metal plate. As sound waves pass over it, the changes in high and low pressure cause the diaphragm to move back and forth and vibrate. This movement is measured by the device and converted into audio data. The data is then interpreted by your computer. The following figure shows an example of a microphone:

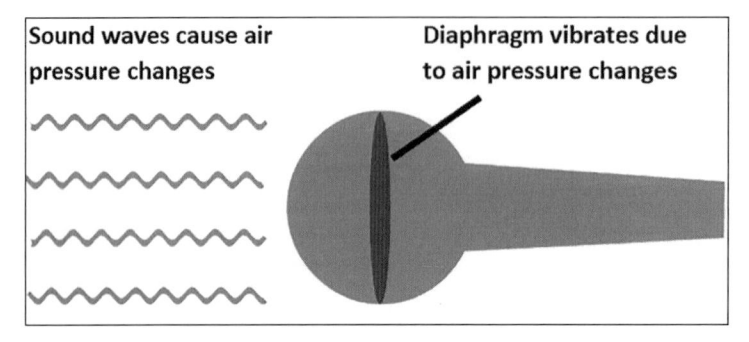

Figure 5.3 – Microphone

Your ears work in a similar fashion to a microphone. Your eardrums encounter air pressure changes, which cause them to vibrate. Your brain interprets these vibrations as sound.

When audio waves meet, they can react to one another. This can result in the following effects:

- **Constructive interference** is where two sound wave crests combine to make one crest with a higher amplitude than the original one. This makes the sound seem louder.
- **Destructive interference** is where the crest and the trough of two sound waves encounter each other and cancel each other out.

Noise cancellation technology in headphones works by analyzing the sound around you and generating a sound wave that destructively interferes with the original sound wave to cancel it out. Essentially, one sound makes another sound quieter.

Increases in loudness are not linear. Sound needs to be about 10 times the intensity in order for it to appear twice as loud. **Decibels (dB)** are the units measuring the loudness of a sound. Take the following examples:

- Near total silence: 0 dB

- A whisper: 15 dB
- Normal conversation: 60 dB
- A lawnmower: 90 dB
- A car horn: 110 dB
- A rock concert or a jet engine: 120 dB
- A gunshot or firecracker: 140 dB

The maximum loudness you can generate in air is around 194 dB. In water, it's around 270 dB. Why? Remember that sound is energy and sound waves exert pressure. So, when we say 194 dB in air, we're talking about a huge amount of pressure. Anything higher than that and the medium that the sound is traveling through starts to break down, making the measurement no longer meaningful.

The **Doppler effect** is where the pitch of a sound changes as you get closer or further away from the sound. As you get closer, the pitch of the sound increases, and it decreases as you move further away. Imagine the siren of a police car. As the car approaches you, the sound gets louder and the pitch gets higher. As the car gets further away, the sound gets quieter and the pitch gets lower. Some instrument effect plugins mimic the Doppler effect. They do this by simulating how the loudness and pitch appear to increase as the object gets closer. This effect is frequently used in movie sound effects.

We now know that sounds are composed of waves and that our ears can interpret these waves. But how do we create music out of sounds?

How do instruments create sound with different pitches?

In order to understand how instruments create pitches, we need to understand how instruments create sound waves. There are two types of sound waves. **Traveling waves** are observed when a wave is not confined to a given space. If you were to shake an unattached, loose rope, the resulting random ripple in the rope would be a traveling wave. The wave could have any wavelength as there's nothing restricting the length.

Standing waves, on the other hand, occur when a wave is confined to a fixed space in a medium. The medium restricts the wavelength to hit recurring wavelengths and frequencies. If you were to shake a string that's attached to a pole, the resulting constrained ripple would be a standing wave.

This medium restriction produces a regular wave pattern that repeats. We call this a standing wave (as though it were standing still). You can see an example of a standing wave in the following figure:

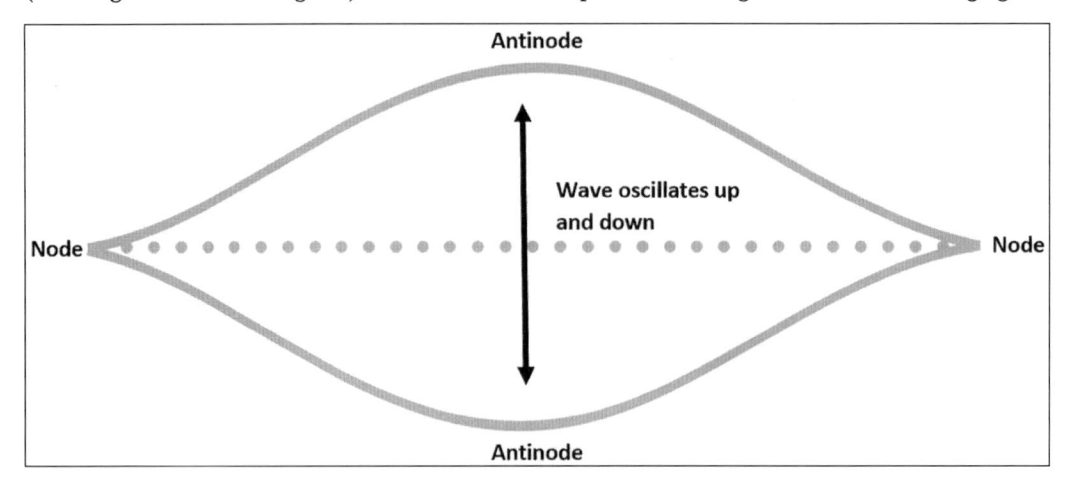

Figure 5.4 – Standing wave

You can think of a standing wave as a guitar string. The string is attached to both ends of the guitar and so each string end has no movement. Only the middle of the string can move. Physicists call the point of no movement on a wave a **node**. The part of a wave that moves is called the **antinode**. The wave appears to vibrate in a repeating movement where only the amplitude of the wave is changing.

If you tune a guitar, it will tighten the string, restrict the wavelength, and cause the string to vibrate a certain number of times per second. What you're doing by tuning the guitar string is shaping the frequency of the wave. When you hear the frequency of the wave, you recognize the sound as a specific pitch. When you press down on the guitar string in different places, you cause the active part of the string to change lengths, resulting in a new note pitch.

In wind and brass instruments, there are no strings to vibrate. Instead, the air molecules are restricted within the space of the pipe. This space confines the size of the wavelength and amplitude. The shape of the pipe dictates the nature of the standing wave. The following figure shows a wave confined within a pipe:

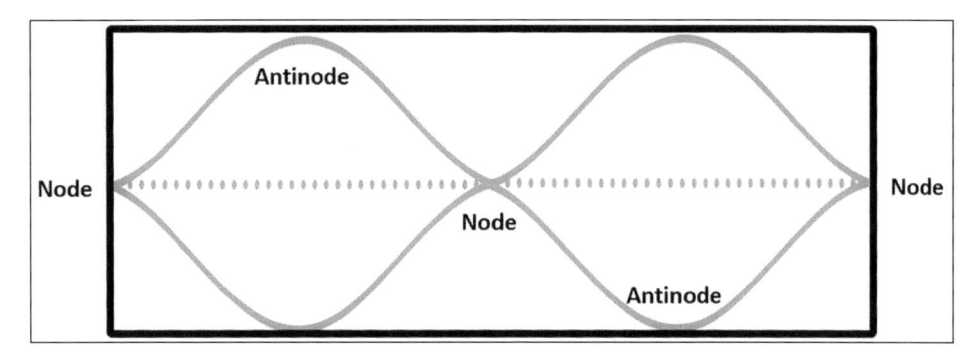

Figure 5.5 – Standing wave in a pipe

In a pipe (like a woodwind or brass instrument), the end of the pipe acts as the fixed node. The wave reflects back off the end of the pipe and creates the waveform. An open-ended pipe can reflect a wave too, even if there isn't a solid surface for the wave to reflect off.

There are a number of variables to play around with that can shape the wave, such as how long the pipe is, whether the pipe is open or closed, and how many openings are open or closed. Imagine a flute. When you blow into a flute, the sound changes depending on how many holes you cover. The pitch is dictated by the number of open holes.

If we adjust the medium the wave is traveling through (such as making the pipe longer or shorter), we can get a different number of wave nodes and antinodes. This is a way to change the pitch we hear. The lowest number of nodes and antinodes that can exist in a wave is two nodes and one antinode. We call this the **first harmonic**, also known as the **fundamental**:

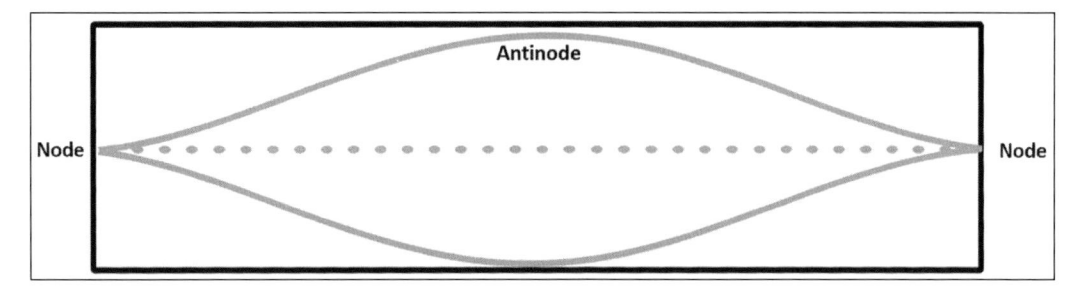

Figure 5.6 – First harmonic (fundamental)

If we add a single node and antinode to our wave, we get a wave like the one in the following figure. You can see that there are now three nodes and two antinodes:

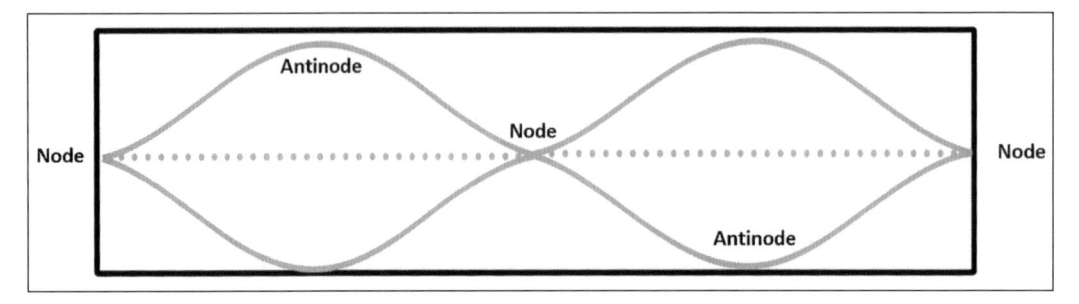

Figure 5.7 – Second harmonic (first overtone)

We call this the **second harmonic**. Another name for this is the **first overtone**. Music theory often uses the term **harmonic**. Physics often uses the term **overtone**, but they both mean the same thing. Notice we have increased the frequency of the wave. The first harmonic only had half a wavelength, while the second harmonic has a full wavelength, but it's the same total distance. This means the pitch of the sound would be higher. How much higher? Exactly one octave. If, for example, our fundamental had a pitch of middle C, meaning it had a frequency of 261.6 Hz, the second harmonic/first overtone would be 523.2 Hz, or a C note that is exactly one octave higher.

If we add another node and antinode, we get a wave as in the following screenshot:

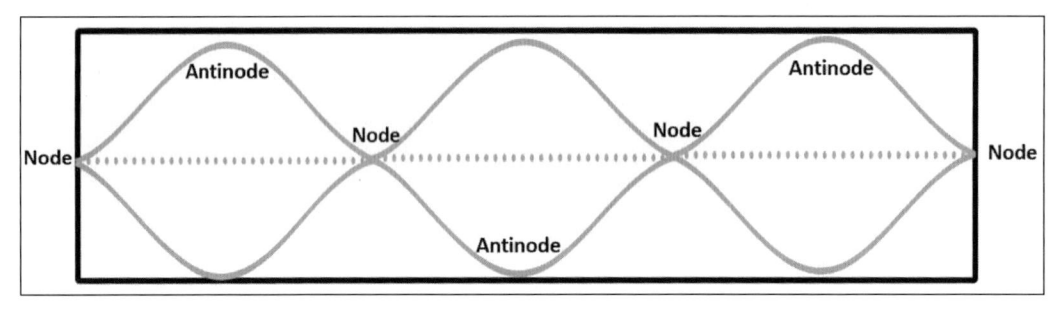

Figure 5.8 – Third harmonic (second overtone)

A wave with four nodes and three antinodes is known as the **third harmonic**, also known as the **second overtone**. Note that the frequency has increased again; the amount would again be another octave higher.

What all of this means is that instruments can create different pitches by modifying the sound wavelength and frequency of the wave.

Why do different instruments playing the same pitch sound different?

Different instruments emphasize different harmonics/overtones. They emphasize some overtones louder than others. The waveforms of different instruments have different amplitudes, which also shape the sound. Also, remember that air is able to support many sound waves simultaneously. This variation in the combination of waveforms played simultaneously also shapes the sound we hear.

In our diagram examples, we've looked at sine waveforms. There are many kinds of waveforms. Instrument plugins can generate different types of waves, such as square waves, saw waves, and any sort of strange concoction developers can think up. The type of waveform will affect the resulting sound.

When you experiment with synthesizer plugin instruments, what the plugin is doing is creating different wave shapes. It adjusts the wavelength, amplitude, frequency, harmonics, and combination of waveforms it plays. Once the waveform is created, there are additional ways to modify sound waves using what are called sound envelopes.

Modifying sound envelopes

A **sound envelope** is a term describing how sound changes over time. When playing around with instrument plugins, you may come across the acronym **ASDR**. This stands for **attack**, **sustain**, **decay**, and **release** and refers to the four stages of a sound envelope.

The best way to understand a sound envelope is to modify one yourself:

1. Grab a single sound sample and load it up into the channel rack. Later on, after we've adjusted the sample envelope, we'll add it to the playlist.

I'm going to use an acoustic guitar sample, as shown in the following screenshot:

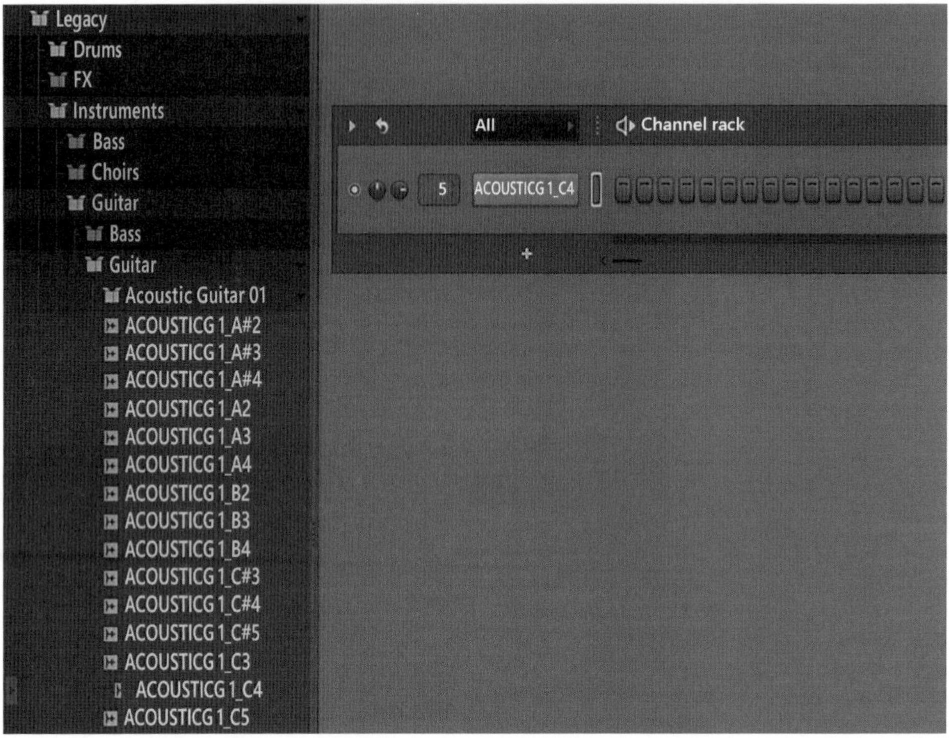

Figure 5.9 – Guitar sample

Note tha t I say channel rack, not playlist. It's important that you don't drag the sample directly into the playlist at this stage as you won't be able to see the envelope controls.

2. Once loaded, left-click on the sample in the channel rack to bring up the sample properties. Select the envelope/instrument settings toggle button at the top left of the window, as shown in the following screenshot:

Figure 5.10 – Envelope settings

You will now be able to see the sample envelope as shown in the preceding screenshot. By default, the **Volume** envelope is highlighted. Directly underneath the volume button, you can see a list of knobs with controls for changing the volume envelope.

You can think of an envelope as a container for sounds. Imagine you have a bunch of objects that are all different, but they're shipped in a standard format container, just like how boats ship items overseas. The container itself has a bunch of properties regardless of what it carries, such as how long it is or how quickly it gets delivered. The container has an influence on how we interact with the object inside. An audio envelope is a little like that. The envelope allows us to interact with the sound using some universal controls.

3. Experiment with changing the delay, attack, hold, decay, sustain, and release knobs while playing the sample at the same time.

You'll be able to hear how the envelope manipulates the sound.

Here's a brief description of the envelope controls in order, from left to right:

- **Delay:** The time it takes for the note to go from the maximum level to the sustain level.
- **Attack**: The time it takes for the note to reach its maximum level (in this case, volume). By increasing the attack, you'll hear the sound become more punctuated.
- **Hold**: How long to hold the maximum level when the audio reaches its peak.
- **Decay:** The time taken from the attack level to the sustain level.
- **Sustain:** The level at which the note is held. Some instruments allow you to maintain a level continuously at the end.
- **Release:** The time it takes for the note to fall from the sustain level to silence after being released.
- **Tension:** The first tension knob adjusts the time between the delay and the attack. The second tension knob adjusts the time between the sustain and the release.

When dealing with envelope controls, you may come across a term known as a transient. **Transients** refer to modifying the attack and release controls of a sound volume envelope to increase or decrease them. If increased, this will make the sound more punctuated. If decreased, it will make the sound less punctuated and less intense.

Any sample can have its audio envelope manipulated in this fashion. Most instrument plugins include envelope controls. Understanding the terminology described so far in this section will allow you to learn about instrument plugins and effects much quicker.

Using Mod X and Mod Y for automation

FL Studio provides you with control knobs that you can use to automate any other FL Studio plugin knob. Essentially, you can create an automation once and have control knobs on different plugins copy the automation.

> Warning: this next feature is a little on the advanced side. If you find this confusing, don't worry, as you'll only need it when you want to create your own custom sound design.

In the same menu window as before, in *Figure 5.10*, you can see options for manipulating the envelope of **Panning, Volume, Mod X, Mod Y**, and **Pitch**. Just like the volume, you can adjust the envelopes for any of these parameters.

Chapter 5

Panning determines whether you want the audio to come out of the right or left speaker. **Pitch** determines how high or low the sound is.

Mod stands for **modulation**. **Mod X** and **Mod Y** may seem a little unintuitive at first glance. From a big-picture understanding, X and Y are essentially placeholder names for whatever control is assigned to them. They allow you to create automation now, and later figure out what control you want to link the automation to.

What does it mean to modify the envelope of **Mod X** and **Mod Y**? Let's take a closer look at these. **Mod X** and **Mod Y** allow you to create an automation clip that other controls can use. The easiest way to understand this is through an example:

1. Route the sample we're currently using to a track in the mixer. We discussed routing in *Chapter 4*, *Routing to the Mixer and Applying Automation*.

2. Select the **Mod X** button to open up the Mod X envelope controls, as shown in the following screenshot:

Figure 5.11 – Mod X

On the right side, under **Filter**, you'll see two knobs that say **MOD X** and **MOD Y**.

3. Right-click on the **MOD X** knob and select **Create automation clip**:

Figure 5.12 – Mod X automation

An automation clip is created in the playlist.

4. Create a curve in the automation; any type of curve will do. If you need a refresher on how to create automation curves, we discussed it in *Chapter 4, Routing to the Mixer and Applying Automation*.

5. Add the sample that you modified to the playlist. Your playlist should now look similar to the following screenshot:

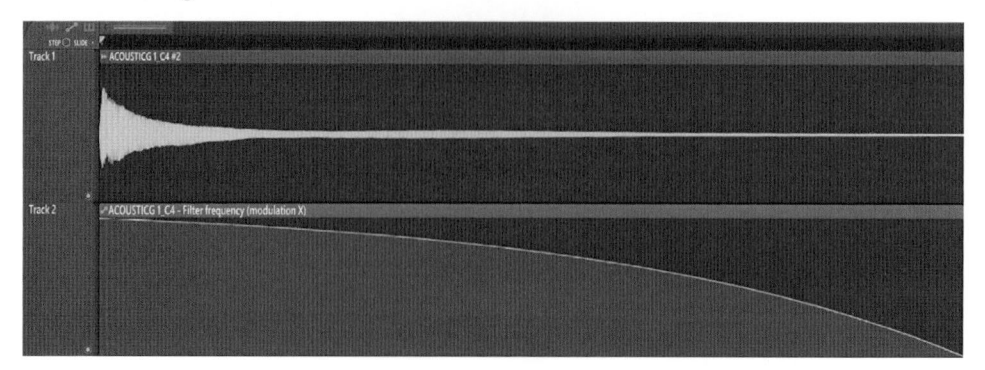

Figure 5.13 – Playlist

So far, we've set up the Mod X control with automation for a sample. Essentially, it's saying that we have automation that will change over time. But what do we want to automate?

6. In the mixer channel where you sent your instrument, add an FL Studio effect plugin to the sample. I'm going to choose **Fruity parametric EQ 2**, but you can pick any native FL Studio plugin:

Figure 5.14 – Fruity parametric EQ 2 effect on the sample

7. We can now pick any control knob in our native plugin effect and link it to our Mod X automation clip. Right-click on any adjustable knob in your effect plugin. In my example, I'm going to right-click on the band **5** peaking knob. Select **Link to controller...**:

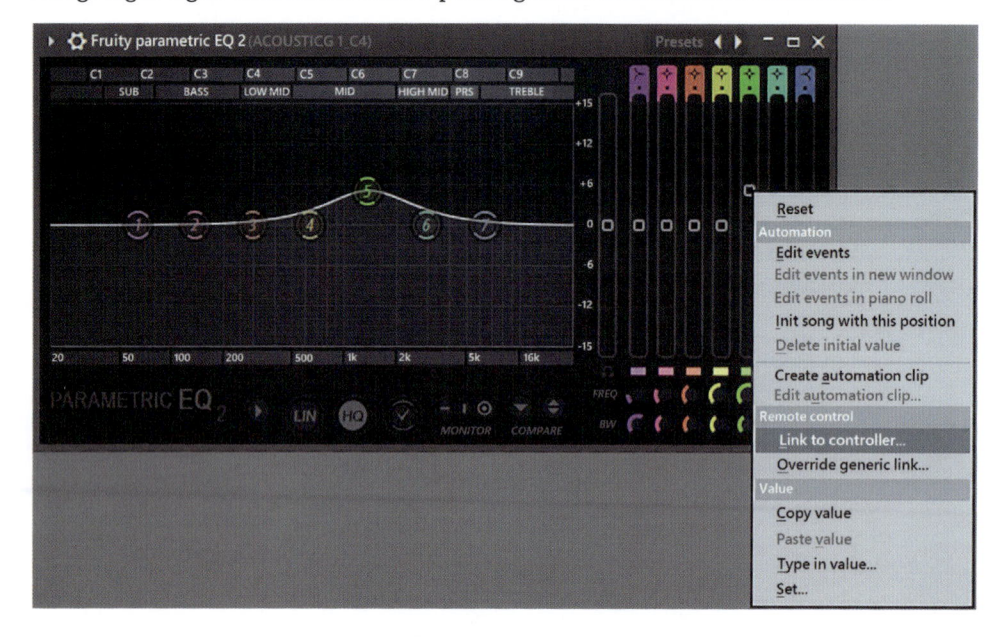

Figure 5.15 – Link to controller

8. Once selected, the **Remote control settings** window will pop up, as shown in the following screenshot. Under the **Internal controller** heading, you'll see the automation clip that you created in the playlist, as well as any other automation clips present:

Chapter 5

Figure 5.16 – Internal controller

9. If another control knob is already linked to your automation clip, you'll need to uncheck the **Remove conflicts** button at the bottom. This won't be an issue if this is your first time doing this. Once your automation clip is selected, click **Accept** at the bottom.

10. Go back to your playlist and play the song. The following screenshot shows our sample, the automation of Mod X, and the effect knob that is being modified:

Figure 5.17 – Effect is being modulated

What you've done is created an automation clip and linked the automation clip to an effect control. As you play your song, the plugin effect knob that you linked will adjust according to the automation clip. In my example, band 5 of the **Fruity parametric EQ 2** effect moves according to the automation clip.

You aren't restricted to linking one control to an automation clip. You can have multiple effect controls linked to the same automation clip using the same technique.

What's the point of Mod X and Mod Y?

We used Mod X and Mod Y controls to create automation clips in our example, but this could have been any kind of automation clip. Mod X and Mod Y don't control anything on their own; they're just empty controls to be assigned.

Mod X and Mod Y are simply further tools that can be used when arranging your songs. Most commonly, they're used to show how an effect changes over time to bring interest to the arrangement. For example, if you know that you want the intensity to build up before reaching the chorus but you don't yet know what effects you want to apply, you could set up the Mod X automation ahead of time and add effects later.

The only difference in using Mod X and Mod Y versus some other automation control is that they are specifically referenced in several FL Studio plugins, such as **Patcher**, **Slicex**, **Sytrus**, and **Harmor**. When you use those plugins, you'll find the names **X** and **Y** appear in several places of the plugin. If you're planning on doing surround sound 3D space, Mod X and Mod Y are logical control candidates to use to identify your x and y axes' position.

Overall, Mod X and Y are useful for creating automation that you can later assign controls to. You now know how to modify a waveform using Mod X and Y, and have learned how, by doing this, you can pass around automation between plugins.

Summary

In this chapter, we explored how sound works. We learned about sound waves, how we hear sounds, and how instruments create sounds. We learned about audio envelopes and how to adjust the audio envelope of any audio sample. With this information, you will be able to start using instrument plugins quickly and have an intuition of how they work. Finally, we learned how to link any FL Studio instrument plugin control to an automation clip.

In the next chapter, we will learn about music mixing techniques and explore plugin effects that can be applied to your sounds.

6

Compression, Sidechaining, Limiting, and Equalization

When you hear music performed live, there's variation in the volume. Some sounds are loud, some are quiet. Some may be muffled, distorted, shrill, or filled with echo, but you probably won't notice when you're enraptured by the performance visuals. If you were to record the performance live on your phone and play it back later, you'd notice that the sound quality of the recording is poor. There's background noise, the lyrics are hard to make out clearly, and the bass sound likely overpowers the higher instrument sounds.

When you prepare a song for production, you want to achieve the highest-quality sound you can get. You want the audio to be as clear as possible and emphasize the best parts of your sounds and reduce the unpleasant parts.

Mixing is the name of the process we use to polish our sounds. It includes combining and grouping recordings of instruments in a tool called the mixer. The mixer balances the volumes of each instrument relative to the others and applies effects to your sounds. The two categories of effects that you can apply to your sounds are compression and **equalization (EQ)**. These are broad categories. There are several types of compression: simple compression, gating, sidechaining, and limiting.

In this chapter, you'll learn mixing techniques with compressors and equalizers. Compressors allow you to tame extremes in your sounds and make your sounds appear balanced and full. Equalizers allow you to shape and refine your sounds. Sidechaining reduces the volume of a sound based on the input of a second sound source.

Limiting creates a cap on the volume of a sound, constraining the volume to a certain value threshold.

In this chapter, we'll cover the following topics:

- Understanding compression
- Applying gates and expanders
- Applying sidechaining
- Using limiters
- Applying equalization

Understanding compression

When mixing, we call the range in volume from loud to quiet the dynamic range. **Compression** is an effect to be applied to a sound to reduce the dynamic range. After compression is applied to a sound, the loudest parts of the sound become quieter relative to the quieter parts. The volume of the whole sound is then raised. Reducing the dynamic range means that you have less change between the quietest and the loudest parts of your sound.

Why would you want to use compression? Imagine you were having a conversation with someone and wanted someone else to hear a recording of the dialog. In the recording, some parts of the dialog might be really loud while others might be quiet. You might whisper in some parts and yell in others; you might move close to or further away from the microphone. All of these factors will affect the volume of the end result of the recording. For someone listening to the recording, you don't want them to be struggling to hear the whispering and then having their ears blasted off in the louder parts. You want to have a consistent volume throughout to ensure an easy listening experience.

Applying compression to a sound helps to remove these problems. By applying compression, the volume of the loud parts of your audio will be brought down so that they don't overpower your listener. After compressing, we can bring up the volume of the whole sound, including the quiet parts. The volume of the whispering parts will be increased to a level that is comfortable to hear. The overall result is a recording that's easy to listen to, with the loud peaking parts tamed and the quiet parts made more audible.

Any sound with extreme peaks in the dynamic range may benefit from compression. After applying compression, sounds generally appear thicker and fuller, which is desirable. The trade-off is that you won't have as much contrast between sounds.

Let's see what compression looks like visually. The following figure shows the waveform of a kick drum audio sample before it is compressed:

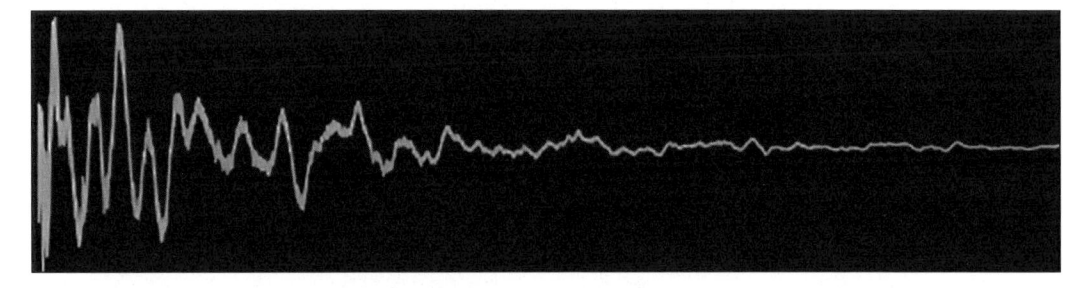

Figure 6.1 – Uncompressed kick sample

The following figure shows the waveform of the same sample after it has been compressed:

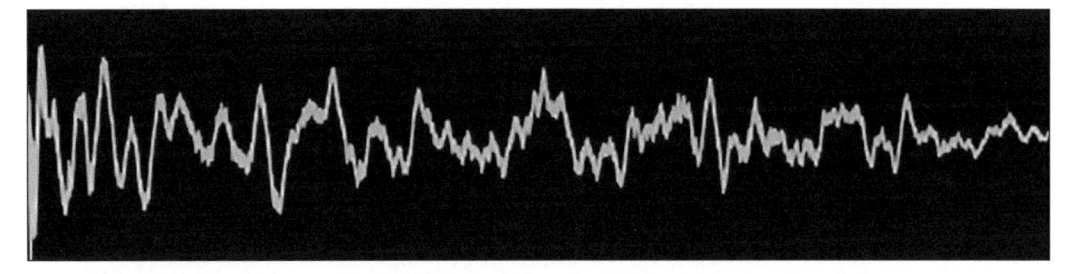

Figure 6.2 – Compressed kick sample

The amplitude (height) of the waveform indicates the loudness. In *Figure 6.1*, you can see that the dynamic range is large. It's loud in the beginning but tapers off over time until it becomes nonexistent.

In *Figure 6.2*, you can see the dynamic range is smaller. It's loud in the beginning and the volume stays high for the duration of the sound. The volume of the loud part at the beginning has decreased and the quiet tail end of the sound has increased.

When we compress, we bring the loud and quiet parts closer together so that there's less variation between the highs and lows (less dynamic range), and then usually increase the overall volume of the sound.

Applying compression with Fruity Limiter

Let's learn how to apply compression to a sound. To illustrate the examples in this chapter, we will use **Fruity Limiter**, a plugin that comes with FL Studio. Fruity Limiter has multiple tools, including compression, gating, sidechaining, and limiting. We will explore these topics in detail in the upcoming pages. Understanding how to use these tools will give you generally applicable skills used in many synthesizer plugins and effects.

Let's get started with applying compression with Fruity Limiter:

1. Drag any audio recording sample into the playlist and route the audio to a mixer channel. In my example, I'm using a single kick sound sample found in the Pack folder in the browser. If you need a refresher on routing audio to mixer channels, see *Chapter 4, Routing to the Mixer and Applying Automation.*

2. In the mixer channel that you routed your sample to, insert the **Fruity Limiter** effect plugin, and select the **COMP** setting (which stands for **compression**), as shown in the following screenshot:

Figure 6.3 – Fruity Limiter

Fruity Limiter is made up of several components: the **LOUDNESS** section, the **ENVELOPE** section, and the **NOISE GATE** section.

The **LOUDNESS** section is a compressor. The following are descriptions of the controls from left to right:

- **GAIN**: Increases or decreases the overall volume. After applying compression to the sound, the louder parts will be quieter. This means the loud and quiet parts of the sound are closer together in amplitude. You can then increase the volume of the sound as a whole by increasing the gain.
- **SAT (saturation)**: This is a form of mild distortion. It affects the louder parts (higher amplitude) of the sound more than the quieter parts. In electrical hardware, this occurs by overloading the electrical component. The more signal you apply, the more the sound gets saturated. If you combine saturation with compression, the compression brings down the volume of the louder parts. This results in the quieter parts of the sound being closer in amplitude to the louder parts and allows more of the sound to receive saturation.
- **THRES (threshold)**: This sets the level above which the signal will be compressed. If the threshold is set to **0** dB, it disables the threshold and no compression will be applied.
- **KNEE**: This determines the transition between no compression and full compression. It allows you to fade in the amount of compression.
- **RATIO**: This determines how much compression should be applied once the threshold is exceeded.

By adjusting the threshold, knee, and ratio controls, you can compress the sound of the audio. The following screenshot shows an example of applying compression:

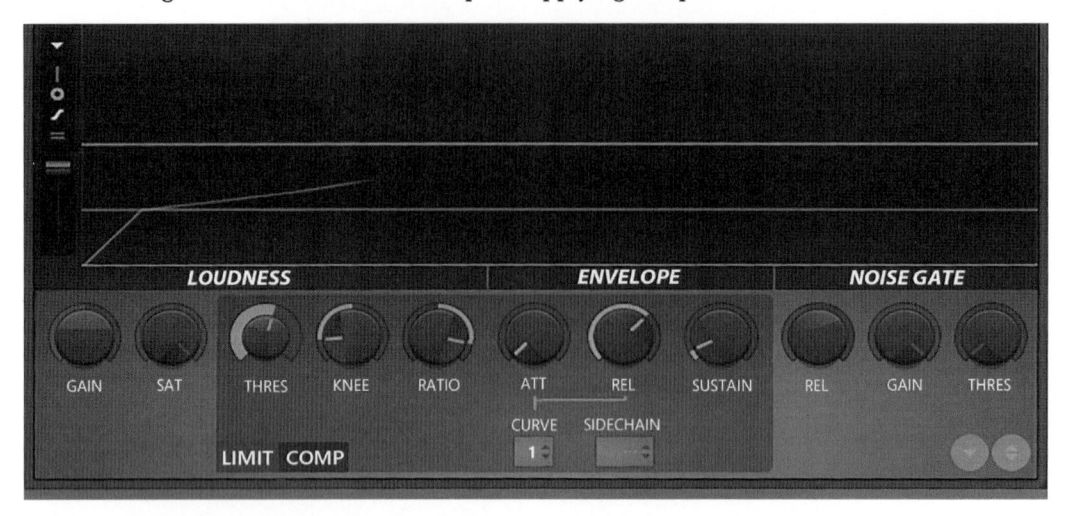

Figure 6.4 – Threshold

To apply compression similar to the preceding screenshot, do the following:

1. Have the sample playing while applying the compression.
2. Set the **THRES** control level to a value below **1.0**. This determines what volume to start applying compression at. Anything above the threshold level will have compression applied to it. You can set the **KNEE** control if you want the compression to fade in instead of coming in abruptly. The lower the value you set the threshold to, the more you will notice the sound of the compression.
3. Set the **RATIO** level to a value greater than **1.0:1**. This will determine how much the sound is compressed. If the ratio is set to **2.0:1**, this means that for every dB in volume, the signal will be reduced to half. If the ratio were **3.0:1**, then the signal would be reduced by a third, and so on.
4. Increase the **GAIN** level of the sound. After adjusting the threshold and ratio controls, the volume of the sound has decreased. The loud parts of the sound have been lowered to a level closer to the volume of the quieter parts. We now apply what is called the **makeup gain**. This will increase the overall volume and result in an ending sound where the quieter and louder parts are brought closer together. This makes the sound appear fuller with less dynamic variation.

Congratulations, you just applied compression to your sound!

Chapter 6

Let's continue exploring the Fruity Limiter plugin. To the right of the **LOUDNESS** section, you can see the **ENVELOPE** section, as shown in the following screenshot:

Figure 6.5 – Envelope

Transients are the short burst of energy that you hear at the start of any sound. The envelope provides control over the **ATT (attack)**, **REL (release)**, and **SUSTAIN** levels of the transients.

The **ENVELOPE** section here is applied to the compression. You won't hear any difference when you use these controls unless you compress the sound first.

By decreasing the attack of the compression, you cause the compression to come in quicker. This will reduce the punchy articulation of the sound.

By decreasing the release time, the sound becomes shorter and brings focus to the loud, punchy peaks of the sound. This is because decreasing the compressor release means that the quieter part of the sample isn't amplified for as long. The opposite is also true – by increasing the release time, the sound becomes longer, and you can hear more of the compressed tail after the makeup gain.

The **SUSTAIN** control allows the compression to last longer or shorter.

In the bottom-right corner of Fruity Limiter, you can see two circle icons with arrows, called **store in spare state**. These buttons allow you to flip between two states of the plugin to give you a before-and-after comparison. Essentially, you get two alternative setups that you can switch between and compare.

Fruity Limiter contains several presets in the top-right corner of the plugin. I encourage you to experiment with the presets to see examples of compression.

Understanding parallel compression

If you look up the term **compression** online, you may come across the term parallel compression. **Parallel compression** is where you have two identical sounds being played simultaneously. One of the sounds has compression applied to it, while the other doesn't. You have a compressed sound and an uncompressed sound.

The benefit is that you get the emphasized part of the compressed sound without losing the original transients. When you compress a sound, you make a trade-off. You lose the impactful loudness peaks of the original sound and trade it for a thicker, fuller-bodied sound that emphasizes more of the quieter parts. The hope is that the fuller-bodied compressed sound is more pleasing to the ears.

In parallel compression, you don't have to make this trade-off. You layer the uncompressed version with the transients with the compressed sound that doesn't contain the transients. You gain all of the benefits of compression while leaving the delicate transients intact. The result is a thicker, fuller sound that still maintains the punchy articulations. Parallel compression is most often used on drum instruments to maintain transient punchiness.

So far, we've covered simple compression and parallel compression. Let's look at another type of compression, called a gate.

Applying gates and expanders

To the right of the **ENVELOPE** section in Fruity Limiter, we can see the **NOISE GATE** section:

Figure 6.6 – Noise Gate

Gates and **expanders** are useful tools for music producers and can be used in a wide variety of situations. They can be used independently from the rest of the controls in Fruity Limiter.

To understand gating, let's compare it to simple compression. Simple compression works by reducing the loudest parts of a sound above a threshold level. Gates and expanders do the opposite. Expanders reduce the parts of a sound below a threshold level. Gates completely remove the audio below the threshold (*don't allow anything through the gate*). Expanders reduce the audio below the threshold but don't eliminate it completely. From here on in, we will refer to examples using gates, but the same overall concept is used with expanders too.

Why would you want to use a gate? Imagine you had a dialog recording in a room. In addition to the dialog, there might also be some ambient room noise. Perhaps a gentle hum, some subtle static, a little wind: these undesired sounds detract from the overall focus of clearly hearing the dialog. Gating allows you to remove the undesired background noise. Gating reduces sounds that are not the desired focus.

To use the **NOISE GATE**, do the following:

1. Set the **THRES (threshold)** level to a value below 0 dB. This is the level below which sound will be reduced. If your sample has some background noise you want to remove, set the threshold level slightly above the volume of the unwanted sound but still below the sound of the main subject. For example, if the dialog volume is at least -10 dB, you could set your threshold to somewhere below -10 dB.
2. Decrease the **GAIN** level. This will reduce the volume of the sound below the threshold level and make the unwanted sound quieter.
3. Adjust the **REL (release)** control. This will determine how long you want the gating effect to be applied after the initial reduction.

The end result of using a gate is that we are able to remove unwanted background noise, leaving behind just the desired louder noise.

When to use gating

You want to use noise gating in any situation where you have unwanted background noise. For example, when you record live vocals or a live instrument, before applying any other effects to your sound, you should consider applying a gate. Unless you have a soundproof studio, there will usually be some unwanted background noise that can be removed through gating.

Gating is always the first effect that you should apply in a series of effects. You want effects to be applied only to your desired sound and not to unwanted background noise.

So far, we've learned how to use compressors and gates. Next, let's learn about sidechaining.

Applying sidechaining

Sidechaining (also known as **ducking**) is a compression technique where you use the input of one sound source to determine when to compress a second sound. This technique is used extensively in pop and electronic dance music to sidechain bass instruments whenever a kick drum sound occurs. The result is a rhythmic pumping bass sound associated with the urge to tap your feet and bob your head.

Sidechaining in electronic dance music uses the following rationale: sidechaining the bass sound reduces the bass sound when the kick drum comes in. This frees up space to allow the kick sound transient to punch through and focuses your ears' attention more on the kick.

It should be noted that sidechaining can be applied to any sound and doesn't have to involve percussion at all. A sidechain pumping sound of an instrument can be used on its own. For example, you may want to sidechain the bass instrument, even if you don't have any percussion playing.

The fastest way to understand sidechaining is to use it in an example. In order to do the following example, you will need a bass instrument and a kick sound sample. You can use any bass instrument synthesizer and kick sound sample you like. In my example, I will be using the FL Studio **Harmless** synthesizer and use the default instrument setting when the plugin is loaded. The kick sample used is one that comes with FL Studio in the Pack folder found in the browser:

1. Load your kick sample and bass instrument into the channel rack. Create a clone of the kick sound sample in the channel rack. If you need a refresher on loading instruments, we covered it in *Chapter 2, Exploring the Browser, Playlist, and Channel Rack*.
2. Add a note every 1/4 bar for both of the kick samples.
3. Add the pattern to the playlist and name it Kick.
4. Route all channels in your channel rack to the mixer. Consider coloring your instruments and patterns for visual convenience. After completing these steps, your playlist and channel rack should look similar to the following:

Figure 6.7 – Sidechaining setup

5. Create a new pattern and name it Bass.

6. For the bass instrument (in my case, **Harmless**), add notes every 1/8 bar. Aim for the sound to have low bass by decreasing the pitch until the sound of the instrument is low. For Harmless, notes in the pitch of A2 are low enough. After adding bass instrument notes, your screen should look similar to the following:

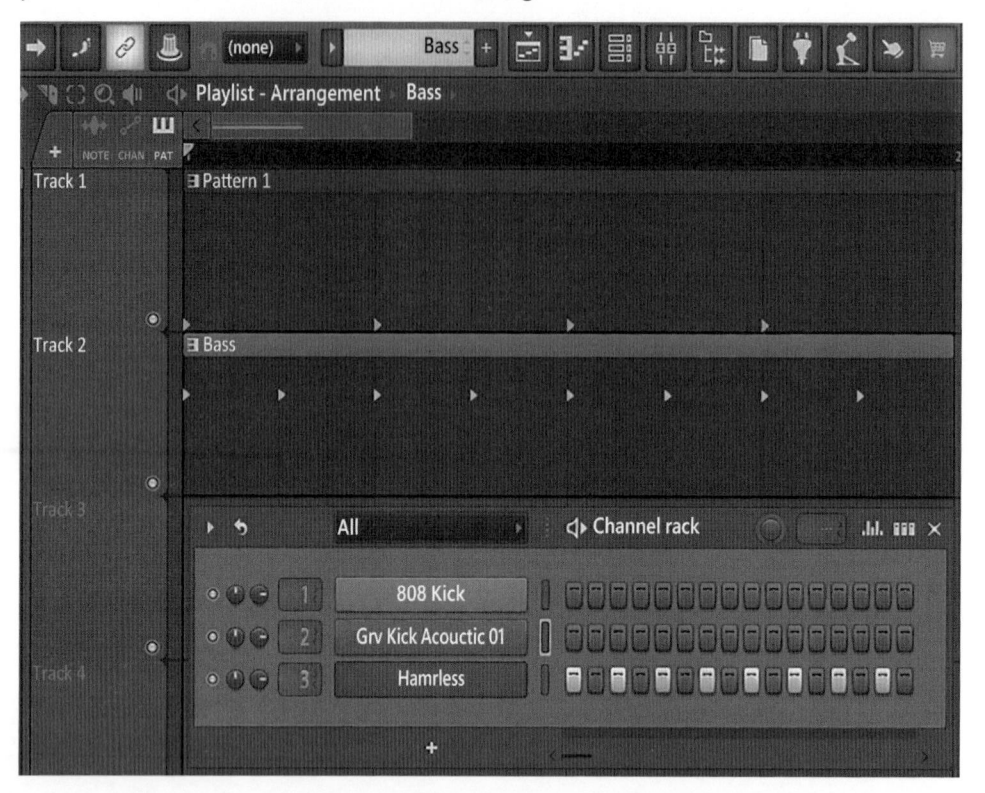

Figure 6.8 – Bass notes in the channel rack

7. Add the pattern with the bass instrument to the playlist. Your playlist should look similar to the following with both the **Kick** pattern and the **Bass** pattern added. Note how the **Kick** and **Bass** notes line up each bar:

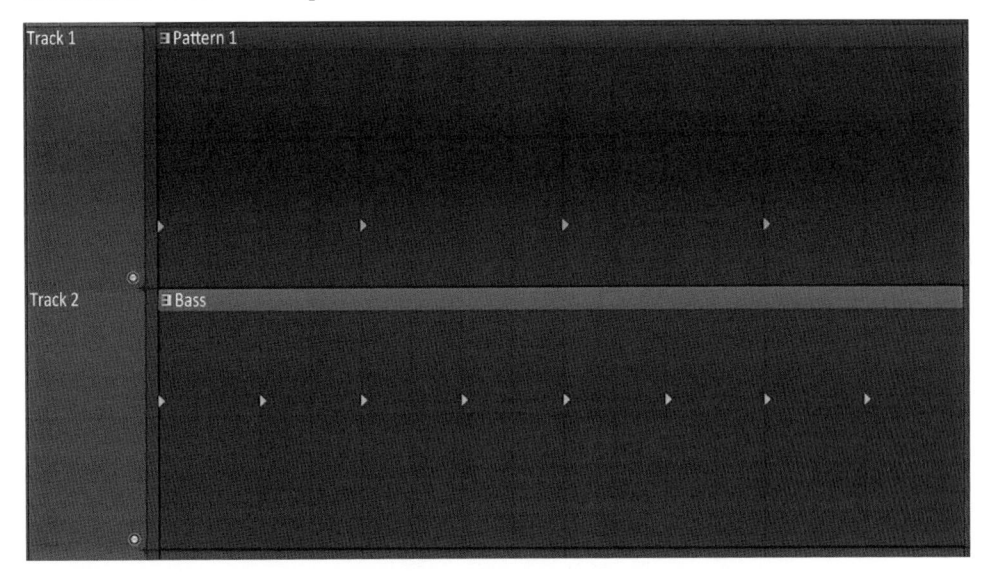

Figure 6.9 – Playlist with both the bass instrument and kick

You can now play the playlist and hear the bass instrument and the kick sounds.

8. Next, we're going to apply sidechain compression to the bass instrument. This will cause the volume of the bass instrument to decrease whenever the kick drum occurs.

9. In the mixer, select one of the kick channels. Then, right-click on the arrow at the bottom of the bass instrument channel (**Harmless**) and select the **Sidechain to this track only** menu drop-down option:

Figure 6.10 – Sidechaining kick to the bass instrument

What we've done is told the signal of the kick drum to no longer route to the master channel. The signal from the kick sample is now being sent exclusively to the bass instrument channel to be used as an input for sidechaining.

10. Add the **Fruity Limiter** plugin to the **Harmless** mixer channel. Select **COMP** in **Fruity Limiter**.

Chapter 6

11. In the **SIDECHAIN** control of **Fruity Limiter**, scroll to select **1**. This will tell Fruity Limiter to listen for the kick audio. Your screen should look similar to the following:

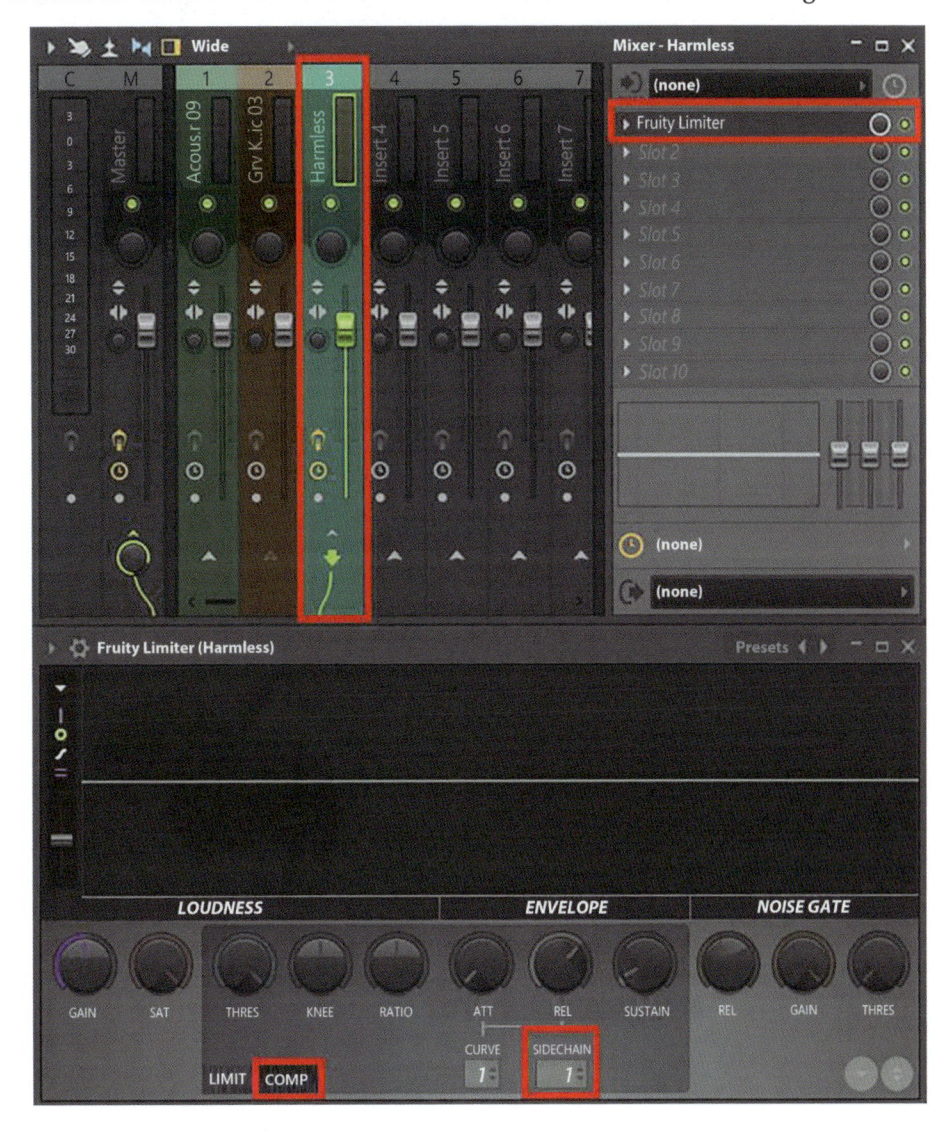

Figure 6.11 – Fruity Limiter now accepts kick as a sidechain source

12. Play the song. At the same time, under the **LOUDNESS** and **ENVELOPE** sections of **Fruity Limiter**, add compression to your sound using the techniques we learned earlier in this chapter. The exact compression control adjustments will depend upon the sounds you are using, but when you're done, it could look similar to the following:

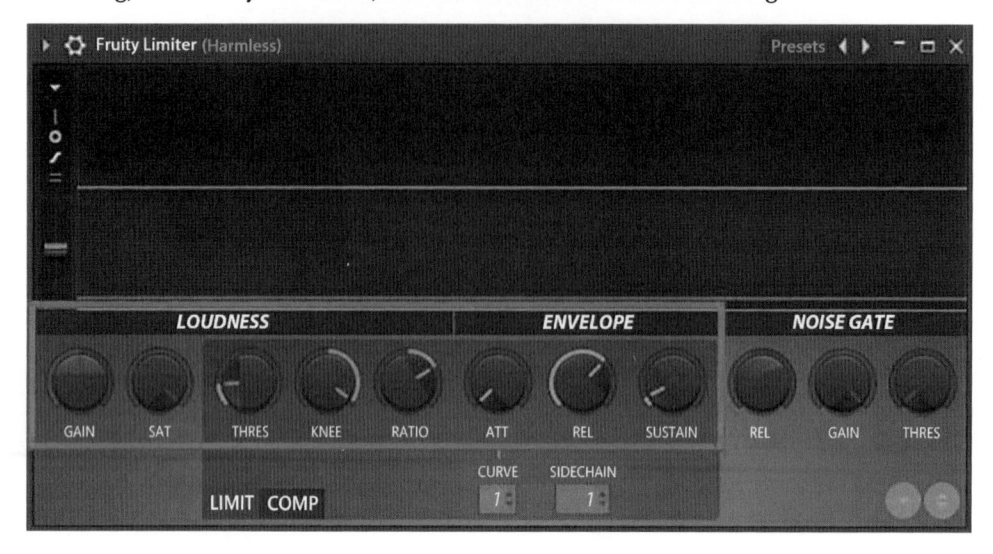

Figure 6.12 – Fruity Limiter LOUDNESS and ENVELOPE sidechain settings

In the **LOUDNESS** and **ENVELOPE** controls, we've added compression to the sound. Remember, compression reduces the loudness of the sound.

We used a kick sound as an input for sidechaining. This is a little different from the simple compression we did in an earlier example. We're using sidechaining to cause the bass instrument to compress only at certain times, rather than constantly throughout. The bass instrument gets compressed when it receives input from the sidechained kick channel. When the bass channel receives signal input from the kick channel, it tells the compression to start.

If you've done everything correctly, when you play your playlist, you should be able to hear the rhythmic pumping action of your bass instrument ducking every time the kick drum sound occurs. I encourage you to try adding sidechaining compression on your own on various bass instrument setups until you feel very comfortable with the technique. Sidechaining bass sounds is a technique you will use on many songs. Congratulations, you've successfully used sidechaining! Next, let's learn how to use limiters.

Using limiters

So far, we've discussed simple compression, parallel compression, and sidechain compression. Fruity Limiter offers another tool, called a **limiter**. Limiters are tools used to lower the amplitude peak of a sound. Limiters have a threshold level, and when it's reached, the average volume of the audio is compressed and then raised until it reaches the threshold. The result is that the overall sounds appear louder but are contained under the threshold.

The difference between a compressor and a limiter is that in a compressor, you set the compression ratio to an exact value (for example, reduce by a 3:1 ratio), whereas in a limiter, the ratio is not specifically set by you. The ratio of compression adapts until the overall volume is raised up to the threshold.

Why would you use limiters? One reason to use limiters is to prevent unwanted distortion. If the volume of your final audio exceeds 0 dB, unwanted distortion occurs. In hardware, this causes a signal overload. Limiting reduces your audio signal to prevent this.

Another reason to use limiters is to increase the overall perceived volume of your completed song. Audio that appears louder is easier to hear and is preferred.

A limiter is used on your master channel. Limiters are used to bring up the overall volume of the finished song in the mastering process. Before exporting your final song in mastering, the last plugin effect that the sound is processed through is always a limiter.

180   Compression, Sidechaining, Limiting, and Equalization

Let's use a limiter in our project:

1. Create any project with some music playing.
2. If it isn't there already, add **Fruity Limiter** to your master channel:

Figure 6.13 – Fruity Limiter in Slot 10 of the master channel

Under the **LOUDNESS** section, you can see three controls: **GAIN**, **SAT** (saturation), and **CEIL** (ceiling). **GAIN** and **SAT** perform the same function as they do in a simple compressor. The **CEIL** control sets the maximum level that the volume of the sound can reach. Any sound that reaches the ceiling is compressed until it no longer exceeds the ceiling level. By default, the ceiling level is set to **0** dB. This means the maximum volume that can be reached is 0 dB. Anything above 0 dB could result in unwanted distortion, so you never want to set the ceiling above 0 dB. You can leave the ceiling at the default of **0** dB in most cases. Setting a ceiling threshold is sometimes known as setting a *brick wall*: a metaphor to mean that no sound gets through.

3. Increase **GAIN** slightly. You'll need to experiment with how much to increase the gain. If you increase the gain too much, you'll find your overall sound feels squashed. Increase the gain until you find a comfortable balance between making your song as loud as you can while still maintaining the desired dynamic range.

The end result of using a limiter is that our sound is louder and easier to hear. We've covered the main types of compression. Next, let's look at equalizer plugins.

Applying equalization

In *Chapter 5, Sound Design and Audio Envelopes*, we learned that frequencies are related to the pitches we hear. By increasing the frequency, we increase the pitch of a sound.

Equalization (shortened to **EQ**) is a category of filter effect used to increase or decrease targeted frequencies of a sound. EQ is used to enhance the frequencies of sounds you like and reduce those unwanted ones you don't.

One way that EQ can be used is to clean up muddy mixes. When multiple instruments are playing, instruments may sound like they're trying to play over one another. The overlapping of sounds makes it difficult to hear any of the competing instruments clearly. This is known as *mud in the mix* and is undesirable. EQ can help fix muddy mixes by removing competing frequencies of instruments playing at the same time. This helps to designate an area of frequency space for each instrument so that you can hear each one clearly. This is known as *cleaning up the mix* or *removing the mud*. The result is a desirable, clearer sound.

FL Studio comes with an excellent EQ plugin called **Fruity parametric EQ 2**. It has lots of features to satisfy most of your EQ needs. Let's use Fruity parametric EQ 2 to demonstrate how to apply EQ to your sounds:

1. Route an instrument or sound sample to an empty mixer track and add the **Fruity parametric EQ 2** effect.

2. Play your sound. When your sound is played, your plugin will look like it does in the following screenshot:

Figure 6.14 – Fruity parametric EQ 2

The EQ plugin visually shows the frequencies of the sound as orange/pink vertical lines. Louder frequencies will appear brighter and quieter ones duller. Directly below the frequency visual, you can see a scale of frequencies ranging from **20 Hz** to **10k** Hz. Above the frequency visual, you can see the note pitches and labels associated with the corresponding frequencies.

Along the horizontal line in the middle of the frequency visual, you can see circle icons with the numbers **1** to **7**. Each of these icons is supposed to represent a frequency range known as a band. You can drag these band icons with the mouse to move them. The bands allow you to increase or decrease the sound of frequencies at the corresponding position.

3. While playing your sound, left-click on one of the EQ bands and drag it upward. You'll notice that the sound increases in volume in the area of the affected frequency. This is known as *boosting the frequency*. Dragging the band down will decrease it. This is known as *cutting the frequency*.

Chapter 6

4. When used in practice, you want to experiment with increasing and decreasing EQ bands to increase frequencies that you like the sound of and reduce those that you don't.

5. A way to determine offensive frequencies is to select a band and increase the value. Then, move the band (sweep it) left and right to find the frequency that is most offensive. For example, you may find that at a certain position, you hear undesired shrill whistling. At this position, experiment with decreasing the level of the band below 0 dB. The amount to reduce will depend on your specific scenario. The hope is that this will cut out the offensive frequency sound.

6. On the EQ band that you moved upward in position, hover over the band and scroll with your mouse wheel. Doing so will adjust the slope of the EQ band fading in. The slope makes the change in frequency more or less abrupt. The terminology associated with adjusting the slope is known as **bandwidth (Q)**. You can adjust the slope (bandwidth) to make it wider or narrower.

7. Right-click on the same EQ band. A menu of additional features will appear, as shown in the following screenshot:

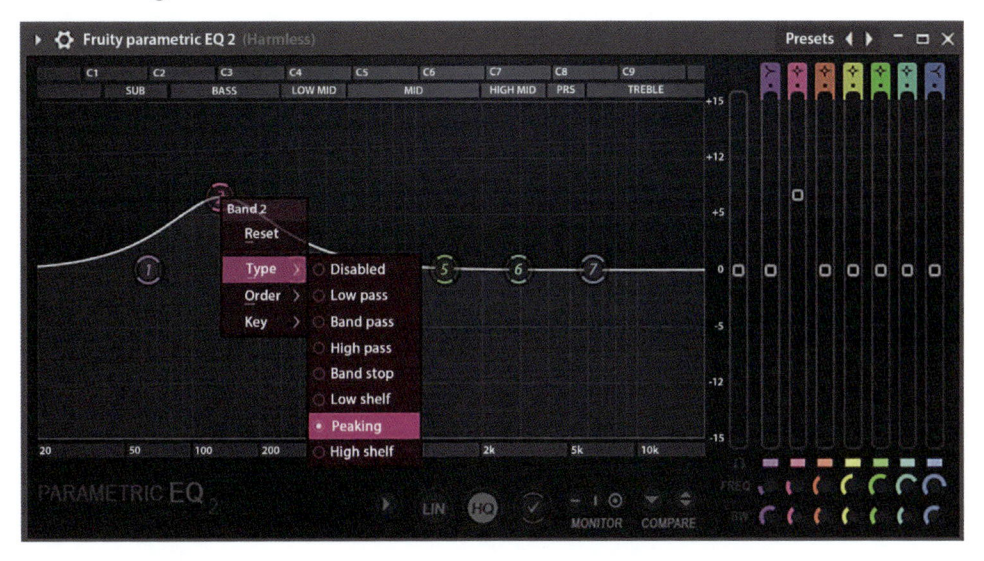

Figure 6.15 – EQ passes and shelves

By default, the type of EQ band is set to **Peaking** and allows us to add or reduce specific frequencies. You can see that there are other options types for **pass**, **stop**, and **shelf**.

A **pass** is a filter that restricts which frequencies are allowed. Only frequencies within the pass filter range will be heard. A low pass only allows frequencies that are below the filter. A high pass only allows frequencies that are above the filter. A **stop** is where all frequencies in the chosen band are removed. A **shelf** is where you increase all frequencies that occur within the shelf filter range.

Passes are very useful. Instruments are intended to occupy a specific frequency range. The scale above the frequency visual has labels for common frequency ranges: **SUB**, **BASS**, **LOW MID**, **MID**, **HIGH MID**, **PRS**, and **TREBLE**. Outside of the frequency range, instrument frequencies may be competing with other instruments, which could result in muddy mixes. In such cases, it is advised to consider adding a pass to remove the unneeded frequencies. This can help to prevent muddy mixes. For example, a sub-bass instrument likely benefits from a low pass filter. This removes high frequencies from the instrument and helps prevent the sub-bass instrument sound from overpowering higher instruments' sounds.

The **Band** menu has an **Order** option. **Order** lists various slopes into the band. This does the same thing as hovering over the EQ band and scrolling with your mouse wheel.

The final **Band** menu option is the **Key** category. Since frequency is the same thing as pitch, you can choose to increase or decrease specific pitches. By selecting a specific pitch in the menu, you can choose an exact pitch position for an EQ band.

The right side of **Fruity parametric EQ 2** has knob controls for precise control over individual bands. Moving the sliders up or down allows you to move the frequency bands.

At the top right of **Fruity parametric EQ 2**, you'll see a menu of presets. I encourage you to experiment with presets to see examples of the EQ possibilities.

At the bottom of the plugin, you'll see the options and settings. One worth mentioning is the **COMPARE** button. This allows you to flip back and forth between two states of the plugin. It can be used to show a before-and-after state to see whether the EQ improved your sound.

EQ best practices

The fewer instruments you have playing at any given time, the less likely you are to run into competing frequencies. If you add in a lot of instruments playing simultaneously, you're going to have to spend more time with the EQ to carve out and create frequency space for each instrument.

Your ears pay more attention and can more easily detect changes in high frequencies than in lower frequencies. You only ever want to have one instrument at a time playing in the sub-bass frequencies. Your ears won't be able to distinguish multiple melodies going on in the sub-bass region. Consider using a high pass filter on everything that is not a bass instrument.

EQ general rules

Here are some general EQ suggestions:

- Cut frequencies if you're trying to make things sound better. Best results are usually achieved by eliminating offensive elements in a mix.
- Boost frequencies if you're trying to distinguish sounds from each other.
- Find the most important element in a song and emphasize it. Everything else acts as support. Competing frequencies should be removed. This leading instrument element may change throughout the course of the song, for example, from vocals to a guitar solo. You'll usually want to create frequency space for the vocals and favor them over other instruments.

When two instruments are playing at the same volume and occupy the same frequency range, they are competing for attention. To fix this, consider the following potential solutions:

- Consider putting one of the instruments in a different section. Mute one competing instrument and bring it in later.
- Set one of the instruments further back through the use of reverb.
- Focus each instrument on its own frequency and tailor the offending instrument to focus on a different frequency range.
- Pan the competing instruments to different locations.

The following is a list of terminology commonly associated with frequency ranges. For example, if an audio engineer says that a sound feels muddy, they're probably referring to the range around 250 Hz:

Frequency Octave Range	Popular Definition
31 Hz	Sub-Bass
63 Hz	Bottom
125 Hz	Boom, Thump, Warmth
250 Hz	Fullness or Mud
500 Hz	Honk
1 kHz	Whack, Nasal
2 kHz	Crunch
4 kHz	Edge
8 kHz	Sibilance, Definition, *Ouch*
16 kHz	Air

Figure 6.16 – Frequency range terminology

You can use this terminology when you are collaborating with another musician on a song mix and need to refer to a specific frequency range.

Acoustic instruments generally occupy a set range of frequencies. The following chart shows some examples:

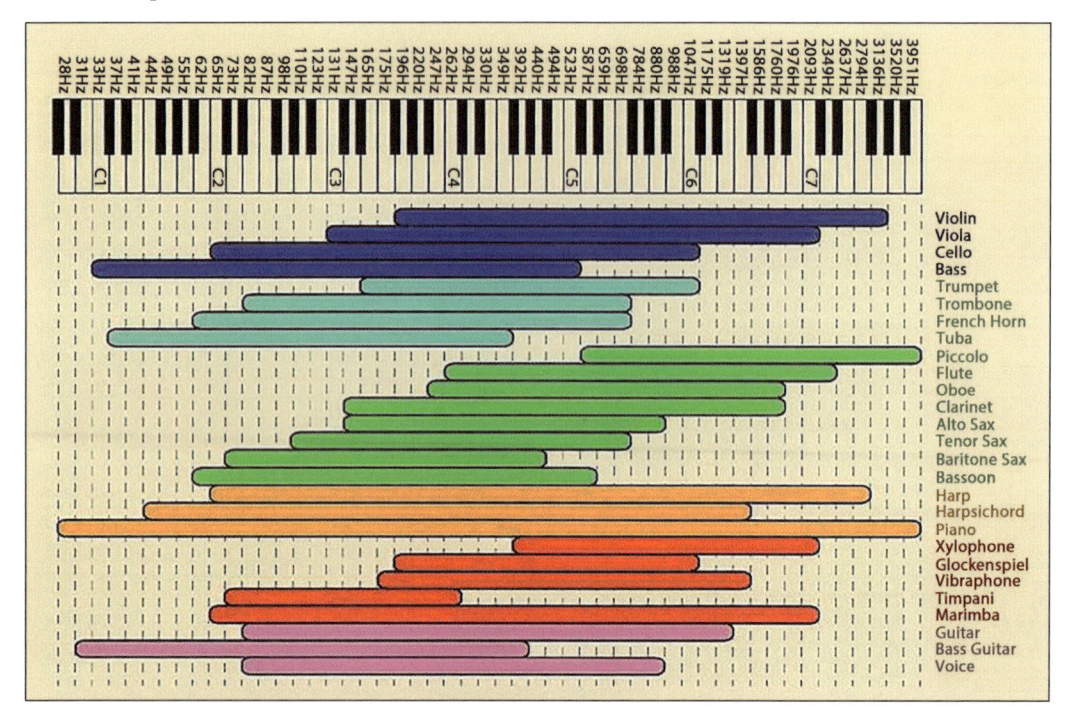

Figure 6.17 – Instrument frequency chart (source: https://commons.wikimedia.org/wiki/File:Estensione_Strumenti_Musicale.jpg)

When thinking about mixing, you generally want to only have a minimal number of instruments occupying the lower bass frequencies at any one time, as these tend to blur with one another. If you must have competing low-frequency instruments playing simultaneously, this is where sidechaining can come in handy so that the instruments don't compete with one another.

In this section, we explored Fruity parametric EQ 2, which is a *parametric equalizer*. Parametric means that you have continuous control over the frequencies and can adjust any chosen frequency. It should be mentioned that there is another type of equalizer, called an analog equalizer, and you will likely come across many of these plugins. In the beginning, before digital audio workstations, all equalizers were analog equalizers. Analog equalizers allow you to adjust frequencies of sounds just like parametric EQs but are restricted to predetermined frequency intervals.

Summary

In this chapter, we learned about the various types of compressors and equalizers. Compressors can make your sounds appear thicker and fuller. Gates can reduce unwanted background noises. Sidechaining can be used to give your bassline a pumping groove. Limiters can be used to raise the volume of your mix. Equalizers can be used to enhance desired frequencies and reduce unwanted ones.

In the next chapter, we will investigate additional mixing techniques with stereo width.

7

Stereo Width (Panning, Reverb, Delay, Chorus, and Flangers) and Distortion

Imagine you're at a rock concert. The sound feels huge. The stage itself is large. There are echoes and reverberations throughout the theater. It's an impressive experience. When mixing music for production, we want to recreate that feeling. How can we make our music sound huge when the listener is listening to it in a small environment? If the audience is listening with headphones, the actual space that sound can bounce off is tiny. What we have to do is trick our ears into thinking the sound is in a space much larger than it is.

Stereo width describes the perceived width of a sound. By increasing the stereo width, your sound gains the impression of being in a larger space. This can be done with several tools, which we will explore in this chapter. We will discuss the tools in isolation, but you can and should consider layering these tools on top of each other to increase the stereo width further.

In this chapter, we will cover the following topics:

- Panning audio
- Using reverb
- Applying digital reverb with Fruity Reeverb 2
- Applying convolution reverb with Fruity Convolver
- Using Luxeverb
- Using delay effects

- Using Fruity Delay 3
- Using chorus effects
- Using Vintage Chorus
- Using flanger effects
- Using phaser effects
- Using Vintage Phaser
- Using distortion effects
- Using Distructor
- Understanding mix buses

Panning audio

The simplest tool to increase stereo width is a technique called panning. Before we can explain panning, we need to understand what mono and stereo mean.

Monophonic sound (known as **mono**) is the term used when different audio channels play the same sound equally. Regardless of whether you are listening out of your right or left speaker/headphone, the audio is identical. Mono is used for radio talk shows and telephone calls.

When identical audio is played out of two audio speakers, as with mono, your ears perceive the sound as originating from a location in the middle of the two sources. This is known as a **phantom center**.

Stereophonic sound (known as **stereo**) means you have different sounds coming out of each audio channel. If your left speaker/headphone has a different sound coming out of it from the right, your sound is said to be in stereo. The benefit of stereo sounds is that it creates the illusion of audio coming from multiple directions just like in real life. If you were to watch a band playing live, the instruments are positioned on the stage at different locations. The audio reaches each ear at different intensities depending on how close each instrument is. Stereo sound is used in films and music players.

Panning means choosing the direction in which sound comes out of audio channels. We can set audio to pan left, meaning that the audio comes out of our left channel, or pan right so the audio comes out of our right channel. In film score mixing, you may have additional pan controls to include up and down as well, but this requires a special speaker setup such as in a movie theater, with speakers surrounding the listener above and below them, as well as to the left and right.

By default, audio coming out of any channel in the mixer is set to monophonic. If you were to have two identical sounds where one is panned all the way right and one is panned all the way left, you would hear a mono sound. Duplicating a track and hard panning each in opposite directions do not make a sound stereo. In order to hear a stereo sound, you need to have different sounds playing out of the left and the right audio channels.

Let's pan some audio:

1. Load any instrument and add some notes to it. Route the instrument to a channel in the mixer.
2. While playing your audio, left-click on the panning control knob and drag it left or right. As you drag, you'll be able to hear the audio volume if you focus on the speaker you're panning toward:

Figure 7.1 – Panned audio

You can pan any sound in the mixer in a similar fashion.

Panning best practices

Low-frequency sounds instinctively are associated with larger instruments. Biologically, this makes sense, as a lion makes a much deeper and larger sound than a bird, which makes a high-frequency and smaller sound. You usually want your low-frequency sounds (sub-bass and bass) to be centered in your mix, meaning we want them to be mono. Why? Human ears struggle to distinguish the direction of subfrequencies. It feels as though subfrequencies just exist all around you regardless of where they come from. Further, if you have differences between the left and right channels of your bass, you might accidentally create phase cancellation when playing your subfrequencies on live speakers.

Your higher-frequency sounds can be panned out more to the left or right. If you have an instrument panned to the right, you should have another instrument panned to the left to balance out the mix. You want to avoid scenarios where you have an instrument hard-panned to one side for long durations of time and nothing panned to the other side. This will result in the mix feeling off-center and sounding unpleasant to users wearing headphones.

If you have two similar sounds occupying the same frequency range playing simultaneously, consider panning the instruments in different directions to spread them out. This can result in sounding like the instruments are playing off each other and add a sense of distinction between them.

Lead vocals should be centered in your mix (mono). Backup vocals and harmonies can be panned and spread out in the mix.

Panning in combination with other stereo-width tools can create interesting effects. For example, using automation to pan a guitar to the right while gradually panning a delay of the guitar to the left can make it appear like the guitar sound is bouncing off a wall and echoing into the opposite ear.

Panning is the simplest tool to use to create stereo width. Next, let's look at a technique called reverb.

Using reverb

Natural **reverb** occurs when sound waves bounce off a surface and reflect back at a listener. The timing and amplitude of the reflected audio exhibit some variation compared to the original. Over time, the amplitudes and frequencies in the sound wave decrease and the sound dissipates.

You can think of reverb as making your sound feel further away. The more reverb you add, the further away your sound will feel and the larger the space the sound will appear to exist in. Reverb is actually a separate sound that is played (you can play just the reverb of a sound without hearing the original source), but our ears get tricked and interpret the original and the reverb as if they are connected as a single sound.

In general, reverb is the last effect you want to apply in the signal chain to your sound.

There are two kinds of reverb: algorithmic digital reverb and convolution reverb. Let's take a look at each of these.

Applying digital reverb with Fruity Reeverb 2

Algorithmic digital reverb plugins work by generating delayed versions of the original sound. The number of reflections of the reverb is determined by sending the delays through a feedback loop. In a natural environment, your ear expects to hear sound echoing throughout the room and to hear echoes of echoes. Feedback resembles echoes of echoes. Unless specifically labeled otherwise, reverb plugins are digital algorithmic types and not convolution types.

Let's take a look at using reverb with **Fruity Reeverb 2**:

1. Load up a sample or an instrument with notes and route it to a new mixer track.
2. Apply the **Fruity Reeverb 2** effect to the mixer channel and play your sound:

Figure 7.2 – Fruity Reeverb 2

When playing your sound, you'll notice your sound has echoes and the appearance of being further away.

3. Click on the cylinder image to the left of the reverb plugin and drag the image around. You'll notice the cylinder changes shape and the reverb controls adjust accordingly.

Let's take a look at the reverb controls (from left to right):

- **MID/SIDE**: Determines how your reverb affects your sound in mono or stereo. By default, it is set to **MID**, meaning the reverb is mono. If you have a sound that is panned to the right or left, you should use the **SIDE** option. This will affect your left/right stereo field but leave your center untouched so it doesn't wash your sound out.
- **H.CUT**: Stands for *high cut* and allows you to remove high frequencies before applying reverb.
- **L.CUT**: Stands for *low cut* and allows you to remove low frequencies before applying reverb. Effective when used on drums to remove low rumble muddiness.
- **DELAY**: The more delay you add, the longer it takes to hear an echo and the further away sound will appear. There is a **TEMPO** button to sync the echo to fit it to the song's BPM.
- **SIZE**: Determines the space of the reverb. A higher setting means a larger reverb sound.
- **MOD**: Stands for *modulation* and removes metallic reverb ringing sounds that can occur.
- **DIFF**: Stands for *diffusion* and determines the density of sound reflections. Low values make the reflections appear spread out; high values make the reflections appear more concentrated as though coming from a more central place.
- **SPEED**: Determines the speed of the modulation control.
- **BASS**: Determines the number of bass frequencies you want in the reverb.
- **DEC**: Stands for *decay* and determines how long it is before a sound dissipates. Smaller values give the impression of a smaller room, while larger values make it sound like the listener is in a larger room.
- **CROSS**: Determines the threshold below which bass frequencies get boosted.
- **DAMP**: Stands for *high damping* and is the rate at which high frequencies decay. Turning this to maximum bypasses (turns off) the high damping control.
- **DRY**: Sets the input signal level. If you turn it all the way down, you can hear just the reverb on its own, without the original source.

- **ER**: Stands for *early reflections* and sets the level of the first reflections.
- **WET**: Sets the overall level of the reverb.
- **SEP**: Stands for *stereo* separator and pans the reverb. The dry signal is unaffected.

So far, we've discussed digital reverb. There is another type of reverb called convolution reverb.

Applying convolution reverb with Fruity Convolver

Convolution reverb is more realistic than digital reverb. To create convolution reverb, developers travel to physical locations and collect audio recordings of sounds reflecting around the space. By measuring the impulse timings, developers can recreate a simulated environment that mimics the real one. Then, when a sound is sent into the simulated environment, it reflects off the surroundings just like it would in a real space. This creates very realistic reverbs but can potentially be more CPU-intensive.

Let's apply a convolution reverb with **Fruity Convolver**:

1. Load up a sample or an instrument with notes and route it to a new mixer track.
2. Add the **Fruity Convolver** effect to the mixer channel and play your sound:

Figure 7.3 – Fruity Convolver

3. In the top-right corner of the **Fruity Convolver** plugin window, left-click on the **Default** presets. You will see the list shown in the following screenshot:

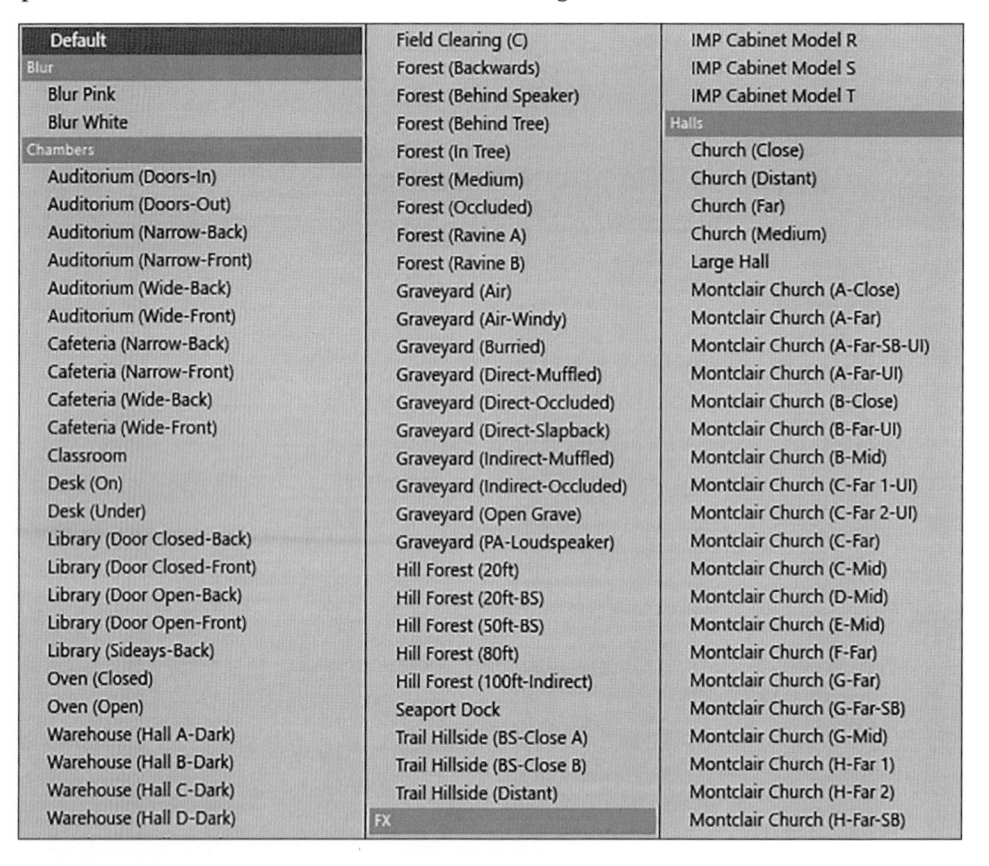

Default	Field Clearing (C)	IMP Cabinet Model R
Blur	Forest (Backwards)	IMP Cabinet Model S
Blur Pink	Forest (Behind Speaker)	IMP Cabinet Model T
Blur White	Forest (Behind Tree)	Halls
Chambers	Forest (In Tree)	Church (Close)
Auditorium (Doors-In)	Forest (Medium)	Church (Distant)
Auditorium (Doors-Out)	Forest (Occluded)	Church (Far)
Auditorium (Narrow-Back)	Forest (Ravine A)	Church (Medium)
Auditorium (Narrow-Front)	Forest (Ravine B)	Large Hall
Auditorium (Wide-Back)	Graveyard (Air)	Montclair Church (A-Close)
Auditorium (Wide-Front)	Graveyard (Air-Windy)	Montclair Church (A-Far)
Cafeteria (Narrow-Back)	Graveyard (Burried)	Montclair Church (A-Far-SB-UI)
Cafeteria (Narrow-Front)	Graveyard (Direct-Muffled)	Montclair Church (A-Far-UI)
Cafeteria (Wide-Back)	Graveyard (Direct-Occluded)	Montclair Church (B-Close)
Cafeteria (Wide-Front)	Graveyard (Direct-Slapback)	Montclair Church (B-Far-UI)
Classroom	Graveyard (Indirect-Muffled)	Montclair Church (B-Mid)
Desk (On)	Graveyard (Indirect-Occluded)	Montclair Church (C-Far 1-UI)
Desk (Under)	Graveyard (Open Grave)	Montclair Church (C-Far 2-UI)
Library (Door Closed-Back)	Graveyard (PA-Loudspeaker)	Montclair Church (C-Far)
Library (Door Closed-Front)	Hill Forest (20ft)	Montclair Church (C-Mid)
Library (Door Open-Back)	Hill Forest (20ft-BS)	Montclair Church (D-Mid)
Library (Door Open-Front)	Hill Forest (50ft-BS)	Montclair Church (E-Mid)
Library (Sideays-Back)	Hill Forest (80ft)	Montclair Church (F-Far)
Oven (Closed)	Hill Forest (100ft-Indirect)	Montclair Church (G-Far)
Oven (Open)	Seaport Dock	Montclair Church (G-Far-SB)
Warehouse (Hall A-Dark)	Trail Hillside (BS-Close A)	Montclair Church (G-Mid)
Warehouse (Hall B-Dark)	Trail Hillside (BS-Close B)	Montclair Church (H-Far 1)
Warehouse (Hall C-Dark)	Trail Hillside (Distant)	Montclair Church (H-Far 2)
Warehouse (Hall D-Dark)	FX	Montclair Church (H-Far-SB)

Figure 7.4 – Fruity Convolver room presets

Here you can see a list of reverb room presets with various room types to choose from.

4. Select one of the presets. A reverb will be applied to your sound that simulates how your sound would echo if played in the chosen room.

For most users, these presets will supply more than enough reverb options. For those who want more though, **Fruity Convolver** offers a vast array of features that extend beyond the scope of this chapter. For example, the **Impulse** section of **Fruity Convolver** allows you to record a sound and simulate your own custom reverb room.

Chapter 7

> For a detailed breakdown of all **Fruity Convolver** features, see the Image Line documentation videos at `http://support.image-line.com/redirect/FruityConvolver_Videos`.

Next, let's explore the FL Studio reverb plugin, Luxeverb.

Using LuxeVerb

Luxeverb is a cutting-edge reverb plugin that comes with FL Studio All Plugins Edition. Luxeverb is a reverb plugin with tons of features and controls. One distinguishing feature that sets Luxeverb apart from most reverb plugins on the market is that you have the ability to adjust the pitch and dynamics of the reverb. Let's take a look at the features offered by Luxeverb:

Figure 7.5 – Luxeverb

As always, on the top right, you'll find a list of presets to explore.

By default, Luxeverb is split into a top blue reverb control section and a bottom envelope control black section. You can choose to hide the envelope section by clicking the bottom edges and dragging upward.

Let's take a look at each section, starting with the **INPUT** and **REVERB** sections.

Figure 7.6 – Luxeverb INPUT and REVERB panels

Here's a description of the controls.

The **INPUT** panel:

- **WET GAIN**: Controls how much input sound to feed into Luxeverb.
- **HIGH CUT**: Filter to remove high frequencies.
- **LOW CUT**: Filter to remove low frequencies. Low frequencies can make your sound muddy when applying reverb. Consider using this when you automate to pitch down as this can create an over-the-top rumbling sound.

The **REVERB** panel:

- On the far right, you'll see an enable and disable control for the reverb effect.
- **DECAY**: Controls how long you want the reverb to last in seconds.
- **BRIGHTNESS**: Controls how pronounced you want the high frequencies to be present in the reverb tail. 100% will simulate a space with hard surfaces. By decreasing the value, you simulate an environment with soft surfaces which will reduce high frequencies.
- **SIZE**: Increases the space between echoes of the reverb. 0-10 values simulate a small plate-sounding space, 10-50 simulate an acoustic space, and > 50 simulate an over-the-top large space.
- **DIFFUSION**: Simulates obstacles in the room in the path of the echoes. Creates more irregularity in the echo.

- **CHARACTER**: Values of 0.5 create a smooth diffuse reverb tail. Values < 0.5 create more prominent echoes. Values > 0.5 allow the reverb to collect and create a fuzzy echo effect. You'll hear a stronger effect if you increase the **SIZE** value.
- **P. DELAY**: This stands for predelay. You can enable tempo sync, which usually sounds better.
- **MOD AMP**: Modulates delay line lengths. Creates a chorus effect in the reverb. You'll hear the effect more when the **CHARACTER** control is all the way up or down.
- **MOD FREQ**: The frequency of modulation delay line lengths.
- **FREEZE MODE**: Allows infinite reverb duration. It has 3 modes:
    - **NORMAL**: Standard. **FREEZE MODE** disabled.
    - **FREEZE**: Uses the current input and sustains the reverb at the moment when freeze control is enabled. The sound will sustain until the freeze control is disabled.
    - **SUSTAIN**: The same as **FREEZE**, but allows input to continue so sound will build.
- **HQ**: *On* gives higher resolution on higher frequencies. *Off* makes a grittier sound where high frequencies die out faster. More noticeable when **FREEZE** or **SUSTAIN** is in use.

Next, let's look at the **FEEDBACK** and **OUTPUT** panels:

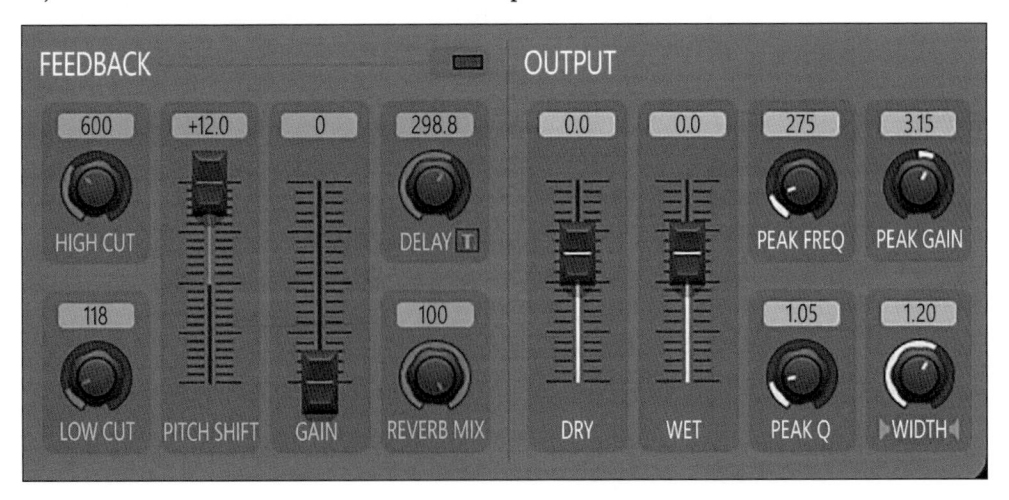

Figure 7.7 – Luxeverb FEEDBACK and OUTPUT panels

The **FEEDBACK** panel is where you can do pitch-shifting effects:

On the far right, you'll see an enable and disable control for the panel.

- **HIGH CUT**: Filters to remove high frequencies from being refed back into the plugin.
- **LOW CUT**: Filters to remove low frequencies. Otherwise, the output can get muddy when pitching down.
- **PITCH SHIFT**: Feeds reverb output back as input audio with pitch-shifting. Values of 12+ create ethereal, rising sounds. Values of 0 are normal. Values of -12 create dark evil sounds. You can automate this control to hear the reverb pitch of your sound increase or decrease.
- **GAIN**: The amount of gain on feedback. A value of 0 means no feedback.
- **DELAY**: Controls the amount of delay to apply. Tempo sync can be enabled, which usually sounds better.
- **REVERB MIX**: Controls how much effect to feed back into the loop.

The **OUTPUT** panel:

- **DRY**: The amount of original input sound to output.
- **WET**: Defines how much effect to apply.
- **PEAK FREQ**: Peaking filter center frequency.
- **PEAK GAIN**: Allows you to add gain.
- **PEAK Q**: Sets the resonance peak. Values of 1 result in an octave-wide peaking filter. Values of 2 create a half-octave-wide filter. The greater the value, the smaller the filter peak.
- **WIDTH**: The amount of stereo width. A value of 1.25 is the default. Larger creates more width.

In the lower section of Luxeverb, you'll find the envelope section.

Figure 7.8 – Luxeverb envelope

Here you'll find controls to manipulate the reverb output. This allows you to create gated or side-chained sounds.

Let's take a closer look at the controls.

Figure 7.9 – Luxeverb envelope controls

Here's a description of the controls:

- **MODE**: Type of modulation

    - **OFF**: No modulation
    - **WET**: Output is modulated
    - **DECAY**: Decay time is modulated

- **SIDECHAIN**: Lets you choose which insert track to use as a sidechaining source. In order to use this, you must previously route a mixer track to the same mixer track as Luxeverb. See *Chapter 4, Routing to the Mixer and Applying Automation*, if you need a refresher on how to route mixer tracks.
- **THRESHOLD**: The threshold value, above which any audio gets modulated. Just like how a compressor works.
- **SCALE**: Controls the amount of envelope to apply. Positive values create a gated reverb. Usually used to make space for percussion sounds.
- **LOW CUT**: Filters to remove low frequencies.
- **OFFSET**: With a value of 0, you have mono-polar modulation. If the value > 0, you have bipolar modulation.
- **ATTACK**: Controls when audio starts to be affected. Usually, you leave this alone.
- **DECAY**: Controls decay – how long before the reverb level drifts back down to the input level.
- **SMOOTH**: High values increase smoothness, while low values allow more fluctuation.

At the bottom right, you'll find the display panel.

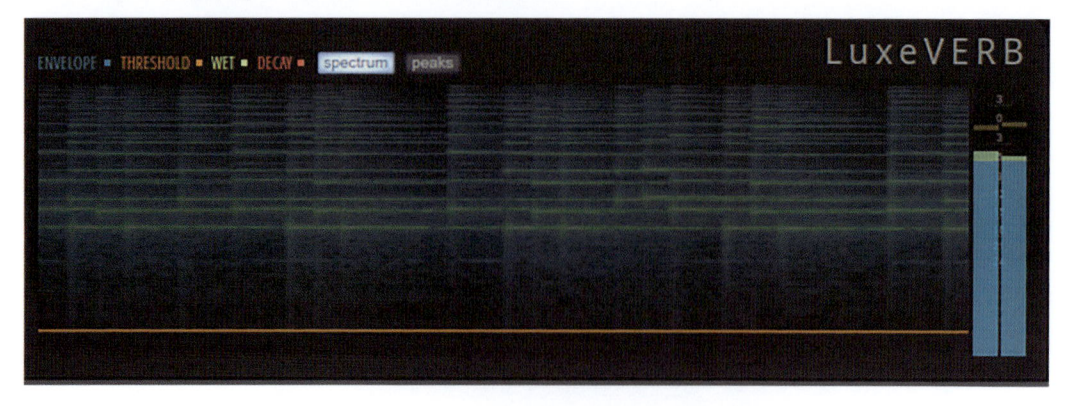

Figure 7.10 – Luxeverb envelope

Here's a description of the envelope display:

- **ENVELOPE (blue)**: The input signal or the sidechain signal (if selected).
- **THRESHOLD (orange)**: The level above the threshold is where modulation begins.
- **WET (green)**: Shows the modulation of output. The **MODE** switch will determine if **WET** or **DECAY** is modulated. Change the **SIZE** control to see changes.
- **DECAY (red)**: The **MODE** switch will determine if the **Wet** or **Decay** is modulated. Change the **SIZE** control to see changes.

We've looked at the reverb plugins we can use to increase stereo width. Next, let's look at using delay.

Using delay effects

A **delay** is the repeat of a sound played back after a few milliseconds. That's it, pretty simple, right? With a delay plugin, you can control how long to wait before hearing the echo. It can be synced with the tempo of your project.

The following terminologies are used to describe certain types of delays:

- **Straight delay**: Delaying the original material.
- **Slapback delay**: Delay times of between 70 ms and 120 ms. Generally, this complements dry sounds.

- **Doubling delay**: Delay times of between 20 ms and 50 ms. It creates an artificial doubling of the track.
- **Ping-pong delay**: Creates a call-and-response reaction between the repeats of the delay. For example, the initial call is 300 ms and the follow-up call is 600 ms.
- **Stereo-widening delay**: Short delays of around 10 ms. Sounds like the original sound to the listener, but spreads out more in the stereo field.

Applying delay effects with Fruity Delay 3

Fruity Delay 3 is a delay plugin that comes with FL Studio. It is a beast of a plugin and offers above and beyond the delay effects that you will need for your projects.

Let's apply a delay effect to our audio using **Fruity Delay 3**:

1. Load up a sample or an instrument with notes and route it to a new mixer track.
2. Add the **Fruity Delay 3** effect. When you play your instrument, you will be able to hear a delay effect:

Figure 7.11 – Fruity Delay 3

Fruity Delay 3 is an analog delay plugin. It has the ability to sync with the BPM of your song. It offers filtering and distortion effects and allows self-feedback to create special effects. Check out **Presets** in the top-right corner of the plugin for examples of delay effects.

Each section of the delay plugin is labeled; let's take a look at each section. As you read the control descriptions, make sure you play with the plugin to hear how the sound changes:

- **INPUT**: Determines the *dryness* or *wetness* (the level of audio input into the delay plugin). You can create an automation to turn on and off audio being inputted so that only certain parts of the audio receive the delay.

- **DELAY TIME**: Determines the time between echoes. The **TIME** knob allows you to adjust the delay from 1 ms to 1,000 ms. **TEMPO SYNC** limits the values of the **TIME** knob to fixed intervals. Having **TEMPO SYNC** on and the **TIME** knob set to **4:0** is generally pleasing for most cases. As the **TIME** knob changes values, the pitch will adjust. You can maintain the pitch with the **KEEP PITCH** button. **SMOOTHING** determines how fast the pitch changes. Long values create a *tape-style* delay. **OFFSET** controls the panning of the delay. It depends on the **DELAY MODEL** setting.
- **DELAY MODEL**: Lets you choose how panning effects will be used with the delay.
- **Mono** creates delays in mono, where the audio is the same out of all speakers. The offset creates a left-to-right, bouncing, panning effect. **Stereo** creates stereo delays. **Offset** controls pre-delays for left-to-right bouncing effects (in the **Delay Time** section). **Ping pong** is a type of stereo delay. The left and right channel audio outputs flip back and forth in isolation, creating a bouncing effect. **Off** is for no delay; you can still use filters, saturation, limiting, sample rate, bit reduction, and tone effects later on in the plugin. The **STEREO** spread knob controls how much of the mono or stereo effect is applied to the sound.
- **FEEDBACK**: Works by sending a signal outputted from the plugin back into the plugin to be processed again. **LEVEL** controls how much delay is sent into the feedback. **CUTOFF** allows you to limit the frequencies sent into the feedback. How you limit is determined by the filter types discussed in the following:
    - **RES** stands for resonance and it creates a boost in the frequency at the point of the cutoff value, drawing attention to it. This will increase feedback.
    - The following options for filter types are available:
        - **LP**: Stands for *low-pass filtering* and it allows only frequencies below the cutoff value.
        - **HP**: Stands for *high-pass filtering* and allows only frequencies above the cutoff value.
        - **BP**: Stands for *band-pass filtering*, and it allows only frequencies around the cutoff value.
        - **Off**: No filtering.
        - **SMP RATE** stands for *sample rate* and removes rumbles created by feedback. **BITS** stands for *bit depth* and it controls the number of bits used in the waveform file. On max, your audio will be of regular quality. Lower values add a crunchy, grainy feel to the sound. If you want to make your sound feel like it's coming from an old broken device, this can be one way to create that effect. The value needs to be above 10 ms to be noticeable.

- **MODULATION**: This offers controls affecting the delay timing and feedback.
- **RATE** sets the modulation time, from 0 to 20 Hz. **TIME** determines how much modulation to apply to the decay time. Increasing this value results in flanging and chorus effects. **CUTOFF** modulates the feedback cutoff value.
- **DIFFUSION**: Controls the blending of the delay sound.
- **LEVEL** smears the echoes and **SPREAD** sets the time of the smearing.
- **FEEDBACK DISTORTION**: Distorts the delay each time that it's passed back into the plugin. You can choose between the following two types of distortions:
- **Limit** sets the maximum level value of the waveform. If this is selected, you won't hear much distortion.
- **Sat** or *saturation* determines the maximum level of distortion. This is affected by the **KNEE** and **SYMMETRY** controls. **KNEE** controls how extreme the transition is between non-distorted and distorted audio. **SYMMETRY** controls the waveform properties, making the distortion equal in the positive and negative waveform cycles. **LEVEL** determines the value that limiting or saturation starts. The lower the value, the quieter the sound.
- **OUTPUT**: Controls the level of sound outputted from the plugin.
- **WET** controls the output signal level. **TONE** sets a low- or high-pass filter for the wet signal. And finally, **DRY** determines how much of the original sound to output. If you set this to **0**, you can hear the delay on its own without the original sound.

Delay effect best practices

- Unless you're trying to go for a crazy effect, you generally want to apply compression to your sounds before you apply delay.
- Delay effects should be applied before reverb effects. You want to have the reverb of a delay, as this will sound realistic, but not a delay in reverb.
- Short delays under 100 ms make the original sound appear larger and help to fill empty space.
- Single sounds, such as orchestral hits, explosions, and impacts, benefit from delay effects to make them feel huge.
- Delays can be used to add grooves to your melodies when used at intervals of the 8th or 16th note.
- You can use the delay of a sound on its own, using the wet signal and removing the dry signal. Effects can be applied to delay sounds, including phasers, flangers, pitch correction, and automation to create movement. Then you can tame harsh frequencies with EQ and compression to make them sound appealing.

We've discussed using echoes and delay to increase stereo width. Next, let's look at how playing with the waveform itself can increase stereo width.

Using chorus effects

In *Chapter 5, Sound Design and Audio Envelopes*, we discussed phase cancellation and interference. This is where multiple waveforms interact with each other and cause the sound to become louder or quieter. In-phase audio makes the sound louder while being out of phase causes the sound to become quieter. These are the two extreme phase possibilities, but there is a range between them. Plugins that play with the sound phase include chorus plugins, flangers, and phasers. We will discuss each of these over the next few pages.

Chorus plugins play with the signal phase. A chorus plugin creates duplicates of the audio signal, using the same phase position, amplitude, and frequency. The copied signal is delayed to create a difference in phase. With this delayed sound, we can adjust a bunch of properties such as the timing or pitch. There is a control included called the **Low-Frequency Oscillator (LFO)**, which controls the delay timing.

Using Fruity Chorus

Let's apply a chorus effect to an instrument:

1. Load up a sample or an instrument with notes and route it to a new mixer track.
2. Add the **Fruity Chorus** effect. When you play your instrument, you will be able to hear a chorus effect:

Figure 7.12 – Fruity Chorus

3. To hear examples of chorus effects, left-click on **Presets** in the top right of the plugin while playing your sound.

Here's a description of the **Fruity Chorus** plugin controls:

- **DELAY** determines the time for which to wait before playing the copy of the audio.
- **DEPTH** sets the range for the delay. The chorus effect sweeps back and forth between the **DELAY** and **DELAY + DEPTH** values. Higher depth values will create more noticeable chorus effects.
- **STEREO** controls the stereo image width.
- **LFO FREQ** (short for *frequency*) determines the modulation speed.
- **LFO WAVE** lets you choose the waveform.
- **CROSS TYPE** lets you choose whether to work on the low or high area of the sound frequency.
- **CROSS CUTOFF** sets the cutoff frequency value for use in **CROSS TYPE**.
- **WET ONLY** lets you choose whether to allow the original audio to be outputted or not.

Chorus effect best practices

Chorus effects can be great on accompanying instruments to surround your lead instrument or vocal. As a general guideline, consider applying chorus effects to guitars, electric pianos, snare drums, bass guitars, and backing vocals. Adding chorus effects increases the perceived stereo width of a sound, making it appear larger.

When chorus effects are applied to vocals, it sounds similar to vocal doubling. Natural vocal doubling is where a singer's vocals are repeated by backup singers. With natural vocal doubling, there is a variation in timing and pitch with the backup vocals. A chorus effect resembles this sound by also creating variation in timing and pitch. The overall effect is a larger-sounding vocal.

When mixing, you want to place chorus effects before your delay and reverb effects in the signal chain. This way, the chorus effect feels tied to the vocal. Delay and reverb feel more tied to the environment that the sound is existing in.

Using Vintage Chorus

FL Studio Signature Edition has a chorus effect plugin called Vintage Chorus. Let's discuss the Vintage Chorus effect plugin.

Vintage Chorus is a chorus effect plugin that emulates the Roland Juno 6's **Bucket Brigade Delay (BBD)** Chorus effect:

1. Load up a sample or an instrument with notes and route it to a new mixer track.
2. Add the **Vintage Chorus** effect. When you play your instrument, you will be able to hear a chorus effect:

Figure 7.13 – Vintage Chorus

As usual, there is a list of presets in the top-right corner of the plugin to get you started.

Let's take a look at the components of Vintage Chorus.

Figure 7.14 – MODE

In Vintage Chorus, there are three modes to choose from. These modes are various chorus effects that can be applied. By default, **MODE 1** is selected.

MODE 1 creates the **Juno 6 Chorus I** effect. **MODE 2** creates the **Juno 6 Chorus II** effect. You can apply both mode effects at the same time by left-clicking **MODE 1** and holding *Shift* while left-clicking on **MODE 2**.

If **MODE 1** or **MODE 2** is selected, the **DELAYS** and **MODULATION** panels will be disabled. If you select the **EDIT** mode, then you'll be able to edit the **DELAYS** and **MODULATION** panels.

Chapter 7

Let's take a look at the **DELAYS** panel.

Figure 7.15 – DELAYS

Here's a description of the **DELAYS** controls:

- **TIME 1**: Sets delay time 1.
- **TIME 2**: Sets delay time 2.
- The chorus will create a modulation between times 1 and 2.
- **FEEDBACK**: Incorporates feedback from the output audio back into the input audio, creating a flanger chorus sound.
- **H PASS**: Sets a high-pass filter cutoff. This allows you to exclude low-frequency sounds from receiving the chorus effect.

The next panel is the **MODULATION** panel.

Figure 7.16 – MODULATION

Here's a description of the controls:

- **START PHASE**: Sets the time at which to restart the phase.
- **L/R PHASE**: The phase difference. Bigger values make a larger stereo effect.

- **TYPE**: Allows you to choose between a saw and a SINE wave to use in the chorus LFOs.
- **TEMPO Sync**: Syncs the LFO waveform with the project's tempo.
- **SPEED**: Changes the speed of the chorus LFO.

The last panel is the **LEVELS** panel.

Figure 7.17 – LEVELS

Here's a description of the controls:

- **MONO INPUT**: Creates a mono sound.
- **INVERT WET**: Inverts audio polarity.
- **NOISE GATE**: Adds a noise gate to remove hissing sounds when no audio is playing.
- **NOISE**: Amount of hissing noise.
- **GAIN**: Loudness.
- **MIX**: Controls how much effect to apply.

Next, let's look at another plugin that plays with phase: flangers.

Using flanger effects

Flanger effects are similar to chorus effects and create a copy of the original sound, adjusting the delay times. The copied sound is delayed usually between 5 and 25 ms. A low-frequency modulator is applied to the delay time to oscillate between shorter and longer delay times. Since the waveforms are the same, wave interference occurs as discussed in *Chapter 5, Sound Design and Audio Envelopes*. At certain interfering frequencies, resonances are created. You can think of **resonance** as an intense tone made more pronounced than other frequencies. The low-frequency oscillator moves around the waveform to find different resonances. We call this sweeping resonance sound a **flanger**. Flangers take advantage of the feedback to resend the output sound back into itself and create additional resonance.

Chapter 7 211

As a general guideline, consider applying flanger effects to hi-hats, guitars, and pads. These often complement the sound of the instrument. When mixing, you want to place flanger effects before your delay and reverb effects in the signal chain.

Let's apply a flanger effect to an instrument:

1. Load up a sample or an instrument with notes and route it to a new mixer track.
2. Add the **Fruity Flanger** effect. When you play your instrument, you will be able to hear a flanger effect:

Figure 7.18 – Fruity Flanger

3. To hear examples of flanger effects, left-click on **Presets** in the top right of the plugin.

The following is a description of the **Fruity Flanger** plugin controls:

- **DELAY** controls the minimum time to wait before playing the copied delayed sound.
- **DEPTH** controls the modulation of the *wait* before playing the delayed sound.
- **RATE** adjusts the speed of the modulation.
- **PHASE** widens the stereo image.
- **DAMP** allows you to filter the selected frequencies.
- **SHAPE** adjusts the shape of the low-frequency modulator between a sine wave and a triangle LFO. Sine waves are smooth, while triangle waves have more abrupt pitch transitions.
- **FEED** (short for *feedback*) sets the level of feedback on the sound fed back into Fruity Flanger.
- **INV FEEDBACK/INV WET** allow you to invert the output signal phase.
- **DRY/WET/CROSS** control the level of the output signal.

Next, let's discuss phaser effects.

Using phaser effects

Phasers sound similar to chorus and flanger effects and are used in almost the same way. In phasers, a copy of the original sound is moved in and out of phase with the original. The focus of a phaser is to sweep frequencies across the spectrum.

When mixing, you want to place phaser effects before your delay and reverb effects in the signal chain.

Let's apply a phaser effect to an instrument:

1. Load up a sample or an instrument with notes and route it to a new mixer track.
2. Add the **Fruity Phaser** effect. When you play your instrument, you will be able to hear a phaser effect:

Figure 7.19 – Fruity Phaser

3. To hear examples of phaser effects, left-click on the default presets in the top right of the plugin.

The following is a description of the **Fruity Phaser** plugin controls:

- **SWEEP FREQ.** (short for *frequency*) sets the frequency of the low-frequency modulator.
- **MIN DEPTH** and **MAX DEPTH** choose the range for the phaser to sweep in.
- **FREQ. RANGE** sets the range for the sweeping frequency.
- **STEREO** controls the stereo image width.
- **NR. STAGES** (meaning the *number of stages*) sets the number of phases to go through. As you increase the number of stages, the effect becomes more extreme.

- **FEEDBACK** sets how much output is fed back into the phaser.
- **DRY-WET** controls the level of phaser output.
- **OUT GAIN** allows you to increase the output signal.

Using Vintage Phaser

FL Studio Signature Edition comes with a phaser plugin called Vintage Phaser. It's modeled after the Electro-Harmonix Small Stone Phase Shifter guitar pedal.

Let's explore Vintage Phaser and add a phaser effect to an instrument:

1. Load up a sample or an instrument with notes and route it to a new mixer track.
2. Add the **Fruity Phaser** effect. When you play your instrument, you will be able to hear a phaser effect:

Figure 7.20 – Vintage Phaser

The following is a description of the controls. The layout is very similar to the layout of the FL Studio plugin Vintage Chorus.

The **PHASING** panel lets you change the modulation range.

Figure 7.21 – Vintage Phaser PHASING panel

- **MIN**: Lets you set the minimum frequency for the oscillator.
- **MAX**: Lets you set the maximum frequency for the oscillator.
- **HQ**: Allows oversampling. Oversampling is when the plugin converts the audio into a higher sample rate. This helps removes negative artifacts from the audio, such as aliasing.
- **MANUAL**: Swaps out the **MIN** and **MAX** control with a knob that lets you manually adjust the phaser frequency. You can then automate the frequency if you want precise control.

The **MODULATION** panel lets you change the modulation speed/choose how the phase moves between the min to max frequencies.

Figure 7.22 – Vintage Phaser MODULATION panel

- **START PHASE**: Chooses where to restart the phase from.
- **TYPE**: Lets you choose between a triangle and a sine wave.
- **L/R PHASE**: If increased, this will increase the stereo effect.
- **FEEDBACK**: Lets you choose how much output sound is fed back into the input. More means a larger phasing effect.

The **DELAY** panel controls delay effects.

Figure 7.23 – Vintage Phaser DELAY panel

- **ACTIVATE**: Turns on delay effects.
- **MIX**: Adjusts the amount of delay effect applied.
- **FEEDBACK**: Feeds delay output back into the input to increase the delay effect.
- **HP/LP**: Controls high-pass and low-pass filters to cut off frequencies.
- **KEEP PITCH**: Allows you to maintain the pitch when delay modulation changes.
- **TIME**: Sets the delay time.
- **TEMPO SYNC**: Sets the delay time as beat units instead of milliseconds.

The **LEVELS** panel controls the output.

Figure 7.24 – Vintage Phaser LEVELS panel

- **NOISE**: Simulates the noise that the analog device would normally produce.
- **NOISE GATE**: Only allows analog noise when there is an active sound being fed into the plugin. Otherwise, it will create phasing effects without input sound.
- **MONO INPUT**: Sets the input to mono.

- **MIX:** Controls how much effect to output.

Figure 7.25 – Vintage Phaser Advanced Options

Selecting the **Advanced Options** gear icon unlocks additional controls. The original guitar pedal was battery-powered and sounded different depending on the amount of remaining battery level. The phaser sound was more rich and crisp when at a high battery level and more crunchy and laggy when on a low battery level.

The additional controls allow you to create sounds similar to how the pedal effect changed due to battery level:

Figure 7.26 – Vintage Phaser Additional Controls

- **COLOR GAIN:** Sets the gain.
- **COLOR FREQ:** Sets the frequency.
- **INPUT HP:** Sets a high-pass filter on the input audio.
- **FEEDBACK:** Sets how much output audio to feed back into the phaser input to increase the effect.
- **RATE FREQ 1:** Maximum frequency value.

- **RATE FREQ 2**: Minimum frequency value.
- **LFO SCALE**: Sets how much to lower the volume as the frequency increases.
- **LFO PULL**: This controls the LFO *pull down*, which affects how often the phaser frequency gets 'pulled down' to 0.

We've finished discussing stereo-width effects. Next, let's discuss applying distortion effects.

Understanding distortion effects

Distortion is an audio effect created by overloading audio. It changes the waveform and compresses sound in a way often described as "warm or dirty" sounding.

There are several types of distortion:

- **CLIPPING** occurs when your audio is louder than the sound system can handle. Unintended clipping is an unpleasant sound to the ear. You've heard clipping whenever you hear audio feedback from phone or video calls. This type of audio can occur when the audio gain is turned above 0 dB. Unintended clipping distortion is undesirable; however, there are many kinds of desirable distortion that can be used in creative effects for your music to add unique character to your sounds. For the purposes of this chapter, we will be talking about intended distortion being used as a creative effect, rather than unintended clipping distortion.
- **SATURATION** adds harmonic frequencies to your sound. It adds some compression and smooths transients.
- **TUBE DISTORTION** is slightly heavier distortion than regular saturation.
- **BIT CRUSHING** reduces the sample rate and bit depth. You can think of it as though you are reducing the resolution of the sound. A comparison might be watching a 720-resolution video instead of a 1,080-resolution video. Why would you want this? Sometimes, you want to create a retro sound where less precision in sound is desirable.
- **HARMONIC DISTORTION** is where you add new tones to the original sound. The distortion multiples the original signal's frequencies.
- **OVERDRIVE/FUZZ** distortion makes your audio sound more aggressive. This is what you think of when you hear a metal band playing guitars with lots of distortion effects.

Using Distructor

FL Studio has a distortion effect plugin called **Distructor**. Distructor is an effect rack that takes effects from several FL Studio plugins and groups them together conveniently in an easy-to-use interface.

Let's apply a distortion effect to an instrument using Distructor:

1. Load up a sample or an instrument with notes and route it to a new mixer track.
2. Add the **Distructor** effect. When you play your instrument, you will be able to hear a distortion effect:

Figure 7.27 – Distructor

Distructor is a collection of 4 modules of effects. Distructor contains distortion, filter, chorus, and speaker effects. Upon loading, Distructor is populated with 4 effects, which work on the audio chain from left to right. For example, in the initial setup, the audio passes through the distortion module, which then passes the audio to the filter module, then to the chorus, and finally to the speaker. As usual, in the top-right corner of the plugin, you'll find effect presets, which you can instantly apply to your audio.

You can swap out the type of module by left-clicking the module title and choosing which effect module you want to use, as shown in the following screenshot.

Figure 7.28 – Distructor module

All Distructor effect modules have the same bottom-panel buttons, allowing you to control how much input audio and output audio you want the effect to use. These are controlled by the **IN**, **MIX**, and **OUT** knobs. They all also have volume meters to the left.

Below the **IN**, **MIX**, and **OUT** knobs are the **Move module left** option to remove a module and **Move module right**. These allow you to rearrange the order of the effects applied to your audio.

Below those are **SOFT CLIP OUTPUT**, which helps to stop audio from peaking above 0 dB, and the **SHOW PEAKMETERS** button, which enables you to toggle the audio volume visual on or off.

Let's take a look at each of the Distructor effects – first up, the Distortion effect module.

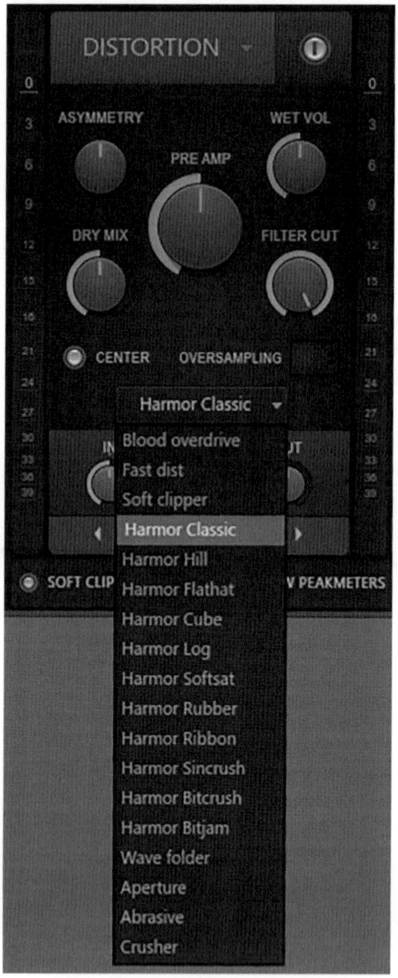

Figure 7.29 – DISTORTION effect

In the preceding screenshot, we've clicked on the algorithm section, which reveals a drop-down menu of various distortion presets. The controls in the effects module change depending on which preset is selected:

- **BLOOD OVERDRIVE**: Creates an overdrive distortion, creating compressed soft sounds.
- **FAST DIST**: Creates a gritty punchy effect.
- **SOFT CLIPPER** avoids clipping by applying a soft knee compression to the audio. It can cause saturation distortion when the audio exceeds the threshold level.

Chapter 7   221

Most of the presets are effects from other FL Studio plugins that have been copied into Distructor. By default, the **Harmor Classic** preset is selected. If you want to learn more about Harmor, here is a link to the documentation:

```
https://www.image-line.com/fl-studio-learning/fl-studio-online-manual/html/
plugins/Harmor.htm
```

The next Distructor module is the **FILTER** module.

Figure 7.30 – FILTER effect

The filter module contains a variety of presets and provides a cutoff and resonance knob to adjust the control values.

In general, the cutoff control allows you to select which frequency to act the filter on. The resonance control lets you choose what peak to use for the cutoff frequency. Here's a description of the controls:

- **Low pass**: Only allows frequencies to be heard below the filter value.
- **High pass**: Only allows frequencies to be heard above the filter value.
- **Low shelf**: Boosting or cutting frequencies below the cutoff value.
- **High shelf**: Boosting or cutting frequencies above the cutoff value.
- **Notch**: A band of frequencies where frequencies are cut at the cutoff frequency. The resonance knob controls the width of allowable frequencies.
- **Peak**: A band of frequencies where frequencies are allowed to pass through. The resonance knob controls the boost.
- **Phaser 1, 2, 3**: Phaser effects.
- **Vowel**: Makes a sound like a spoken vowel sound. The cutoff knob controls the A, E, I, O, and U sounds. The resonance parameter controls shifting/offsetting.
- **Comb +**: A series of band peaks that look like a comb.
- **Comb -**: A series of band cuts that look like a comb.
- **All pass**: Changes the phase of sound frequencies. The resonance knob controls the width.

You can always see what value a control is set to by clicking the control and looking at the top-left corner of your screen to see the hint panel, as shown in the following screenshot.

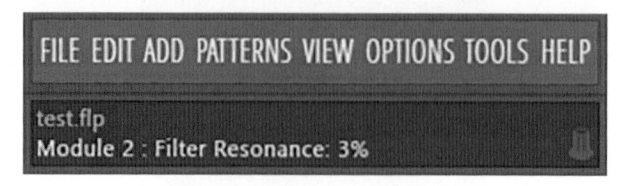

Figure 7.31 – Control value

Next, let's look at the chorus effects module.

Figure 7.32 – CHORUS effects

Chorus effects are created by delaying copies of a sound and detuning them.

- **DELAY**: Controls the minimum delay.
- **FEEDBACK**: Determines how much you want the original sound to be mixed with the delayed sound.
- **SPEED**: Chooses the modulation speed.
- **DEPTH**: High values create a stronger modulation of the voice delay.
- **BLUR**: Controls the number of chorus voices.
- **COLOR**: Turning it left creates a low-pass filter, and the reverse creates a high-pass filter.
- **MONO**: Creates chorus voices that are in mono, making audio the same in the left and right speakers.
- **STEREO**: Chorus voices are set to stereo, allowing differences between the audio in the left and right speakers.
- **WIDE**: Creates a wide stereo chorus effect.

Next, let's look at the speaker effect module:

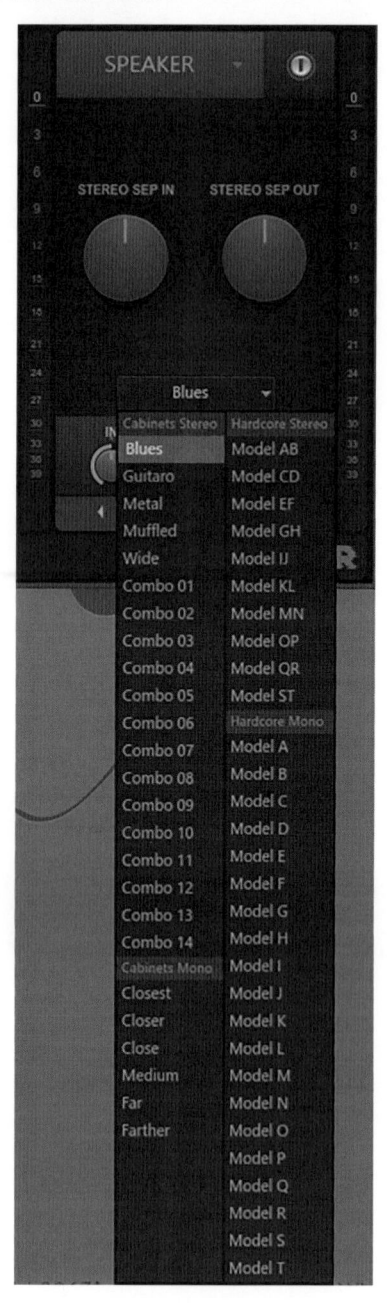

Figure 7.33 – SPEAKER effects

The speaker effects module creates reverb effects using convolution technology. The idea is that it replicates an environment for your sound and plays your audio in the environment to simulate the reverb. The presets are effects taken from the Fruity Convolver plugin.

- **STERO SEP IN**: Controls the stereo amount of the input sound.
- **STEREO SEP OUT**: Controls the stereo amount of the output sound.

Distortion best practices

Adding distortion effects is useful when you want to make your sounds more aggressive or warm, or cut through the mix. Brass instruments can sometimes benefit from sounding a little more aggressive with the aid of a little distortion.

Distortion is most often added to guitar instruments. It can be used on vocals depending on the genre of music you're trying to make. If used on vocals, it's recommended that you add distortion to the vocals on a parallel mixer track to your vocals so that you retain all your vocals' original nuances without losing them. So far in this chapter and the previous chapter, we've discussed applying effects to individual instruments. Next, let's discuss how to apply effects to multiple instruments at once.

Understanding mix buses

When you have two or more mixer channels routed into a single mixer channel, we call the combined audio a **bus**, also known as a **mix bus**. Buses are useful for combining sounds together and making them appear related to one another.

The master channel is a type of bus that collects audio from all the other mixer channels. Most of the time, when we talk about a bus, we aren't referring to the master channel, though.

You can generally think of a bus as a checkpoint along the way to the master channel. Does the audio coming out of the bus sound good so far up to this point? In most songs, you will have a bus for your drums, a bus combining the layering of your instruments, and a bus for your vocals.

Let's set up a mix bus in our mixer:

1. Load up two instruments in the channel rack, add some notes, and copy those notes to both instruments.
2. Route both instruments to separate new mixer channels.
3. In the mixer, select both mixer tracks. You can select multiple mixer channel tracks at once by pressing *Ctrl* + *Shift* + left-clicking on the desired mixer tracks.

4. With the mixer tracks still selected, right-click on the arrow at the bottom of the mixer track you would like to make into a bus, as shown in the following screenshot:

Figure 7.34 – Mix bus

The audio signals from your two instrument channels have been sent to be combined in a mixer channel. You've just created a mix bus.

Chapter 7 227

5. Make it easy for yourself to identify that the mixer track is being used as a bus. Right-click on the mix bus channel and change the name and color by selecting the **Rename, color and icon...** option. This will make it easy for you to organize:

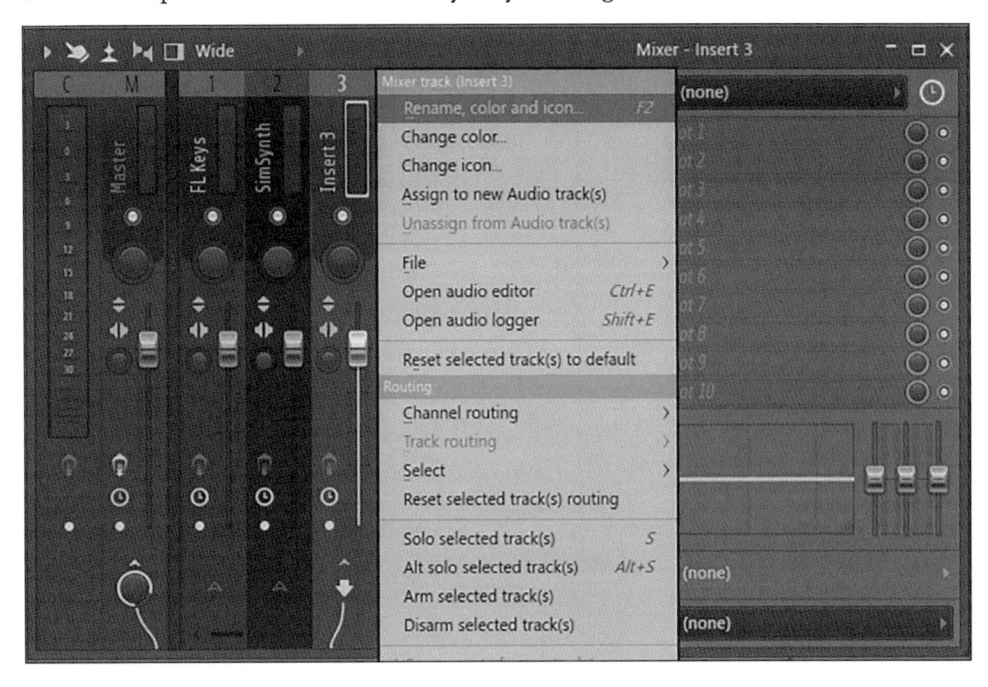

Figure 7.35 – Rename and color your mix bus

6. In this bus mixer channel, add any effect plugin. The effect plugin will affect all instrument sounds routed to the bus. In the following screenshot, we can see that I've added the **Fruity Delay 3** plugin. This will apply a delay effect to both instruments routed to the bus channel:

Figure 7.36 – Adding the Fruity Delay 3 plugin

Mix bus best practices

Compression effects should be applied to the bus to gain a sense of cohesion between the instruments. For example, drum instruments are often grouped together in a bus and then compression is applied to them. Note that the compressor is going to change the volume and frequencies of all instruments sent to the bus. To save yourself some time, if you know you're going to be adding bus compression, add the compressor first before doing additional mixing, such as volume and EQ tweaks.

You can apply EQ effects to a bus. You can create low- or high-pass filters to avoid your instruments interfering with instruments in other buses. For example, you can add a high-pass filter to remove the subfrequencies from your non-sub-bass instruments. This will make any remaining bass instruments' subfrequencies stand out unimpeded.

You can make subtle EQ cuts, such as at around 200 Hz, to remove muddiness. If you find yourself making large EQ cuts, you should probably be doing EQ on the individual instruments themselves rather than on the bus.

When reverb effects are applied to a bus, it gives the impression that all instruments in the bus exist in the same physical space. Consider applying convolution reverb at this stage to make your instruments feel like they all exist together.

Adjusting the volume of a bus will change the volume of all instruments in it at once. This can be useful when balancing the volume of different instrument groups. For example, you can adjust the volume of the drum bus relative to the vocal bus.

Congratulations, you've created a bus and used it to apply effects to multiple instruments at once! You now know how to group your instruments together and apply effects that make the grouped instruments sound more cohesive.

Summary

In this chapter, you learned how to make your sounds feel large and trick your ears into thinking your digital instruments were played in actual physical environments. This will make your sounds feel natural and more enjoyable to listen to.

We discussed stereo width and the effects you can use to make your sounds feel larger. We explored tools used to manipulate stereo width, including panning, digital reverb, convolution reverb, delay effects, chorus effects, flangers, and phasers. We also discussed distortion effects. Finally, we discussed how to use mix buses to combine your instruments to make them more cohesive and appear related to one another.

In the next chapter, we'll jump into recording live audio and the vocal processing best practices.

8

Recording Live Audio and Vocal Processing

Vocals are the most recognizable part of a song and can single-handedly determine whether people love it or hate it. You'll want to devote careful attention to making sure you get the best-sounding vocals possible. In this chapter, we will learn how to record live audio and process vocals.

In the pages ahead, we'll discuss the setup and preparation you need to take care of before recording. We'll look at how to record in FL Studio, learn how to mix your vocals, and finally, look at the best practices to apply effects.

In this chapter, we'll cover the following topics:

- Understanding microphones
- Setting up your recording environment
- Recording audio in FL Studio
- Using pitch correction with Newtone
- Retiming audio samples with Newtime
- Vocals effect processing best practices

Technical requirements

To follow the examples in this chapter, you will need the FL Studio Producer Edition or higher. You will also need headphones and a microphone to record into.

Understanding microphones

You need a microphone to record live audio. What are microphones? **Microphones** are electronic devices you use to record audio. They contain a material called a **diaphragm** that vibrates when struck by sound waves. They convert the sound waves into electrical currents that can be played by devices that replay sound.

If you were to Google search *What microphone should I buy?*, you may feel overwhelmed by the number of search results. There are many competing brands of microphones that each have their own advantages. Prices range from tens of dollars to thousands of dollars.

Personally, in my experience, if you do a good job in terms of recording, mixing, and applying effects to your audio, most listeners won't be able to tell how expensive the microphone you used to record is. The thing you're recording and what you do with it is much more important than the price of the mic you use. That said, there are different types of microphones you will come across, and they are used for different purposes.

Let's discuss the types of microphones available so you can make an educated choice when selecting one for yourself.

Dynamic microphones

Dynamic microphones are microphones intended for use in stage performances. They consist of a wire coil coupled with a diaphragm. A minimum amount of energy is required to initially cause the diaphragm to vibrate from sound waves. The diaphragm is subject to inertia in that once it starts vibrating, it continues to vibrate. This inertia problem means the microphone won't be able to pick up on subtle transients as they are too brief.

Dynamic microphones can be used to record loud sounds such as sounds from drums and guitar amps. They record audio from one direction and reject incoming sounds from other directions. This allows them to focus on a singer/instrument and ignore background noise. If placed further than 1 foot away from the sound source, the sound becomes thin, so you need to place them close to the source. They are materially tough as they are expected to withstand being roughly handled and smacked around a bit onstage. They can withstand extreme sound pressure without distorting. If you're doing live shows, a dynamic mic is the right choice for you. If you're recording in a studio, a dynamic microphone is the wrong choice for you.

Condenser microphones

Condenser microphones are intended for use in quiet recording environments. They consist of a diaphragm next to a metallic alloy. Sound pressure causes the diaphragm to vibrate. The vibration changes the space between the two surfaces and an electrical charge accumulates between the two. The discharge is translated into an electrical current, which gets interpreted later as sound. They are more expensive than dynamic microphones and are delicate and sensitive to nuanced tones. If recording in a studio, a condenser microphone is a good choice for you.

Ribbon microphones

Ribbon microphones are delicate and fragile microphones that are usually quite expensive. They too need to be placed within 1 foot of the source to avoid sounding thin. They record audio bidirectionally and pick up all sound in their proximity. If placed close to the audio source, they may receive an increase in bass frequencies. They consist of a ribbon (of conductive material) between two magnets. The ribbon functions as both a diaphragm and a conductor. As a result, ribbon mics are not subject to the inertia problem of dynamic microphones. This means they can pick up subtle transients. If recording in a studio, a ribbon mic is another good choice.

Condenser microphones and ribbon microphones require a device called a **microphone preamp** or an audio interface to plug your microphone into. These devices provide electrical power to the microphone, known as **phantom power**, to increase the volume of the recorded audio. Without phantom power, your microphone's audio will be too quiet to use. If you use a condenser or ribbon microphone, you will need to investigate how to connect to phantom power. The phantom power device will then have an output that can be connected to your computer.

USB microphones

USB microphones are a special type of condenser microphone. These are mics you can plug directly into your computer via a USB port. This makes it easy to record audio as you don't need to worry about getting a microphone preamp. They tend to be cheap and beginner friendly but offer less control over recording compared to the higher-priced condenser mics. If you are new to music production and just playing around, unsure of whether you want to get serious or not, get a USB mic. They're cheap and you can just plug them into a computer and use them right away without worrying about phantom power. When you need to record professionally, look into getting a condenser or ribbon mic.

Setting up your recording environment

Before recording your audio, you want to be in a location free from background sounds. Ideally, you would be in a soundproof environment.

If you record audio and find there is some consistent background static or hum, it's not the end of the world. If the unwanted sound is at a low volume level, you may be able to remove the unwanted noise using a gate plugin effect. We discussed gates in *Chapter 6, Compression, Sidechaining, Limiting, and Equalization*.

You'll need to obtain headphones so that you can listen to your music playing while you record your instrument or vocals. You don't want to hear your song playing in the background on speakers while you're recording sounds, or else the background noise will appear in the recording.

Recording instruments

Recording instruments appears simple on paper, but it takes a surprising amount of effort to do. If you're recording an acoustic instrument, position the microphone as close as you can to the instrument and record. With electric instruments, position the microphone close to the instrument amp/speaker.

The following photo shows an example of how you can set up a microphone to record an electric guitar amp:

Figure 8.1 – Recording guitar amp

Note that the microphone is positioned slightly off-center of the speaker. Each speaker has a sweet spot in terms of where the best sound comes from, and it's usually not directly smack dab in the center.

Recording drum kits

Drums kits are fiddly for recording. When recording a drum kit, you want to designate a microphone for each drum kit item. This way, you can record each part in isolation, which gives you the freedom to play with individual sounds when mixing. There's a bit of an art to arranging microphones so that they are close to the drum kit but don't impede the drummer when playing it.

The following photo shows an example of how you could position your microphones to record a drum kit:

Figure 8.2 – Drum kit microphones

In the preceding photo, you can see that each drum and cymbal has its own dedicated microphone.

In addition to recording each instrument, you also want to record the instrument in the context of the room to hear the natural reverb. To do so, place microphones some distance away from the instrument as shown in the following photo:

Figure 8.3 – Drum kit room microphones

In the preceding photo on the far left and right, you can see microphones recording the drum kit at a distance. These microphones capture the room reverberations of the drum kit. The same idea applies to any instrument. Ideally, you would record both close to the instrument and further away to capture the natural reverb.

Preparing to record vocals

Before recording your vocals, make sure your body is physically prepared. You're going to record many takes of the song and then mix and match the best parts from all the takes. Recording vocals takes a while and is energy-intensive. You should warm up beforehand. Consider doing some of the following activities prior to recording vocals to get your lungs and throat in peak performance condition:

- Go for some brief cardio exercise beforehand, such as a quick run, to get the blood circulating.
- Hum.
- Consider doing vocal exercises such as singing scales.
- Have a hot shower.
- Drink a hot beverage.

Using pop filters

When recording vocals, you should obtain a pop filter. A **pop filter** is a mesh screen used to filter your vocals while recording. Pop filters help to remove undesired popping sounds created while talking. You can get pop filters cheaply. Any kind of mesh fabric can work as a pop filter; you can even create your own at home by following a YouTube tutorial. You can see a pop filter in the following photo:

Figure 8.4 – Pop filter

To use a pop filter, place the pop filter directly in front of the microphone and sing into the pop filter while recording.

So far, we've discussed microphones, recording instruments, and getting ready to record vocals. Next, let's record audio into our digital audio workstation.

Recording audio into FL Studio

Let's record audio into FL Studio:

1. Select the position in the playlist of your song that you want to begin recording from. Left-click to place your cursor on the playlist timeline.

2. Check that the **Countdown before recording** button is selected as shown in the following screenshot. This will give you a few seconds to prepare when you are recording:

Figure 8.5 – Record countdown

3. Open your mixer and left-click on a new mixer track to select it. When you record, your audio will be recorded into this audio mixer channel and then sent to the playlist. If you have effect plugins on the mixer channel, like pitch correction plugins such as **Autotune**, this will be applied while recording the audio file. Usually, you'll want to apply effects later in mixing, but it is possible to do so at this point. If you're going to record with audio effects, it's recommended to record on two channels simultaneously (one channel with the effect applied, and one on a channel to capture the raw audio).

4. Once you've chosen your mixer channel, ensure that **Song** is selected on the **Transport** panel, and then press the record button at the top of the screen as shown in the following screenshot:

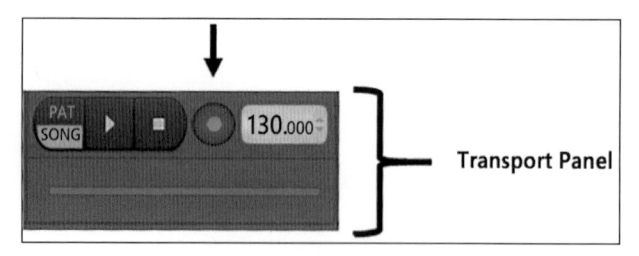

Figure 8.6 – Record button

After hitting record, a menu will pop up as shown in the following screenshot:

Chapter 8   239

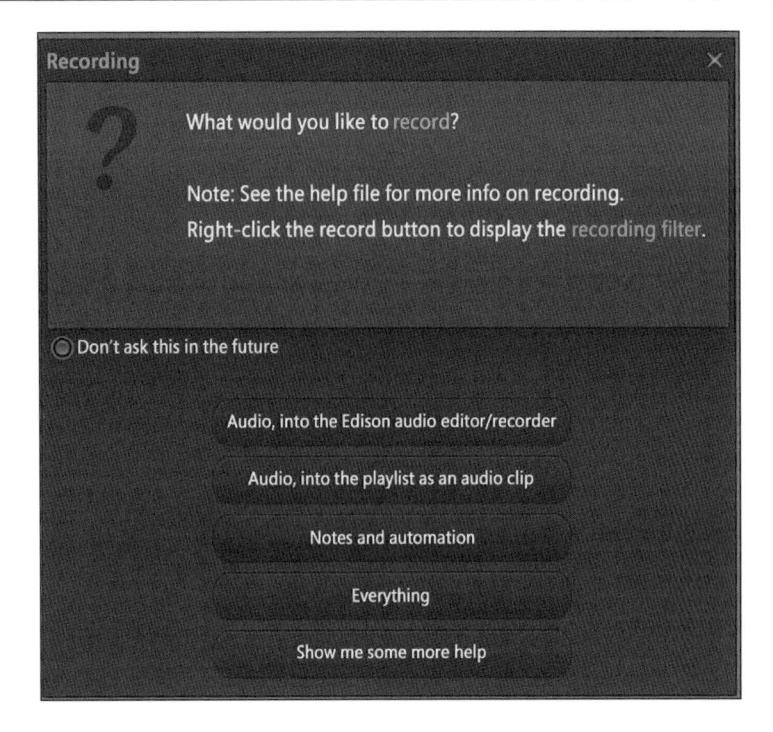

Figure 8.7 – Recording options

5. The simplest recording option is to select **Audio, into the playlist as an audio clip**. Once you do this, you will be prompted with a list of all available microphones in the mixer:

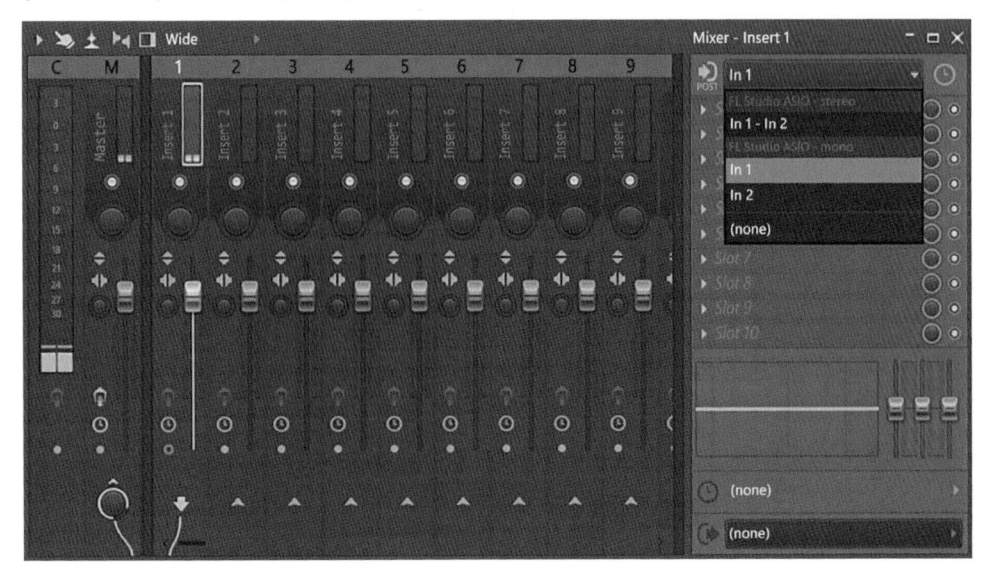

Figure 8.8 – Choose a microphone to record with

Once you've selected a microphone, your recording will begin and the song will start playing and recording.

If you record into the playlist using the previous method and you have **BLEND NOTES** and **LOOP RECORD** both engaged (in the **Transport** panel), your audio takes will be on a loop, and you can then hear one take after another. After pressing **Stop**, you can delete the takes you don't want.

When you press the **Stop** button, which is next to the **Record** button in the **Transport** panel, your song will stop playing and your recorded audio will appear in the playlist.

Your recorded audio is saved as a file on your computer. You can see all audio recordings in the **Browser** under a folder called **Recorded**. Unless you delete these audio files, they will continue to accumulate throughout your projects. Over the years, this could result in a large amount of memory being used, so you should occasionally check for and delete unused files. If you want to remove all unused audio samples in a single project, go to **Tools | Macros | Purge Unused Audio Clips**.

Congratulations! You now know how to record audio.

Recording with Edison

Edison is an audio editor and recorder available with FL Studio. It's an alternative to the previous recording method and has lots of functionalities to give you fine control over your audio recording:

1. If you want to record with Edison, go into the mixer and load **Edison** onto a mixer channel. Alternatively, you can click on a mixer channel and press *Ctrl + E*. At the top-right of the mixer, choose the microphone you want to use to record into Edison. The following screenshot shows Edison having been loaded onto a mixer track and the selection of a microphone to use:

Figure 8.9 – Loading Edison

2. In **Edison**, press the record button. Now play your song in the playlist (press play on the **Transport** panel). As the song plays, Edison will record audio.

3. Edison will continue to record until you tell it to stop. This means that you can play your song, pattern, or selected segment of the playlist on repeat multiple times and continue to record in **Edison** throughout. When you've finished recording, press the record button again in Edison to stop. An audio wave will appear in **Edison**.

4. When you've stopped recording, send the audio from Edison into the playlist by clicking the **Send to playlist as audio clip / to channel** button, as highlighted in the following screenshot. Your audio will appear in the playlist:

Figure 8.10 – Drag from Edison into playlist

Alternatively, select the **Drag/copy sample/selection** button and hold left-click to drag and drop the audio into any other FL Studio window.

Congratulations! You've just recorded audio with Edison.

Loop recording with Edison

In Edison, you can loop a segment of your playlist and record over that segment to get multiple takes before choosing the best one. To do this, execute the following steps:

1. In your playlist, highlight the segment you want to loop and record over by left-clicking and dragging on the playlist timeline.
2. Press the **Loop recording** button at the top of the screen. This will keep the playlist looping through your song.
3. In the preceding screenshot of Edison, to the right of the record button at the top, you can see the text **On Input**. If you click on that text, you can see some more recording options. Select the option that says **On Play**.
4. Hit record in **Edison** and press play in your playlist. As the playlist loops through the selected segment, Edison will record multiple takes of your recording.

Chapter 8   243

5. Press record again in **Edison** to stop recording. You'll see the recording in **Edison** has been split up into multiple takes. You can see an example of how your audio might look in the following screenshot:

Figure 8.11 – Edison recorded multiple takes

6. Choose which recording take you like best by pressing the left and right arrow keys on your keyboard. If you press *Delete*, a take will be removed. You can press *Shift + C* to send your audio take to the playlist.

Congratulations! You've just recorded multiple audio recordings and chosen the best one using Edison.

We've covered the features that I personally use in Edison. However, the Edison plugin has a lot more tools available that I don't use often, such as denoising and blurring. These go beyond the scope of this book, but if you want a detailed breakdown, check out the FL Studio documentation or the YouTube channel *In The Mix* for tutorials on using Edison at www.youtube.com/c/inthemix.

Using pitch correction with Newtone

When you record, a singer's melody will sometimes drift out of pitch from the song scale. Usually, this is undesired and makes the vocal sound bad. **Pitch correction** is a tool used to bring note pitches back into the song scale. There are several pitch correction tools on the market. Some well-made pitch correction plugins include Antares's **Autotune** and Celemony's **Melodyne**. The most widely known and used pitch correction tool in the industry is Antares's Autotune. It is a little pricey for beginners, though. If you're interested in purchasing Autotune, visit www.antarestech.com.

FL Studio has a pitch correction plugin called **Newtone** that comes with the FL Studio Signature Edition. If you are new to processing vocals and don't have access to Autotune or Melodyne, Newtone is a beginner-friendly option to give you an introduction. It offers the ability to adjust pitch in a timeline graphical mode as well as enabling you to convert audio to MIDI notes.

Let's pitch-correct with Newtone:

1. Add a vocal sample to the playlist and route it to a new mixer channel. Left-click on the top-left corner of the audio sample and select the option **Pitch-correct sample**. This will import audio into Newtone.

Figure 8.12 – Importing audio into Newtone

The method described in the preceding screenshot is what I find to be the easiest method of getting audio into **Newtone**.

Alternatively, you can load up a sample in **Newtone** directly by going into **Newtone** and clicking **File | Load Sample** and finding your audio sample.

Once the sample is loaded into Newtone, Newtone automatically divides the audio into note pitches. You can click on any of the notes and change the pitch by dragging the note up or down. If you click on the left or right edge of a note, you can shorten or lengthen the note. You can also delete a note by left-clicking on it and pressing *Delete* on your keyboard.

Figure 8.13 – Audio in Newtone

The following screenshot shows the control panel of Newtone:

Figure 8.14 – Newtone controls

Let's take a look at the controls in the top-right corner of Newtone from left to right:

- **Send to piano roll** identifies the note pitches used in the audio and creates MIDI notes in the piano roll. This can be handy if you want to to take the pitch and timing of the vocal notes and translate them to an instrument instead.

    To use this feature, select an instrument in the channel rack that you want to send notes to.

Press **Send to Piano roll**. MIDI notes will appear for the instrument you selected in the channel rack and piano roll. You can then go into the piano roll and edit the notes.

- **Save As** saves the file.
- **Drag Selection** allows you to drag audio after editing in Newtone to a new location such as a mixer channel.
- **Send to Playlist** sends the audio to the playlist.
- **CENTER** adjusts note pitches in the audio to force fixed pitch intervals. This control affects the entire audio sample.
- **VARIATION** increases or decreases the amplitude of the waveform to control how drastic pitch jumps are. If **VARIATION** is turned all the way down, it sounds robotic. This control affects the entire audio sample.
- **TRANS** (transition) controls the speed of moving between notes. This control affects the entire audio sample.
- **Slice** allows you to chop notes into smaller pieces.
- **Advanced Edit** enables access to an additional set of pitch control options. When **Advanced Edit** is enabled, you can click on a note and you'll be able to edit the volume and pitch variation.
- **Slave Playback to Host** syncs Newtone with the playlist timing. When you play your playlist, Newtone will play in time.
- **Scroll to Follow Curser**, when selected, moves along the Newtone timeline as the audio plays.

Pitch correction best practices

In your pitch correction plugin, if you have fast retune speeds, you will hear stronger pitch correction and a more robotic vocal sound. This may be a desired effect and is used intentionally in a lot of trap music. If you want more natural-sounding vocals, you'll want to reduce the retune speeds. A lower speed will have a more natural, relaxed sound, letting the vibrato of the vocal through.

Pitch correction won't turn a bad voice into a good voice. Pitch correction is best used to assist vocals that are already near the correct pitch. If your vocal is significantly out of pitch, pitch correction likely won't make the vocal sound great. Great singers combined with autotune can sound amazing. Lousy singers using autotune still sound bad. If your vocals don't sound good before applying pitch correction, you should get some better vocals.

On many pitch correction plugins, you may come across the term **formant**. The term formant is used to describe resonant frequencies. It refers to emphasized harmonics and overtones giving an instrument a distinctive character. This is different from changing the pitch as that can be maintained while changing the harmonics and overtones.

This probably sounds confusing. Let's look at an example. With a human vocal, the shape of the throat, chest, and nasal cavity all contribute to the individual's voice tone to give it a distinctive character. It's tricky to adjust the shape of your body, but with a formant plugin, you can achieve what it would sound like if your body were a different shape. This can be used to make your vocal appear higher, like a chipmunk, or much deeper. Many electronic dance music artists use an extensive amount of formant effects on their vocals to achieve their signature sound. An FL Studio plugin that uses formants is **Pitcher**. We will cover Pitcher in *Chapter 9, Vocoders and Vocal Chops*.

Retiming audio samples with Newtime

When recording live audio or importing samples, sooner or later you'll find audio clip timings don't match up with the rest of your song. Audio mistimings can be corrected using the FL Studio plugin Newtime.

Newtime allows you to map out the key moments in your audio sample and adjust the timing to better fit your song. Let's retime audio samples using Newtime:

1. You'll first need an audio sample clip to retime. Load up an audio clip sample in the playlist. Any will do. In my example, we'll use a drum sample that comes with FL Studio, but you can use any sample that you like. If this is your first time using Newtime I recommend finding a drum loop sample as this is the easiest way to see clear results.

Figure 8.15 – Drum sample

2. In the playlist, left-click on the top left corner of the sample to see the options and choose the **Time-warp sample** option:

Chapter 8

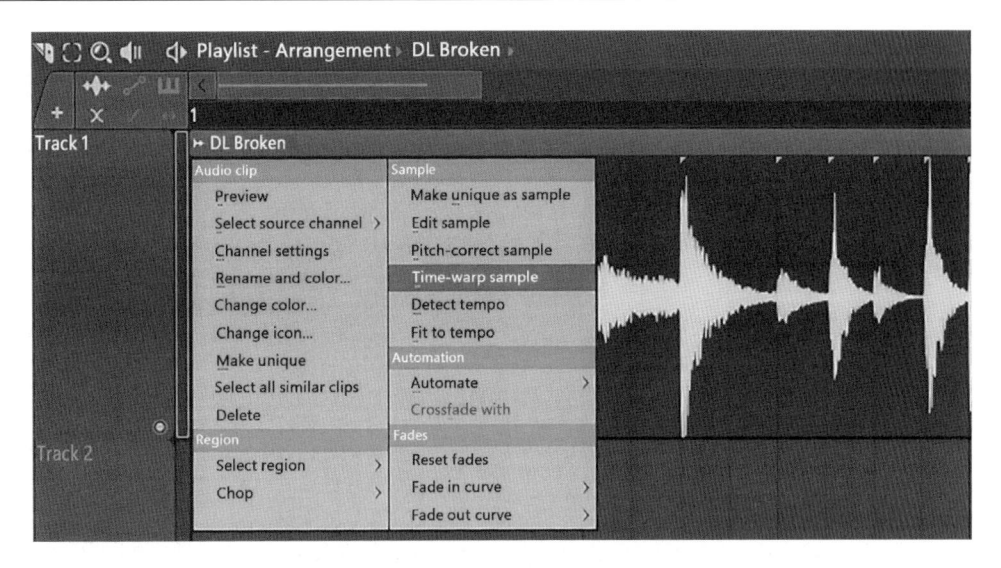

Figure 8.16 – Time-warp sample

This will load the sample in Newtime. You'll see Newtime load the audio clip similar to the following screenshot:

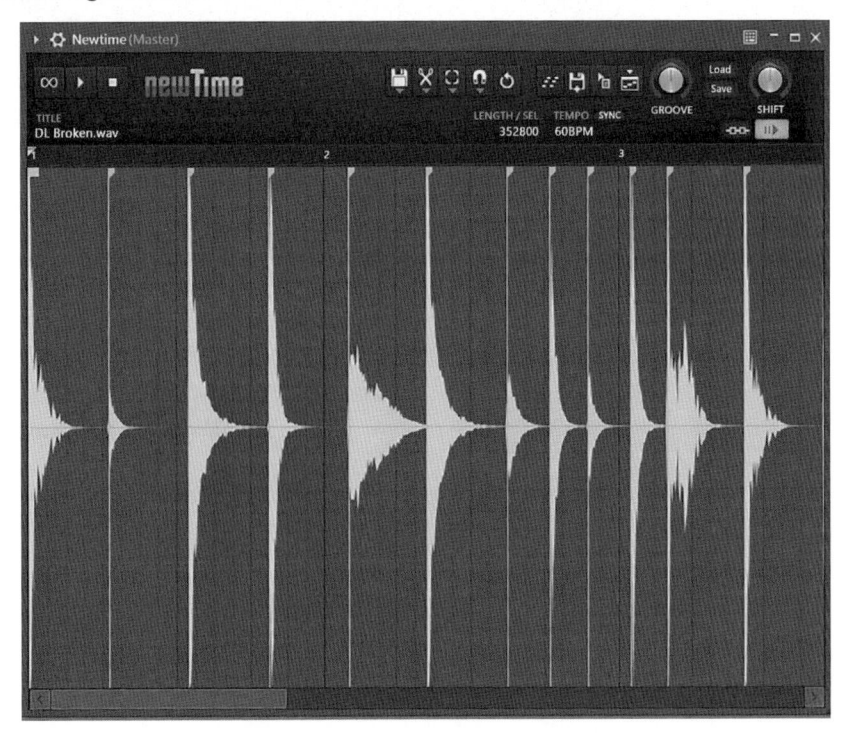

Figure 8.17 – Newtime loaded sample

Newtime splits audio into sections based on transients. It assigns markers (called warp markers) that you can move around to retime the audio.

The interface is very similar to the FL Studio's Newtone plugin, with many of the same controls.

3. Enable the **Slave playback to host** button to sync the Newtime audio playback with your playlist. Once enabled, anytime you play the playlist, Newtime will play the audio in sync. You'll likely want to keep playing the song in the playlist from now on when editing the sample in Newtime:

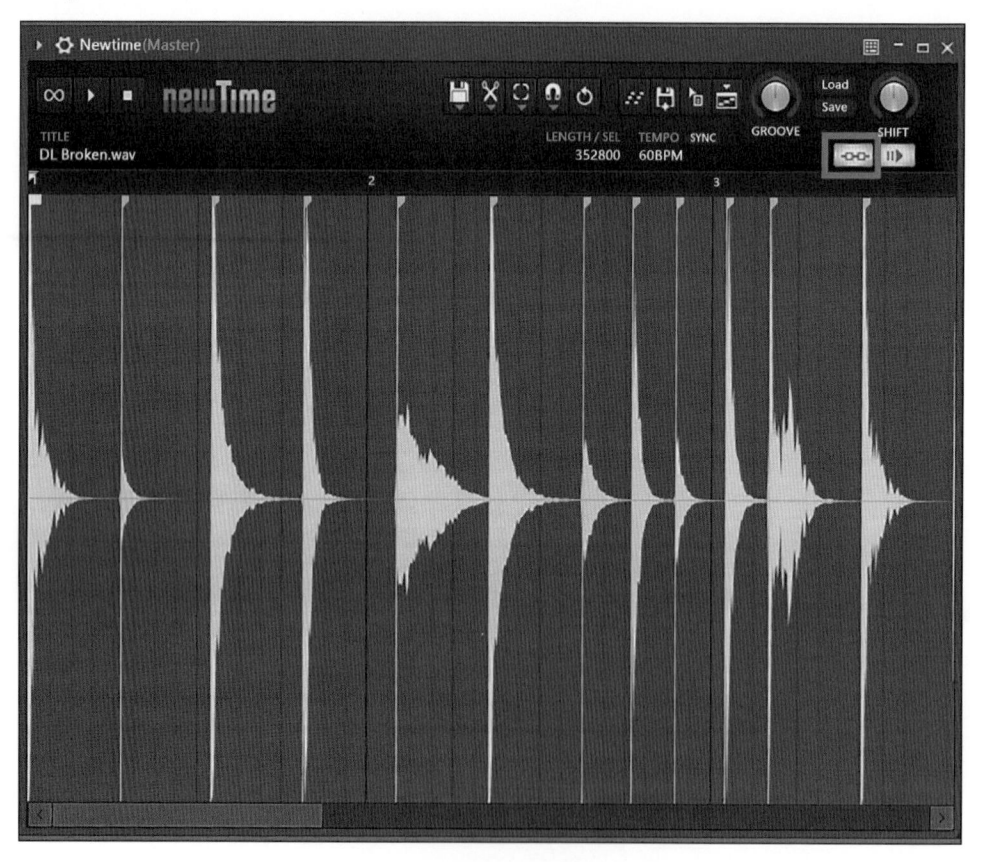

Figure 8.18 – Slave playback to host

Newtime can attempt to match the sample timing to the tempo in the playlist.

4. Select **Tempo Sync**. Newtime will attempt to fit the sample to match the project tempo. The following screenshot shows the selection of the **Select Tempo Sync** button:

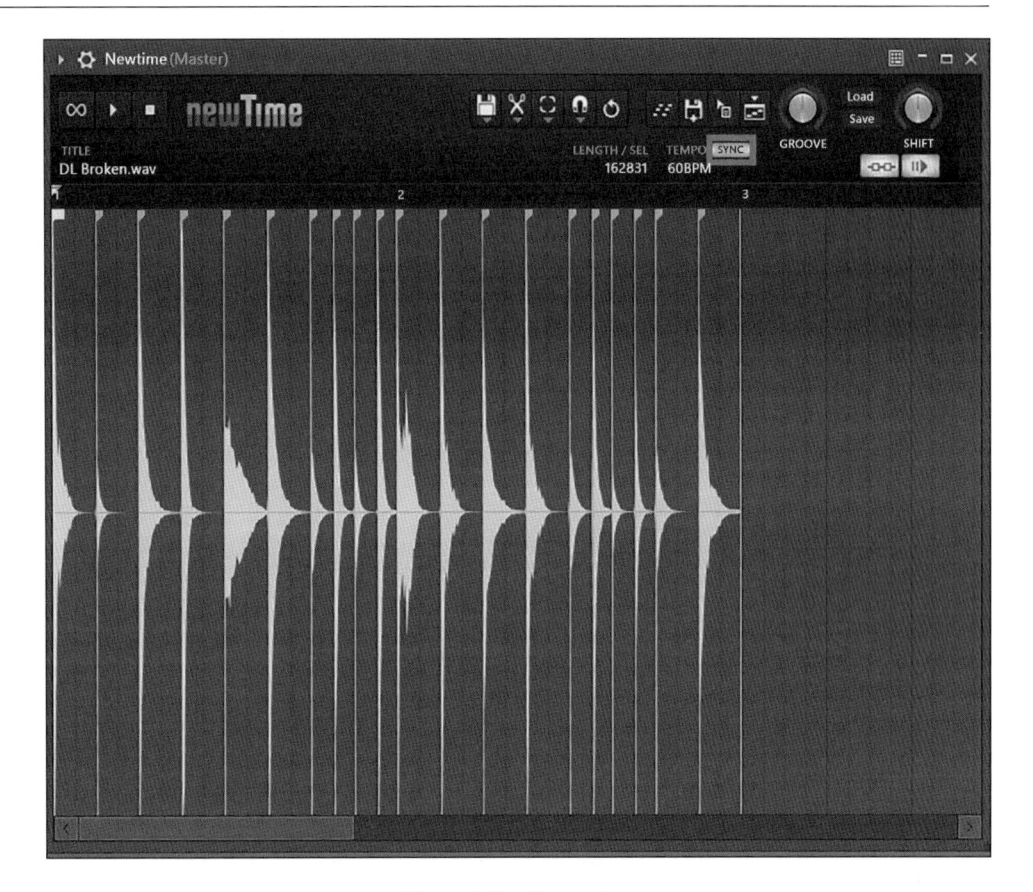

Figure 8.19 – Tempo Sync

The more rhythmic your sample, the more likely Newtime will correctly retime the audio sample. The less rhythmic, the more likely you'll have to manually retime the audio.

The markers (warp markers) can be dragged left or right to retime the audio. This is how you can retime your audio manually. Simply move the markers around until you feel that the sound matches the rest of your song.

By default, the first marker will be highlighted in green to indicate that it is the downbeat marker. The downbeat marker helps with beat detection. If your melody doesn't start on the first beat of the bar, you can reassign the downbeat marker by right-clicking on a marker, and it will reassign the downbeat marker.

If you hold *Alt* while dragging a marker, it will temporarily disable snapping to the grid.

You can double-click anywhere in the grid to add more warp markers.

After left-clicking once in the waveform, you can hold down **shift** while hovering over the audio wave to display a line to help with fine-tuning placement.

You can select multiple marker clips at once by holding *Ctrl*. Then you can drag them all at once.

5. Newtime comes with built-in groove presets available to manipulate your samples. *Grooves* adjust the timing of the sample to match a preset rhythm. Select the **Load Groove Pattern** button as shown in the following screenshot:

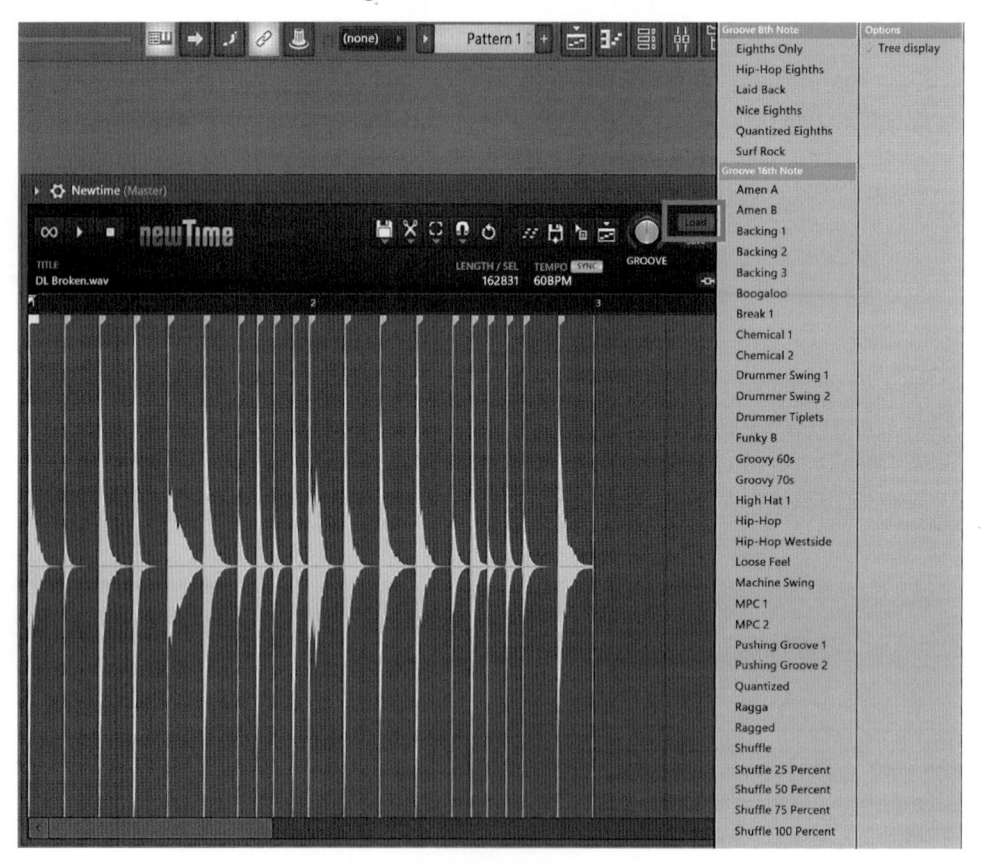

Figure 8.20 – Loading a groove pattern

Once you've chosen a groove, several of the markers will be selected in yellow.

6. Adjust the groove pattern to determine how much groove effect you want to be applied to the sample. An example is shown in the following screenshot:

Chapter 8   253

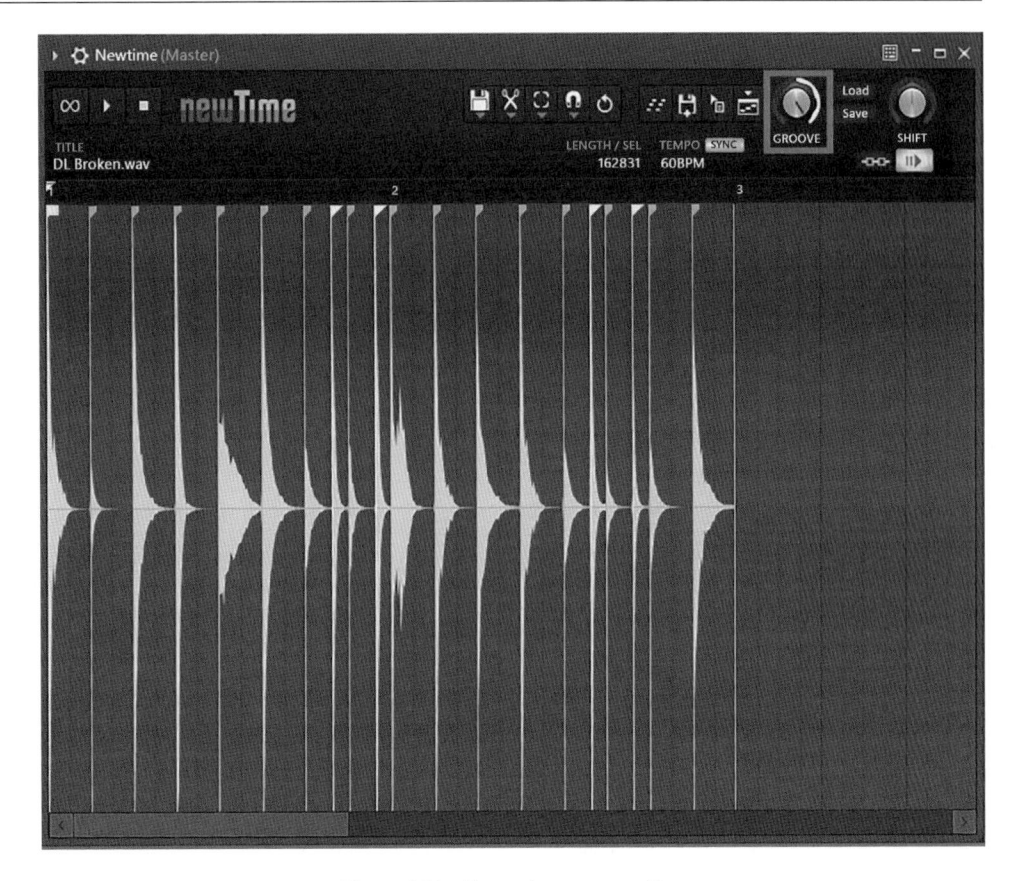

Figure 8.21 – Example groove pattern

Increasing the groove control adjusted the timing of the notes. I encourage you to experiment with trying out different grooves and seeing how it sounds with the rest of your song.

7. You've finished tweaking the timing of your audio sample. Now it's time to export it out of Newtime and back into the rest of your song. There's multiple options to export from Newtime as shown in the following screenshot:

Figure 8.22 – Export from Newtime

- **Send to piano roll** sends the MIDI timing of the Newtime markers to the piano roll. This is useful if all you care about is the timing but not the audio itself. This might also be useful if you want the groove to be played by an instrument.
- **Save as** allows you to save the audio as a file.
- **Drag selection** allows you to drag the Newtime audio into any other plugin that requires an audio sample.
- **Send to playlist** sends the audio into the playlist. This is usually the option that you'll want to use.

You now know how to retime your audio samples.

Vocals effect processing best practices

Let's discuss some best practices to process your vocals.

It's best to record dry vocals without any effects. You can always add in and swap out effects later. If you need to hear how an effect will sound for reference while recording (such as when using an autotune or vocoder tool), record the dry vocals at the same time as the effected vocals on two separate channels so that you end up with access to the dry vocals, in addition to any effected vocals.

When applying effects on vocals, there's an order that's usually followed. The following order is a suggestion, not a mandatory rule. This order is here to help you get a natural sounding vocal where each effect helps to build on the previous one rather than interfere. If you find any of the following terms confusing regarding compressing or EQ, revisit *Chapter 6, Compression, Sidechaining, Limiting, and Equalization*.

Here's a suggested order to apply effects to vocals:

1. **Pitch correction** corrects pitch and adjusts mistimings.
2. **Gate effects** or **expander effects** remove background and unwanted noises. For example, Fruity Limiter can be used as a gate. The gate effect always comes before the compressor. Why? A gate needs a dynamic range of volumes to help decide what to filter out. A compressor reduces the range of volumes, so having the compressor before a gate would be counter-productive.
3. A **compressor** balances out the dynamic range of the vocal and reduces the difference between its loud and quiet parts. The amount of compression used is down to personal taste and depends on the genre of music you make. You may also consider using parallel compression if you want to preserve vocal transients.

Chapter 8

4. A **de-esser plugin** removes sibilance, makes surgical resonant cuts, and tames and controls harsh frequencies. De-essing is done using a multiband compressor. It compresses common problematic frequency areas. On the FL Studio Maximus plugin, there is a preset for de-essing that can help you get started.

5. **Vocal effects** include harmony creation, vocoders, and saturation effects, to name a few. We will discuss vocoders in *Chapter 9, Vocoders and Vocal Chops*.

6. **EQ** cuts out unwanted frequencies and boosts desired ones. You can add an EQ high pass filter to remove the sub-bass frequencies that are not the focus of the vocal. This high pass filter is usually placed around 80 Hz–120 Hz.

7. You may want to make an EQ boost somewhere around 12 kHz–16 kHz. If there are unwanted resonances in your vocals, you may want to cut somewhere in the low-mid to high-mid frequencies to remove them. Where and how large the cut or boost is will depend on the vocal you work with.

The following screenshot shows an example of how your EQ curve may look when applied to vocals:

Figure 8.23 – EQ on vocals

In the preceding screenshot, you can see we've rolled off the low-end frequencies, creating an EQ cut around 350 Hz and a boost around 12 kHz. This is not a fixed rule to blindly apply, though. Your vocal EQ curve will look a little different in every situation.

8. **Delay**, if desired, adds additional stereo width. Pan out your delay to achieve side delays so that they don't conflict with the lead vocal frequencies in the center.
9. **Reverb** makes the vocal sound as though it were in a realistic environment. Some mixing engineers like to have minimal pitch correction on the original dry vocal and another hard pitch-corrected version with the speed set to full to use on the vocal reverb.

Backing vocals effects best practices

Backing vocals are mixed the same as lead vocals with a few subtle differences:

- With the backing vocals, you don't need to hear as much breathiness as the lead vocal because it may distract from the focus.
- Backing vocals, if desired, can be subtly panned out left and right, whereas you want to leave the lead vocal directly mono in the center.
- Have more relaxed pitch correction on the backing vocals than the lead vocals. Harder pitch-corrected vocals are generally more noticeable, and you don't want your backing vocals to take focus away from the lead.

Once you've set up your effect plugins in your mixer, you can save the project as a template to save time and reuse it. Create a template by saving the project under `C:\Program Files (x86)\Image-Line\Data\Templates`. Then, in the future, you can reopen the template by going to **File | New** from your template and selecting your project. Your exact folder location may differ depending on your computer.

We've covered best practices for vocal processing. Congratulations! You now know how to mix vocals.

Summary

In this chapter, we learned about recording audio so that you can record your instruments and vocals. We learned about microphones and how to prepare for recording. We learned how to record into FL Studio. We learned about pitch correction and how to pitch-correct using Newtone. We learned how to retime audio samples using Newtime. Finally, we learned a series of tips and best practices to mix your vocals.

Some key points to think about:

- The order you apply effects can be important, so the plugin effects should complement and build on each other instead of undoing the previous plugin's work.

- After adding effects, you should always test turning your plugin effects on and off to check that they actually made your sound better.
- Once you've finished setting up your mixer effects chain, you can save the mixer track by right-clicking on the mixer track and selecting **File | Save mixer track state as**. Then, you can easily load it in the future by right-clicking on a mixer track and selecting **File | Open mixer track state**.

For the ambitious who want to go further, you can look into learning about **gain staging**: `https://www.izotope.com/en/learn/gain-staging-what-it-is-and-how-to-do-it.html`.

In the next chapter, we will learn about special effects that you can do with your vocals using vocoders and vocal chopping.

9
Vocoders and Vocal Chops

In this chapter, we'll learn about special effects that can be applied to vocals. These effects can make your songs distinctive and memorable. We'll discuss how to create vocal harmonies and how to use vocoders to modulate your vocals with an instrument. Lastly, we'll look at how to create vocal chops.

In this chapter, we'll cover the following topics:

- Understanding vocoders
- Understanding MIDI
- Using vocoders
- Using Vocodex
- Creating vocal chops

Understanding vocoders

What are vocoders? If you've heard a voice that has been transformed to sound like a robot, then you've probably heard a vocoder. They sound awesome and are my favorite weapon to wield when making music. Vocoding is used extensively in electronic dance music, especially in the house, electro, and dubstep genres. If you're unsure about what a vocoder effect sounds like, consider checking out the following songs:

- **Daft Punk** – *Harder, Better, Faster, Stronger*
- **Don Diablo** – *You're Not Alone ft. Kiiara*

Vocoders create effects that modulate an existing sound. The input sound (usually a vocal) splits into frequency bands and is analyzed for its frequency level and content. We call this the **modulator**. The vocoder breaks this information down into a series of band pass filters to be used later. In other words, the vocoder figures out what frequencies were used in the vocal.

A second sound (usually an instrument) is fed into the vocoder. We call this the **carrier**. We use this as the sound that we're going to modify. We use the modulator filter to filter the incoming carrier audio. In other words, we allow the instrument sound to play frequencies that line up with our vocal frequencies.

If you find this confusing, you can think of your own voice as a vocoder. Your throat and mouth shape act as a vocoder, modulating the sound in the air as it leaves your body. As you adjust the shape of your mouth, the sound changes.

There are several vocoder plugin effects on the market. If you like the ones that are demonstrated in this chapter and want to buy more vocoders, I recommend the following:

- The best one I've found is the **iZotope** VocalSynth plugin, available at `www.izotope.com`.
- **RAZOR** is another excellent vocoder plugin by Native Instruments, available at `www.native-instruments.com`.

Understanding MIDI

In order to use vocoders, we need to first know how to use **Musical Instrument Digital Interface (MIDI)**. MIDI is a way for software and electronic devices to pass music information from one device to another so that the new device knows what notes to play. In *Chapter 3, Composing with the Piano Roll*, we discussed how to record MIDI information to the piano roll. Once entered, notes in the piano roll act as MIDI information that can be passed between instrument plugins.

Passing MIDI information between plugins is useful in a few scenarios:

- Passing MIDI information is how you can communicate with hardware instrument devices. Hardware instruments use MIDI to give and receive information to and from your computer. If you want to play notes directly from FL Studio to or from your hardware device, you use MIDI. FL Studio has documentation and video tutorials to help connect your hardware MIDI devices at `http://support.image-line.com/redirect/MIDI_Out`.

- MIDI notes defined in one place can be sent to one or more instrument plugins at once. For example, channel rack **layers** allow you to use the same MIDI notes for multiple instruments.
- Some plugins require external MIDI input to work. Vocoders usually require the use of MIDI to operate. We will explore this feature extensively in this chapter.

Using vocoders

In this section, we will prepare MIDI for use in plugins. Then we'll route the MIDI notes into additional instruments and effects, such as vocoder effects. Although we'll specifically discuss vocoders in this chapter, any plugin that uses MIDI as an input will follow the same steps.

In our examples, we assume that you are using a vocal audio sample to feed into the vocoder. However, you do have the option of using any other sound instead of a vocal, such as a guitar, and this can be used to create interesting effects.

Harmonizing vocals with Pitcher

To illustrate vocoding, we will use a built-in FL Studio plugin called **Pitcher**, which comes with FL Studio Signature Edition and higher. Although it's not advertised as a vocoder, it has vocoder features, and most closely resembles how you use other vocoder plugins on the market. Let's learn how to use Pitcher:

1. Load up a vocal sample in the playlist. Either use an existing vocal sample or record a new audio vocal. We covered recording audio in *Chapter 8, Recording Live Audio and Vocal Processing*. This vocal will be the source that we will modulate in the vocoder.
2. Route the vocal to a free mixer track.
3. Let's create chords so that we have some MIDI notes. Load an instrument, such as FL Keys, in the channel rack and create some chords in the piano roll for the instrument.
4. Route the instrument to a free mixer channel.

5. The following screenshot shows an example of the chords you could create in the piano roll:

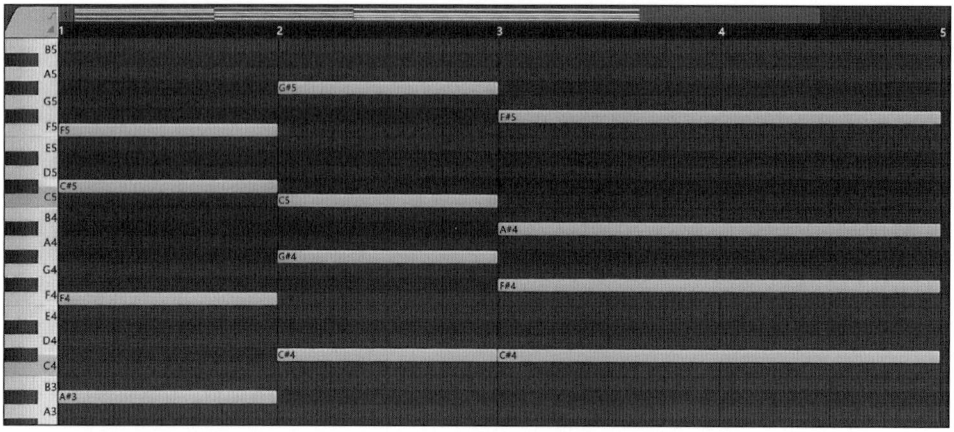

Figure 9.1 – Piano roll chords

The notes used in the chords should be in the same key as the rest of your song. When you play the notes, they should complement any other instruments playing. If the chords don't fit the rest of the song, your vocoding will not sound good when done.

The chords must complement the song. The vocal, however, can be in any key (even one from a different scale). It doesn't matter what note pitches the vocal uses as they will be changed by the vocoder. The only notes that matter are the notes that the carrier (vocoder plays), not the notes used by the vocal.

6. Add the vocal and the piano roll notes to your playlist so that they are in time with each other. Your playlist will now look something like the following screenshot:

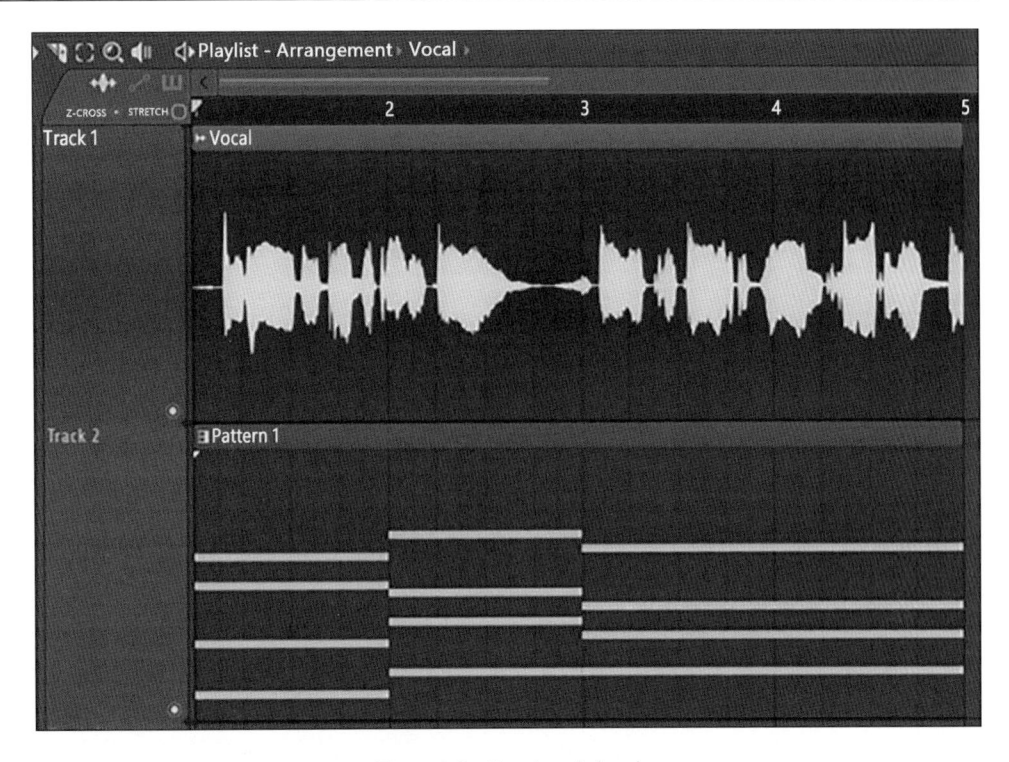

Figure 9.2 – Vocal and chords

In the preceding screenshot, we can see a vocal running in time with the chords we just created.

In the previous chapters of this book, we thought of the piano roll notes as belonging to the instrument playing them. It turns out that we can take these notes and send them anywhere, such as to plugin effects. We can do so with the **MIDI Out** plugin.

7. In the channel rack, load the **MIDI Out** plugin by pressing the + symbol and selecting **MIDI Out**.

8. Copy the chord notes from your FL Keys to **MIDI Out**. When you open up **MIDI Out**, you will see the following plugin:

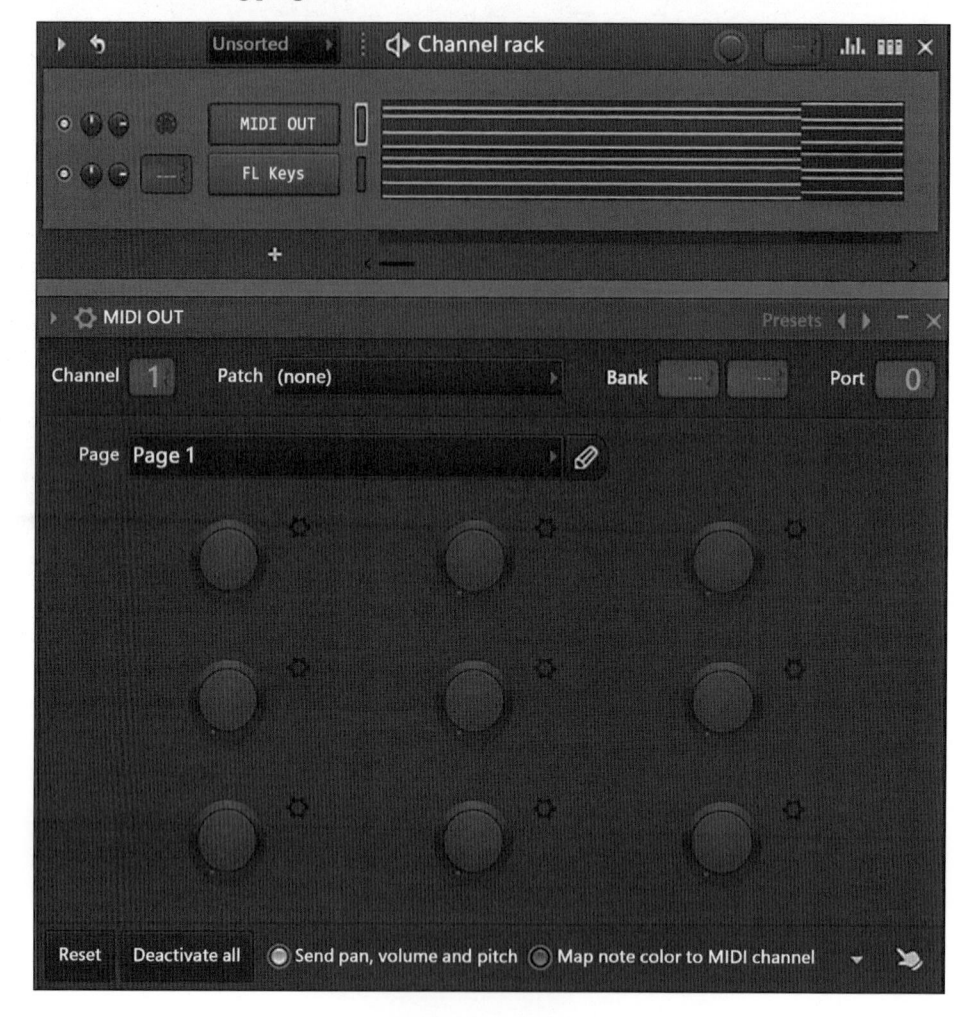

Figure 9.3 – MIDI Out

MIDI Out does not make any sound when you play it, as it is not an instrument. Rather, it's a controller that sends notes to other plugins.

9. At the top right of **MIDI Out**, you can see a **Port** value. Change this **Port** to a value other than **0**. Any MIDI notes played in **MIDI Out** will become available to any instrument or effect that receives signal from that port value:

Figure 9.4 – Assigning a port value

In the preceding screenshot, you can see I've chosen port 1. Remember the port value that you've chosen; you will need it in a moment.

10. In the mixer, select a channel track and left-click on any open slot, and then add the vocoder plugin effect of your choice. Once done, name it Vocoder. I am going to use FL Studio's **Pitcher**. Once added, your effects rack should look similar to the following screenshot:

Figure 9.5 – Loading Vocoder

11. Route the signal from the vocal channel to the vocoder channel. Do this by first selecting the vocal channel, then right-clicking on the **Vocoder** mixer channel arrow and choosing the **Route to this track only** option, as shown in the following screenshot:

Figure 9.6 – Routing the vocal to Vocoder

Our vocal has been routed to the vocoder channel and is accessible to the Pitcher plugin. Now we need to notify our vocoder plugin of the MIDI notes that are available to be used. Note that the instrument is not routed to Pitcher in this example, only the vocals. This is very important.

12. Open up the **Pitcher** plugin:

Figure 9.7 – Pitcher

13. Left-click to press down each of the **MIDI**, **OCTAVES**, and **HARMONIZE** buttons, as shown in the preceding screenshot.
14. At the bottom of **Pitcher**, the text **MIDI Input Port Number: ...** will appear. Left-click on **...** and drag to change the value to the **MIDI Out** port value you chose earlier. In my case, the value is **1**. It could be something different depending on how you routed the signal.
15. Play your playlist and be blown away by how Pitcher harmonizes your vocals.

Whoa, that sounds cool! What just happened to my vocals? Pitcher is a pitch-correction plugin. When it comes to generating harmonized vocals using MIDI, it's spectacular. It allows you to generate up to four voices controlled by the MIDI note melodies.

Pitcher uses the MIDI notes as filters. It generates copies of the vocal that is fed into it and filters them to hit only the MIDI note pitches.

Let's take a closer look at some of the Pitcher harmonizing controls, as shown in the following screenshot from left to right:

Figure 9.8 – Pitcher harmonizing controls

- **VOICE PANNING** allows you to pan the vocals left or right, from the highest-pitched MIDI note to the lowest. Panning the vocals will increase the stereo width and make the harmonies appear larger.
- The **REPLACE MIX** switch allows you to hear the original vocals or to just play the harmonized vocals.
- **VEL** (velocity) controls the harmonized vocal velocity. You must turn off **OCTAVES** for this feature to work.
- **STEREO SPREAD** allows you to increase the overall mono or stereo effect.
- **GENDER** allows you to control the formant effect. Turning left will make the vocal deeper, while turning right will make the vocal sound higher. **FORMANT** turns on or off the gender control. If you see a bright orange light on the **FORMANT** button, then this means it's *on*.
- **FINE TUNE** adjusts the output tuning of the plugin.

So far, we've looked at how you can generate harmonies for your vocals using vocoding. We've had an introduction to vocoding. Now let's really get our hands dirty with another vocoder. Next, we'll explore the FL Studio plugin Vocodex.

Using Vocodex

Vocodex is a traditional vocoder and allows you to modulate a vocal. It is used a little differently than most vocoder plugins though, as it doesn't require MIDI Out to operate. Instead, you can directly use an instrument sound in the mixer.

Let's begin using Vocodex:

1. To start, you will need to already have a vocal and an instrument playing chord MIDI notes routed to the mixer. We already did this in *steps 1–6* in the preceding section on *Harmonizing vocals with Pitcher*; go through those steps first if you haven't already.

   In the **Vocoder** mixer channel that we created earlier, mute any other effects and add the Vocodex plugin, as shown in the following screenshot:

   Figure 9.9 – Adding Vocodex

2. Select the **FL Keys** mixer channel and the **Vocal** mixer channel and route them to the **Vocoder** channel by right-clicking on the **Vocoder** mixer channel arrow and selecting the **Route to this track only** option, as shown in the following screenshot:

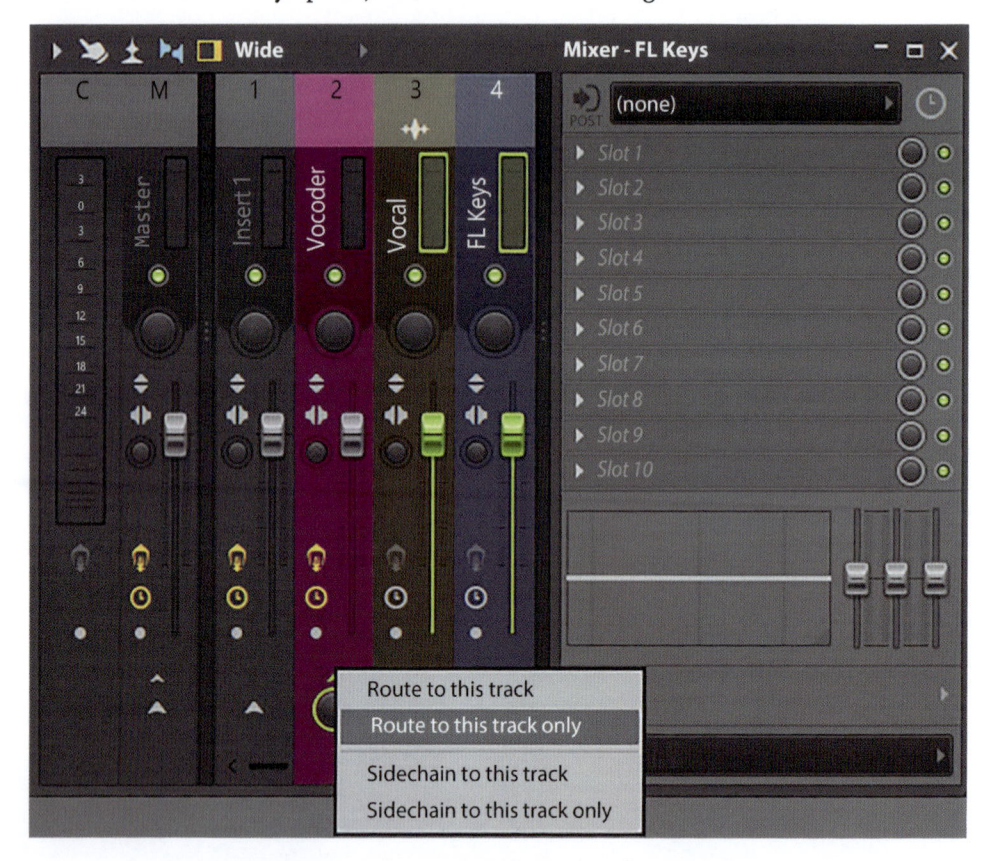

Figure 9.10 – Routing the instrument and vocal to Vocoder

3. Open **Vocodex**. At the top, you'll see the modulator sidechain input port numbers next to the text **L-R ENCODING**. These are waiting to receive the modulator (instrument sound) and the carrier (vocal sound).

    L-R ENCODING refers to the left and right channels in your mixer. Right-click on one of the sidechain input number boxes and you'll see your available options. Choose the vocal for the modulator (**MOD**) sidechain input number box and the instrument for the carrier (**CAR**) sidechain input number box:

Figure 9.11 – Setting up ports in Vocodex

When you play your sound, you'll hear your vocals harmonized using the MIDI notes and with vocoding effects applied to it. There are lots of controls that you can play with to tweak the vocoder sound.

The following is a summary of the controls starting from the top:

1. **WET** controls the amount of vocoding that is applied. **SG (Sound Goodizer)** applies compression as used in the Sound Goodizer plugin. **MOD** (modulation) controls how much modulator input is outputted; increasing the level of this will allow more of the dry vocal through.

   Modulator pass-through high-pass frequency (high-pass filter) sets the high-pass filter threshold cutoff. Only sounds higher than the threshold of the modulator will be used.

2. **CAR** (carrier) pass-through low-pass frequency (low-pass filter) sets the low-pass filter threshold cutoff. Only sounds lower than the threshold of the carrier will be used.

3. The carrier-added noise highpass (**HP**) frequency allows noise to pass through. A little noise can help make speech easier to understand.

4. **Contour** turns the volume envelope on the modulator and carrier on or off. **DRAFT** lowers the CPU usage but may result in lower quality. **THREADED** allows multi-core processing.

5. Under the **Options** (down arrow) in the top right of Vocodex, you'll see an option for **Detect modulator noise level**, which generates a noise mapping from the source to try to identify the background noise. Use this on a quiet section of your audio; then you can select the subtractive denoising option to denoise the background noise.

6. Back on the left side, you'll see the **HOLD**, **ATT**, and **REL** time controls, which adjust the sound envelope. **HOLD** allows the note to play for a longer length of time. The attack control determines how quickly the carrier responds to the modulator. Increasing the value will create a smoother sound. The release control determines how long the vocoder effect will last. **PEAK** and **RMS** determine whether you want the envelope to respond to the audio peaks or RMS level (more of an average sound).

7. The bandwidth control determines how wide the frequency bands are. Smaller values create a thinner sound. Larger values create a fuller sound. The *modulator bandwidth multiplier* adds more resonances at a low level and airy sounds at higher levels.

8. *Modulator pitch shift* increases the **FORMANT** value. *Modulator unison shift* allows you to add levels of voices. Drag on the modulator unison order box to increase the number of voices.

9. The *unison panner* allows you to pan the unison voices. **ORDER** allows you to choose how much you want the vocoder to sound like a synth or like a human vocal.

10. **Bands - Distribution** sets the number of bands to be used. Lowering the band distribution will make the vocoder sound more synthetic. A higher value will make it sound more like a human.

11. Below **Envelope Follower**, you can see the *Editor target*, which contains additional controls, as follows:

    - *Band gain multiplier* allows you to choose the volume for selected frequencies.
    - *Band panning* lets you pan the sound for selected frequencies.
    - The *band gain offset* allows you to choose how much of the carrier sound you want to hear for selected frequencies. Increasing it will allow you to hear more of the carrier sound.
    - The *modulator noise level* determines the minimum threshold level that needs to be reached before you can hear the sound. By default, it's set to **0**.
    - *Modulator pass-through* determines how much of the modulator you can hear.
    - The *envelope follower* contains envelope controls for setting the hold, attack, and release.
    - *Band distribution* allows you to choose how many bands are used for selected frequencies.
    - *Bandwidth* allows you to determine the size of the bands around selected frequencies.
    - *Modulator pitch shift* allows you to adjust the pitch of selected frequencies.
    - *Saturation mix* allows you to add distortion.
    - *Carrier Tone* provides you with several filter sounds that can be used to shape the carrier sound.

Vocoder best practices

Here are some tips for using any vocoder plugin:

- Vocoders are an excellent way to design creative vocal instruments. If you want a song to stick out and be instantly recognizable, using a vocoder effect is a way to do so.
- Vocoder vocals tend to take center focus of the listener's attention. If you're using vocals, plan for them to be the lead melody or layered with the lead melody.
- When subtly layered and played at the same time with a regular vocal, vocoder sounds can add thickness to the lead vocal.
- If you find that your vocoder sound is not quite right, consider changing the instrument used as the carrier sound.
- Vocoder effects on vocals work really well when combined with vocal chopping, which we will discuss next.

Creating vocal chops

In this section, we'll learn how to create vocal chops. **Vocal chops** are chopped-up fragments of vocal samples. You hear them most often in electronic dance music, and they are often applied to vocal samples after being processed through a vocoder.

If you're unsure what vocal chops are, consider listening to some of the following songs, which use vocal chops:

- **Porter Robinson & Madeon** – *Shelter*
- **Skrillex** – *First Of The Year (Equinox)*
- **Skrillex** – *Summit (feat. Ellie Goulding)*

In the upcoming section, we will assume that you are creating vocal chops, but the same techniques can be used to chop up any audio sample. For example, you can just as easily slice up a guitar or drum audio sample.

If your aim is simple, you could slice and dice samples on the playlist just by cutting up a sample manually with the slice tool.

On any sample in the playlist, you can quickly chop up the sample by left-clicking the top-left corner of a sample, navigating to **Chop**, and then choosing one of the chopping presets:

Chapter 9 275

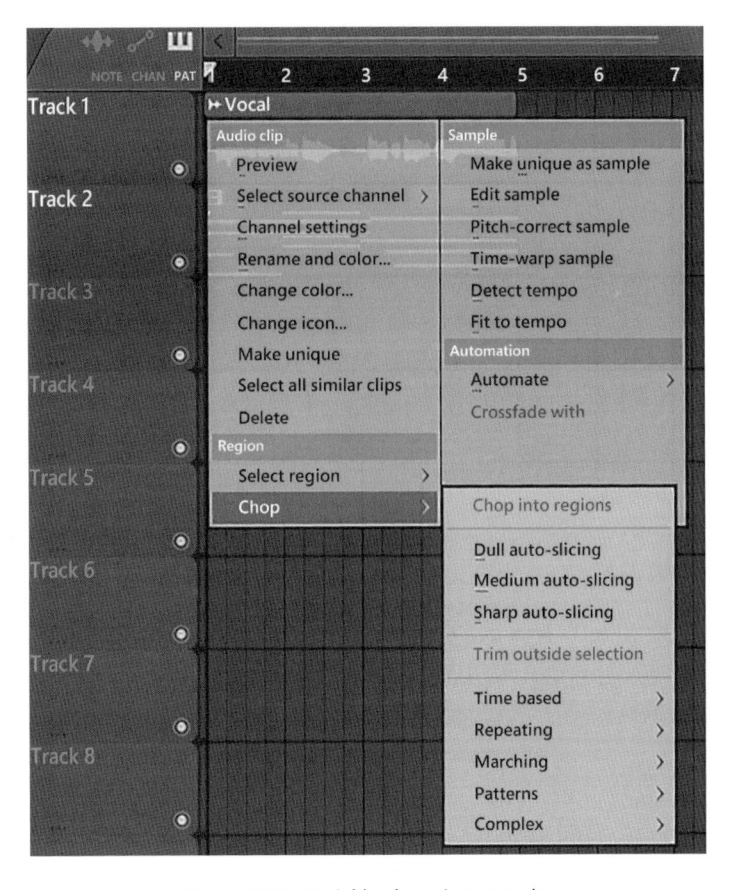

Figure 9.12 – Quickly chopping samples

You have options for **Time based, Repeating, Marching, Patterns,** and **Complex** vocal chopping presets. If you just need some quick glitchy sounds, this chopping approach may be all you need.

There are tools, such as **Slicex**, that provide you with more precise control over chopping samples. Most specifically, it gives you control over chopping and the pitch of the vocal chop. We will explore Slicex next.

Using Slicex to create vocal chops

Slicex is a native FL Studio plugin that is intended for slicing and dicing samples. It's especially useful for creating vocal chops.

Before creating vocal chops, you need to have a vocal audio sample. You can use any audio sample. If you are applying effects to the vocal before chopping it, you will need to render the sound into an audio wave before chopping. If you need a refresher on rendering (freezing) audio, we covered it in *Chapter 4, Routing to the Mixer and Applying Automation*.

Let's create vocal chops with Slicex:

1. Create a new pattern and add it to the playlist.
2. In the channel rack, insert the **Slicex** plugin. Make the **Slicex** plugin detached by going to the top-left corner of **Slicex**, clicking the plugin option down arrow button, and then choosing **Detached**.
3. If you're like me, the first time you see Slicex you'll instantly feel overwhelmed. What is this monstrous beastly plugin? Don't worry—you won't need to use most of these features, except in very special cases where you want to tinker with the finest details. Most of the time, chopping vocal samples is a very straightforward task, and we'll look at the easiest way.
4. Drag your chosen audio sample (such as a vocal) into **Slicex**. One way is to drag it directly from the browser. Another way is to load the sample up directly in **Slicex** by finding its location on your computer and dragging it in. A third way is to double-left-click on the audio sample in the playlist to reveal the waveform and drag the audio from there into **Slicex**, as shown in the following screenshot:

Figure 9.13 – Dragging the sample into Slicex

Once you've dragged in your audio sample, Slicex may attempt to automatically slice up the sample. This occurs if there are obvious transient sounds. If this doesn't occur automatically, you can force Slicex to do an auto-slice by clicking the **Medium auto-slicing** button, as shown in the following screenshot:

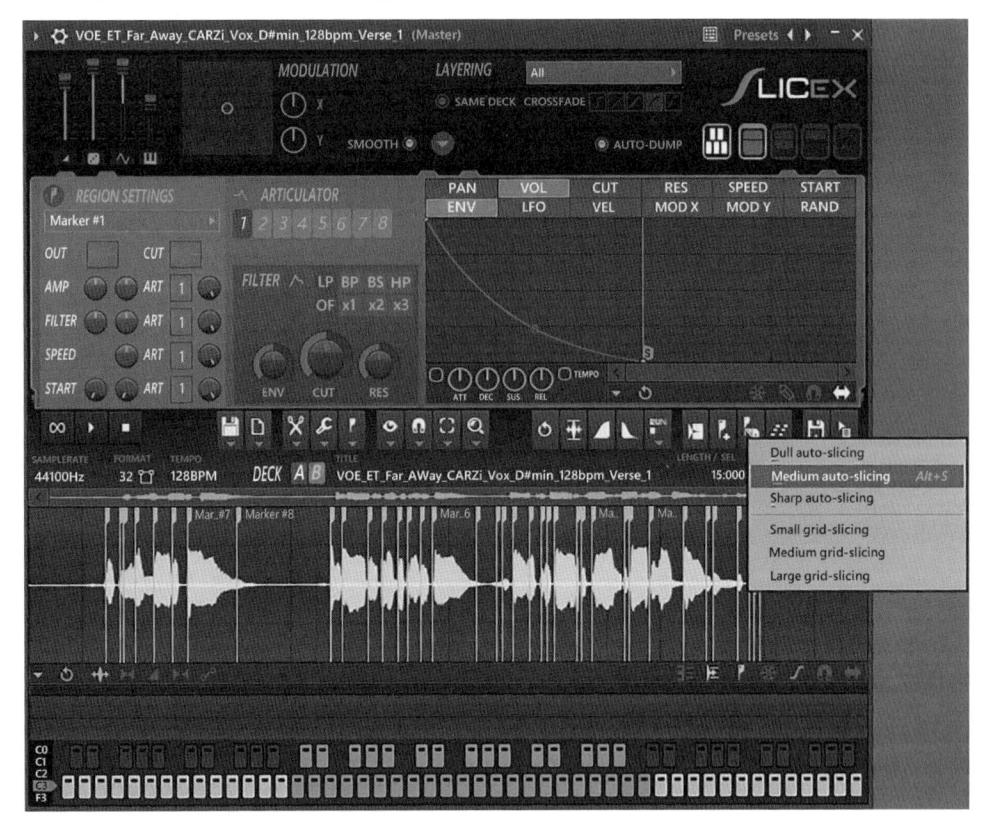

Figure 9.14 – Dragging the sample into Vocodex

Auto-slicing may or may not do a good job of slicing. Maybe this is good enough for you. If not, you will have to go in and manually assign markers to create chops, which we will discuss next.

If you play your pattern, you'll see the cursor in **Slicex** move through the slices of sampled audio.

Every time you see a marker, this is the start of a new chop. Slicex contains many controls that can be used to place markers and choose where a chop begins and ends. For example, on the waveform, you can left-click and drag to move the position of a marker left or right. You can right-click at the top of a marker and see the available options, such as deleting the marker.

5. By right-clicking on the waveform, it will play a selected sample chop. You can replay the sample by pressing *Space* on your keyboard. You can then move forward and backward through the chops by using your left and right keyboard arrows.

6. Once you're happy with the chops themselves, we can arrange the chop timing. In the channel rack, find the **Slicex** plugin and open it up in the piano roll:

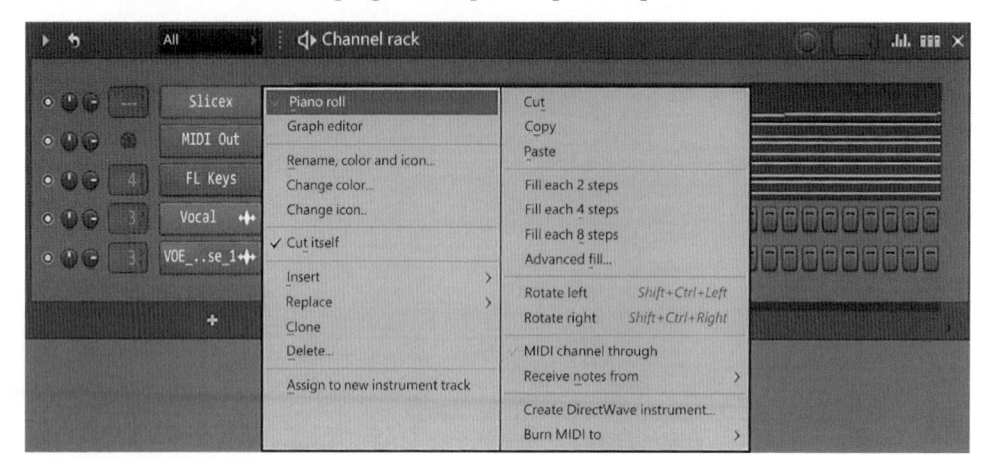

Figure 9.15 – Slicex in the piano roll

In the piano roll, you'll see that the audio sample has been sliced up by markers, as shown in the following screenshot:

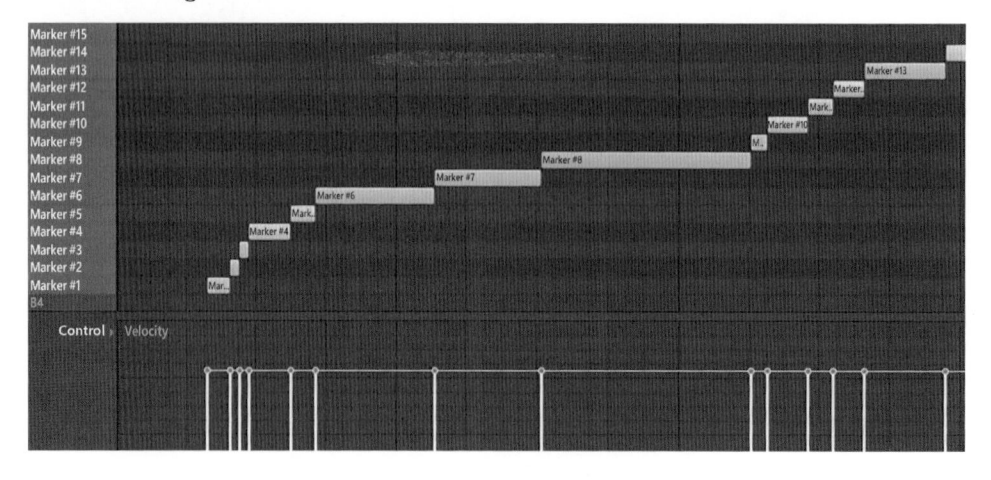

Figure 9.16 – Vocal chopping in the piano roll

7. Play the pattern.

You'll see that the vocal chops played just like instrument notes moving from left to right. Each marker represents a chop. You can trigger chops to play by adding notes. You can trigger a chop to occur multiple times by adding additional notes. For example, in the following screenshot, we can see that I've triggered **Marker #1** chops by playing the same note three times:

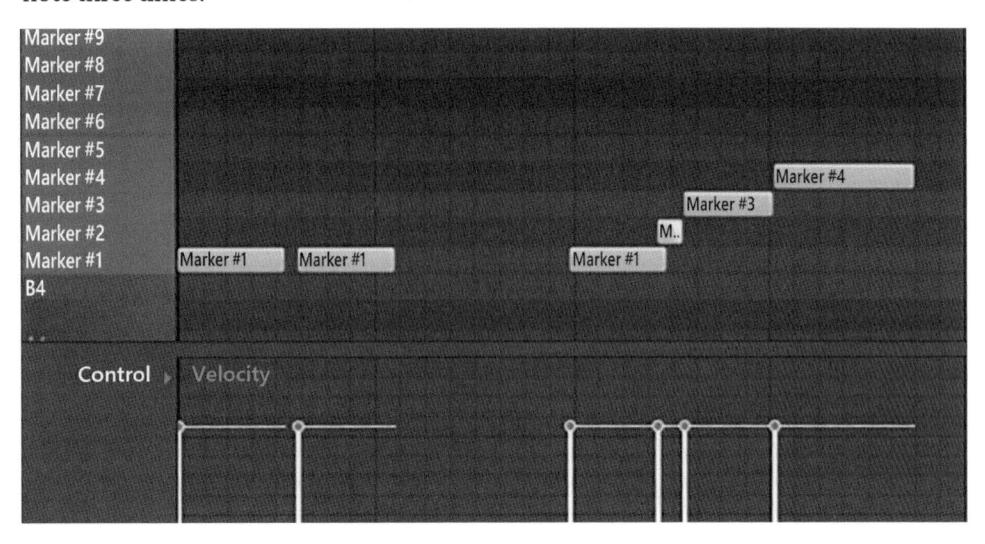

Figure 9.17 – Retriggering a vocal chop

8. By arranging the timing of your chops, you can create rhythmic vocal chop melodies. For the icing on the top, you can adjust the pitch of any given vocal chop. To do so, left-click on the **Control** button at the bottom left of the piano roll and choose the **Note fine pitch** option:

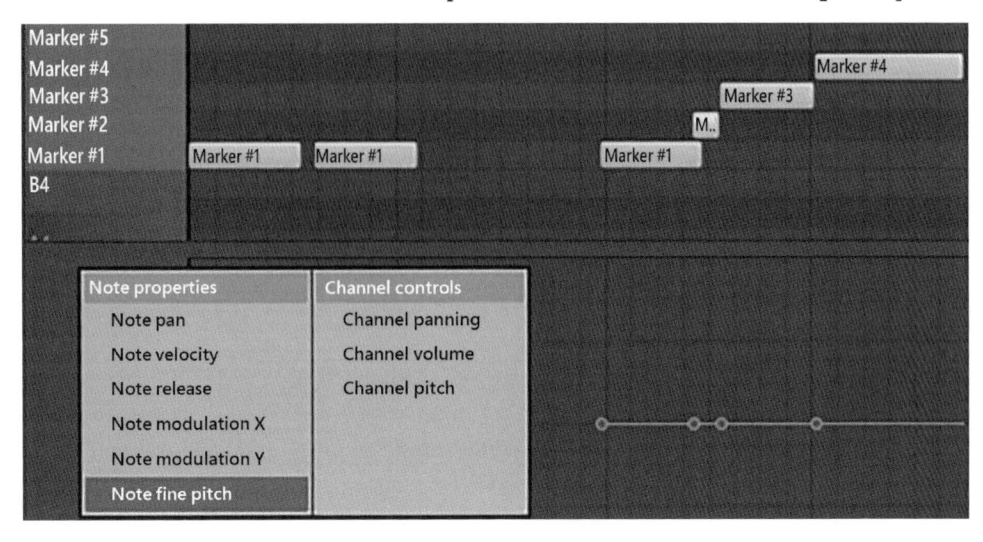

Figure 9.18 – Note fine pitch

9. You can adjust the pitch of notes by left-clicking in the **Event Editor**. Anything higher than its default position will increase the pitch; anything lower will decrease the pitch. You can see an example of this in the following screenshot:

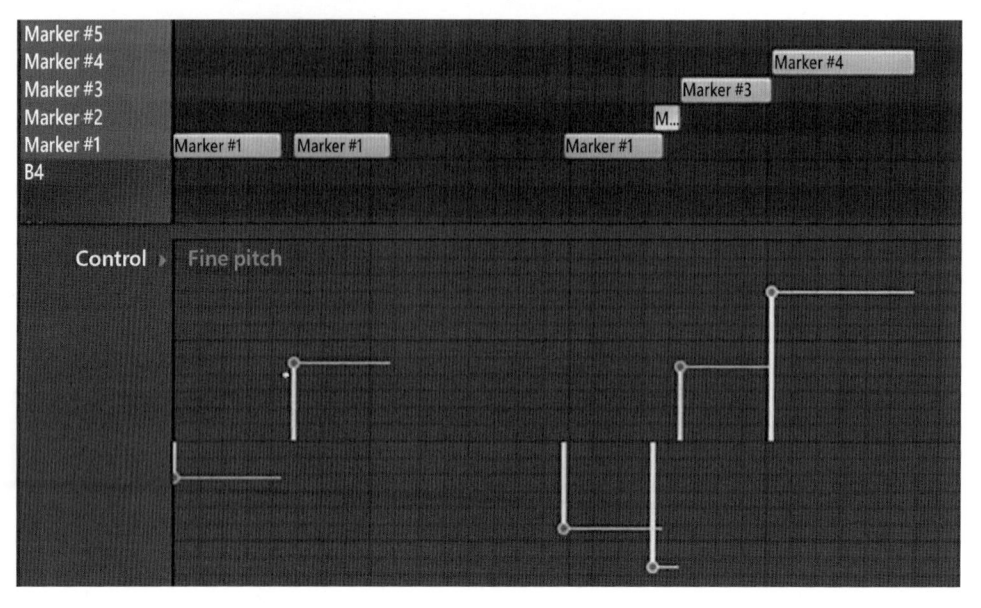

Figure 9.19 – Adjusting note fine pitch

You can see the amount of pitch change in the hint panel at the top left of the screen. In the following screenshot, you can see that we've adjusted the pitch by 700 percent:

Figure 9.20 – Pitch change value

100 percent means 1 pitch higher. So, 700 percent means 7 pitches higher than the original sample pitch.

This is all you need to create vocal chops. You could stop here and have more than enough to work with. For the ambitious though, there are lots of additional controls in Slicex.

Chapter 9

Let's take a brief look at some of the most useful features:

- The *drag/copy sample/selection tool* allows you to take any highlighted chops as individual audio samples and drag them anywhere, such as the playlist. In the following screenshot, you can see that **Marker #29** has been selected and can now be dragged:

Figure 9.21 – Dragging the chop

Why might you want to drag an individual chop? Sometimes, you may find it easier to edit the timing of a vocal chop in the playlist. Dragging a chop into the playlist could make it easier to arrange the timing of the sample, rather than having to create an additional Slicex pattern each time you want to use the chop.

Figure 9.22 – Slicex global controls

At the top of **Slicex**, you can see the global effects that get applied to all chops in Slicex:

- *Master level* adjusts the output volume level.
- *Master randomness level* increases any randomness effects applied in the audio editor.
- *Master LFO* increases any **Low Frequency Oscillator** (**LFO**) effects applied in the audio editor.
- *Master pitch* changes all slice pitches.

- **MODULATION X** and **Y** controls can be automated and linked to parameters later on in the plugin.
- The **LAYERING** section allows you to create multiple decks of sample chops if you wanted to play a drum pad with samples.

The audio editor section contains controls that allow you to manipulate the sound of individual vocal chops. In the following screenshot, we can see that we're looking at a chop labeled **Marker #29**.

Figure 9.23 – Region settings

All the following settings that we have adjusted will be applied to that specific chop sample:

- **AMP** (panning) allows you to control the panning. The knob to the right of the panning button lets you control the volume.
- The **FILTER** knobs let you control the frequencies and resonance.
- **SPEED** controls the pitch.
- **START** controls the delay time for when the sample begins.
- To the right of **AMP**, **FILTER**, **SPEED**, and **START**, you can see the word **ART** (articulator), which allows you to assign an articulator variable control value. For each articulator, you can also adjust the envelope. Essentially, this is just there to help you map controls together.

The **FILTER** section provides a series of envelope controls that allow you to choose between different types of filters that can be applied to the sound.

On the right in the editor target section, you can see a visual grid that allows you to automate any of the controls as they are played.

Chapter 9

The **Tools** button (the wrench symbol) has a list of features, as shown in the following screenshot. I encourage you to experiment with them:

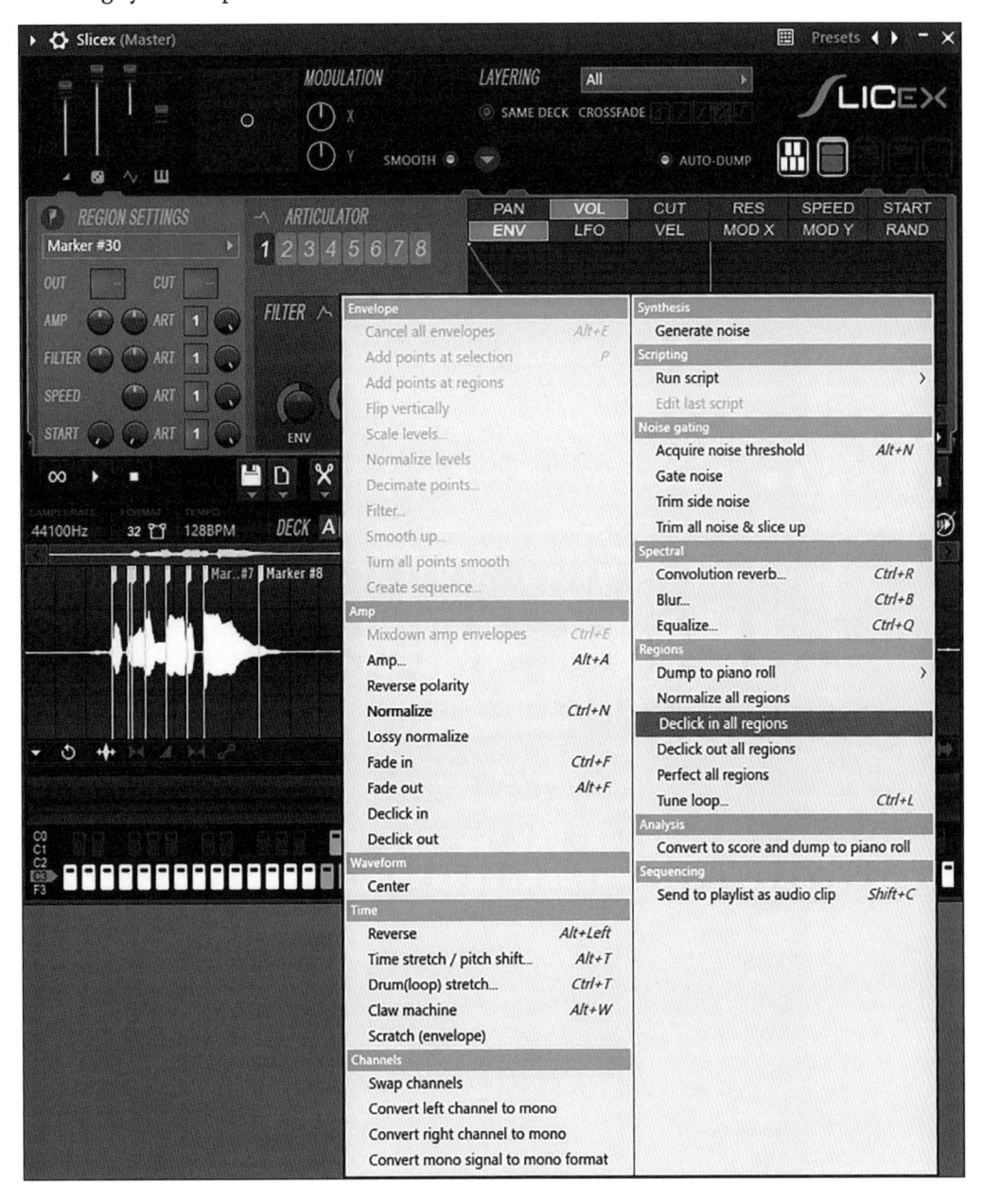

Figure 9.24 – Tools options

Of the many controls listed, here are some of the most important ones:

- **Gate noise** removes unwanted background noise. **Trim side noise** will remove unwanted noise before or after your chop.
- **Normalize all regions** will normalize your audio volume and increase its loudness level.
- **Declick in all regions** and **Declick out all regions** can help remove unwanted clicking sounds that occur when chopping.

Under the regions section (marker icon), you can assign the chopped-up sample to another device to be played back, as shown in the following screenshot:

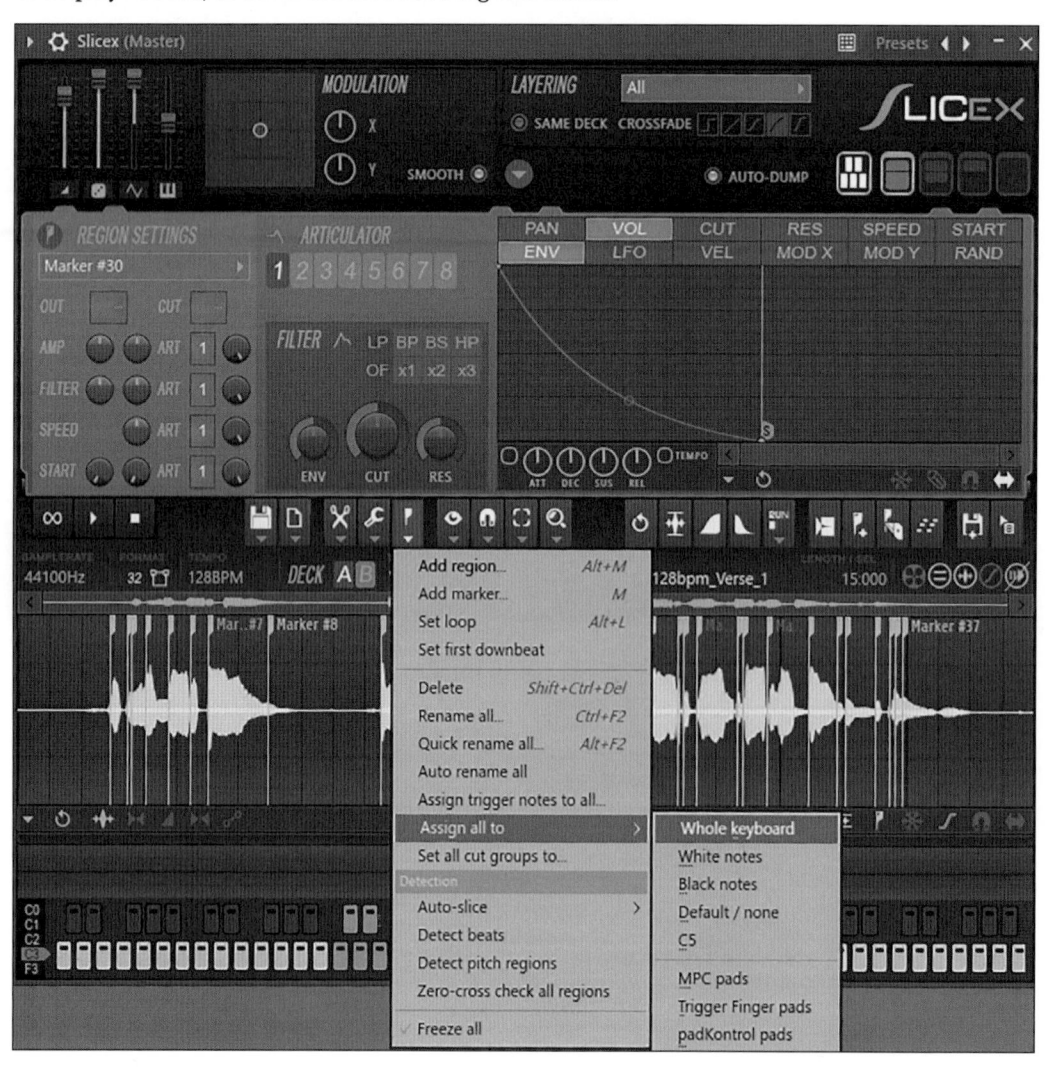

Figure 9.25 – Slicex global controls

Once assigned, you can trigger the playback of individual sample chops on another device, such as an MPC pad. If you like playing live and using hardware, then this is for you.

Vocal chopping considerations

Here are some things you should consider when creating vocal chops:

- Vocal chops tend to take the center focus of the listener. Plan for this accordingly.
- Vocal chops may sound better at different pitches; consider transposing the vocal chop pitch higher or lower.
- Consider adding distortion effects.
- Sidechaining can be applied to the vocal chops.
- You could apply any effects and filters to your samples before chopping them up. In this chapter, we suggested using vocoders before chopping up your samples.
- You can chop up any sample, not just vocals. Guitars, drums, and synths work great too.

Congratulations! You now know how to chop up samples.

Summary

In this chapter, we learned about some plugin effects that you can apply to your vocals. These effects can enhance your vocals and give your songs a distinctive quality.

We learned how to route MIDI notes to other instruments and effects. We also learned how to generate harmonies for your vocals using Pitcher. We learned how to use vocoders, such as Vocodex. Finally, we learned how to create vocal chops and slice up your samples using Slicex.

In the next chapter, we will explore glitch effects and create our own instruments and effects.

10
Creating Your Own Instruments and Effects

In this chapter, we'll learn how to create effects with sounds, transform samples into playable instruments, and create custom instruments and effect chains that can be reused in other projects. We'll start off with a relatively simple effect called glitch effects, and work toward more advanced effects such as Patcher.

In this chapter, we will cover the following topics:

- Understanding what glitch effects are
- Creating glitch effects with Gross Beat
- Creating instruments with DirectWave
- Creating custom effect chains with Patcher
- Using Patcher presets
- Using VFX Sequencer to create arpeggiated patterns

Understanding glitch effects

Glitches are the sound of audio device failure. When a hardware music player fails to work, various sounds can occur, such as stuttering, scratching, stretching, and reversing. When unintended, these indicate that something went wrong. When intended, glitch sounds can be a creative tool to make your sounds feel more artificial and more mechanical.

Glitch effects can be used in a lot of situations, such as the following:

- Transitioning between one song section to another
- Fading instrument sounds in or out
- Creating movement within a sound

Here are some of the best glitch plugins on the market:

- FL Studio's **Gross Beat**. Included with FL Studio Signature Edition and higher. We'll learn how to use Gross Beat in the upcoming pages.
- Izotope's **Stutter Edit**, available at `https://www.izotope.com/`.
- dBlue's **Glitch 2**, available at `https://illformed.com/`.
- Sugar Bytes's **Effectrix**, available at `https://sugar-bytes.de/effectrix`.

Creating glitch effects with Gross Beat

Gross Beat is a plugin for creating effects such as beat-synced glitches, stutters, repetitions, scratches, and gating effects.

The easiest way to understand what Gross Beat does is by using it on an audio sample:

1. Add an audio sample to the playlist.
2. Route the audio sample to an empty mixer track.
3. Add the **Gross Beat** plugin to the mixer channel. Open Gross Beat. You will see a screen similar to the following:

Chapter 10

Figure 10.1 – Gross Beat

The left side of Gross Beat lists the time and volume effect presets. The right side contains a visual grid allowing you to draw and modify time- and volume-based effects.

Gross Beat contains two types of effects: **time-travel envelope** effects and **volume envelope** effects. Time-travel effects play with the speed of the audio playthrough. You can speed it up, slow it down, or reverse it with precise control. Volume effects control the level of the audio. They can be used separately or in combination. You can tell which type of effect is currently selected by the symbols and text at the bottom.

In the following screenshot, we can see that the time-travel envelope is currently selected because the time envelope symbol is highlighted:

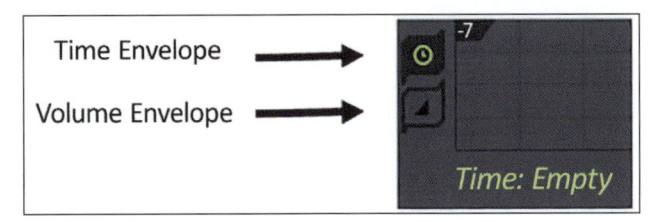

Figure 10.2 – Time and volume

4. Time and volume effect presets are listed on the left-side panel. While playing your sound in the playlist, left-click on some of the presets to see how they affect your sound. Time-based effects will slow down or repeat the previous beats of your sample. Volume effects will add volume variation, such as volume gating effects, sidechaining, or fading. I encourage you to experiment by trying out different effect presets:

Empty	Basic 1	Basic 2	Basic 3
Basic 4	Basic 5	Basic 6	Basic 7
Basic 8	Basic 9	Basic 10	Basic 11
Complex 1	Complex 2	Complex 3	Complex 4
Complex 5	Complex 6	Complex 7	Complex 8
Complex 9	Complex 10	Complex 11	Complex 12
Chaos 1	Chaos 2	Chaos 3	Chaos 4
Chaos 5	Chaos 6	Chaos 7	Chaos 8
Chaos 9	Chaos 10	Chaos 11	Chaos 12
Empty	2 Beat Gate	1 Beat Gate	1/2 Bt Gate
1/3 Bt Gate	1/4 Bt Gate	1/6 Bt Gate	1/8 Bt Gate
Trance Gt 1	Trance Gt 2	Trance Gt 3	Trance Gt 4
Saw Gate 1	Saw Gate 2	1st Step	1st Stp Fade
2 Step Gate	Off Beat	1/4 Dynamic	1/4 Swing
1/4 Gate Out	1/4 Gate In	Spd Up Gate	Slw Dn Gate
End Fade	End Gate	Tremelo Slw	Tremelo Fst
Sidechain	Drum Loop	Copter	AM
Fade In	Fade Out	Fade Out In	Mute

Figure 10.3 – Time and volume presets

If you want to automate how an effect is turned on and off throughout your song in the playlist, go through the following steps:

1. Left-click on the time or volume effect you want to add. Right-click on the preset effect. Menu options will appear. Select **Copy value** – this will copy the effect.
2. Right-click again on the effect preset and select **Create automation clip**, as shown in the following screenshot:

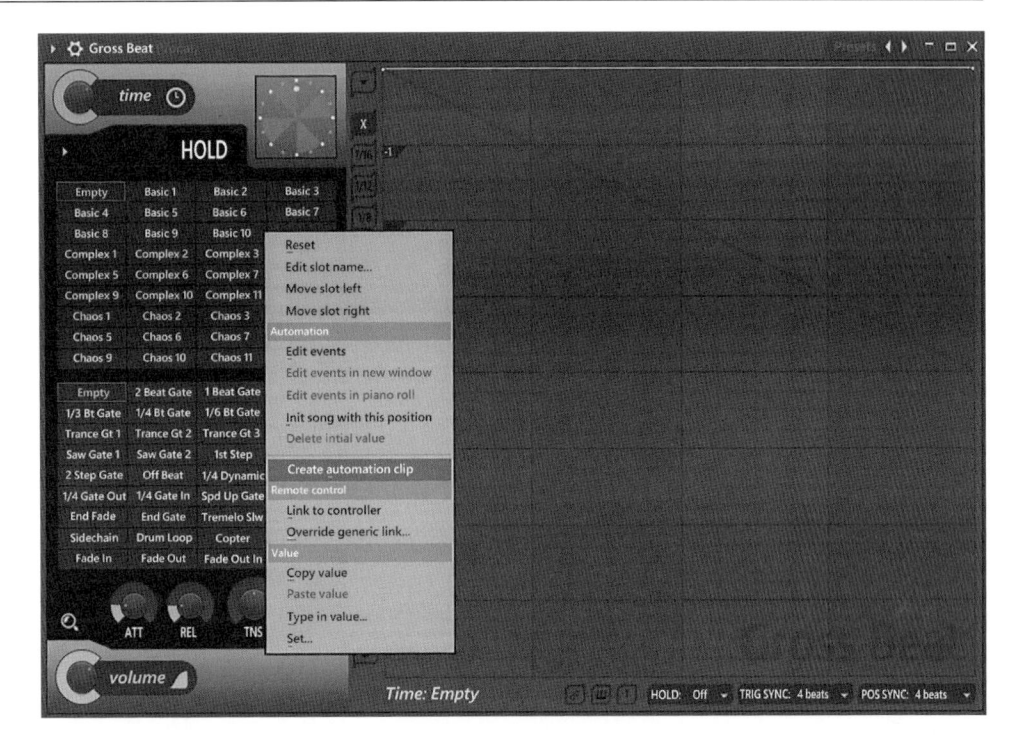

Figure 10.4 – Automate effect

An automation clip will appear in the playlist. By default, the effect is turned on:

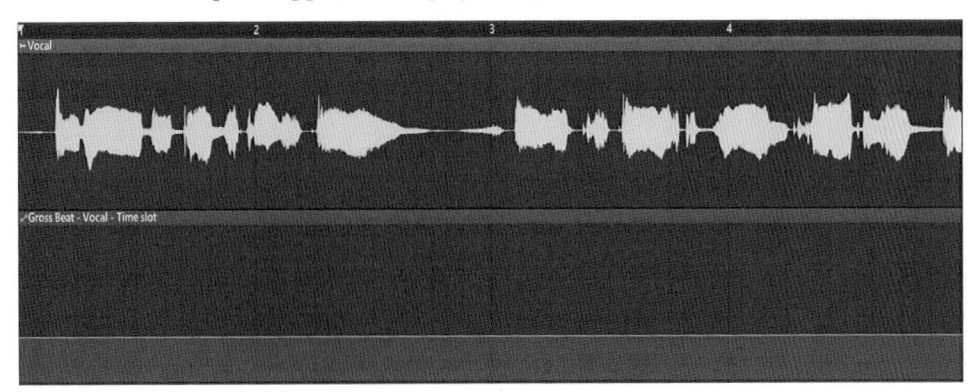

Figure 10.5 – Automation in the playlist

3. Left-click and drag the automation key points down to **0**, as shown in the following screenshot. This will turn the effect off:

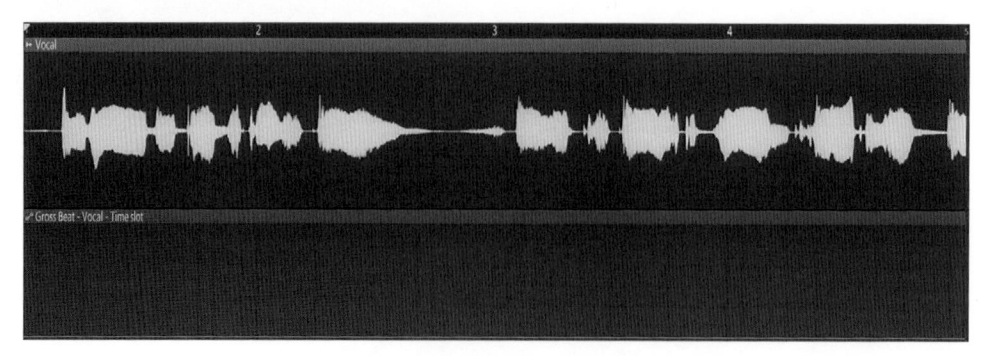

Figure 10.6 – Reduce level to 0

4. At the position that you want the glitch effect to activate, right-click in the automation clip twice and paste the value that you previously copied from Gross Beat. This will paste the preset effect you copied earlier.

5. Adjust the automation curve so that it looks like the following screenshot:

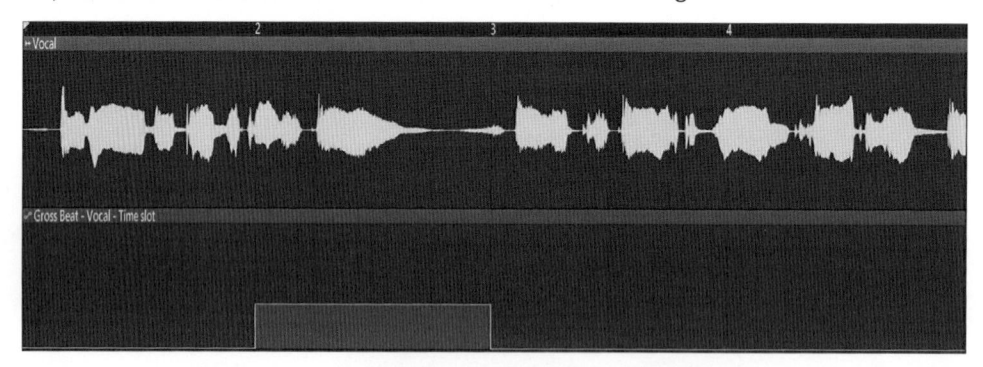

Figure 10.7 – Pasting the value that was copied in Gross Beat

In the preceding screenshot, the Gross Beat effect activates in bar 2 and deactivates in bar 3.

Congratulations! You can now turn Gross Beat effects on and off. Using this method, you can switch between Gross Beat effects at different stages of your song by copying and pasting different effect values. This method can be applied anywhere in your mixer, including in a mix bus to affect multiple sounds at the same time.

Gross Beat presets

In the top corner of Gross Beat, you'll find the **Presets** dropdown. Clicking it will display a list of presets:

Chapter 10

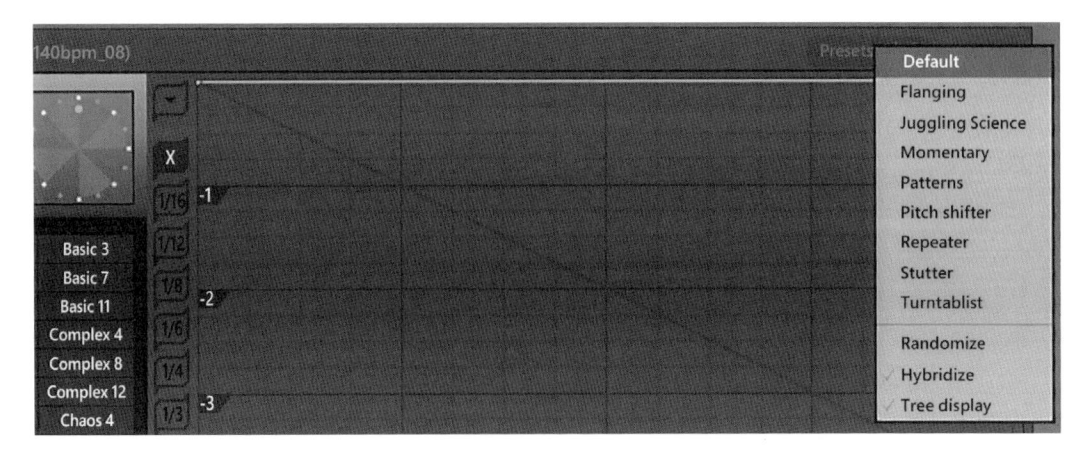

Figure 10.8 – Gross Beat presets

Selecting one of the options will change the dashboard of time and volume effects available to choose from. In the following screenshot, we've selected the **Momentary** preset:

Figure 10.9 – New time and volume effects

On the left-side dashboard, a new list of time and volume effect presets will populate. There are a ton of time and volume effects available. I encourage you to explore the dropdown presets to see all the options that are available.

Mapping time and volume effects to a sample

You can drag an audio sample into Gross Beat. Doing so will generate time or volume effects based on the waveform. This is easiest understood by seeing it in action:

1. Find an audio sample in the browser. Use a drum loop sample or a loop with punctuated transients for the best results.
2. In Gross Beat, choose either the **time travel** envelope or **volume** envelope symbol. This will determine the type of effect we are generating.
3. Left-click and drag the sample audio waveform into Gross Beat. Gross Beat will analyze the sample and generate an automation point based on the sample. You can see how Gross Beat looks after you have dragged in a drum sample in the following screenshot:

Chapter 10

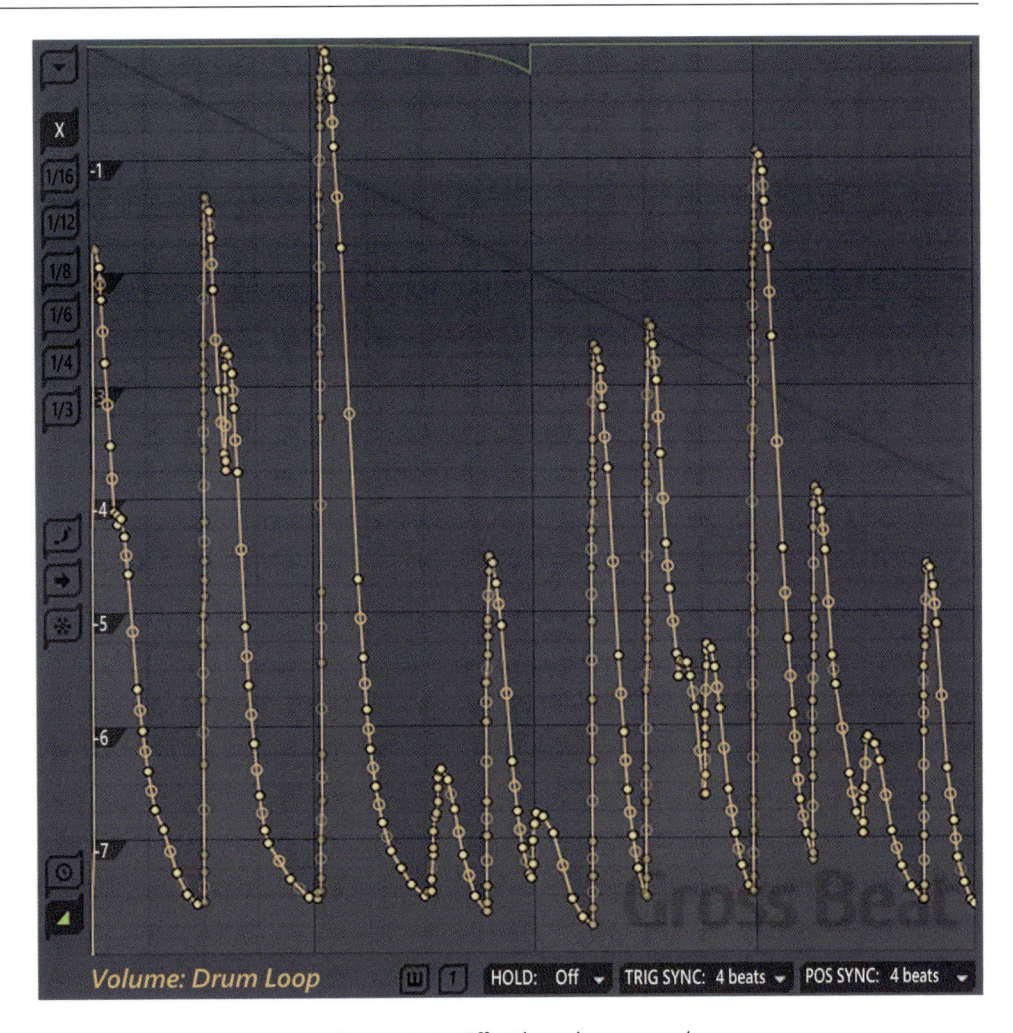

Figure 10.10 – Effect based on a sample

If you play the sample in the playlist, you'll be able to hear the Gross Beat effect applied.

Gross Beat sequencer

Gross Beat contains a sequence generator to produce automation curves that can be used for **time** and **volume** effects. This allows you to quickly create new effects with ease.

To load up the sequencer, go to **Options | Create sequence...** as shown in the following screenshot:

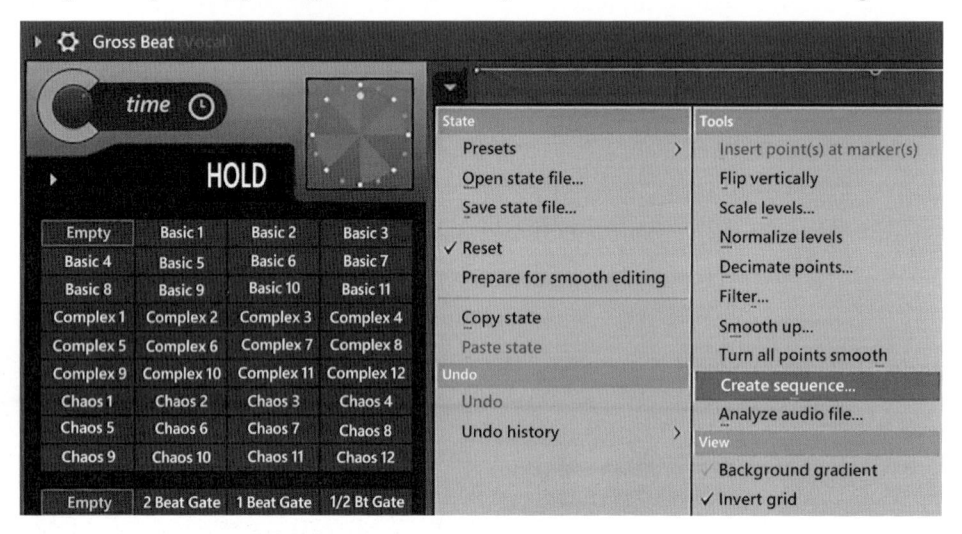

Figure 10.11 – Load Gross Beat sequencer

A window will pop up showing additional controls:

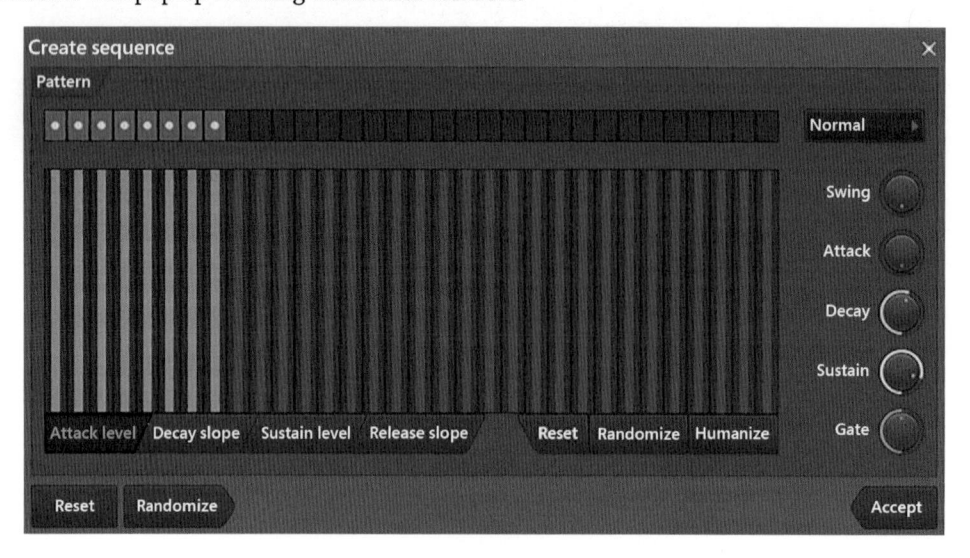

Figure 10.12 – Gross Beat sequencer

In the sequence generator, you'll discover some controls for creating Gross Beat automation curves. Here's a brief description of the controls. These are intuitive, so you will quickly learn their function if you adjust them while playing the sample:

- *Off/on hold/stick* allow you to create additional automation curves. You can add or remove them by left-clicking on the buttons.
- **Mode** allows you to toggle between a single or double version of the automation curves.
- The *arpeggiator increment* allows you to increase the size of the curves. What the curve changes is dictated by the **Attack level**, **Decay slope**, **Sustain level**, or **Release slope** that is selected.
- **Randomize** generates random curves.
- **Humanize** tries to make the automation curves feel less robotic.
- On the far right, you'll see global envelope controls for **Swing**, **Attack**, **Decay**, **Sustain**, and **Gate**.
- At the very bottom, you'll see a **Randomize** button, which generates random settings for all the parameters.

We've just scratched the surface of what Gross Beat can do. If you want more features and examples, check out the FL Studio Gross Beat video tutorials at http://support.image-line.com/redirect/GrossBeat_Videos.

We've learned how to create glitch effects. Next, let's learn how to create your own instruments from audio samples.

Creating instruments with DirectWave

DirectWave is a native FL Studio plugin sampler. Among other things, it allows you to take any single audio sample and generate additional pitches for the sound. Let's create instruments with DirectWave:

1. Add the DirectWave plugin to the channel rack.
2. Locate an audio sample you'd like to convert into an instrument. This works best with one-shot samples or sampled instruments. You can find a list of samples and instruments intended for use in DirectWave in the browser, under the Packs folder.

3. Drag the sample or sampled instrument into DirectWave in the channel rack, as shown in the following screenshot:

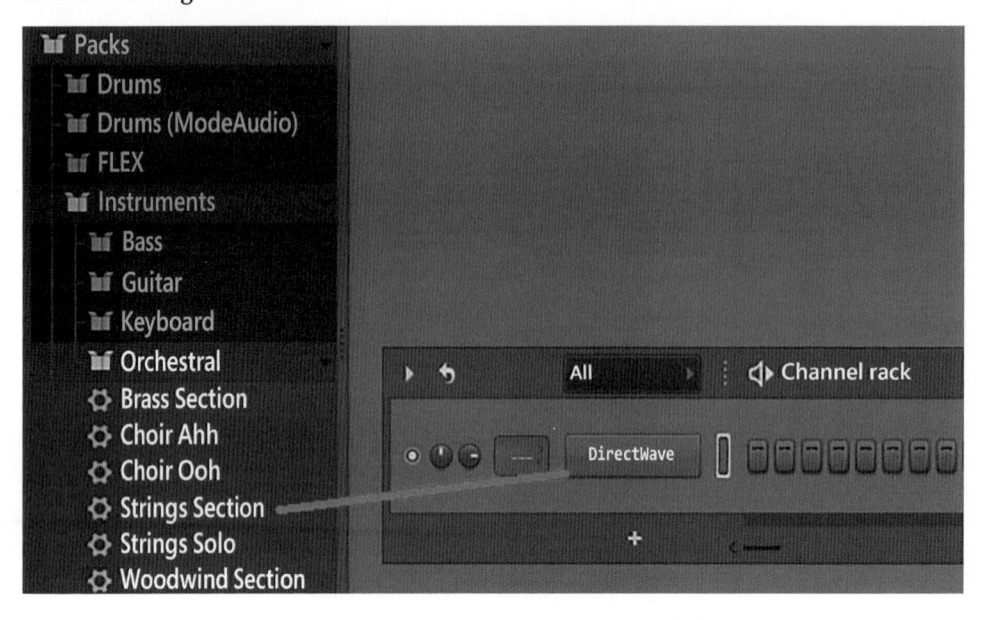

Figure 10.13 – Gross Beat sequencer

If you want to quickly swap out one sample for another, you can do so by clicking on the sample in the browser with the scroll button on your mouse.

Once the sample or sampled instrument has been dragged in, DirectWave will open, as shown in the following screenshot:

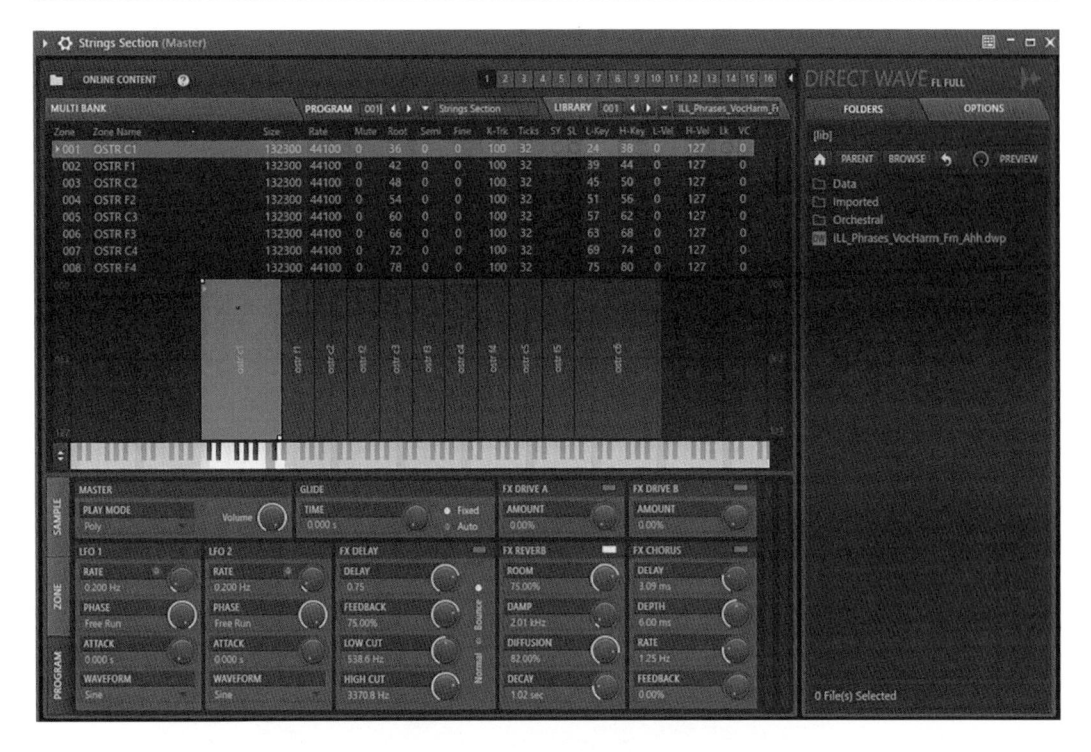

Figure 10.14 – DirectWave

If you play some instrument notes on your MIDI instrument or in the piano roll, you'll hear that DirectWave has analyzed the audio sample and generated transposed pitches above and below the original sample. Essentially, DirectWave creates an entire instrument that you can play. This is a big deal. You can go out and record any audio sample and DirectWave will turn that sound into an instrument by creating additional note pitches.

FL Studio even provides samples that can be dropped directly into DirectWave. You can find a list of samples available in the browser `Packs` folder as shown in the following screenshot:

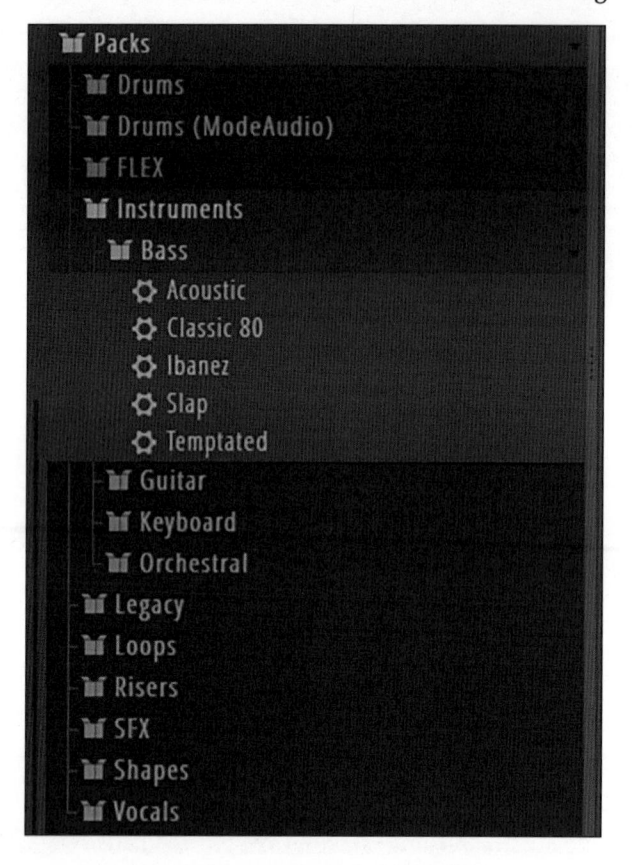

Figure 10.15 – Samples for DirectWave

The preceding screenshot shows browser samples that come with FL Studio. There are bass samples, guitar samples, keyboard samples, and orchestral samples, as well as a folder of legacy samples. I encourage you to experiment with left-clicking and dragging them into DirectWave. This will convert the sample into a fully playable instrument.

> FL Studio has lots of instrument samples that can be imported into FL Studio, both for free and for a price. To download the samples, go to **Online Content** in the top-left corner of DirectWave.

After DirectWave has created your instrument, it offers a large array of controls to modify the envelope of your sound, as well as a series of effects, as shown in the following **PROGRAM** panel:

Figure 10.16 – PROGRAM panel

The **PROGRAM** panel contains lots of effects to adjust your sampled sound. Of interest is the **PLAY MODE** panel, where you can choose to hear your sound as **Mono** (plays single notes at a time), **Poly** (allows you to play multiple notes at a time), or **Legato** (allows single notes to smoothly glide into the next note). The **GLIDE** panel then controls how smooth the glide between notes is.

We've learned how to create your own instruments. Next, let's learn how to create your own effects.

Creating effects with Patcher

Patcher is an FL Studio plugin that allows you to chain instruments and effects together. Patcher allows you to create your own custom instrument and effect chains, link everything together, and save them for reuse in other projects. Patcher is related to modular synthesis. **Modular synthesis** is where you have individual instrument and effect components and link them together to connect everything.

Patcher can be loaded into the channel rack or onto a mixer channel. If loaded into the channel rack, you can load instrument plugins and Patcher will play the instrument using MIDI notes sent to it from the piano roll. If Patcher is loaded in the mixer, it's intended to be used as an effect rather than to play MIDI notes. In the following examples, we assume that you want to use Patcher as an instrument and accept MIDI notes, and have loaded Patcher into the channel rack:

1. In the channel rack, load up Patcher. Open it up and you'll see the following screen:

Figure 10.17 – Patcher

2. To add a synthesizer, right-click on an empty space in Patcher, select **Add plugin** from the menu options that appear, and select a synthesizer plugin. In my case, I'm going to add the **FLEX** plugin, as shown in the following screenshot:

Figure 10.18 – Added FLEX

Chapter 10 303

You'll notice that a blue arrow line and a yellow arrow line have been added. The blue line indicates that MIDI input coming from FL Studio is being sent to FLEX. If you don't see this, it means you opened Patcher in the mixer as an effect and not the channel rack. The yellow line shows where the audio is going. In this case, the audio is leaving FLEX and being sent back to the channel tack.

If you play some MIDI notes, you will hear FLEX play. If you left-click and drag the yellow line, you can adjust the level of output (volume).

3. If you double-left-click on a plugin in Patcher, it will open up. You can then tweak any controls you like.

You can add effects or multiple synthesizers. Once you've added them, choose where you want MIDI or audio to be routed. Let's look at a quick example.

Add an effect plugin, such as **Fruity Convolver**, in the same way that you added the FLEX instrument. Redirect audio from FLEX to it by left-clicking the yellow audio arrow from FLEX and dragging it to Fruity Convolver. In the following screenshot example, I've added the Fruity Convolver effect and redirected the audio from FLEX to go to Fruity Convolver. I then routed the audio from Fruity Convolver to return to FL Studio:

Figure 10.19 – Routing audio from FLEX to Fruity Convolver

If you play some MIDI notes, you can hear the notes played with FLEX with an effect added by Fruity Convolver.

Creating custom dashboards in Patcher

In **Patcher**, you can create dashboards with gadgets to navigate your instruments and effects. The benefit of using a dashboard is that you have a list of custom controls and effects in one place instead of opening up plugins one at a time. This is useful when you're playing live, and you want to change your instruments and effects all in one place. It also unlocks automation abilities within Patcher as you can automate controls added to the dashboard. To understand this, let's look at an example:

1. Go to the **Surface** tab at the top of Patcher:

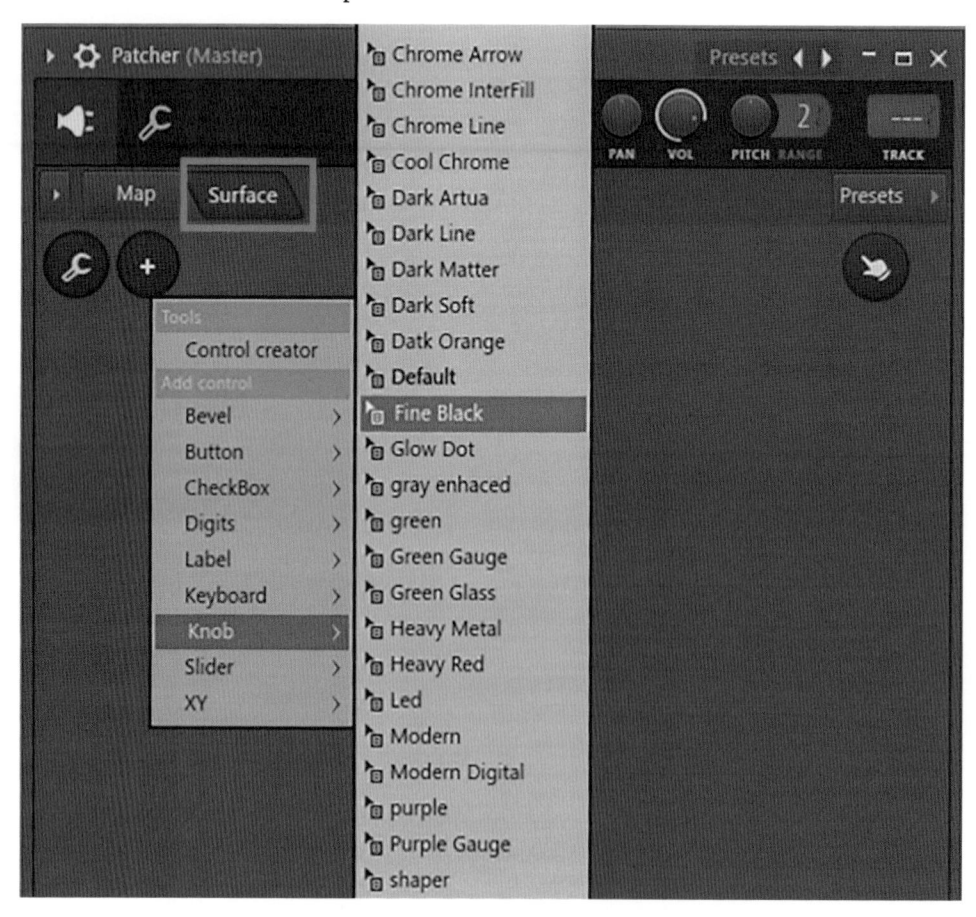

Figure 10.20 – Adding a knob

Chapter 10

2. Click the plus sign icon. A menu will pop up showing you the controls that you can add. There is also an option called **Control creator**, which allows you to design your own controls.

3. Select a knob. In the preceding screenshot, I've chosen one called **Fine Black**. A knob will appear.

4. Left-click on the wrench symbol at the top left of **Patcher** to finish placing the knob. We've created a gadget. Now we need to tell the gadget to connect to a plugin control so it knows what to do.

5. Click the **Map** tab at the top left to return to your instruments and effects. You'll see that a red circle appears to the right of the **Surface** object. This is the output port of the dashboard and is connected to the knob that we just created:

Figure 10.21 – The Surface object now has an additional output

6. We're now going to connect our knob to a control in an instrument. Double-left-click on the FLEX instrument in Patcher. FLEX will open up.

7. Right-click on any control in FLEX. A menu will appear. Choose the **Activate** option. This will tell Patcher that we want an input port to lead to this control. This is shown in the following screenshot:

Figure 10.22 – Activating a control

8. Close FLEX. Back in Patcher, you'll see that a red circle has appeared to the left of the FLEX instrument. This is the input controlling the knob we just activated:

Figure 10.23 – New input to FLEX

Chapter 10 307

9. Left-click on the red circle output of the **Surface** object and drag it onto the FLEX red input port circle we just created. When you're done, it will look like the following screenshot:

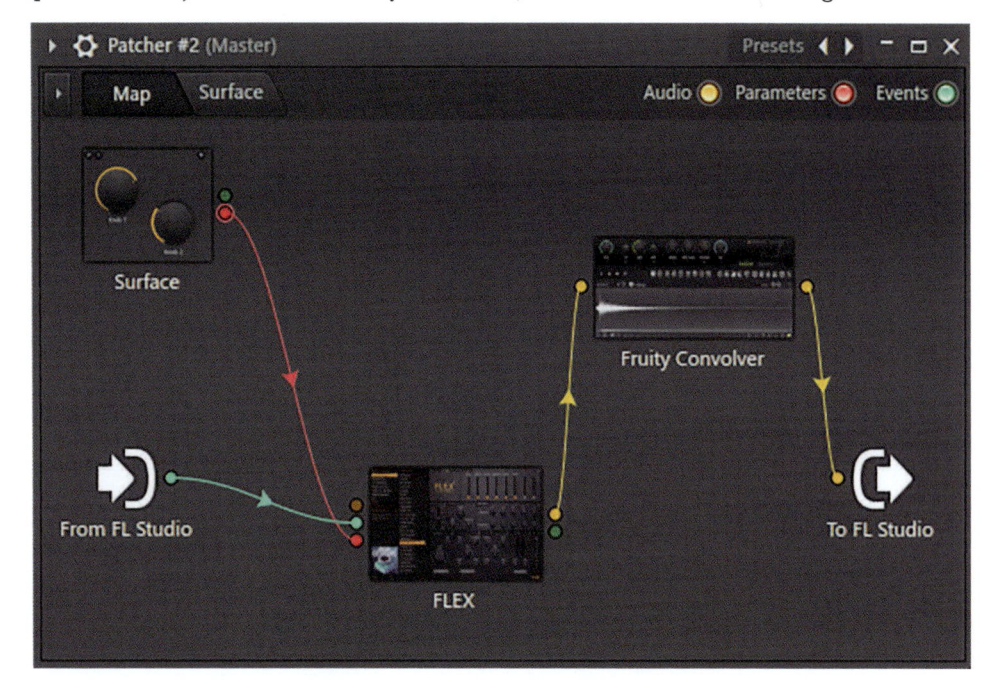

Figure 10.24 – Connecting the knob on the Surface dashboard to FLEX

What we've just done is connect the knob that we added to the **Surface** dashboard to the control in FLEX. The knob on the **Surface** dashboard now manipulates the control in FLEX.

Left-click on the **Surface** tab again to return to the **Surface** dashboard.

10. From now on, anytime you want to adjust the control in FLEX, instead of opening FLEX, you can play with the knob on the **Surface** dashboard. Play some MIDI notes and adjust the knob on the **Surface** dashboard; you will hear the FLEX control adjusting as the instrument plays. When you're finished adding and routing instruments and effects, it's time to save Patcher.

11. To save it, go to the dropdown arrow at the top left of Patcher and choose **Save preset as** to save your preset.

Later on, in any project, you can go to the drop down arrow again and load your Patcher effects chain. You can even send the Patcher preset to another musician and they'll be able to open your Patcher preset, assuming that they have access to the same plugins you do.

You now know how to create your own instrument and effect chains in Patcher.

Send any instrument to Patcher

There's a very easy way to send any VST plugin into Patcher using the **Patcherize** option. This will allow you to easily start creating chains of instruments and effects:

1. In order to send an instrument into patcher, first load up an instrument in the channel rack.
2. Right-click on the channel rack instrument and select the **Patcherize** option as shown in the following screenshot.

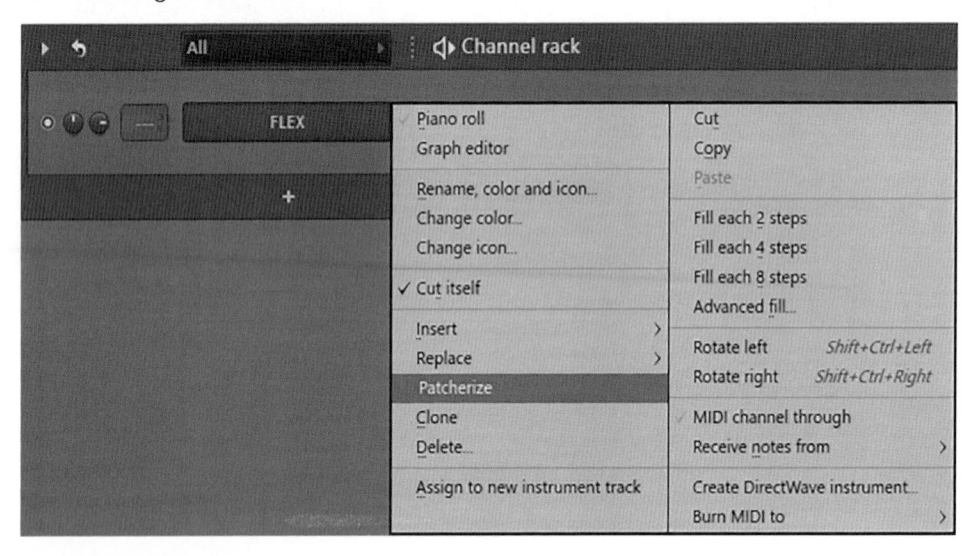

Figure 10.25 – Patcherize

Patcher will open up with the instrument loaded, ready to go.

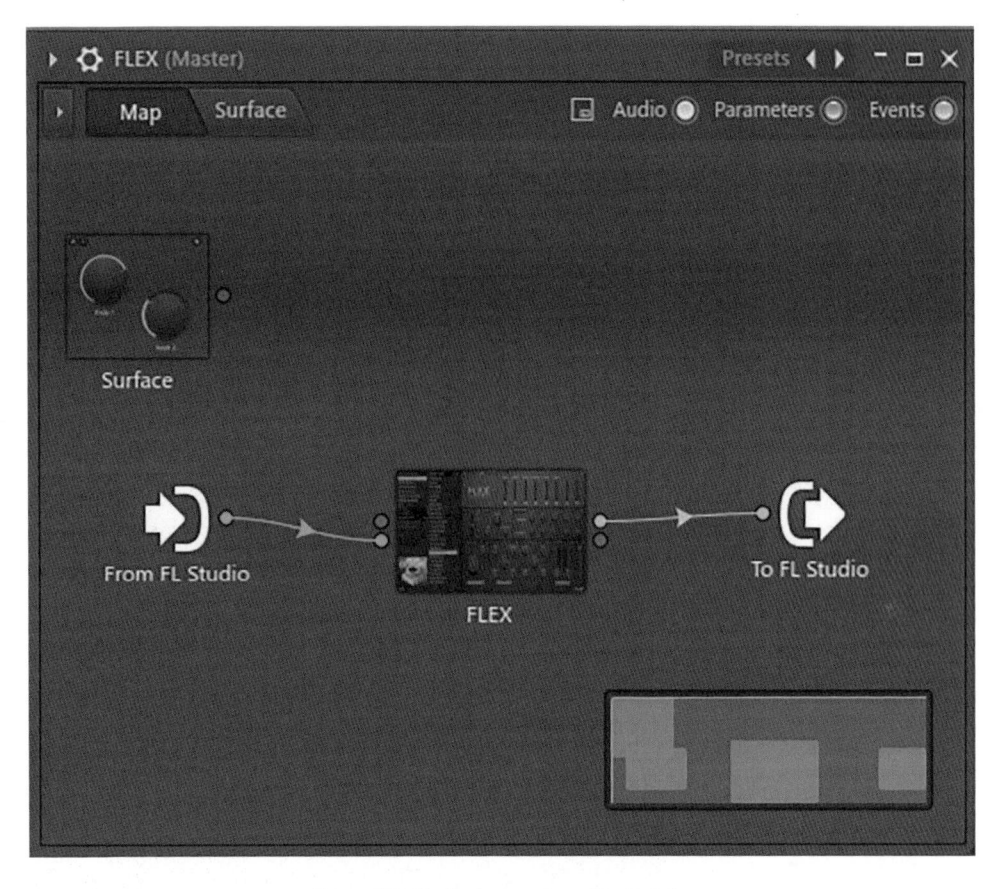

Figure 10.26 – Instrument sent to Patcher

You can even send non-native plugins into patcher using the **Patcherize** option. In the following screenshot, I show an example where I sent a non-native FL Studio VST synthesizer plugin I purchased called **SynthMaster** into Patcher.

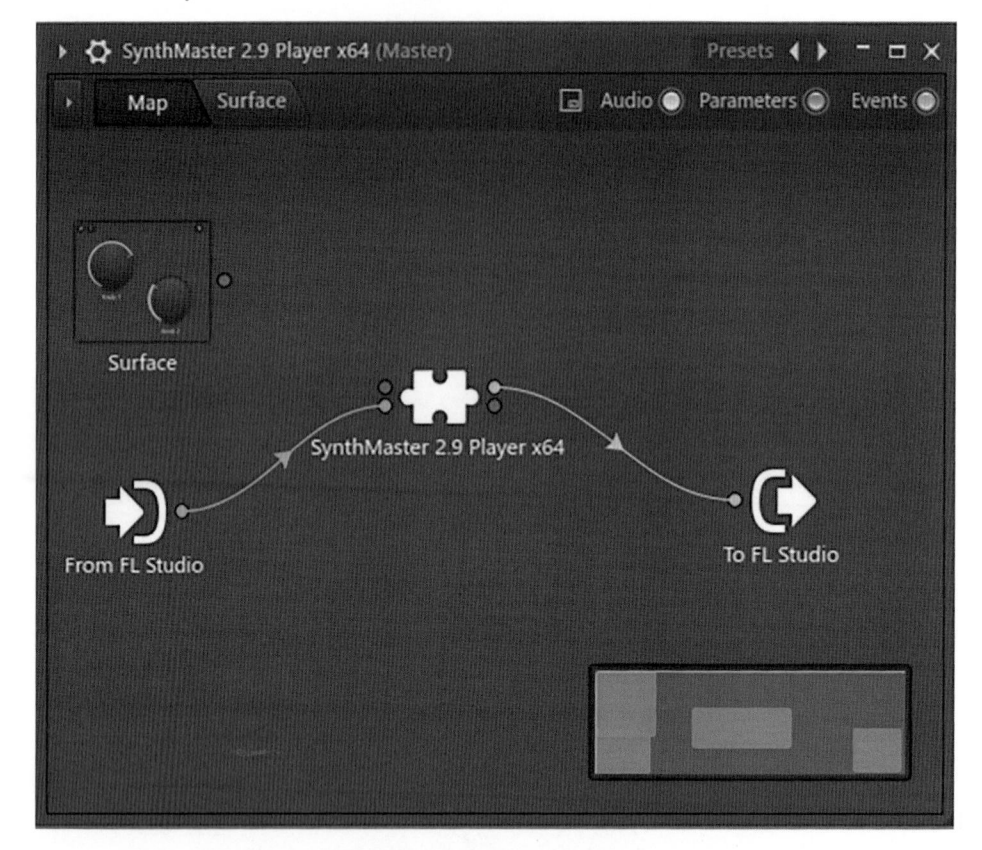

Figure 10.27 – SynthMaster

We've learned how to use load instruments in Patcher; next let's check out Patcher's presets.

Exploring Patcher presets

Patcher contains a variety of powerful presets that are worth exploring.

1. In the channel rack, load up an instance of Patcher.

Chapter 10 311

2. In the top-right corner of the Patcher plugin, select the **Presets** dropdown as shown in the following screenshot:

Figure 10.28 – Patcher presets

These presets are customized versions of Patcher. There are lots of Patcher presets and I recommend you browse through them. First on the list of presets is **Aeropad**. Aeropad is an ambient pad generator. Select the first preset and load up Aeropad and you'll see the following:

Figure 10.29 – Patcher Aeropad

At the top right, you'll see a tab called **Presets**. Anytime you want, you can save a custom preset of Patcher for easy reloading later on. Saving a custom preset will remember the exact knob and effect position of your patcher instance.

At the top middle is a tab that says **Help**. By selecting this, you'll find a detailed set of instructions for what each button does in the preset.

Chapter 10

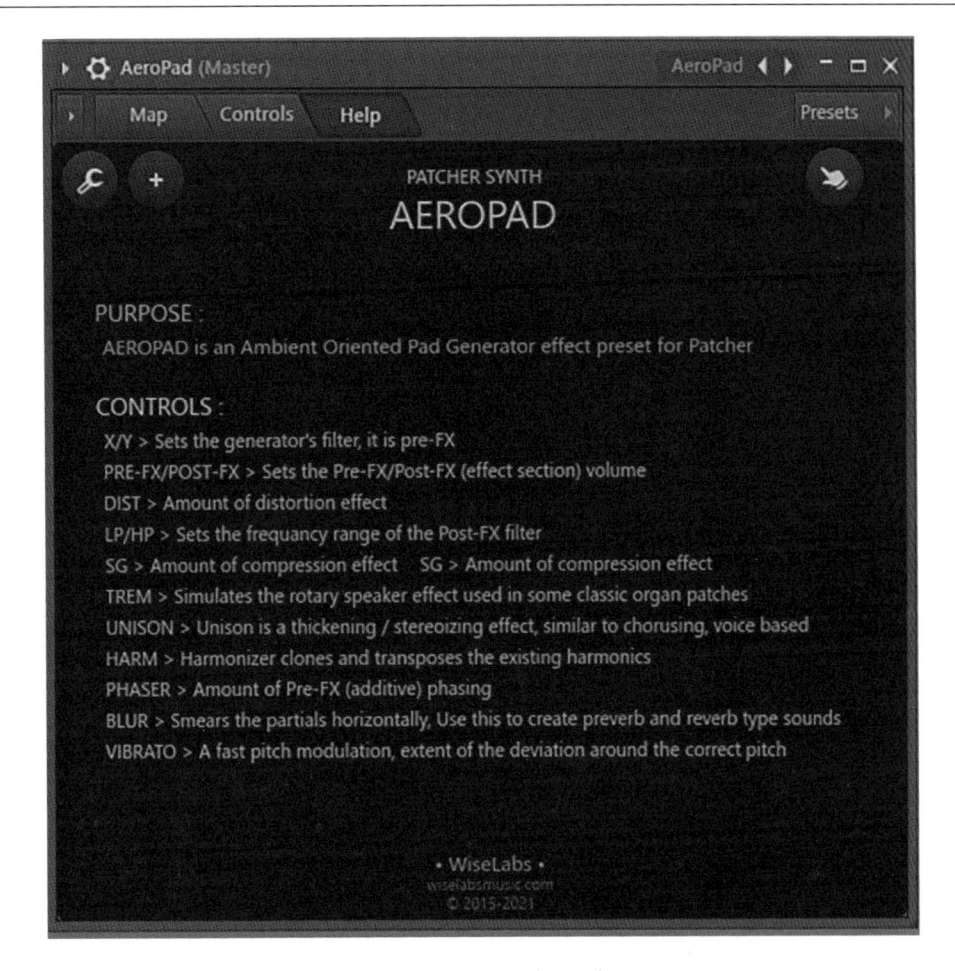

Figure 10.30 – Patcher Help

Let's briefly flip through the rest of the patcher presets:

- **Autoclap, AutoSnare, Cymbalism, Drumbass, Infinitom, Kickmachine, Magic-Hat**, and **PercSeed**, are percussion plugins that create percussion sounds. **SplitKit** is a full drumkit with different instruments assigned to each keyboard MIDI note.
- **Midvore** is a key scale plugin that allows you to select an instrument scale. When you play MIDI notes, it will shift notes received into notes that fit the selected instrument scale. If you're wondering what different scales might sound like, this is an easy way to experiment with playing notes from different scales.
- **Plucker** is a key-based plucked chord generator.

- **Randomless** is based on the **Harmless** plugin. It generates new random presets depending on a random seed value you set.
- **Reezor** is a bass-led synth generator.
- **Vocatcher** is one of my favorites and is seen in the following screenshot. It's a vocal synth generator allowing you to create a synth sound like a vocal with lots of customizing parameters.

Figure 10.31 – Patcher Vocatcher

Lots of trap music uses synths that sound like vocals. If you've been looking for a great vocal synth, look no further than **Vocatcher**.

Chapter 10

Wobbler is a wobble machine generator. It creates wobble sounds that are often heard in dubstep music.

Figure 10.32 – Patcher Wobbler

There are lots of knobs and buttons, but for the control nut, the real beauty of patcher is the endless automation and control capabilities. Remember earlier in this chapter, in *Figure 10.19 – Activating a control*, we created a knob from scratch as a dashboard and hooked the knob to control our FLEX synth plugin. You can do the same thing with any patcher preset.

In the case of Wobbler and some of the other presets, you can automate controls directly within the channel rack. In Wobbler, if you right-click inside **OSC**, you can use **Create automation clip** as shown in the following screenshot:

Figure 10.33 – Patcher Wobbler automation

This will create an automation clip in the playlist, which you can then adjust.

Next on the Patcher Presets is **YottaSaw**. YottaSaw is another of my favorite patcher presets. It's a key-based chord generator.

Figure 10.34 – Patcher YottaSaw

With YottaSaw, regardless of what note you hit, the plugin will create a full saw chord from that note. You can then customize the sound.

The great thing about patcher presets is that although you can endlessly customize them inside of Patcher, at the end of the day, they're just instruments that exist in the channel rack. So you can treat them just like any other instrument in the channel rack. You can add MIDI notes for them to play in the piano roll, and later add effects in the mixer, should you choose.

We've explored Pather's presets. Next, let's look at a powerful Patcher arpeggiator plugin called VFX Sequencer.

Using VFX Sequencer

VFX Sequencer is a powerful MIDI sequencer plugin that runs inside Patcher.

In general, an arpeggiator plays a series of notes whenever it receives a MIDI note. For example, you could play a chord, and the arpeggiator could then cycle between playing notes inside the chord. A sequencer is an advanced arpeggiator giving you lots of control over how the note patterns are created.

VFX Sequencer allows you to generate MIDI notes for any instrument. Let's explore VFX Sequencer:

1. Open up an instance of Patcher in the channel rack.
2. Inside Patcher, right-click and select the option **Add plugin**:

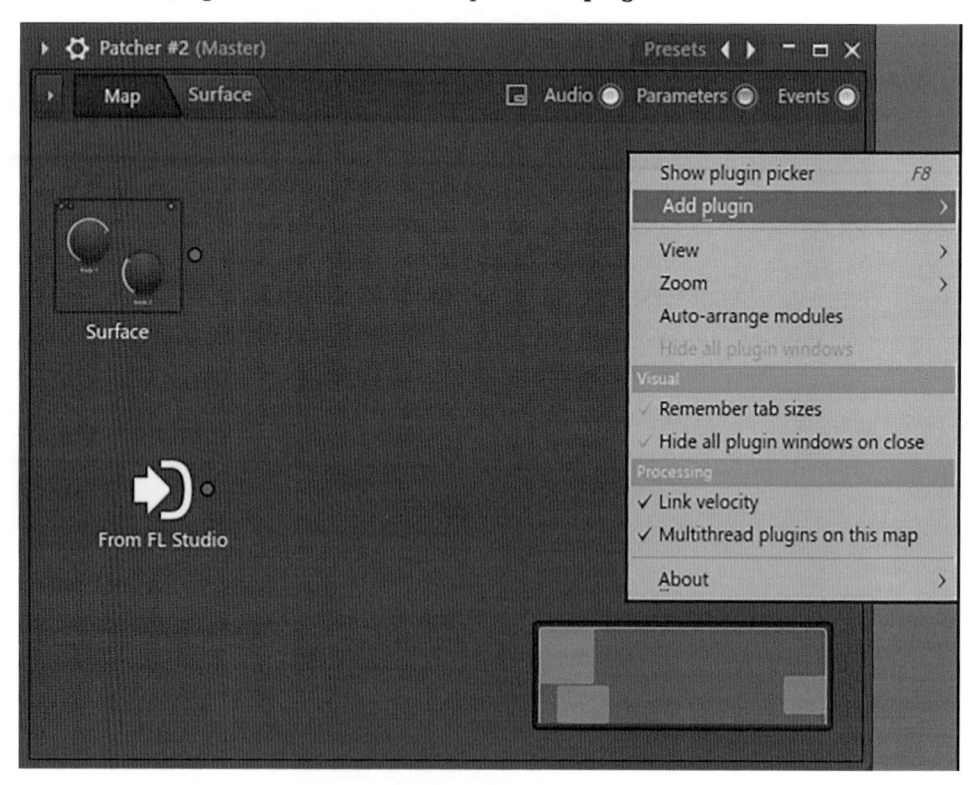

Figure 10.35 – Add plugin in VFX Sequencer Patcher

3. Locate VFX Sequencer and select it. You'll see that VFX Sequencer is added to patcher, as in the following screenshot:

Figure 10.36 – Patcher added VFX Sequencer

You'll notice by default that VFX Sequencer doesn't output audio the way that synthesizer plugins like FLEX do. Hitting MIDI notes won't make any sound by default. This is because VFX outputs MIDI notes, but doesn't output audio. VFX generates MIDI sequences to be played by a synthesizer plugin. We need to add an instrument for VFX Sequencer to generate notes for. Let's do that next.

4. Right-click on the green circle to the right of VFX Sequencer, as shown in the following screenshot. Add a synthesizer plugin of your choice. In the following example, I'm using the FL Studio plugin **FL Keys**, but I encourage you to try FLEX, Harmless, or another synth plugin.

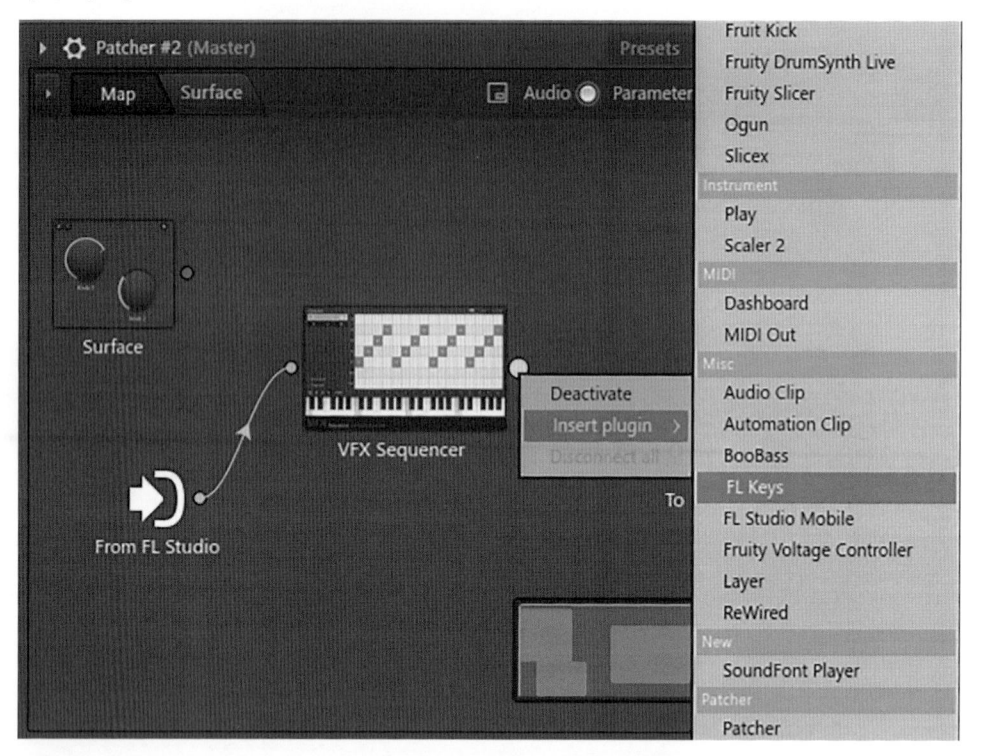

Figure 10.37 – Add instrument for VFX Sequencer

This will create an instrument synthesizer inside Patcher and automatically set up the MIDI routing. It will route any MIDI output from VFX and send it to the new instrument before routing to the Patcher audio to the Patcher output. The result is shown in the following screenshot.

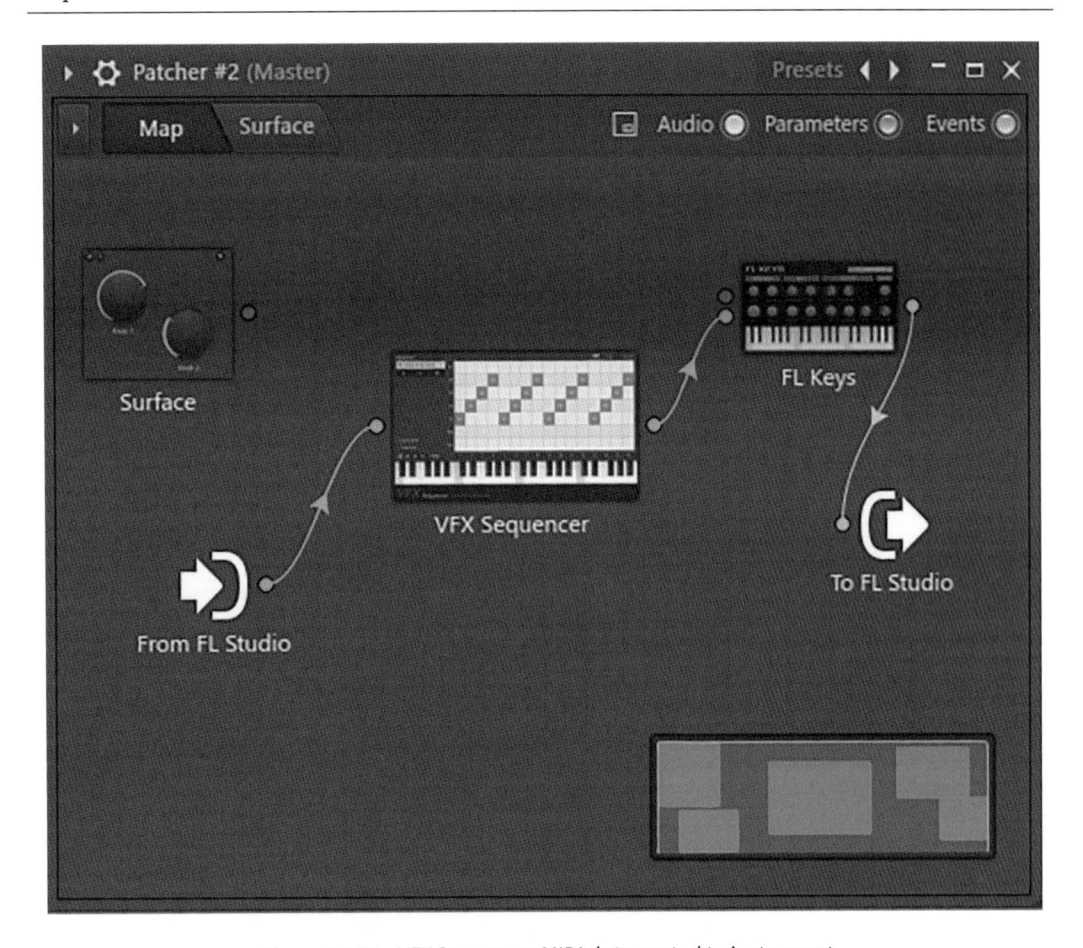

Figure 10.38 – VFX Sequencer MIDI data routed to instrument

In the preceding screenshot, we can see that MIDI notes are received from the piano roll. This is what **From FL Studio** means. The MIDI notes are passed to VFX Sequencer. VFX Sequencer performs any arpeggiation transformations it wants to and then passes the MIDI information along to FL Keys. FL Keys plays the MIDI notes and creates audio, which is then output from Patcher and sent through **To FL Studio** to be sent to the mixer.

Okay, we're all set up and ready to get started using VFX Sequencer. Let's check out the arpeggiation abilities of VFX Sequencer. Double-right-click on VFX Sequencer to open the plugin.

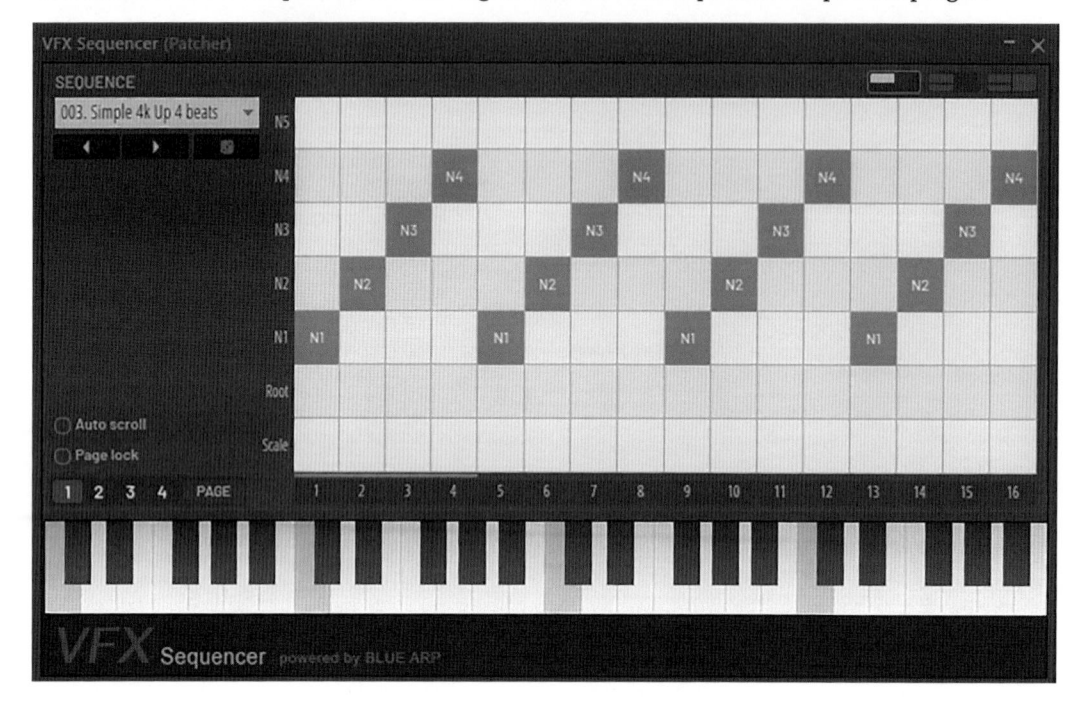

Figure 10.39 – VFX Sequencer single panel

By default, VFX Sequencer opens up in single-panel mode. If you left-click on one of the keyboard notes, you'll hear VFX sequencer playing an arpeggio starting with the selected note.

In the middle, you'll see the grid of notes for VFX Sequencer to play. You can left-click on blank spaces in the grid to change the arpeggio being played.

At the top left, you'll see a dropdown menu of various arpeggio presets that can be selected. Below are arrows to go to the next sequence preset, go to the previous sequence, or to generate a random sequence of notes.

At the top right of VFX Sequencer, you'll see various display modes. Select **DISPLAY MODE COMPLETE**. You'll see the following:

Chapter 10

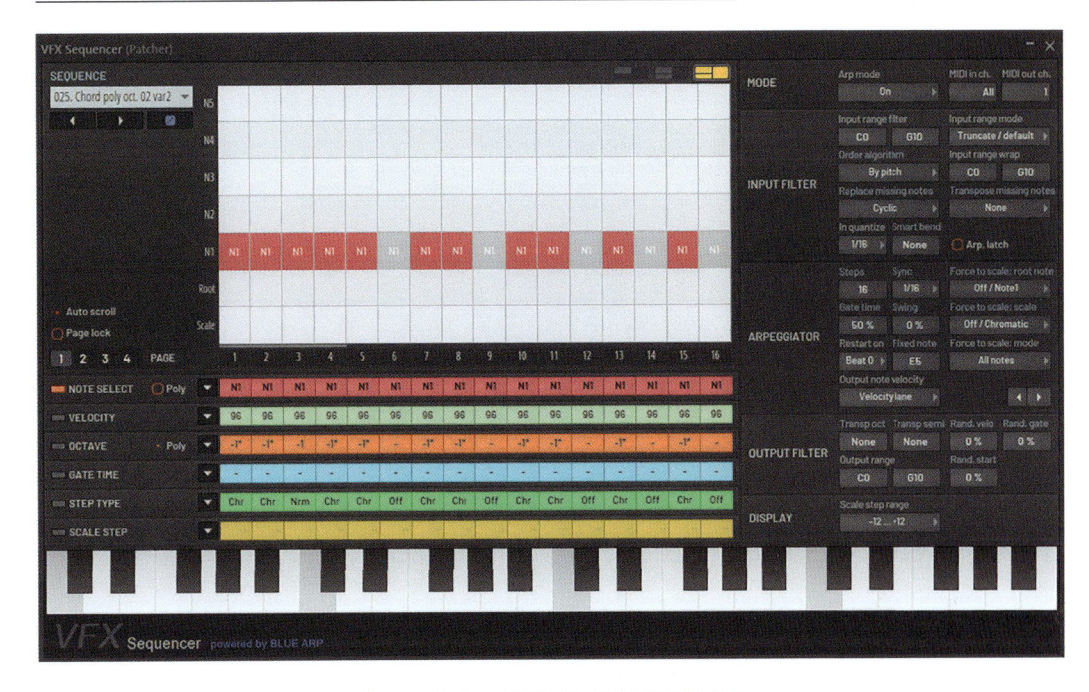

Figure 10.40 – DISPLAY MODE COMPLETE

This will unlock additional panels. Let's take a look at the panel at the bottom left:

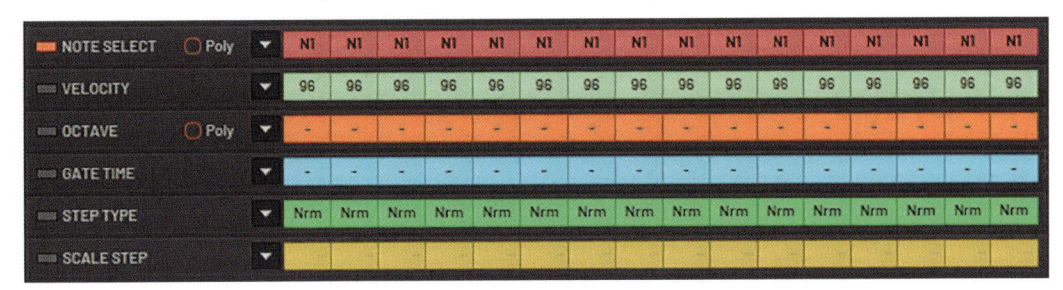

Figure 10.41 – Note select

On the left side, you'll see the controls **NOTE SELECT**, **VELOCITY**, **OCTAVE**, **GATE TIME**, **STEP TYPE**, and **SCALE STEP**. As you select one of these, you'll see the display change to give you a view of the control. By default, you'll see **NOTE SELECT**. If you select a different control, the display will adjust accordingly.

The colored bands of notes to the right of the controls allow you to scroll or drag to change the values of individual arpeggio note parameters.

NOTE SELECT and **OCTAVE** have an enabling button for **Poly**. This is so you can enable multiple notes to be played simultaneously instead of the default single note.

Figure 10.42 – Shift up

To the right of the controls are dropdown options allowing you to create global changes to your arpeggio notes affecting all the notes at once instead of accessing them individually.

Next, let's check out the right-side panels.

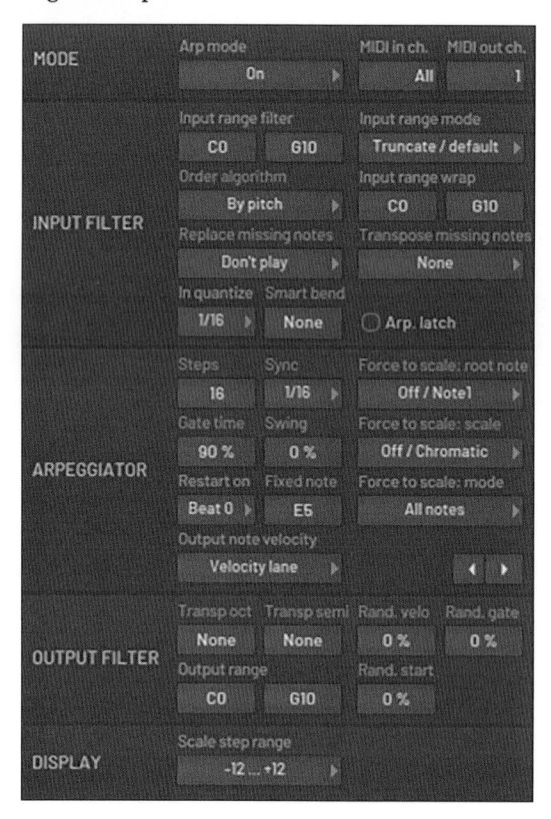

Figure 10.43 – VFX Sequencer advanced controls

Chapter 10 325

Here's a description of the controls. They're a little confusing to understand by just reading them. If you want to understand, I recommend playing some arpeggiated notes while toggling between the settings.

The **MODE** section contains the following controls:

- **Arp Mode**: Chooses how to arpeggiate. The options are:

    - **On**
    - **Off**: Ignore any input
    - **Thru**: Allow notes, but don't arpeggiate. Still allow other settings such as **Input Range**, **Output Range**, **Transpose**, and **Force** to scale.
    - **2/3 auto on/off**: Only play when 2 or 3 notes are being played or otherwise turn off.
    - **2/3 auto on/thru**: When 2 or 3 notes are played, the arpeggiator runs, or otherwise allows single notes to pass without arpeggiation.

- **Midi in ch**: Use MIDI input channel (All/Omni or 1 to 16).
- **Midi out ch**: Use MIDI output channel (All/Omni or 1 to 16).

The **INPUT FILTER** section contains the following controls:

- **Input range filter**: Sets the range of notes for the arpeggiator to play within.
- **Input range mode**: Contains the following options:

    - **Truncate**: Only arpeggiates notes within the selected range.
    - **Pass thru**: Notes within the range are not arpeggiated.

- **Input range wrap**: Transposes notes up or down an octave until they fit within the range. For example, with a bass instrument, you'd want to keep notes in the lower range.
- **Order algorithm**: Sets how to order notes. The options are as follows:

    - **By pitch**: The lowest note is N1.
    - **By pitch desc**: The last note set is N1.
    - **As played**: Plays chords from low to high.
    - **As played desc**: N1 is played last.
    - **By velocity**: Max velocity is N1.
    - **By velocity desc**: Minimum velocity is N1.
    - **Chord (normalized)**: Ignores chord inversions.
    - **Chord (as played)**: Allows chord inversions.

- **Replace missing notes:** Decides what to do when there are multiple input notes simultaneously. The options are:
    - **Don't play:** Mute notes for arpeggiation.
    - **Cyclic:** Cycle between notes for arpeggiation.
    - **First key:** Use the first note for arpeggiation.
    - **Last key:** Use the last note for arpeggiation.
    - **Fixed key:** Use the fixed note for arpeggiation set under the arpeggiator.
- **Transpose missing notes:** The options are:
    - **None:** Don't transpose notes
    - **+1 / -1 Octave:** Replace notes an octave relative to input
- **In quantize:** Allows you to re-time notes.
- **Smart blend:** Works with **Force to scale: scale**. Adjusts notes to fit into a selected scale. If **Force to scale** is set off, then it is a chromatic scale.
- **Arp. latch – OFF:** Arpeggiator stops when input stops. **ON:** Arpeggiator keeps playing the last input notes. Can assign a switch to a keyboard pedal to activate it for live performance with a little tinkering.

The **ARPEGGIATOR** section contains the following controls:

- **Steps:** 0-64.
- **Sync:** Step fraction of a bar.
- **Force scale: root note - Off/Note1:** Create a chord from the N1 pitch.
- **Force to scale: scale:** Sets scale. Works with **Force to scale: root note**:
    - **Off/chromatic**
    - **Detect from chord:** Use input notes to create a scale.
    - **Explicit options:** Choose from a list of scales.
- **Force to scale: mode:** Works with the **Force to scale: scale**:
    - **All notes:** Transposes everything.
    - **Semi-transposed:** Steps with '**Scale Step > '-'' (no change)** selected, won't be transposed.
- **Gate time:** Select a step with the range of 1 to 125%.

- **Swing**: Choose the swing range. Swing shifts the timing of even steps.
- **Restart on**: When to restart pattern. Contains the following options:
  - **Beat 0**
  - **Notes**: Whenever a new input note is received.
  - **1st Note**: Continues until FL Studio playback is restarted.
  - **Play**: Upon Fl Studio playback.
- **Fixed note**: Using the **Note Select Lane** on the far left of VFX Sequencer allows you to replace input notes with a fixed key value instead.
- **Output note velocity**: Velocity can be thought of as how much emphasis you're using on a percussive sound. More velocity means you're hitting the instrument note harder. Velocity options:
  - **Velocity lane**: Use velocity lanes.
  - **Input note**: Use input note velocities.
  - **Lane + input note**: Scale input by velocity lane.
- **Pattern shift**: Rotate the pattern. Useful if the pattern doesn't fit the downbeat.

The **OUTPUT FILTER** section contains the following controls:

- **Transp oct**: Transpose the sequence by octaves.
- **Transpsemi**: Transpose sequence by semitones.
- **Rand. vel**: Randomly assigns velocities within a range. Creates some realism so note velocities are less repetitive.
- **Rand. gate**: Randomly assigns gate values within the range.
- **Output range (wrap)**: Notes outside the range will be transposed until they fit into the range.
- **Rand. start**: Randomizes note start times within the selected range.

You now know how to use VFX Sequencer to create arpeggiated patterns for any instrument.

Summary

In this chapter, we started with how to come up with creative sound effects by using glitch effects with **Gross Beat**. Glitch effects are an excellent way to create variation when transitioning between one section of a song and the next or simply to add interesting rhythmic sequences.

We learned how to create our own instruments from samples using **DirectWave**. Finally, we learned how to create our own instrument and effect chains with **Patcher**. We learned about various presets available in Patcher. And we learned about creating arpeggiating MIDI sequences using VFX Sequencer in Patcher.

In the next chapter, we will learn about intermediate mixing topics and sound design plugin effects.

11
Intermediate Mixing Topics and Sound Design Plugin Effects

In this chapter, we'll cover some of FL Studio's latest plugins. For the ambitious and those eager to explore cutting-edge sound design, FL Studio offers an abundance of tools. This chapter explores advanced FL Studio plugin effects for those who feel they already have a decent grasp of FL Studio and want fine control over their sound design. These are advanced topics, so don't feel bad if it goes a little over your head the first time you read about these topics.

In this chapter, you'll learn how to create real-time pitch-shifting effects using Pitch Shifter. You'll learn how to create metallic sounds and shift frequencies with Frequency Shifter. You'll learn how to stretch audio waves to create complex audio effects with Fruity Granulizer. You'll learn how to create delay effects with Multiband Delay. Finally, you'll learn how to use Frequency Splitter, a tool designed to give you precise control over multiband processing in the mixer.

In this chapter, we will cover the following topics:

- Real-time pitch shifting with Pitch Shifter
- Shifting frequencies with Frequency Shifter
- Stretching audio waves with Fruity Granulizer
- Delay effects with Multiband Delay
- Multiband processing with Frequency Splitter

Using Pitch Shifter

Pitch Shifter is a pitch-shifting effect. It contains two pitch shift algorithms, one for monophonic sounds such as vocals, and one for polyphonic sounds. It can be used for pitch correction and, in my opinion, creates a more natural-sounding result than the FL Studio plugin **Newtone**, which was discussed in *Chapter 8*.

Let's get started using Pitch Shifter:

1. Load up an audio sample in the playlist and route it to the mixer.
2. Apply the **Pitch Shifter** effect to the mixer channel and play your sound. You'll see Pitch Shifter load up, as shown in the following screenshot:

Figure 11.1 – Pitch Shifter

On the far-left side, you'll see the tabs **Music** and **Voice**. **Voice** is for the monophonic pitch-shifting algorithm (single note at a time). You'll usually want this if you're applying pitch-shifting effects for vocals. If you have a polyphonic sound (more than one note at a time), then you'll probably want the **Music** tab. You'll see a different plugin interface depending on whether the **Voice** or **Music** tab is selected. By default, the **Music** tab is selected.

Chapter 11

When the **Music** tab is selected, a *granular* pitch-shifting engine is used. Incoming audio is sliced into waves, which can be looped. Loops are called grains. The pitch is controlled by the speed of playback of the grains. Playing a granular loop faster will increase the pitch of it. Playing it slower will decrease the pitch of it. The duration can lengthen the sound by repeating grains or skipping grains to shorten it. Move the duration slider and see how it affects the sound when played.

> You can find **plugin presets** in the top-right corner of the plugin, which I encourage you to check out.

Moving from left to right, here's a summary of the controls:

- **PITCH**: Controls the pitch of the audio. If you want to change the pitch of the audio, this is the knob that you'll want to automate. You can automate by right-clicking and choosing the option **Create Automation Clip**.
- **DURATION**: The length of the grain buffer. Longer works better with low-pitch audio, and shorter buffers work better with higher-pitched audio.
- **DENSITY**: How much smoothness to apply to sound. Larger values smooth the sound more.
- **JITTER**: Adds randomness to the timing grains. At a value of 0, there is no randomness added; if you want to hear more artifices, you can increase the value.
- **RAND**: Adds randomness to the start position of each grain.
- **DELAY**: The amount of delay time to add.
- **FEEDBACK**: How much output signal you want to feed back into Pitch Shifter:
    - **POST**: The signal is delayed and then pitch-shifted.
    - **PRE**: Audio is pitch-shifted and then delayed.
    - **NO SHIFT**: Deactivate feedback.
- **MIX**: How strong an effect to apply.

On the far left, if you select the **VOICE** tab, you'll see the interface go blue and some new controls appear, as shown in the following screenshot

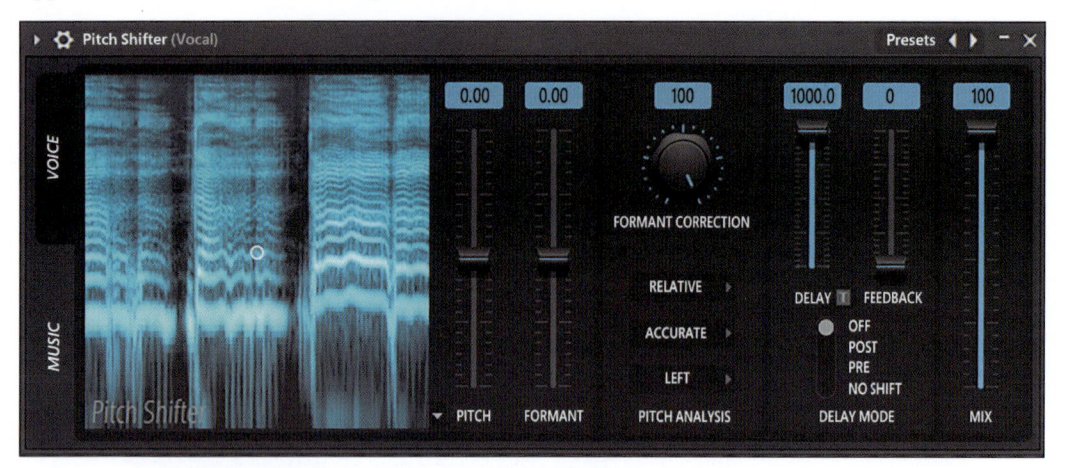

Figure 11.2 – Voice tab

Here's a description of the Pitch Shifter **VOICE** tab controls:

- **PITCH**: Controls the pitch of the audio. You can right-click and select **Create Automation Clip** to automate the control. You can also control this through a keyboard controller or envelope controller. If so, you'll want to enable the Absolute Pitch mode on the plugin. We'll discuss this further in a moment.
- **FORMANT**: Creates the impression of a larger or smaller sound. When you adjust the pitch, you may find the audio sound unnatural; you can adjust the formant to attempt to compensate. For example, as you adjust the pitch up, you can adjust the formant effect lower. Alternatively, many musicians enjoy the sound of playing with the formant effect on its own, regardless of any changes in pitch.
- **FORMANT CORRECTION**: Automates formant correction. If set to 0%, it produces the most natural sound. If you set it to 100%, you'll get the most variability and least natural sound. Normally, formants don't change with pitch, so having the formant compensate automatically sounds unnatural, but could be a creative effect if desired.

- Pitch mode:
    - **RELATIVE**: The incoming pitch is preserved.
    - **ABSOLUTE**: Incoming pitches are flattened to C notes. The intended purpose of this is for the pitch knob to be controlled by an automation clip, keyboard controller, or envelope controller. This will repatch the audio into a new melody. We'll discuss an example next.
- Pitch detector:
    - **FAST**: Keeps live input and pitch-shifted signals in sync. May struggle with lower frequencies below 100 Hz. In general, you should use **FAST** unless you hear problems.
    - **ACCURATE**: May be more accurate when detecting frequencies below 100 Hz.

Controlling Pitch Shifter effects with a controller

You can adjust the pitch effect of the Pitch Shifter using a keyboard controller or envelope controller. This will allow you to use MIDI notes to decide what pitch frequency to hit. This gives you much more precise control than using an automation clip. Let's control the pitch using a keyboard controller or envelope controller:

1. Load up an audio sample in the playlist and route it to the mixer.
2. Apply the **Pitch Shifter** effect to the mixer channel and play your sound.
3. Select the **Voice** tab on the left side of the Pitch Shifter. This will turn the interface blue and show formant controls.

4. In the playlist, create a new pattern that is the length of the audio sample. Your playlist should look something similar to the following screenshot:

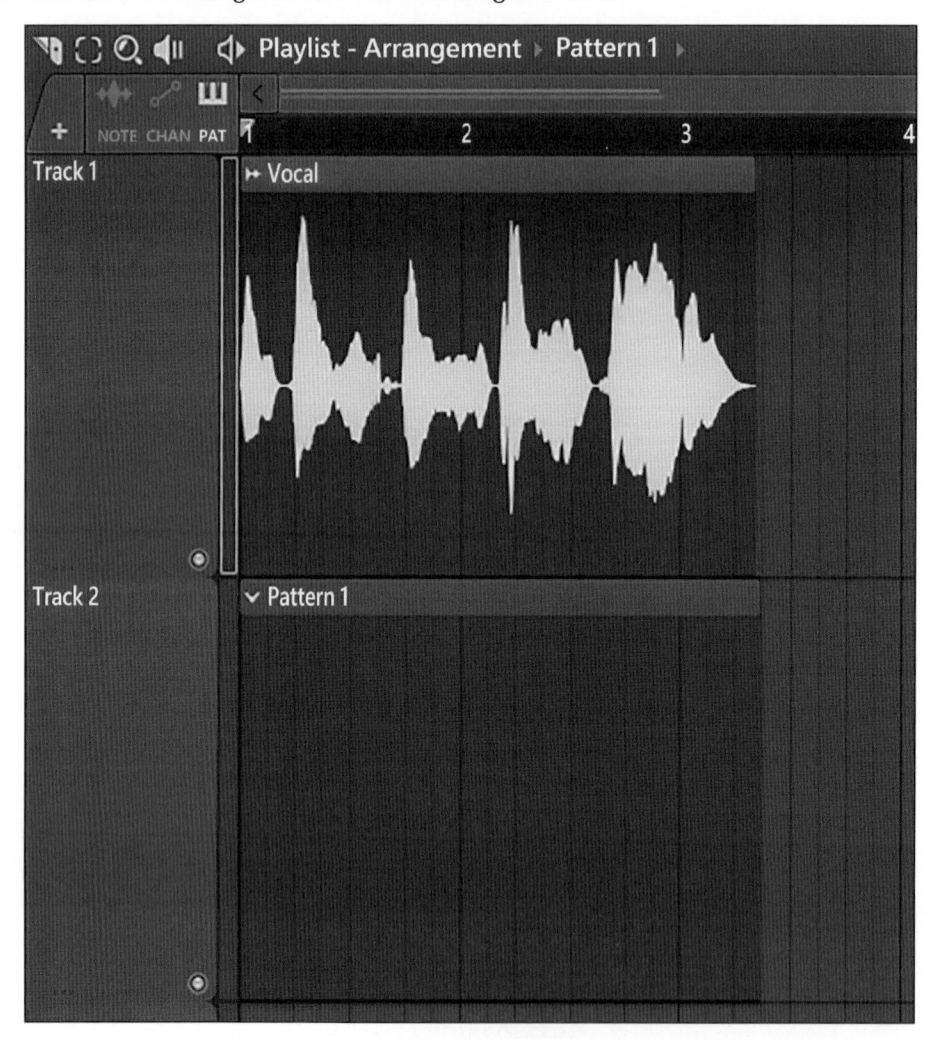

Figure 11.3 – New pattern

5. Open the channel rack and select the pattern, and load up an instance of **Fruity Envelope Controller** or **Fruity Keyboard Controller**. Right-click the controller you added and select the piano roll

Chapter 11

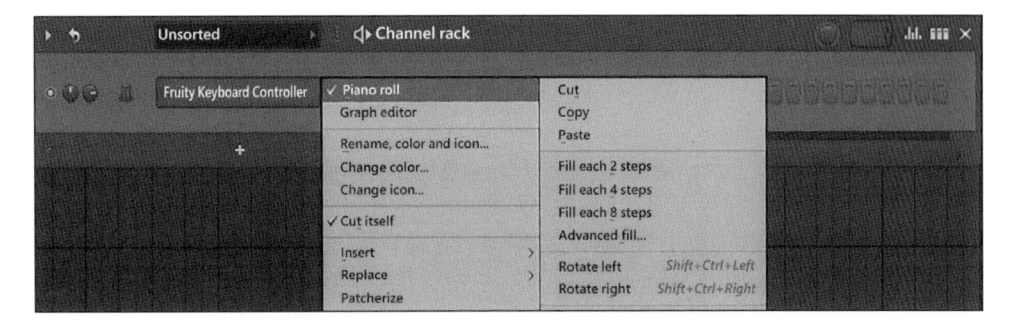

Figure 11.4 – Piano roll

6. In the piano roll, left-click in the grid to add some MIDI notes for your controller to play. These will be the pitches that Pitch Shifter will force the audio to use. An example is shown in the following screenshot:

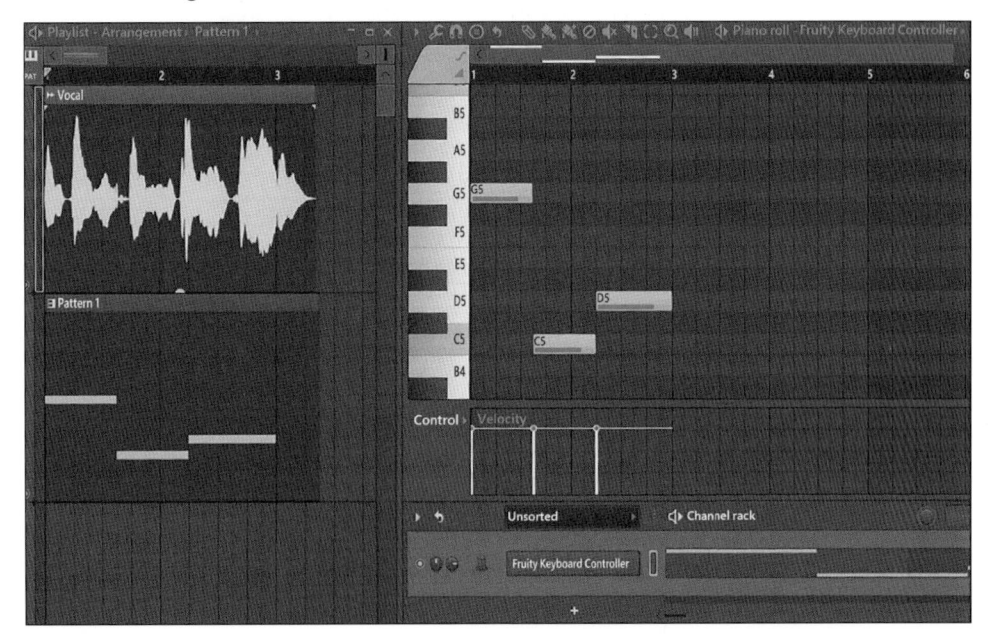

Figure 11.5 – Add MIDI notes

In the preceding screenshot, we can see that we've added MIDI notes to the **Fruity Keyboard Controller**. In the playlist, the pattern playing MIDI notes is placed side by side with the vocal to play at the same time.

7. Open up Pitch Shifter. Make sure that **ABSOLUTE** is selected under **FORMANT CORRECTION**. Then right-click on the pitch knob and select **Link to controller**. An example is shown in the following screenshot:

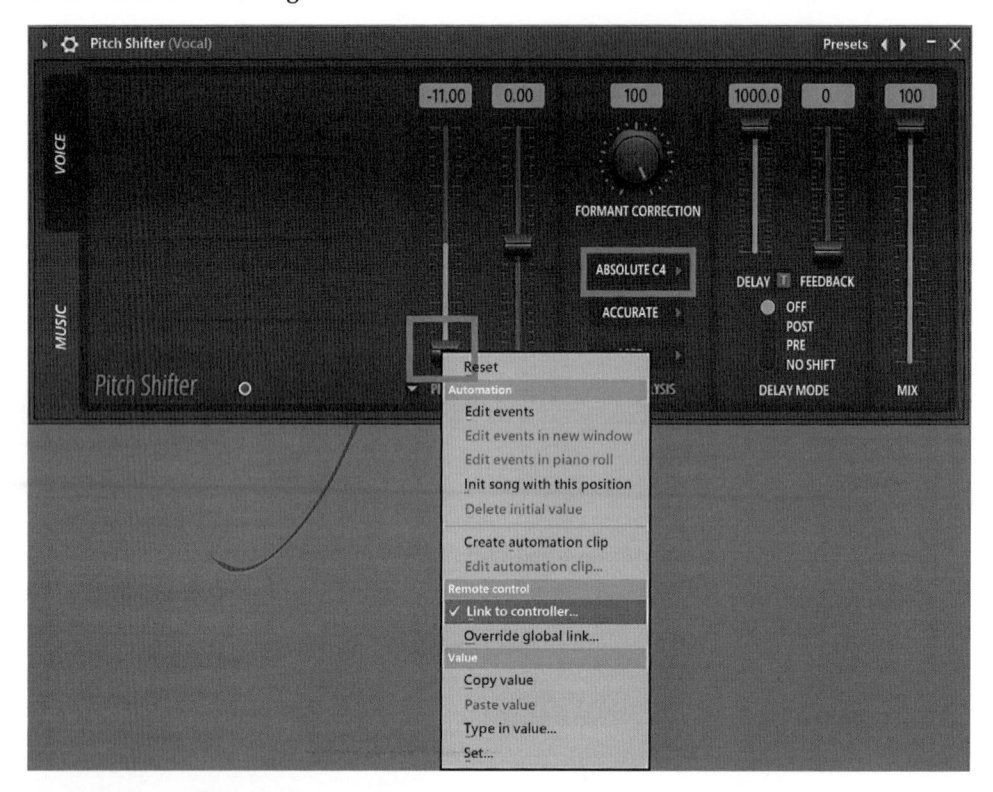

Figure 11.6 – Link to controller

A popup will appear with the **Remote control settings:**

Figure 11.7 – Internal controller

Select the dropdown under **Internal controller**. You'll see the controller that you added in the channel rack. Select the controller. From now on, whenever you play your audio, the Pitch Shifter will be controlled by the MIDI notes that you set in the piano roll for the controller. This is a very convenient way to control pitch shifting. You now know how to use Pitch Shifter.

Using Frequency Shifter

Frequency Shifter is a special effect that shifts all frequencies of a sound by the same amount. It operates similarly to the FL Studio plugin Pitch Shifter, except that it doesn't preserve the pitch key when shifting frequencies; instead Frequency Shifter increments by whatever exact value you tell it to use. It doesn't force specific pitches the way Pitch Shifter does.

Frequency Shifter effects are much stronger on lower-frequency sounds than on higher-frequency sounds. Why? If you have a starting frequency of 100 Hz and shift by 400 Hz, the result is 500 Hz. If you have a starting frequency of 10,000 Hz and the shift is 400 Hz, the result is 10,400 Hz. The relative change is much smaller for the higher frequencies compared to the relative change for the lower frequencies. This is different from how other Pitch Shifters work as they multiply the frequencies by a value instead of just adding. How does this affect the sound? Audio affected by Frequency Shifter effects will sound more dissonant and metallic. This is great for creating dark dubstep bass sounds.

Let's get started using Frequency Shifter:

1. Load up an audio sample in the playlist and route it to the mixer.
2. Apply the **Frequency Shifter** effect to the mixer channel and play your sound. You'll see Frequency Shifter load up as shown in the following screenshot:

Figure 11.8 – Frequency Shifter

> There are **plugin presets** in the top-right corner of the plugin, which I encourage you to check out.

Here's a description of the controls:

- **FREQUENCY**: Amount in Hz to add to the original sound:
    - **20 kHz**: Use for extreme effects.
    - **200 Hz**: Default effect.
    - **TEMPO**: Adds a frequency multiple of the song tempo. A cool effect to consider if you plan on changing the song tempo as will adjust accordingly.
- **FREQ. SHIFTER HQ**: HQ reduces aliasing noises from extreme frequency changes.
- **RING MOD**: Discussed next.
- **SIDECHAIN**: Used in ring modulation.
- **SIDEBAND**: Gives control over whether the frequency shift occurs in just the left or right channel. **L** and **R** can be linked to move simultaneously.
- **ST. PHASE**: Determines the start phase for the sine wave oscillator.
- **L/R PHASE**: Sets the difference between the Left and Right phases. The effect will sound stronger when the Frequency Parameter is 5 Hz or lower.
- **FEEDBACK**: Controls how much output to feed back into Frequency Shifter. This will increase the shifting effect.
- **MIX**: Amount of effect.
- **STEREO**: Amount of stereo width.

If you enable the **RING MOD** setting, you'll notice the interface changes color as shown in the following screenshot:

Figure 11.9 – Ring mod

What is **ring modulation**? Ring modulation multiplies the amplitude of one audio signal by the amplitude of another signal. When modulated by a slow source, a tremolo effect is heard; when modulated by a fast source, new tones are created.

The input source is taken from the sidechain. You'll need to sidechain another audio source to the Frequency Shifter mixer track to use this feature. The following screenshot shows a simplified example of sidechaining one mixer track into another track that has Frequency Shifter:

Figure 11.10 – Frequency Shifter sidechain

Chapter 11

The sidechaining is done by left-clicking the mixer track that has the input source sound, and then right-clicking on the arrow at the bottom of the mixer track that contains the **Frequency Splitter** track.

Frequency modulation can get deep and technical. If you want a further deep dive into the specifics of Frequency Shifter, Convolva's YouTube channel does an in-depth tutorial: https://youtu.be/dqQtP6oJvxo.

Creating granular synthesis with Fruity Granulizer

Fruity Granulizer is an effect using granular synthesis. **Granular synthesis** splits source audio into small pieces called grains. These grains are then looped and played back based on the plugin settings.

Fruity Granulizer is a great effect for bass sound design and for transitions such as risers and falling sound effects.

Let's get started using Fruity Granulizer:

1. Create a new pattern and add it to the playlist.
2. In the channel rack, insert the new instrument, **Fruity Granulizer**:

Figure 11.11 – Fruity Granulizer

3. Load a new sample into Fruity Granulizer such as by clicking in **Click to Load Sample** and navigating to an audio sample you want to use. Alternatively, you can drag and drop a sample from the browser into Fruity Granulizer:

Figure 11.12 – Fruity Granulizer loaded with sample

4. We need MIDI data to tell Fruity Granulizer when to play the sample, so we need to add some MIDI notes in the piano roll. Open the piano roll with Fruity Granulizer, such as shown in the following screenshot:

Chapter 11 343

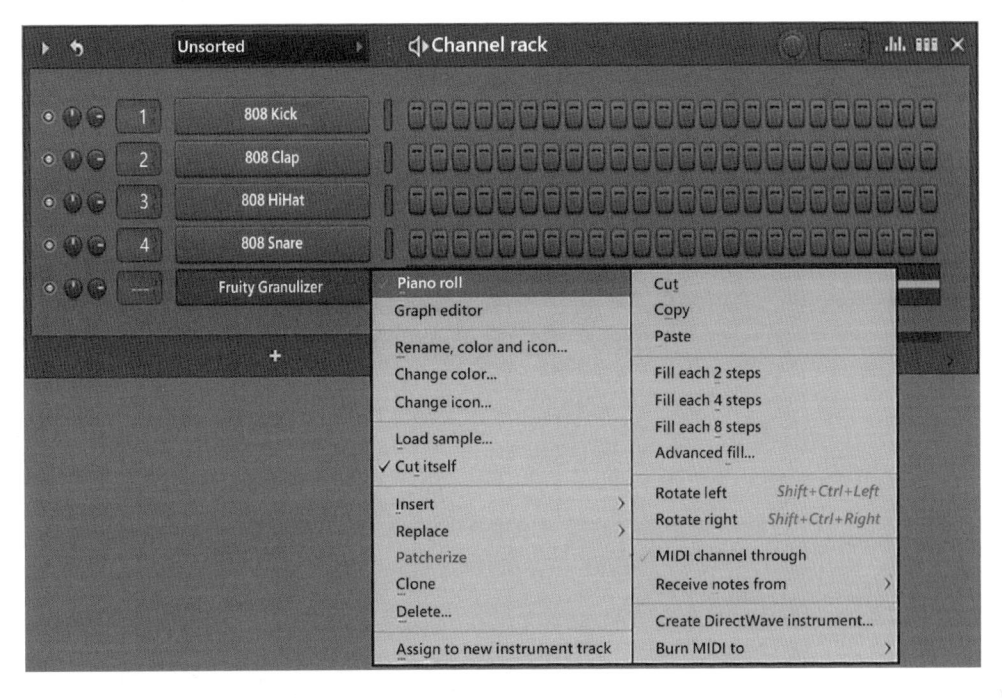

Figure 11.13 – Open Fruity Granulizer in the piano roll

In the piano roll, add some MIDI notes; an example is shown in the following screenshot:

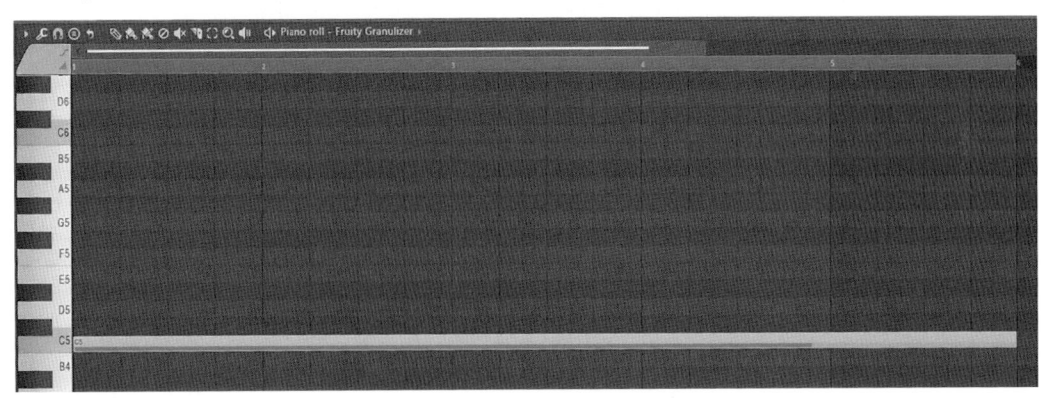

Figure 11.14 – Added MIDI note

Your pattern in the playlist should now show the MIDI note you added for Fruity Granulizer. It should look something like the following screenshot:

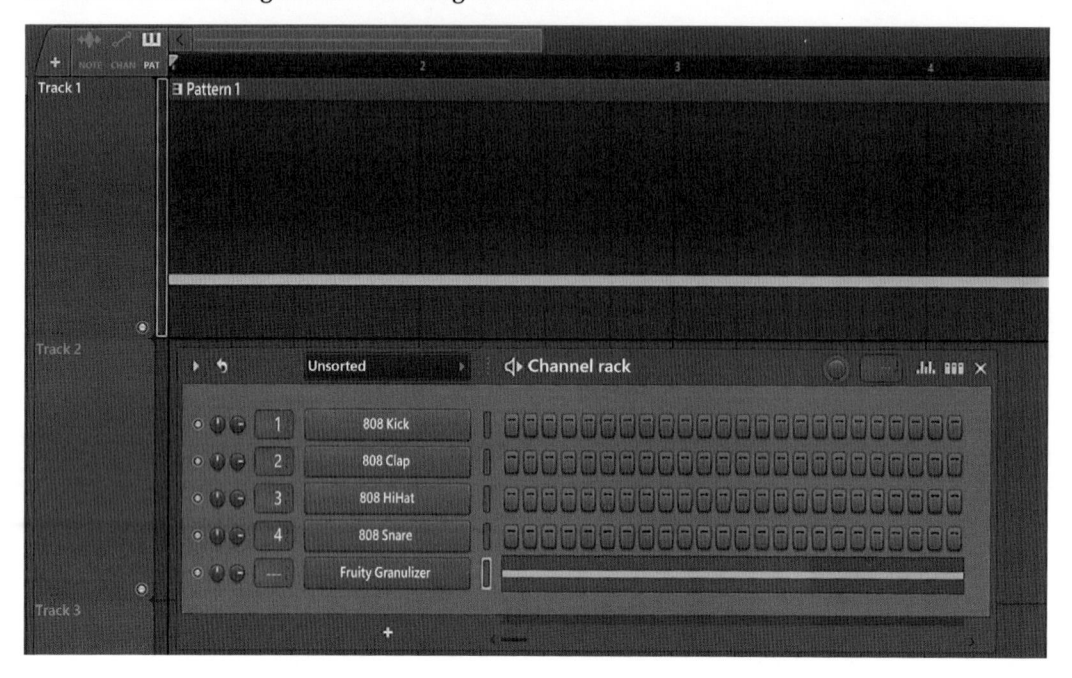

Figure 11.15 – Added Fruity Granulizer pattern in the playlist

Now whenever you play your song, it will tell Fruity Granulizer to play the MIDI notes. A quick recap: we added an audio sample into Fruity Granulizer, and we then told the playlist when to play Fruity Granulizer as if it were any other instrument. Okay, we're set up; now we can play with the Fruity Granulizer settings.

Figure 11.16 – Fruity Granulizer loaded with sample

You should play your song while tweaking Fruity Granulizer so you can hear the effect as it is applied to your audio. This is a plugin where the settings sound a little confusing. The best way to understand this plugin is to tweak knobs while looping over the audio.

> You can find several **presets** available at the top right of the plugin, which I encourage you to check out.

Next, we will go through a list of the controls available in the **Fruity Granulizer** plugin. The **GRAINS** section contains the following controls:

- **ATTACK:** Values for attack length of the grain. It's added to the fade in and out of the **grain**.
- **HOLD:** How long the grain is held before moving to the next grain.
- **GR SPACING:** Spacing of grain. Higher values increase spacing.
- **WAVE SPACING:** Number of grains created from audio. Small values mean more grains are used. Negative values reverse the playback of the grains. Note that this doesn't mean the audio is reversed.
- The **EFFECTS** section contains the following controls:
    - **PAN:** Higher values increase panning. Odd grains are panned left. Even grains are panned right.
    - **DEPTH:** Amplitude of LFO applied to wave spacing. Higher values increase amplitude.
    - **RAND:** Randomizes the order that grains are played back. Higher values increase the effect.

The **TRANSIENTS** section contains the following controls:

- **HOLD:** Determines the length of grain transient.
- Switches:
    - **OFF:** Disable transients.
    - **USE REGIONS:** Use slices loaded from the sample if existing. (It's possible to set transient markers onto samples.)
    - **DETECT:** Autodetect transients.

The **TIME** section contains the following controls:

- **LOOP:** Loops wave when enabled.
- **HOLD:** Playing position won't change if pressed. Same effect as setting the wave spacing to 0.
- **KEY TO:**
    - Key to **Pitch**: Maps keys to pitch. This is the default setting.
    - Key to **Percent**: C5 to C7 are equivalent to 0% - 100%. So you can hit C6 to start at 50%.

- Key to **Step**: Keys C5 and higher offset the sample start with a step (C6 offsets 12 steps, C7 – 24).
        - Key to **Transient**: Keys C5 and higher trigger the sample starting from a specific slice. This assumes that you have previously transient slices built into the audio.
    - **START**: Determines what position to start playing the sample from.

You now know how to create a granular synthesis with Fruity Granulizer.

Creating delay effects with Multiband Delay

Multiband Delay is a sound design delay effect. It works by splitting up the audio into 16 frequency bands. For each frequency band, you can adjust the volume, delay, and panning.

The effect is more noticeable on some sounds than others. For example, the effect is noticeable on flat-sounding acoustic instruments. I recommend trying it with flat piano chords to hear the effect clearly.

Let's get started using Multiband Delay:

1. Load up an audio sample or instrument in the playlist and route it to the mixer.
2. Apply the **Multiband Delay** effect to the mixer channel and play your sound. You'll see **Multiband Delay** load up as shown in the following screenshot:

Figure 11.17 – Multiband Delay

The main idea behind Multiband Delay is that you can set delay, volume, and panning values for individual frequency bands. You can save your band settings in a **BANK** preset. If desired, you can then morph from one preset bank to the next.

> You can find **presets** in the top-right corner of the plugin, which I encourage you to check out.

Here are the descriptions, starting from left to right:

- At the top are switches to turn the frequency band on or off, or lock the band position in place.
- Options dropdown arrow:
    - **Random Curve**: Creates a random curve for the frequency bands.
    - **Reset**: Resets the curve.
    - **Interpolate 1 to 8**: Using the curves from banks **1** and **8**, generates intermediate steps in between.
    - **Wave visualization**: Enable/disables wave display.
- Edit controls:
    - **Pencil mode**: Controls individual bands.
    - **Line mode**: Allows you to left-click and drag lines.
    - **Curve mode**: Allows you to draw smooth curves.
- Band mode:
    - **DELAY**: Top of band is 1000ms delay, bottom is 0ms delay.
    - **VOL**: 0 to 100%.
    - **PAN**: Bottom is panning left, top is panning right.
- Filter type:
    - **GENTLE**: Wider bands. Allows frequencies to appear in more than one band.
    - **STEEP**: Less spillover of frequencies between bands.
    - **LINEAR PHASE**: Splits frequencies while maintaining perfect phase alignment. Will create the most identifiable pitched sounds.

- **SCALE:** For delay times. -100% to 100%.
    - x0.1 Scale range off: 100 ms range. On: 100 ms range.
    - Harmonic scale: Pitches the frequency bands to make them more musically pleasing. This is usually what you'll want.
    - Harmonic weighting: Makes resonances more noticeable.
- **FEEDBACK:** Sends the output back into the plugin to increase the effect.
- **SMOOTHING TIME:** Smooths changes in scaling.
    - Keep pitch: Keeps pitch constant while delaying.
- **MORPH:** Transitions between bank preset settings. Consider adding automation to transition smoothly.
- **WET:**
    - **COMP:** Compress output.
    - **SAT:** Applies saturation.
    - **CLIP:** Allows harsh distortion.
    - **HP:** Filters low frequencies from output.

In general, if you want normal expansive stereo width effects, you want to have the lower frequencies in mono and the higher frequencies can be panned more left and right. You'll usually also want to have the low and high frequencies have less delay applied to them with more effect applied to the mid frequencies. However, Multiband Delay gives you the freedom to break the rules and explore new stereo width options.

Multiband processing with Frequency Splitter

Frequency Splitter is an effect plugin that separates audio into low, mid, and high-frequency bands. Once the frequency bands are split, you can route them to different mixer tracks for additional processing.

Splitting audio into frequency bands has a wide range of applications. Some use cases are as follows:

- In its simplest form, it can be used to perform simple EQ.
- It allows you to perform bandpass sweeping effects.

- It allows you to isolate frequency bands to duck when sidechaining instead of sidechaining the entire sound. For example, reducing the bass frequencies when percussion comes in while still retaining the upper frequencies. More generally, you can apply different effects to low, mid, or high frequencies of a sound.
- It can be used to duck instrument frequencies when a vocal comes so that it can maintain focus on the vocal.
- In mastering, it can be used to isolate frequencies so that you can increase effects such as stereo width, compression, and saturation to each frequency band separately.

Let's get started using Frequency Splitter:

1. Load up a sample or instrument with MIDI notes and route it to a new mixer track.
2. Apply the **Frequency Splitter** effect to the mixer channel and play your sound:

Figure 11.18 – Frequency Splitter

Frequency Splitter shows a visual representation of splitting frequencies up into frequency bands, with red representing the lower, yellow for the mid, and green for the high frequencies.

> You can find **presets** in the top-right corner of the plugin, which I encourage you to check out.

Chapter 11

The far left panel controls what frequencies make up the bands, as shown in the following screenshot:

Figure 11.19 – Frequency bands

- The **SLOPE** will determine the steepness of the frequency curve.
- You can control which frequencies are contained within a band by adjusting the Low/Mid frequency and Mid/High frequency knobs. These adjust the cutoff frequencies for the band.
- The **BANDS** allows you to have either 2 bands or 3 frequency bands.
- The link button connects the frequency knobs so that adjusting one knob will move the other. This is great for when you want to create bandpass sweeping effects.
- The level (loudness) of audio in the frequency band is controlled in the center panel, as shown in the following screenshot:

Figure 11.20 – Loudness in each frequency band

Adjusting one of the knobs will increase or decrease the audio output level of the frequency band. By selecting the checkbox, you can mute/solo the frequency band.

The options arrow at the bottom provides options to see different visualizations of the audio.

On the right panel, you'll find the frequency send controls, as shown in the following screenshot:

Figure 11.21 – Frequency splitter sends

1. To use the frequency sends, you'll want to sidechain the audio from the mixer track that contains Frequency Splitter to another mixer track. Select the track that has Frequency Splitter, then right-click on the arrow at the bottom of the mixer track that you want to sidechain to and select the option **Sidechain to this track**. An example is shown in the following screenshot:

Figure 11.22 – Sidechain to this track

2. Repeat *step 3*, sidechaining audio from the track containing Frequency Splitter to up to three mixer tracks.

Once you've done this, audio from the Frequency Splitter bands will be routed to the sidechained mixer tracks. Back in Frequency Splitter, you'll need to order the frequency band sends. The lowest number is the leftmost mixer track. In the following screenshot, **1** is the low-frequency band:

Figure 11.23 – Order sends

From now on, Frequency Splitter will split audio into frequency bands and send it to the designated mixer track. You've isolated the audio into low, mid, and high frequencies. Now you can perform effects on the mixer tracks targeting only specific frequency ranges.

Using Frequency Splitter for mastering

Frequency Splitter is a great tool for mastering as you can mix each frequency band separately and chain a series of effects. To do so, you'll want to load Frequency Splitter inside of **Patcher**.

If used inside Patcher, the way you add send outputs is by right-clicking on Frequency Splitter and adding an output. An example is shown in the following screenshot:

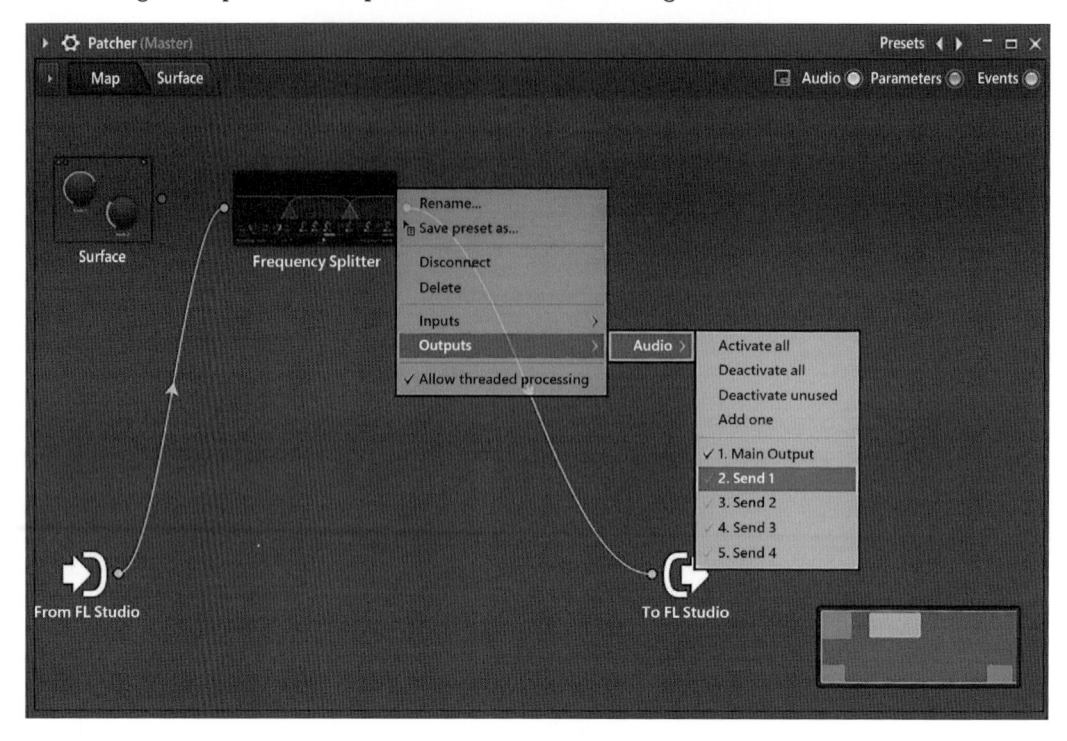

Figure 11.24 – Adding output to Frequency Splitter in Patcher

Once you've added output for Frequency Splitter, you can now apply compression, saturation, and stereo effects to each frequency band separately. For example, consider the following:

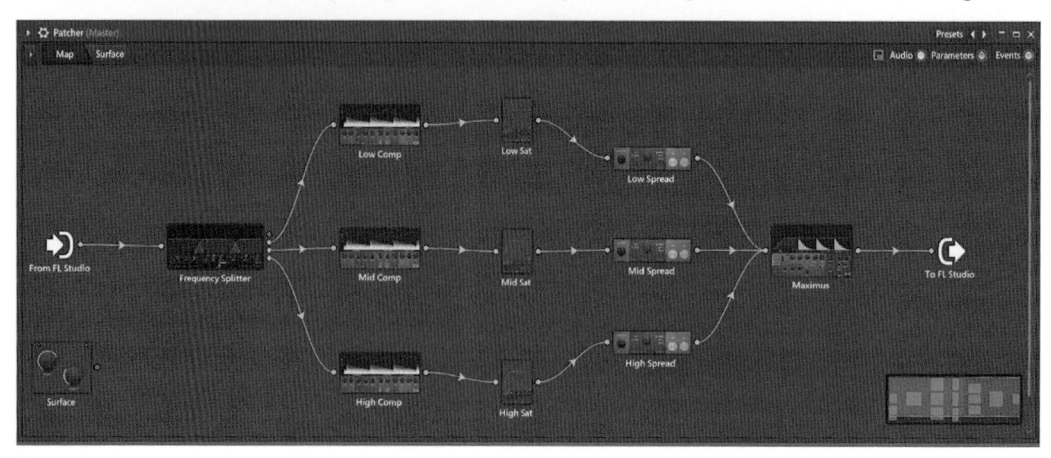

Figure 11.25 – Mastering chain

In the preceding screenshot example, we have different effects applied to the low, mid, and high frequencies.

How you want to master will depend on the song you're working with. The preceding screenshot is just an example of a mastering chain you could come up with; the details aren't important here. We'll discuss mastering in detail in the next chapter. You now know how to use Frequency Splitter.

Summary

In this chapter, we learned how to use Pitch Shifter to apply pitching effects in real time. It's a great effect to apply using automation.

We learned how to create frequency-shifting effects with Frequency Shifter. It can be a fun effect to give a simple sound some texture. We learned how to use Fruity Granulizer to break audio into grains, which can then be looped over. This can be useful when you want a sound to transition from one song passage into the next.

We learned about Multiband Delay to break up the audio into frequency bands and apply individual delay effects. This is useful when you want to create custom stereo width effects and play with the listener's environment experience.

Finally, we learned about Multiband processing with Frequency Splitter. This allows us to isolate frequency bands, which we can then apply effects on. This is useful for techniques like sidechaining that affect only specific frequencies, or for having deeper control over a frequency range when mastering.

In the next chapter, we'll discuss mastering.

Section III

Postproduction and Publishing Your Music

In this section you'll learn how to master music to make it ready for listeners to buy and enjoy. You'll learn music marketing essentials to establish your brand identity as an artist people want to see. You'll learn how to create artwork for your brand using artificial intelligence (Stable Diffusion) and how to create your own music video visualizers. Finally, you'll learn how to monetize and publish your music so you can earn song royalties.

We will cover the following chapters in this section:

- *Chapter 12, Mastering Fundamentals*
- *Chapter 13, Marketing, Content Creation, Getting Fans, and Going Viral*
- *Chapter 14, Publishing and Selling Music Online*

12

Mastering Fundamentals

In this chapter, we will learn about mastering. Mastering is the process taken to ensure our music is at a production-level quality and prepared for distribution. We'll learn the theory behind mastering and generally applicable techniques you can use when mastering music. By the end of this chapter, you'll understand how to master your music.

In this chapter, we'll cover the following topics:

- What is mastering?
- Equalization in mastering
- Using multiband compressors
- What are saturators/harmonic exciters?
- Understanding limiters
- Understanding stereo imaging with vectorscopes
- Exporting audio for third-party mixing and mastering

What is mastering?

Your song is finished being mixed. You're happy with the composition. You've balanced all the levels of instruments and applied effects to enhance your individual sounds. What's next?

When your song is finished being mixed, before publicly releasing it, you take it through a series of steps to enhance it called **mastering**. Mastering is an all-encompassing term for postproduction activities that include the following:

- Making the song sound consistent with other songs in the album
- Editing out flaws

- Equalization to ensure a well-balanced frequency range
- Compression to balance dynamic range
- Stereo width enhancement
- Limiting to raise the overall volume of the mix
- Listening to the audio on different devices and ensuring that there is a consistent quality of sound heard across them
- Any other adjustments necessary to prepare the music for distribution

You should always master your song before publicly releasing it. Mastering should always end up making your music sound better than it did before mastering.

Can you master music yourself?

I personally say yes, or you should at least learn enough about mastering that you know what you're paying for if you use a third party.

Learning to master will help tune your ears, and as a byproduct help you become better at mixing. The activities involved in mastering audio force you to look at your music from a different perspective compared to composing. It makes you imagine how your music will be received from the perspective of a third party. It helps you to hear your music the way your audience will hear it.

When should you master your music?

Master your music when you're done mixing and are ready to publicly release it. If possible, try to give yourself time (at least a day) after finishing mixing the song before you start mastering. This will allow you to approach the song with fresh ears.

How do I get good at mastering?

If you want to get good at mastering, master a lot of music. Just like playing an instrument requires muscle memory in your fingers, mastering requires you to fine-tune your ears. You need to develop a sense of what could be done to improve a song, and to know this, you need to experience what mastering can do. It's not something you can memorize; rather, it's something that you listen to and then make tweaks based on what you want to hear. To master a lot, you either need to make a lot of music and master it or master other people's music.

What equipment do I use to master music?

To do a good job at mastering, you need mastering plugins. Mastering plugins include the following tools:

- Equalizers/dynamic equalizers
- Saturators/harmonic exciters
- Multiband compressors
- Stereo imagers
- Limiters/maximizers
- (Optional) reference tracks

The order of plugins in the effects chain while mastering is usually as follows:

1. The EQ or equalizer
2. Stereo FX – such as widening or mastering reverb
3. Compressors
4. Limiting

We'll learn about mastering concepts in a generally applicable way so that you can use the techniques with any mastering plugin.

I personally use iZotope's **Ozone** suite of tools to master my music. If you are looking for a cutting-edge, all-encompassing mastering suite, iZotope's Ozone is an excellent choice. It's available at https://www.izotope.com/.

Equalization in mastering

When mastering, you will use a parametric equalizer. We learned how to use a parametric equalizer in *Chapter 6, Compression, Sidechaining, Limiting, and Equalization*, so refer to that chapter if you need a refresher. Parametric equalizers show audio levels at each frequency and have band filters to apply EQ to selected frequencies. A **band filter** is a tool used to isolate certain frequency ranges and reject frequencies outside these ranges.

You can then perform effects on selected frequencies in the band filter. The following is an example of a parametric equalizer:

Figure 12.1 – Parametric equalizer

Parametric equalizers break up audio frequencies into multiple filter bands. You can then either increase or decrease the level of a band. By increasing, you'll boost a sound. By cutting, you'll reduce selected frequencies. Boosting frequencies of a sound brings the sound more into focus. Cutting frequencies is useful for removing undesirable, offensive sounds.

You may be thinking *I used compressors and equalizers in the mixing stage, how is mastering different?* When you use compressors and equalizers in the mixing stage, you're tailoring individual sounds as well as combining sounds together. You can make extreme cuts and pass filters to shape your instrument sounds. You fix clashing instruments and balance individual sounds against each other.

When we apply compressors and equalizers in the mastering stage, we're thinking about the mix as a whole and balancing overall dynamics and frequencies. We're thinking about the entire combined sound altogether, rather than individual sounds. We're no longer isolating frequencies; instead, we're simply choosing frequency areas to emphasize over others. While mastering, any changes you make will affect the entire mix. Your boosts and cuts will need to be more subtle than when mixing.

Diagnosing frequency problems

Equalization is all about listening and then making EQ adjustments based on what you hear. When trying to find problematic frequencies, it helps to start by boosting a frequency band. Once you've found an area that sounds unpleasant, you can lightly cut frequencies at that position.

Here are examples of fixes you can do with equalizers:

- Some mastering engineers like to add a high pass filter cutting all frequencies below 20 Hz - 30 Hz as some speakers struggle to reproduce frequencies in that region.
- If the sound is too muddy, try cutting somewhere between 100 Hz and 300 Hz.
- If the sound is too nasal-sounding, try cutting somewhere between 250 Hz and 1,000 Hz.
- If the sound is too harsh, try cutting somewhere in the range of 2,000 Hz to 2,500 Hz.
- If your cutting is more than 4 dB, you probably have an issue that needs to be fixed in the mixing stage rather than the mastering stage and should go back and make mixing tweaks first.

Once you've made a change, always flip back and forth, turning effects on and off to see whether you made the sound better. Also, make sure you compare the ending track after mastering to the pre-mastered track to see whether you made it sound better.

Understanding spectrograms

Spectrograms are a tool allowing you to visualize audio frequencies. You use them when applying equalization and place them after the EQ plugin on the effects chain. They allow you to visualize differences made from EQ cuts or boosts.

If you load up the FL Studio **Wave Candy** plugin on the master channel and choose the built-in **Spectrum** preset, it will load up a spectrogram. In the following screenshot, we can see a spectrogram displaying audio frequencies and energy levels at each frequency:

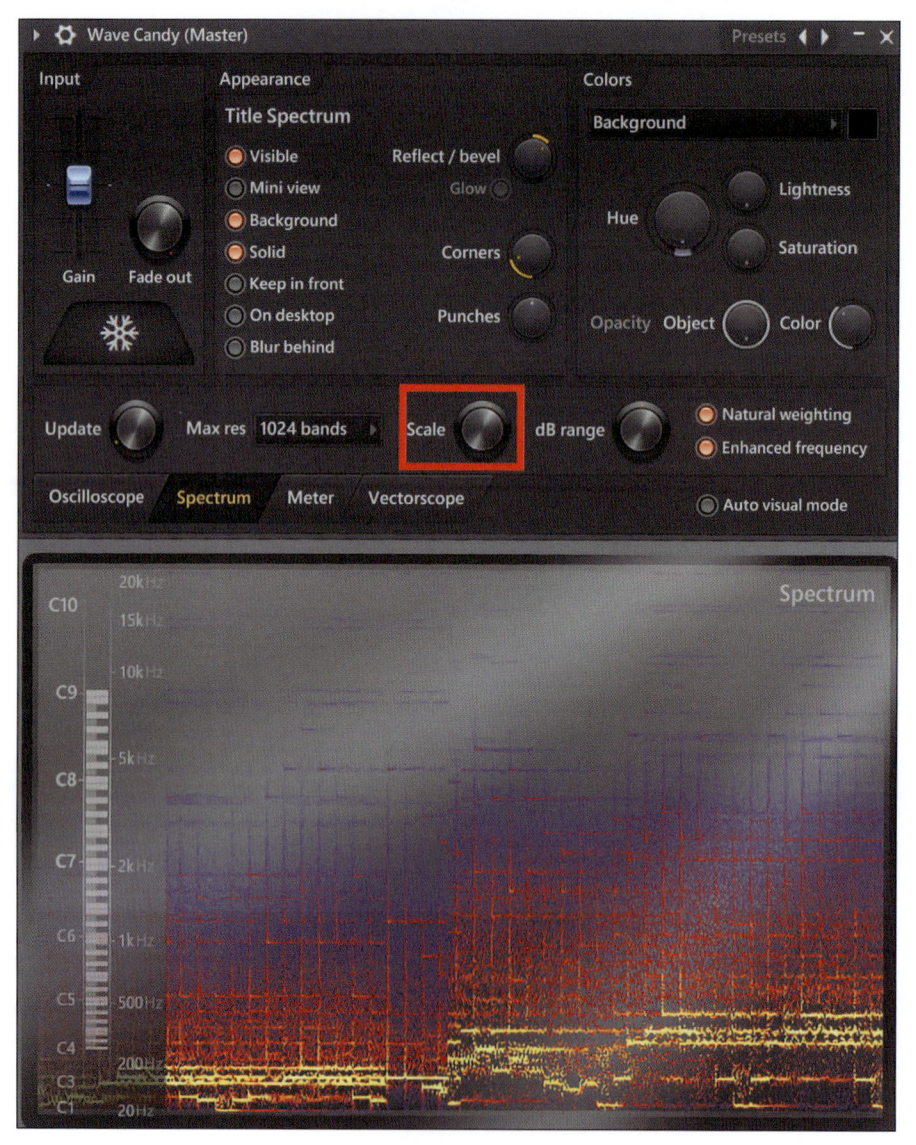

Figure 12.2 – Wave Candy's spectrogram

In the example in the preceding figure, we can see that the highest energy level appears to be in the 200 Hz to 500 Hz range. I've adjusted the scale knob to fit my audio, as seen in the preceding screenshot. You can adjust your scale knob to fit your music.

Here's another example, this time using an **iZotope** plugin:

Figure 12.3 – iZotope's Insight spectrogram

Spectrograms are useful when you're trying to troubleshoot low frequencies that are hard to hear with your ears. For example, let's say you noticed there was some issue in the bass frequencies but weren't sure what was causing the problem; you could look at a spectrogram to try to identify where frequency peaks were occurring.

Adjusting dynamics

Dynamic range refers to how loud or quiet your sound is. When mastering, you need to find a comfortable dynamic range for your listener. If a song has no dynamics, the song will appear flat and lacking in variety. If too much dynamics are present, the listener will need to keep changing the volume to hear clearly, which is an undesirable experience.

One part of mastering is processing the dynamic range of your audio. You want to find a balance between the loud and quiet sections of your song. More specifically, we want to find a balance in dynamic range throughout our frequency ranges. You don't want your low-end frequencies to overpower your high-end ones, or your high-end frequencies to overpower your low-end ones.

You want everything to have clarity while drawing attention to your leading melody.

Using multiband compressors

To find a nice balance between loudness levels and frequency levels, we use compressors, limiters, and expanders to adjust dynamics. Basic compressors work by reducing the dynamic range. We discussed compressors in *Chapter 6, Compression, Sidechaining, Limiting, and Equalization*. Refer to that chapter if you need a refresher on how compressors work. When mastering, we use an advanced form of compressor called a **multiband compressor**. By the end of this section, you'll understand the general principles for how to apply compression with any multiband compressor plugin.

Let's discuss the theory behind using a multiband compressor and then show an example using FL Studio's **Maximus** plugin. Multiband compressors allow you to isolate frequency ranges and apply compression to each region. This way, you can bring up or down the level of the low, mid, or high frequencies separately. For example, say your low-frequency sounds needed compression but not the rest of your frequencies – a multiband compressor allows you to do this.

When you use a multiband compressor, you'll do the following steps:

1. First, split the audio into filter bands based on a frequency range. Usually, there are three or four bands for your lows, mids, and highs. Essentially, we're saying let's break up our audio and look at each frequency area separately.
2. Within each filter band, solo the band so that you can hear the frequencies and level of audio in just that range.
3. Apply compression just to your chosen frequency range. This will help balance out the loud and quiet parts within the band. You can then choose to either raise or lower the level of volume.

I realize this is very confusing without a visual. Let's do the steps described with a multiband compressor plugin.

Applying multiband compression with Maximus

Maximus is a multiband compressor, limiter, noise gate, expander, ducker, and de-esser. Maximus comes with FL Studio Signature Edition and higher. Although you may or may not use Maximus, it is a great tool for learning about multiband compression and works similar to other multiband compressors on the market, so we'll use it in our examples. Let's apply multiband compression using Maximus:

Chapter 12

1. Before using Maximus, you'll need to have a sound to apply multiband compression to. If you have a song already mixed and ready to be mastered, add it to the playlist.
2. On the master channel, add the **Maximus** plugin and play your sound. You'll see something like this:

Figure 12.4 – Maximus

3. Maximus allows you to break up your audio into three frequency bands and apply individual compression to each of them. To apply multiband compression, we first need to break up the audio into frequency filter bands.
4. On **Maximus**, select the **BANDS** tab as shown in the preceding screenshot.
5. Check the **Show output spectrogram** button directly to the left of the **MONITOR** button. This will allow you to visually see the frequency level.

6. You'll see the visual on the right side of the plugin display three distinct colors. These represent the three frequency band filters and are shown from left to right as red, orange, and yellow. Red represents low frequencies, orange represents mid frequencies, and yellow represents high frequencies. This is shown in the following screenshot:

Figure 12.5 – Frequency bands

7. On the left side of **Maximus**, you can see four tabs – **LOW**, **MID**, **HIGH**, and **MASTER** – with the corresponding red, orange, and yellow colors. These tabs allow you to switch between frequency ranges. The **MASTER** tab is the resulting combined sound of any effects applied to the **LOW**, **MID**, and **HIGH** bands.

8. Let's choose a range for a filter band. Left-click to select the **LOW** tab. This will select the low-frequency band.

9. Left-click on the **SOLO** button. You will now be listening to just frequencies existing in the **LOW** filter band.

Chapter 12

10. Now, we need to customize our frequency bands. While the **LOW** tab is selected, left-click on the low filter band visual and drag it around. By dragging, you resize the filter band. The goal here is to isolate the low frequencies of your audio. For example, you could drag until you hear just the sub-bass sounds. Dragging the band will automatically adjust the **LOW** and pregain (**PRE**) knobs:

Figure 12.6 – Adjusting the low-frequency band

11. Left-click on the **MID** tab on the left and adjust the filter band as you did in the previous step until you hear just the mid frequencies.

12. When you drag a filter band around, you'll notice that the **PRE** knob will adjust. This is the volume of your audio before being compressed. You may be wondering whether it's better to increase or decrease pregain. This is something you'll have to discover for yourself. Whether to increase or decrease the volume before compressing will depend on your specific situation. It's a matter of playing around to see whether your sound is improved or not.

13. You have successfully broken down your audio into three filter bands. Next, we can apply individual compression to these filter bands.

14. While the **LOW** tab is selected, we can apply compression to the low frequencies. On the left side, you'll see a visual as follows:

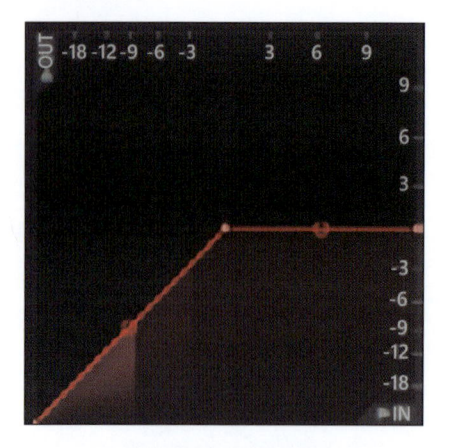

Figure 12.7 – Limiting

By default, limiting is applied to a threshold of 0 dB. By left-clicking and dragging the key points on the visual, you can change how compression is applied.

You can drag points on the line around, add new points, and add curves. This will compress the audio in various ways. An example is shown in the following screenshot. Notice the difference in curve shape between *Figure 12.7* and *Figure 12.8*:

Figure 12.8 – Applied compression

15. Remember that compression can be used to bring the loud and soft parts of a sound closer together. If we like, we can then increase the overall volume of the compressed sound with a makeup gain. On Maximus, makeup gain is done with the **POST** button, as shown in the preceding screenshot. In other words, if you want to increase or decrease the volume of your compressed sound, you use the **POST** button. For example, say after you compressed your sound you discovered that it was too quiet. You could fix this by increasing the **POST** gain.
16. Repeat applying compression to the mid and high frequencies in the **MID** and **HIGH** tabs.
17. You're probably thinking that the sound difference is quite subtle and maybe you don't really hear much of a difference. You're right. Compression in the mastering stage is very subtle. Compression removes dynamic range, so you're hearing the absence of dynamic range.
18. When using a multi-compressor plugin, a good place to start is to select one of the mastering presets, listen to the different possibilities available, then go back and tweak the filter bands and controls to your liking.

19. Maximus comes with several presets. On Maximus, select a preset by clicking **Presets** in the top-right corner:

Figure 12.9 – Maximus presets

In the preceding screenshot, under the **Mastering** header, you can see presets for **Clear master RMS** and **Clear master**. These presets can give your mastering some initial controls to get started.

I've compressed my sound, now what?

The release time of the compressor is an important tool. A fast release time could cause distortion or a pumping sound. A slower release time allows the compressor to compress after the loud peaks pass. You'll likely want your low-end frequency sounds to be compressed differently from your high-end frequency sounds.

Some examples of using multi-compressors are as follows:

- You can set different attack and release times for different frequencies. You can have shorter attack times for high frequencies such as hi-hats or not compress the hi-hat frequencies at all. In general, you'll want shorter attack and release times for high frequencies than low frequencies.
- If you want to increase the loudness of your track but not make the bass sounds overpowering, you can compress the bass sounds more than other frequencies.

There is a trade-off made between making your sound louder and how much dynamic range your sound retains. Overcompressing your mid and high frequencies can ruin transient sounds. **Transients** are the punctuated bursts when a sound first hits. Think about a drum snare hit. In a rock song, you want that to break through the mix and be clearly heard. You don't want the transients to be overcompressed. The way to avoid overcompressing transients is to adjust the release time to be shortened for a less noticeable pumping effect. Maximus contains some presets that can be used to add punchiness to your drums.

This isn't a *one rule fits all* situation though. You may have scenarios where you want your transients to smear together, in which case, you'll want less punchy transients. Your decision comes down to a case-by-case basis for what you want your sound to feel like. This is why reference tracks can be helpful as you have a guide as to what you want your song to sound like.

Using reference tracks

Prior to working, some mastering engineers collect songs they like that are similar to the song being mastered. When mastering the song, they will swap back and forth between the song being mastered and the reference tracks. The goal of reference tracks is to give the mastering engineer a reference point to compare with.

If you want your mastered track to sound similar to an existing song, you can use reference tracks. Instead of applying mastering presets, you compare your song to other similar songs that you'd like your song to mimic. You then tweak your equalization and compression to create a similar mastered sound.

Using reference tracks is easy to do. Simply find some songs that you'd like your song to sound like and periodically compare listening to the two while mastering. Some mastering plugins like Izotope's **Ozone** allow you to quickly switch between the mastered track and the reference song without having to leave the plugin.

You now know how to use multiband compressors. Next, we'll learn about saturators/harmonic exciters.

What are saturators/harmonic exciters?

Saturators/harmonic exciters are effect plugins that are sometimes used when mastering. They're not mandatory, only sometimes used. When applied, they add intended distortion to your audio. Subtle distortion can sometimes add some character to your sounds.

They usually operate like multi-compressors, in that you first select frequency bands, and then apply distortion. Generally, you want less distortion applied to your lower frequencies than your higher frequencies.

Understanding limiters

The idea behind limiting is you choose a threshold volume and compress audio volume peaks that reach the threshold level. Then, you can raise the overall volume of the sound close to the threshold level without going over. This results in your ending sound appearing louder overall to your listener. In general, if your sound is louder, listeners will be able to hear your sound more easily and have a more enjoyable listening experience.

When mastering, the last plugin on your master channel should always be a limiter. Maximus acts as a limiter by default. If you are using Maximus to master your music, it will be the last plugin on your master channel. We also discussed limiters in *Chapter 6, Compression, Sidechaining, Limiting, and Equalization.*

Without a limiter, you risk having your audio go above 0 dB, which can result in uncontrolled distortion on speakers. A limiter ensures that the final sound is contained below a threshold to help prevent unwanted distortion.

On Maximus, on the **MASTER** tab, you can see the final audio being outputted. In the following visual example, on the right side, you can see a scale of the output volume. By default, Maximus limits the output volume to 0 dB as shown by the compression line going horizontal:

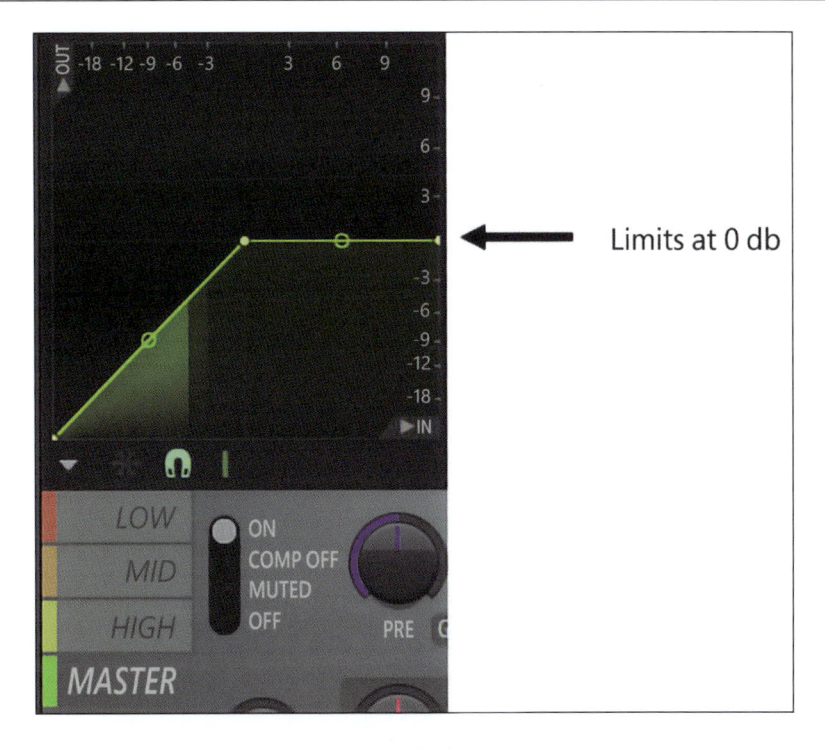

Figure 12.10 – Maximus master

In theory, you can set a limiter ceiling to 0 dB. In practice, there's a chance that the speaker playing the audio may distort when playing the sound, especially if the file format is changed due to file compression. To be safe and ensure there's no peaking, some mastering technicians choose to give a little headroom and set the ceiling threshold somewhere between -0.3 dB and -3 dB, and some as much as -6 dB.

If you find that the overall volume of your audio is then too quiet, you may consider increasing the **POST** gain knob. This will increase the volume of your audio. Note that you can only increase the volume up to the amount of your ceiling threshold. Anything exceeding the threshold will be limited. This means anything that would normally rise above the threshold will now be compressed and you will remove any dynamic range. In other words, your goal is to find a balance between increasing the volume as much as you can before you lose too much dynamic range.

Understanding stereo imaging with vectorscopes

Stereo imaging is another tool that is sometimes used while mastering. A vectorscope can help you to identify where your sounds are positioned in the stereo field (how much mono or stereo).

Stereo imaging is related to stereo width. Stereo imaging is about identifying how your sound is heard out of the left and right channels. This helps you to troubleshoot any issues that may occur, such as sounds unintentionally focused on one side or the other. If there is an issue, you'll then go back to the mixer and investigate what is causing the audio imbalance.

If your goal is to create more stereo width, the vectorscope will allow you to visually see how much stereo width has been created. You'll be able to see how much difference there is between the audio on each side.

The following is an example of FL Studio's **Wave Candy** plugin using the built-in **Vectorscope** preset. It shows the stereo image of your audio:

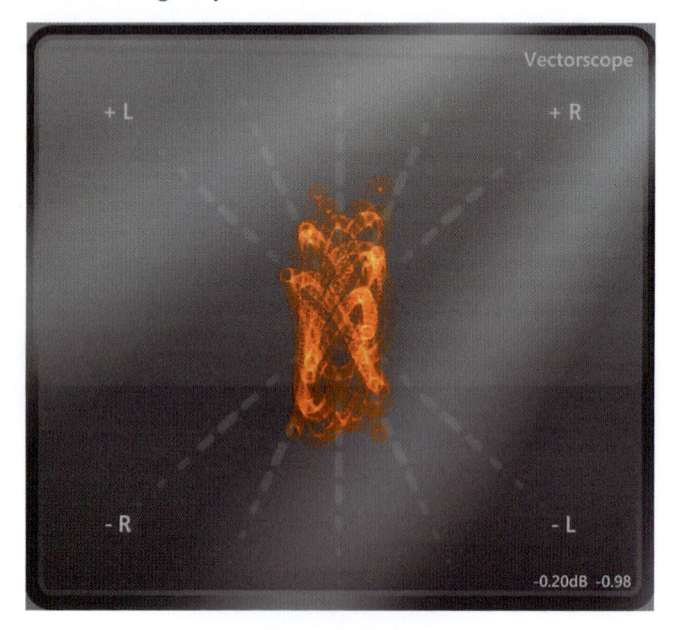

Figure 12.11 – Vectorscope

L stands for left audio channel and **R** for right. In the center, you can see a visual of the audio. If the audio is centered, it will look vertical, as shown in the screenshot. You can think of this as a mono sound where you have equal sound coming out of the left and right channels. If the visual shows a leaning toward the left or right, it means that there is a different sound in the left and right channels.

There are multiple types of vectorscopes that can be used for stereo imaging. The following is another example of a vectorscope, this time using an **iZotope** plugin:

Figure 12.12 – iZotope Insight's vectorscope

In the preceding iZotope vectorscope screenshot, you can see a visual that expands upward and to the left and the right. The left and right positions indicate that there are some distinct differences between the left and right channels.

Stereo imaging best practices

You want most of your sounds to be centered in the stereo field. Why? A lot of the time, your music will be played on a mono device where the same sound comes equally out of all speakers. In such a case, any panning sounds will appear as mono to the listener. Also, if your audience is positioned far from the speakers, the overall impression is still mono.

Does this mean the goal of your music is to be mono? No. It's just important that your song sounds good in mono before you think about stereo effects. Stereo imaging is more like the icing on the cake you can add. Stereo imaging plugins usually come with the ability to increase the stereo width. You can then spread selected frequency ranges out. Ozone has a plugin called **Imager** that spreads out the stereo field of selected frequencies.

Sounds that are centered in the stereo field usually include kicks, snares, lead vocals, and bass instruments. Other higher-frequency sounds may be directed away from the center to give the impression that the sound exists in a larger space.

You can't do stereo imaging on headphones; it can only be done on speakers. Headphones will make it seem like sounds are much wider than they would sound on speakers.

Generally, when mastering, most songs have a very narrow stereo width in the lower frequencies. The mid frequencies have some stereo width, and the high frequencies have the most.

When mastering, make sure you listen to your song in mono as well as stereo. This can help to identify phase cancellation issues that can occur.

Listening to your audio in different environments

One step in mastering is ensuring your song quality is consistent across various devices. For example, does your song sound good coming out of a car radio, earbuds, TV speakers, and any other devices that you can find? Does your music sound good when played on sub-optimal speakers? Everything sounds better on amazing speakers, but does your song hold up when played on bad speakers?

What about formats?

Depending on the type of medium (vinyl, streaming, CD, cassette, and so on) you are exporting to, you may have to choose a different bit depth. Higher bit depth values will give better audio resolution but result in larger file sizes. Usually, you can export at 16- or 24-bit depths. Also, make sure your final master has a resampling rate of 64 points or higher.

This may sound complicated, but it's just a matter of choosing an export setting when you're exporting your finished track, as shown in the following screenshot:

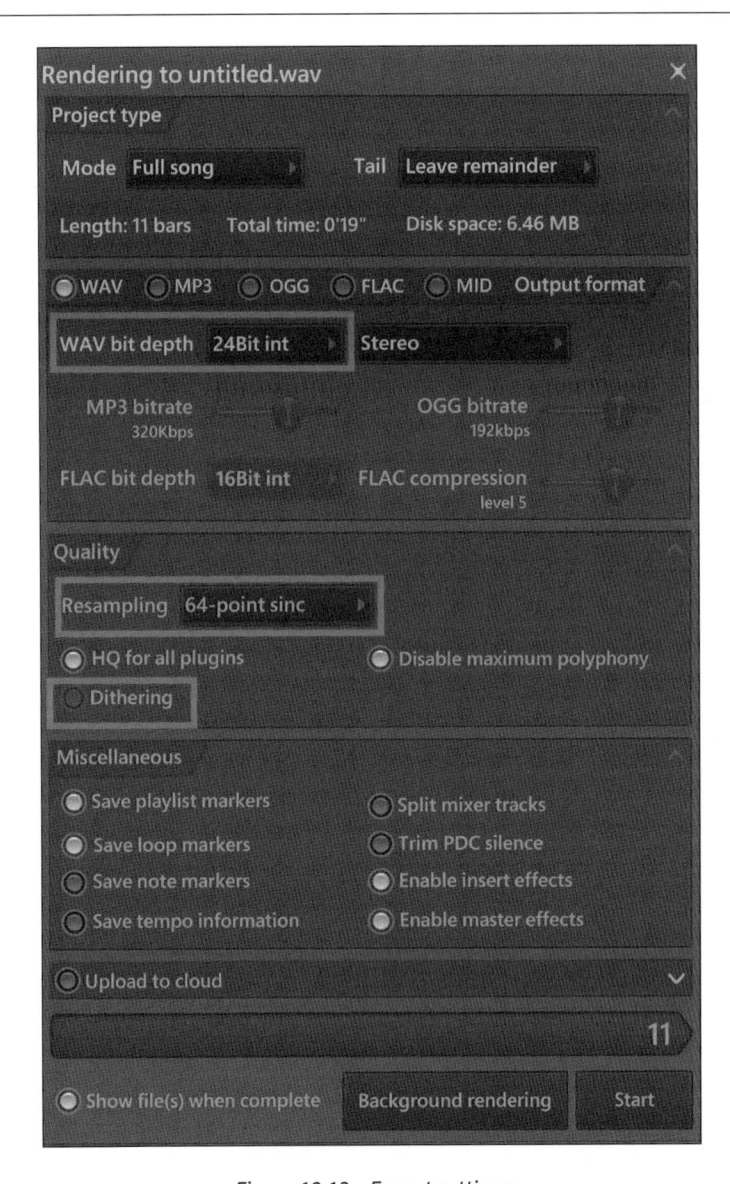

Figure 12.13 – Export settings

If you have a bit depth of 16 bits, turn on dithering on the final master when exporting. How dithering works is beyond the scope of this book, but the general gist is that it makes it appear that your audio is higher-resolution than it actually is.

We've learned skills to master your music yourself. Next, we'll learn about mixing and mastering using third parties.

Exporting audio for third-party mixing and mastering

If you want your music mastered, but don't think you have the skills or plugins to do it yourself, one option is to hire a mastering engineer. One benefit a mastering engineer can provide is an independent set of ears. They will hear your song from an outsider's perspective and may pick up on flaws or ways to enhance your music that you wouldn't think of.

The mastering engineer will request that you do not put any limiters on your mastering track before sending them the track. They will likely request you leave some volume headroom in the master channel – usually at least 3 db - 6 db of headroom so that they have some volume space play around with. They like it when you give them lots of headroom. The more headroom you give them, the more noticeable the mastering effect will be on the song.

If you want to send a song to a third party to mix or master your music, you should send all the audio from the mixer channels in your project. This way, the third party can apply additional effects to your sounds. To export each mixer channel as an individual audio file including the master channel, ensure that you're exporting **WAV** files and that **Split mixer tracks** is checked when exporting, as shown in the following screenshot:

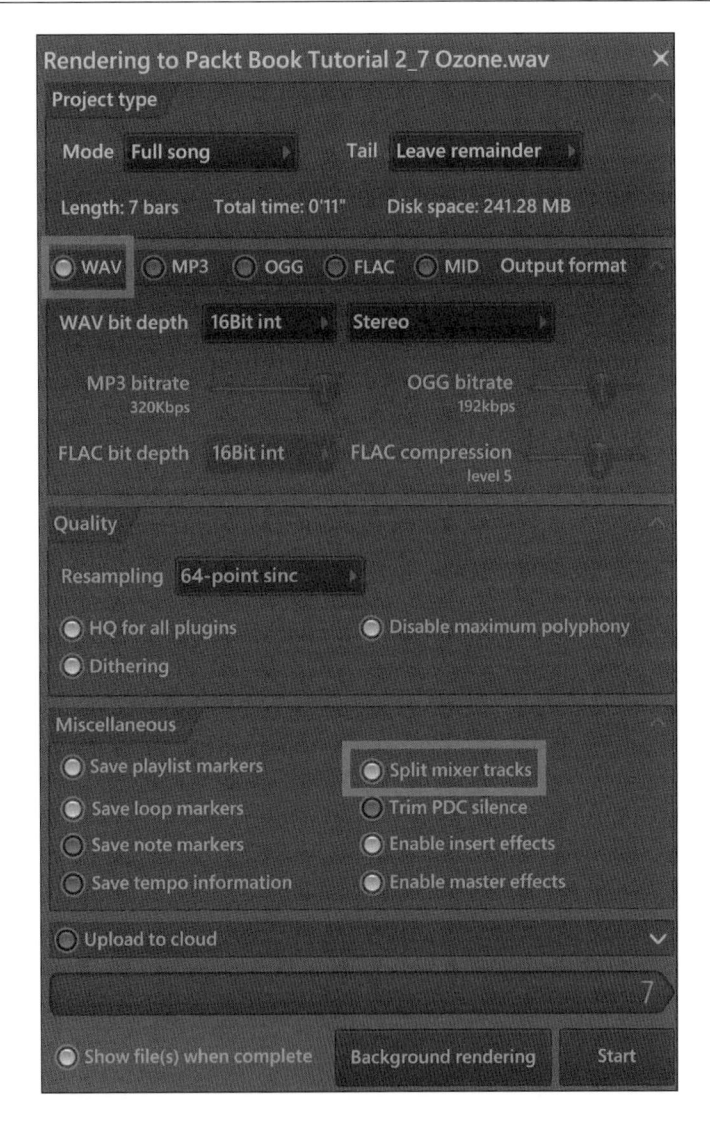

Figure 12.14 – Split mixer tracks

Once they're exported, **WAV** files will be generated from the audio out of each mixer channel. You now know how to export your music for editing by third parties.

Summary

Mastering is the postproduction process you take your music through to enhance your song after it's finished being mixed. Mastering polishes your song into a finished product. This includes ensuring song consistency, removing flaws, balancing frequency ranges, compressing dynamic range, stereo width enhancements, and limiting music. All of which can help to improve the overall reception of your song.

When mastering for the first time, its useful to try out your plugin's existing mastering presets on your song. See whether they improve your song and investigate how the plugin affected the sound. Where did it EQ and compress? Exploring presets and comparing them can give you an idea of what's possible. Then you can tailor the presets and adjust them to your own projects. Listen to songs that you like and think about how the song feels compared to your song. If you were to master your song to sound similar to your reference song, what steps would you need to do?

In this chapter, you learned techniques to master your music, including equalization, multiband compressors to adjust the frequency range, stereo imaging enhancements, and limiting your music. We also learned how to export your song as individual audio stems for use by third parties.

> If you want further reading on mastering topics, consider checking out Izotope's article on LUFS:
>
> https://www.izotope.com/en/learn/what-are-lufs.html

You have completed music. Now it's time to release your music to the world. In the next chapter, we'll learn about marketing your music so that you can ensure that your music reaches as wide an audience as possible.

13

Marketing, Content Creation, Getting Fans, and Going Viral

We've learned how to create music. Now we need to get your music heard. Branding, promotion, and marketing are important tools to launch a career in music. In this chapter, we'll learn about developing your brand, marketing/promoting yourself, and tips to create online content.

In this chapter, we will discuss the following topics:

- Marketing essentials
- Creating a brand
- Making the most of your live performances
- Collaborating with others to promote yourself
- YouTube and TikTok for musicians
- Creating album artwork using AI art generators (Stable Diffusion)
- Creating music visuals with ZGameEditor Visualizer

Marketing essentials

How much you're able to earn is directly connected to how well you're able to market yourself. To market yourself, at a minimum, you'll want to have the following:

- A brand identity.
- A musician website featuring you and your products.
- A YouTube channel.

- A Google email account for business-related inquiries. Give it a professional name.
- Optional but potentially useful: SoundCloud, Patreon, Twitter, Instagram, TikTok, Facebook, and/or Twitch accounts for your brand.

Building a brand isn't something that happens overnight. It takes months or years for you to develop a fan base. So, if you don't have the previously listed items yet, get started creating them.

Creating a brand

Time for the fun part... choosing your identity. What do you want to be known as? How would you like to be recognized? Think about the visuals, logos, genres, and so on. If you don't know what kind of artist you want to be yet, start thinking now.

If you want to get recognized, it helps if you have something to be recognized for. It may sound a little counterintuitive, but the more specific you get with your brand image, the easier it becomes to generate content. By narrowing your options and choosing some rules to work within, it becomes easier to create. This applies to any creative artistic expression. Once you know what direction you'd like to go in, you'll start discovering lots of opportunities to get there.

Making decisions to advance your career can be intimidating and overwhelming when you first start as there are countless paths you could take. Creating a brand makes decision-making easier. Think about how you want to look visually: what clothing, hairstyle, atmosphere, and tone you'd like to convey. Once you pick a style, you'll instinctively start looking for inspiration and tools to help you get there. Your style will help shape the type of live show you deliver when performing and the type of content you want to create when promoting yourself online.

Choosing your artist name

Unless you want to use your real name, you need a professional artist name or band name that you can use when performing. For picking a name, here are two recommendations:

- Pick a name that's easy to spell and pronounce. If people can't remember your name, they'll struggle to search for you and it becomes harder to become famous.
- Pick a name that's unique. Do a Google search beforehand to see if someone else already has a name similar to yours. Pick a name that isn't too similar to something else. Also, check that the website domain name hasn't already been taken. Picking a unique name will help immensely when dealing with search engine optimization as you'll have less online competition.

Creating a website

To promote your brand, you'll want to have a website to showcase your work, enable fans to buy your products and services, and provide contact information for business opportunities.

When creating a website, there are several options available to you. If you have no website-making experience whatsoever, there are website templates and website builders. These will guide you through the process of creating a musician website, and you don't have to worry at all about what's going on in the website backend. If you choose this option, it's easy: just pay money every month and you're done.

If you don't mind getting your hands a little bit dirty and want more customization than what a website builder can offer, I recommend looking into using WordPress. WordPress allows you to import a template of your choosing and then customize the template. It does require some effort to get your template customized, your website hosted, and your SEO optimized, but it is cheaper than using a website builder and you end up with a website that has as many features as you desire. Lots of reasonably priced WordPress templates are available at https://elements.envato.com/.

If you choose to go the WordPress route, you can test your website and host it on your own computer before paying for hosting and publicly deploying it. You can test WordPress sites using a service called **Local**, available at https://localwp.com/.

When you're ready to deploy your WordPress website, you'll need to look into a service that can host it. There are lots of companies dedicated to providing web hosting. At the time of writing, I use a service called **IONOS** by *1&1* for my web hosting. I end up paying about $100 a year for hosting with the domain name included. IONOS by 1&1 services are available at https://www.ionos.ca/.

A website is important to convey the brand identity you want to portray. In addition to being the place for fans to find you, your website will also shape the type of future business opportunities that come your way. Next, let's learn about performing live.

Making the most of your live performances

If you're a live-performing musician, that means you're an entertainer. That means you should be thinking about how to entertain. The music, although important, is only one piece of the act.

If you want to perform live, you need to have something to show. That means you need to put together an act that can be repeated in multiple performances. If someone is watching your show, you need to find ways to keep them engaged. Why should they watch you? Give them a reason.

Think about visuals you can create to captivate your audience. Although you may not be able to control the venue itself, since it changes with each performance, there are many parts of your act that you can control, even when you're first starting out with little to no budget. Here are some suggestions:

- Find a visual costume that is pleasing to look at. You might consider incorporating costume changes throughout your show.
- If you're singing, think about what kind of movement/dancing you could do. Perhaps come up with some signature dance moves.
- If you're playing an instrument, think about how to make the instrument part of the act.
- Between songs, you should have some banter ready to help bridge the gap. If you don't do this, you'll soon discover that the venue becomes awkwardly silent, and you'll lose any momentum you built up.
- Consider humorous dialog between your band members. Perhaps include recurring gag bits you can bring back again throughout the show.
- Consider short games where you interact with your audience members. Prizes and contests are easy and repeatable.
- Think about duets or any other form of collaboration with other artists.
- If you're a DJ, you'll want to look into learning VJ software (video jockey software) to create animated visuals for your performances.

Booking your first gigs

Booking gigs when you're relatively unknown can be a lot of work. You'll have to find bars and venues and send them emails to book stage time. Music venues want to make money. If you want a music venue to let you play a show at their venue, you need to convince them that you're going to bring them customers. If you're wondering why the world isn't beating down your door to give you gigs, it's because you haven't yet proven yourself to be a reliable generator of money for other people. Once people see you're bringing in money, they'll start giving you business opportunities.

There's an old saying that goes like this: *"You need money to make money."* In the music and film business, the saying should be a little different. You don't need to start off with money, but you need to show that you're able to generate money. The saying should go like this: *"You need to show you can make money to make money."*

If you want to increase your chances of booking a slot at a music venue, it helps to have a show that consists of multiple artists. Music venues want an event that will attract a crowd. A larger crowd means more ticket and drink sales.

A show package consisting of several acts increases the likelihood that more people will come to the venue.

So, if you're struggling to get booked at venues, consider teaming up with other musicians. You can then go to a music venue and tell them you have a whole evening of acts ready to play. Even better, tell them how many audience members you expect your show will bring in, and what you'll do to help promote the show. When you do that, you're helping venues see the monetary value you can deliver.

Filming your shows

Every time you perform in front of a live crowd, you should consider recording your performance. You can use the footage in the future for your music videos and post the photos on your social media accounts and website. It's simple enough to do. You just need to get someone to film and take photos periodically throughout your show.

Streaming performances online

If you're considering filming your show, why not take the next step and livestream your show as well? You can livestream on YouTube or Twitch. **Twitch** is a video platform to record live video streaming rather than edited videos. If you livestream your video, you have the benefit of live audience engagement. You can deliver online performances, chat with your audience throughout your show, give live Q&As, and receive donations directly. You can visit Twitch at `https://www.twitch.tv/`.

Another option is **Patreon**. Patreon is a subscription-based model. On Patreon, users pay a subscription fee to you. In return, you provide videos, written media, lessons, or whatever else you want to offer your subscribers. Patreon then takes a small percentage of the profits. You can visit Patreon at `https://www.patreon.com/`.

You now know how to get the most out of your performances. Next, let's talk about self-promotion.

Collaborating with others to promote yourself

Whatever social media you pick, if you want to grow an audience base, it's a lot faster if you collaborate with other content creators.

For example, in many music videos, you'll see videos featuring other singers. Why feature another singer? Why not just do everything solo? By featuring a collaborator, you gain the opportunity to introduce your fans to your collaborator and your collaborator's fans to you. It's a win-win situation, and both of your fan bases increase.

Collaboration is extremely important in building a career in the music and film industries. It presents some golden opportunities, but you need to have the right mindset to see them. Let's take a moment to see how to get the most out of collaborating.

Lots of singers and instrumentalists are talented. There's an endless supply of talent out there. You see countless musicians do very well in TV show competitions, but you rarely hear about the contestants later. Why might this be?

If you want to have a lasting music career, you need to have a network of people supporting you and sharing each other's work. When a musician suddenly wins a TV show contest, they gain momentary fame, but they might not have developed the network to capitalize on that fame. If they have the network, it's easy and they're destined for stardom. But if not, they still have to figure out a way to consistently create and promote new content. The network and content creation part takes a lot of time and nurturing to get right. Most musicians on competition shows don't have this. The goal shouldn't be to get famous until you have a system in place to capitalize on the fame. Fame comes and goes, often by random chance. You want to make sure you're ready to capitalize on it if it comes.

Up until this chapter, everything in this book could be done on your own. You can compose, mix, and master music on your own. But if you want your music to be heard by an audience and keep them coming back, you need other people to help you. How do you get people to want to help you and refer you to opportunities?

Musicians rarely pay other musicians to work with them. Instead, they collaborate and hope to one day share the profits. Perhaps before the internet it was hard to find musicians, but now it's easy to find people who want to collaborate for very little money or even for free. When you collaborate with someone on a music-related project, take it seriously. Even though it might sound like there's no money in collaboration, don't take it lightly. Every collaboration is potentially a golden opportunity. Musicians learn about business opportunities and get referred through other musicians. Friends help friends. You need music friends.

Of course, a song will be lacking when you're brought in to help. If the song were already perfect, they wouldn't need your collaboration. Collaboration is the musician's version of an informal interview, whether you know it or not. If you're a singer or musician and you agree to collaborate with someone else on a project, treat it as though your boss at work gave you a direct order with the highest priority. Deliver above and beyond, and on schedule. Countless times, I encounter a singer who is very talented, but I can't refer them to opportunities because through collaborating with them, I've discovered I can't rely on them.

Unconvinced? Let's look at a scenario I frequently encounter when producing music for singers. Let's say I have two singers working on songs in the early experimental stages of the song-creation process. We have a very basic song beat but it's lacking, and we don't know whether the song will go anywhere.

Singer number 1 is extremely talented: she has the looks, the stage presence... she's got the whole package. But she's difficult to work with. It's frustrating talking with her over phone calls and emails, she rarely gives updates on how her part of the song is coming, delivers the vocals weeks later than she said she would, and sends in only one version of the vocals with no variations.

Singer number 2 is a decent vocalist; she's inexperienced but really pleasant to work with. The initial vocals she sent in were good but not great, but she sent lots of variations to try to improve with several attempts. She's super-responsive to phone calls and emails, keeps everyone updated throughout her work, and delivers the vocals on time. When the song is released, she comes up with a creative way to promote the song on her social media channels.

Who do you think I'm going to call on when I have a future song that needs a singer? Who do you think I'm going to refer to other music producers? Who do you think I'm going to refer for events and promotional opportunities? I'm going to pick singer number 2 over singer number 1 every time. I can rely on singer 2. I trust her. She's going to make me look good because she's great to work with, so I want to do everything I can to promote her. When we refer great people, it makes us look good and strengthens our reputation. Every time I promote her, part of that publicity trickles back to the promoter. It's a win-win situation.

In order for people to refer you, they need to be able to trust and rely on you. Trust is built when you collaborate with others, no matter how big or small the project is or whether there's money or not. The relationship is tested throughout. Even if the current project is a flop, the relationship could result in an opportunity later.

Long story short, go out of your way to collaborate with new people on projects and then deliver above and beyond what's expected to show that you are someone who delivers.

Getting more views on YouTube

On YouTube, if you want to get views you need to create content to entice people to click on the video and watch. Over time, there's been a few common trends on the most successful YouTube channels. Many of the largest YouTube channels use some combination of the following content in their video:

- People reacting to things
- Money-related content

- Pranks
- Challenges that people participate in
- Famous people featuring in the video
- Sex appeal
- Drama

If you can blend a combination of the preceding topics together in your video, you have a better chance of getting more views. Note that all this can be done on little to no budget and doesn't require complicated video effects. All that's required is a little creativity and planning. Even if you do have access to big-budget film shoots, if you want to have a video that reaches a large audience on YouTube, it helps to incorporate this kind of content.

What about YouTube video titles and thumbnails?

Viewers find videos through their titles and thumbnails. Videos with titles that are short and snappy and have shock value tend to result in more clicks. Also, thumbnail images showing people reacting to something also tend to get more views.

TikTok for musicians

TikTok is a video platform for phone and web. It's a useful tool for artists to promote their content and build their fanbase.

How does TikTok work? When a video is uploaded to TikTok, it is randomly shown to a bunch of users, slipping into the video feed between popular videos. If users engage with the video such as watching, commenting, sharing, and downloading it, then the video is promoted to more viewers. Due to the way the algorithm promotes new content, videos on TikTok can potentially reach a high number of viewers even if you have no prior existing followers.

When a user first opens the app, they are shown the **ForYou** page, which is a feed of videos that TikTok recommends to them. The more you use the app, the more personalized the video recommendations become. The algorithm recommends videos to you based on your interaction with videos, accounts followed, comments you posted, and content you created. It also takes into consideration captions, sounds, hashtags, language settings, and country location.

Here are some general guidelines and suggestions for musicians creating video content for TikTok:

- Find a niche. The TikTok algorithm identifies content that viewers have previously watched and shows them similar content.

- Identify trending content and create a related video to join in on the trends. Follow the #trendalert and #tiktokchallenge hashtags to figure out what the current trend is.
- Music video teaser videos.
- Duets.
- Creating music out of household objects.
- Dancing to your own music.
- Demo versus the final version of your song so people can hear the before and after.
- The story behind your song.
- Consider replying to user comments in a video.
- Show behind-the-scenes footage such as your show or music video.

You now know how to promote yourself through collaboration and social media. Next, let's learn how to create visuals.

Creating album artwork using AI art generators (Stable Diffusion)

Whenever you release a song, you need artwork. Great artwork can be instrumental in promoting the song on social media. There are many ways to create album artwork and tons of resources to create art, such as https://www.canva.com/ and https://create.vista.com/ or by hiring artists, but I want to direct your attention to a method of art creation using artificial intelligence that has recently become available.

Stable Diffusion is an open source **artificial intelligence (AI)** art generator. Stable Diffusion is one of the leaders in AI art generators, but there are lots of competitors popping up in the market, such as **Midjourney** and Adobe's **Firefly** (https://firefly.adobe.com/), and even big companies like Microsoft are developing their own version of AI art generators.

Stable Diffusion is available either online at https://stablediffusionweb.com or as a downloadable app on your phone. Any artwork created by Stable Diffusion is open source and falls under the CC0 1.0 Universal Public Domain Dedication.

Let's take a look at using the website version of Stable Diffusion.

On the site, you'll find a text input prompt allowing you to enter the type of art you want to create.

Figure 13.1 – Stable Diffusion

Enter a text prompt for the art you want to create. Once you've finished typing up your prompt, press **Generate image**; it will start creating your art. An example is shown as follows:

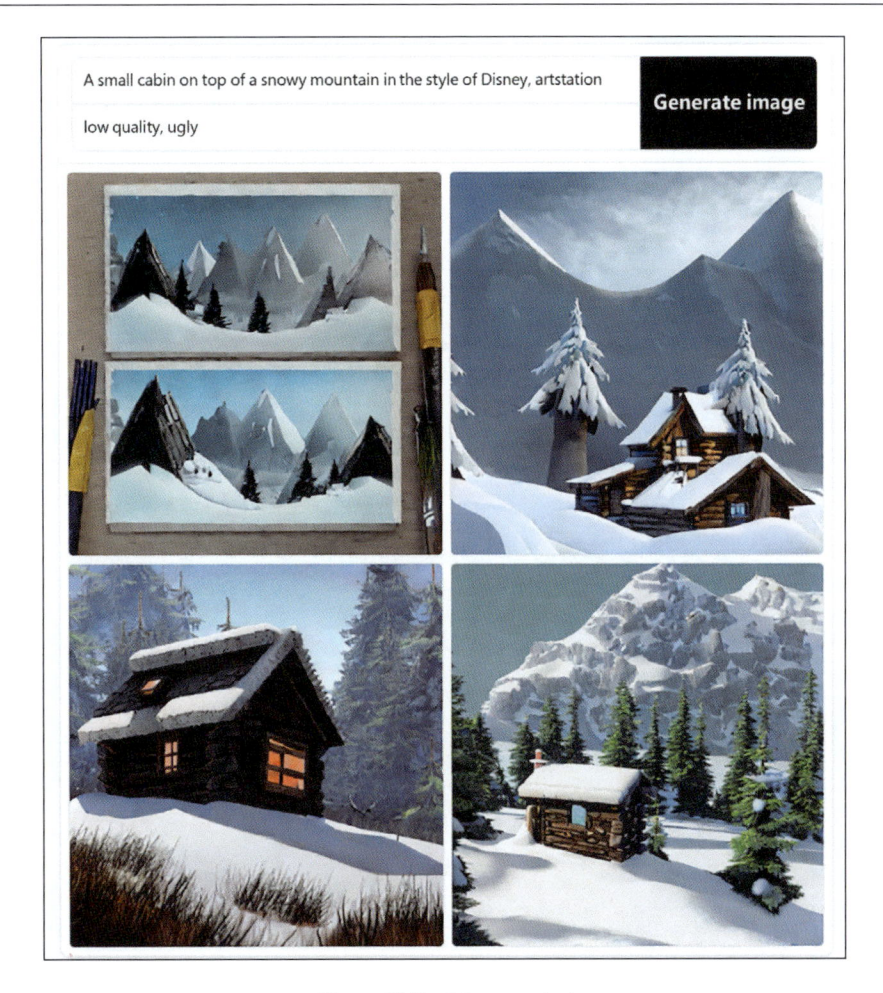

Figure 13.2 – Art generated

Ta-da! The artwork has been generated.

The type and quality of the images depend on the word choice of the prompt you enter. If you want assistance inputting better prompts to get better art results, there are lots of examples that can be found at `https://stablediffusionweb.com/prompts`.

> This is just a taste of what Stable Diffusion offers. If you want to learn more, I teach a full course on creating artwork with artificial intelligence using Stable Diffusion, available at: https://www.chestersky.com/stable-diffusion-masterclass/.

We've learned how to create static album art. Next, let's learn how to create music video visuals with **ZGameEditor Visualizer**.

Creating music visuals with ZGameEditor Visualizer

When you're playing a song, you always need a visual. In the long term, you'll need to invest time and effort into learning about video creation or collaborate with someone who does.

In the short term, when you're just getting started, there's a free tool in FL Studio that can easily generate decent animations called **ZGameEditor Visualizer**. It allows you to sync your music to video and text and add visual effects.

Let's learn how to create animations with ZGameEditor Visualizer:

1. Create a new project and import your finished song into the playlist. You'll want a new FL Studio project as **ZGameEditor Visualizer** can be quite CPU-intensive.
2. On the master bus mixer channel, load up the **ZGameEditor Visualizer** effect plugin:

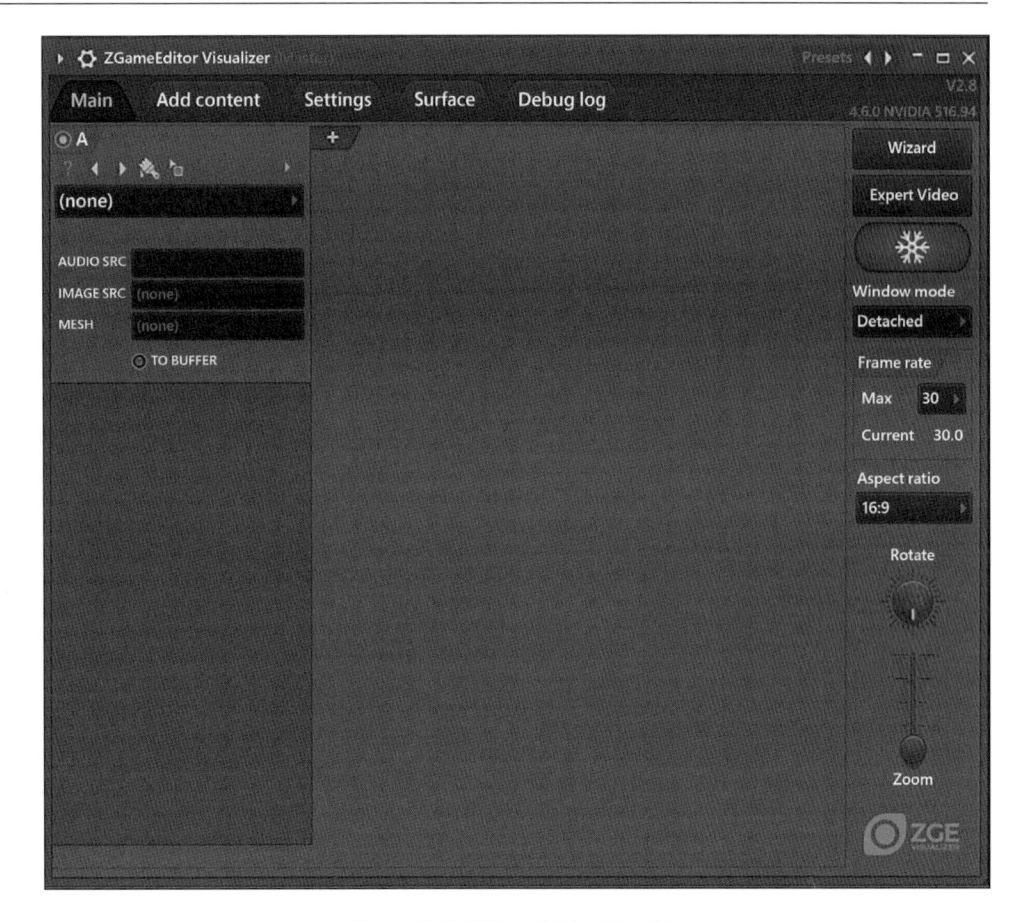

Figure 13.3 – ZGameEditor Visualizer

ZGameEditor Visualizer allows you to load videos, images, and effects in layers. Although you can create animations from scratch, there's an easy way to get up and running quickly using the wizard.

3. Click on the **Wizard** button in the top-right corner. You'll see a window pop up, similar to the following screenshot:

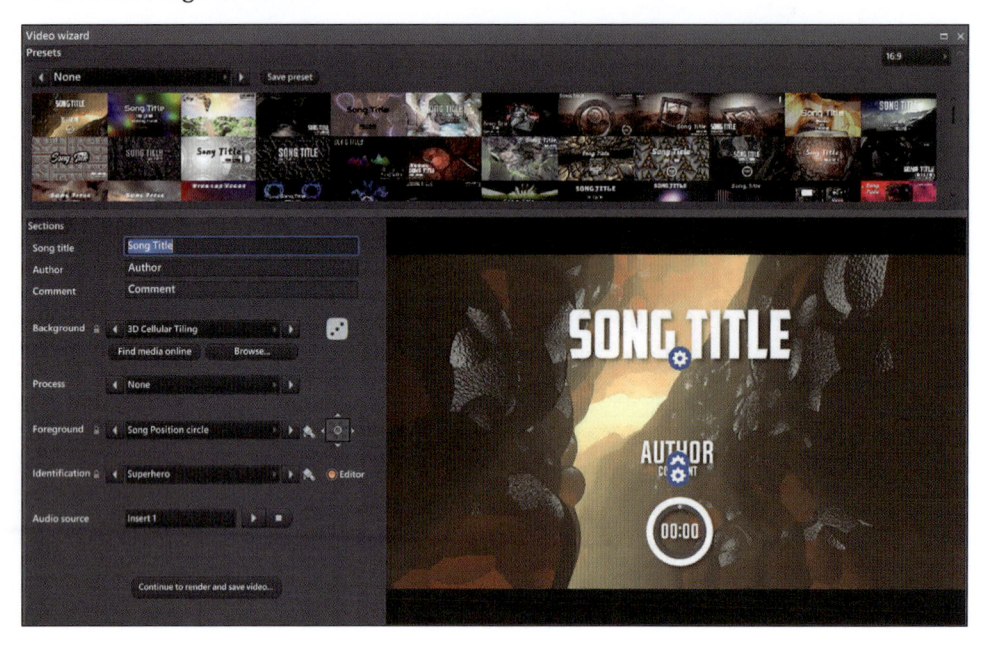

Figure 13.4 – Video wizard

The video wizard allows you to easily add a video or image background and overlay it with a foreground animation and text.

4. At the top, you can see a list of presets that you can scroll through. Under the **Sections** header, you can add your **Song title**, **Author**, and **Comment** settings. **Background** lets you choose between using a picture or video on your computer or media online. If you choose **Find media online**, you'll see a window with free photo and video media that you can use in your visuals, as shown in the following screenshot:

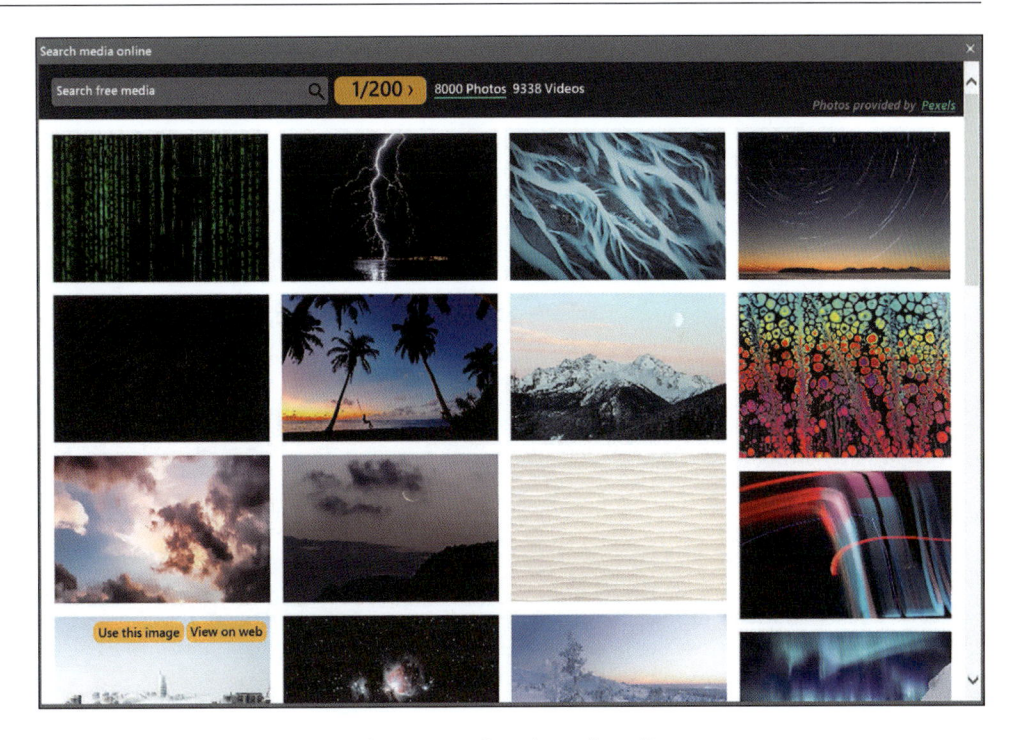

Figure 13.5 – Search media online

Process throws an effect onto your visual. **Foreground** lets you choose an audio-reacting animation visual. To the right of the foreground presets, you can see a **Select Color** paintbrush icon to let you choose your color, and an **X / Y Position** control to let you choose where to position the animation on the screen.

Identification lets you choose the type of font you want for your text. To the right of the font presets, you can use the **Select Color** paintbrush icon to choose a color for your font. **Audio source** lets you choose which audio source you want to use.

Your visual doesn't have to be perfect yet; you can customize everything later. Just find something that you like; that's good enough for now.

5. When you're finished, select the **Continue to render and save video...** option. The following window will pop up, allowing you to choose your export video format:

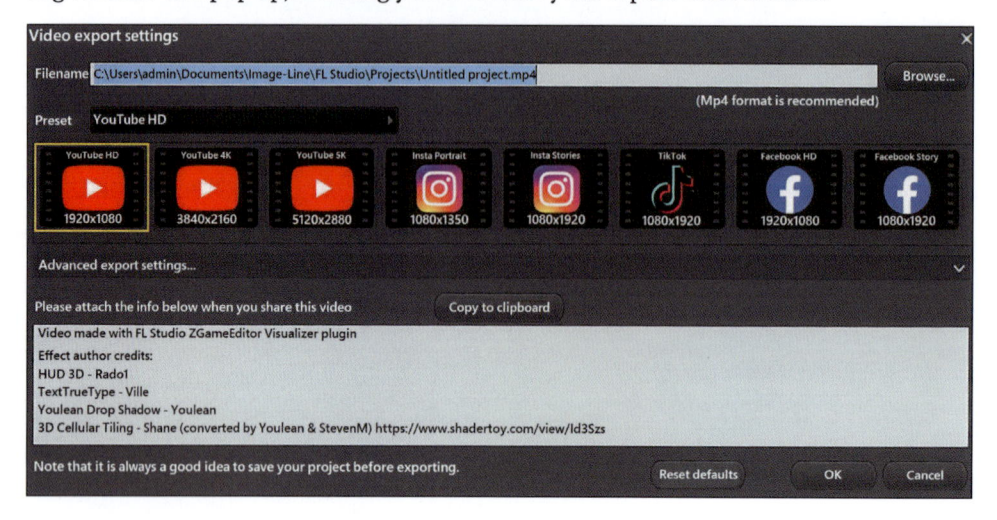

Figure 13.6 – Video export settings

6. Choose the filename location. Under **Advanced export settings**, there are additional controls:

    - Higher **Resolution** and **Video bitrate** values will result in better video quality but larger video files.
    - **Video codec** allows you to choose between H.264 and MPEG-4 files. H.264 files result in higher video quality.
    - The **Uncompressed video** button results in no video compression and huge file sizes. Don't select this.
    - **2x supersample** results in better video quality but takes longer to render.
    - **Audio codec** uses MP3 by default, but you can use FLAC for lossless audio if you plan to use it in another video editor.
    - Higher **Audio bitrate** results in higher audio quality but a larger file size.

7. If you're happy with the video footage, you can choose your desired export format and choose **OK** and your video will begin exporting. If you want to customize your visual more, select **Cancel**. You'll return to the **Main** tab.

8. You'll notice that the **Main** tab of **ZGameEditor Visualizer** has become filled with effects. These effects were added based on what you chose in the video wizard:

Chapter 13

Figure 13.7 – Effects loaded

You can customize any of these effects. The effect layers apply from left to right, with the rightmost layer affecting layers to the left of it.

9. At the top of each effect, you can see the effect selector, as shown in the preceding figure. Here you choose the effect to apply. **AUDIO SRC** sets the audio to use in the effect.

IMAGE SRC sets the media to use in your effect. Here, you can view images or videos that have been already imported into ZGameEditor Visualizer. If you want to use new media, you'll need to navigate to the **Add content** tab and import your media there.

MESH applies 3D meshes that you may have imported. Underneath **MESH**, you'll see the list of effect controls. You can adjust the controls to customize your visual. You can right-click on any control and automate it in the playlist to turn it up or down throughout your song.

10. In the **Add content** panel, you'll see a list of options, as shown in the following screenshot:

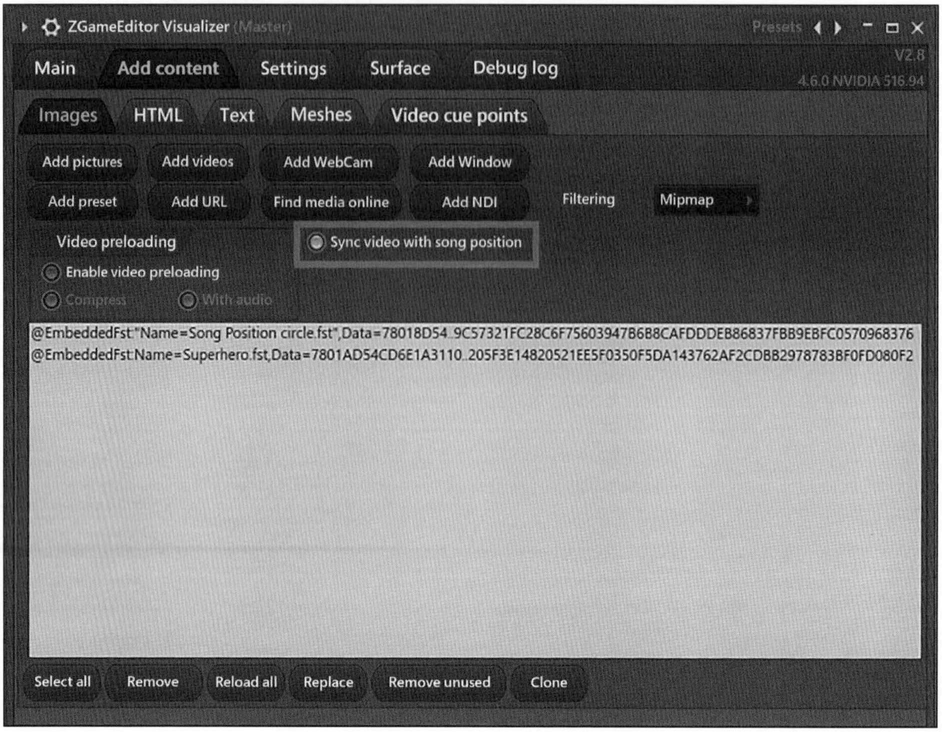

Figure 13.8 – The Add content panel

Here you can import images and video, or even record your web camera for media to be used in your effects on the **Main** tab. If you choose the **Add URL** option, you can grab an image online. There's also an option called **Add Window**, which lets you grab a video playthrough of your mixer, playlist, piano roll, or channel rack while the song is playing.

Note that you'll want to make sure that the **Sync video with song position** setting is selected so that your video always plays in time with your music.

11. When you're finished, go back to the **Main** tab and choose the **Export Video** button on the far right to export.

Congratulations! You now have visuals for your songs.

Summary

In this chapter, we learned about branding, promotion, and marketing. The more effective you are at using these tools, the more publicity and interest you will generate for your music and business.

We discussed choosing an artist identity and an artist name. We discussed preparation for live show performances and booking gigs. We looked at tips to create content on social media platforms and use collaboration as a means of promoting yourself.

We looked at creating album artwork with Stable Diffusion. If you want to go further in learning to create art with artificial intelligence using Stable Diffusion, I offer a full course on the subject at `https://www.chestersky.com/stable-diffusion-masterclass/`. Finally, we learned about creating music video visuals using FL Studio's ZGameEditor Visualizer.

In the next chapter, we'll look at monetizing, selling, and registering your music.

14

Publishing and Selling Music Online

It's never been easier to sell music and collect royalties. **Performance Rights Organizations (PROs)** help you collect royalties from music performances. Digital distribution companies help you sell and stream your music online. In a few minutes, you can release your music online to the world and collect royalty revenues. In the upcoming pages, you'll learn how.

In this chapter, we'll discuss the following topics:

- Registering your music with PROs to collect royalties
- Tagging your music in preparation for distribution
- Selling music on online stores and streaming services using digital distribution companies
- Claiming revenue from songs on YouTube using AdRev

Registering your music

Before uploading your songs and selling them online, you should first register your music with a collection society. Registering your music is how you get paid royalties.

There are different types of royalties that you can collect. How these royalties get retrieved by PROs can be very complex and goes beyond the scope of this book. However, it's straightforward to collect royalties. To ensure you're fully covered for global royalty collection, you should register your music on four platforms that we will introduce you to in this chapter. If you register with all four of these, you should be able to fully collect royalties:

- Register your music as a songwriter with a collection society/PRO (for example, Broadcast Music, Inc. (BMI), or The American Society of Composers, Authors and Publishers (ASCAP) if you're in the US).

- Register your music on SoundExchange to collect digital royalties such as those on Pandora, SiriusXM, and webcasters. Depending on your geographic region, there may be a similar/alternative service to SoundExchange that can collect your digital royalties.

- Register your music with a publishing administrator to collect from global performance and mechanical societies such as Songtrust, or alternatively, get signed with a record label that will manage your publishing royalties.

- Register with a digital distributor (for example, DistroKid or CD Baby) to release your song on streaming platforms and online stores.

First let's talk about registering your music with a music collection society, also known as a PRO. Whenever your music is played in a television show, commercial, movie, video game, or live venue, royalties are paid. PROs collect these royalties. Using the information that you input on the PRO website, PROs trace the music back to you and then distribute the royalty payments to you.

PROs are how you collect royalties from live performance usage. However, this isn't how you collect most of the royalties from online sales or streaming. We'll come to that later in this chapter.

On a PRO website, you will be asked to create an account and list information about your song. For example, they'll ask you for the song name, when it was created, and who was involved in the creation of the song.

The PRO you register with will depend on the country you are located in. For example, in the United States, you would register with one of the following organizations:

- **ASCAP:** https://www.ascap.com/
- **BMI:** https://www.bmi.com/
- **Global Music Rights (GMR):** https://globalmusicrights.com/

You only need to pick one of these organizations to register your music. Which one should you pick? They offer different features and are catered to different clients. Here's a blog comparing them: www.infamousmusician.com/ascap-vs-bmi-vs-sesac-vs-gmr.

In Canada, you register with the **Society of Composers, Authors and Music Publishers of Canada (SOCAN)** (http://www.socan.com/). This still registers you on either BMI or ASCAP at the end of the day, but you need to go through SOCAN if you are Canadian.

If you are in another country, you need to look up the relevant PRO for your geographic region.

In addition to PROs, you should register your music on **SoundExchange** or your country's equivalent service. SoundExchange collects digital performance royalties generated by master recordings on behalf of master owners and performers. When digital content is played online, such as on Pandora, SiriusXM, and webcasters, digital royalty fees are allocated to the rights holders and featured artists. SoundExchange collects these royalties for you.

In order to collect and manage your publishing royalties, you can register your music with **Songtrust**. Songtrust registers songs on behalf of songwriters/publishers with PROs, mechanical collection societies, and digital services worldwide to collect publishing royalties for you.

> Songtrust is available at https://www.songtrust.com/.
>
> SoundExchange is available at https://www.soundexchange.com/.
>
> An article discussing whether Songtrust is a good investment for you can be found at https://passivepromotion.com/what-artists-should-know-about-songtrust.

Tagging your music in preparation for distribution

Before uploading your music online, you should correctly tag it. What's a tag? If you navigate to a song on your computer or phone, you'll see a list of information about the song, such as the name, track number, album, artist, and so on. That information is imprinted upon the file. These are **tags**, also known as **metadata**. In the following screenshot, you can see tag information on songs:

Figure 14.1 – Song tags

You can add custom tags to your songs. The easiest way to do so is with tagging software. I recommend the free tag editor Mp3tag for your songs, which is available at www.mp3tag.de/en.

Chapter 14

When you open up Mp3tag, you'll see a screen like the following:

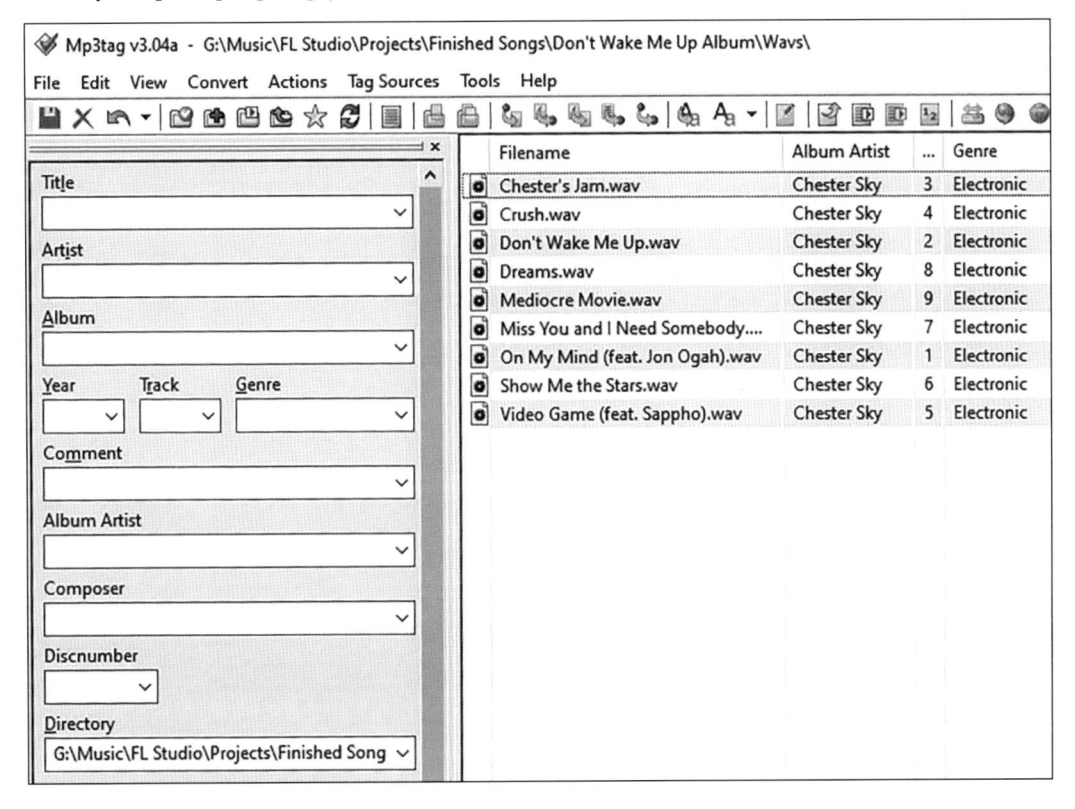

Figure 14.2 – Mp3tag

Mp3tag allows you to add tags for your songs such as **Title, Artist, Album,** and a cover image. The cover image should be square. The image you use for the cover should be a small file size. The size of the image is added to the size of the song. Every time you send the song, the image gets sent along with it, so for speed and convenience's sake, keep your cover image file size small.

You've registered your songs with a PRO and tagged them. Now you're ready to upload your songs for online distribution.

Selling music on online stores and streaming services

Let's talk about selling your music. To sell your music, you have two main options: get signed by a major label/publisher or use a digital distribution company. Labels and publishers each have their own unique way of operating, so I can't speak for them. One way to get in contact with a label is through **LabelRadar**.

Get signed to labels using LabelRadar

If you're interested in getting your songs signed by a label, one way to get the attention of labels is to use the song submission service **LabelRadar**.

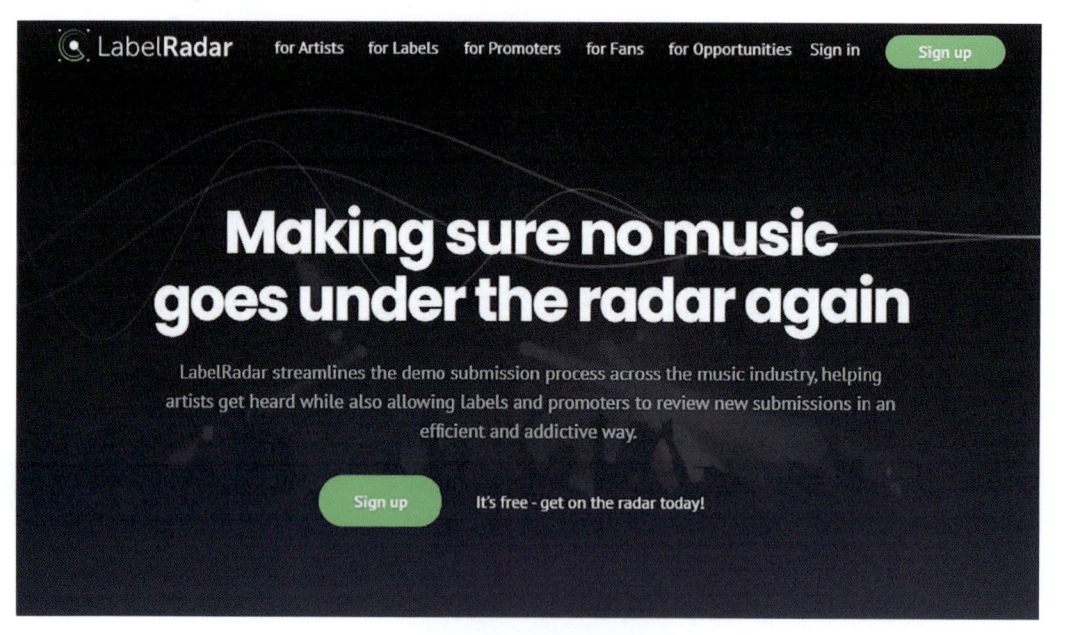

Figure 14.3 – Labelradar.com

LabelRadar is an online service that allows you to upload and submit your songs. Once you've created an account, you can upload a song and submit it to labels or music promoters. The site gives you credits every month allowing you to submit songs to labels and promoters. If you need more credits than what are provided for free, then you can pay to get more.

If you don't want to pay to submit a song, there is another option. If you're interested in a specific label, the site gives you links to label websites so that you can do more research and reach out to them individually.

Some big-name labels listen to music submissions on the LabelRadar platform, including **Monstercat, Armada Music, Ninety9Lives, CloudKid, Blanco y Negro Music, Soave Records**, and **Anjunabeats/Anjunadeep**. If you're a label or a music promoter, you can use LabelRadar to receive new song submissions.

The following is a link to a list of music labels that you can submit songs to using LabelRadar: `https://www.labelradar.com/our-labels`.

Alternatively, if you don't want to submit a song to a label, but just want some music promotion, LabelRadar offers a list of music promoters to whom you can submit your music. Here's a link to a list of music promoters using LabelRadar: `https://www.labelradar.com/our-promoters`.

You can also apply to music contests such as song remix contests. Contest rewards are usually monetary prizes, music gear, song and artist promotion, and getting your name out to labels.

There's no guarantee that the labels will like your song submission. You can increase your chances of being considered by labels by building up a strong artist portfolio and web presence ahead of time. Labels are more likely to want you if you have some kind of fan base and following. Having lots of preexisting fans will put you in a better negotiating position when a label reaches out to you.

Selling music as an independent artist

What if you don't want to submit your songs to labels and want to try self-releasing your music as an independent artist?

In the past, when you wanted to get your music into an online store, you had to upload your songs manually one store at a time. Those days are gone. These days, you upload your songs to a digital distribution company. The digital distribution company publishes your music to lots of online stores and streaming services at once, collects the revenue, and pays it out to you. There are lots of online services that can do this for you. Here are some examples of them:

- **DistroKid** (`https://distrokid.com/`)
- **LANDR** (`https://www.landr.com/`)
- **CD Baby** (`https://cdbaby.com/`)
- **TuneCore** (`https://www.tunecore.com/`)
- **Ditto Music** (`https://www.dittomusic.com/`)
- **Loudr** (`https://www.crunchbase.com/organization/loudr`)
- **Record Union** (`https://www.recordunion.com/`)
- **ReverbNation** (`https://www.reverbnation.com/`)

- **Symphonic** (https://symphonicdistribution.com/)
- **iMusician** (https://imusician.pro/en/)
- **The Orchard** (they work with labels only) (https://www.theorchard.com/)
- **AWAL** (selected applications only) (https://www.awal.com/)

All of these services essentially do the same thing and you only need one of them. They allow you to upload your music, distribute the songs to online stores and streaming platforms, and collect the revenue for you. I recommend comparing the features they offer before enrolling as each has its own niche.

At the time of writing, I use the digital distribution company **DistroKid**. It seems to be one of the cheapest options for me personally. It lets you upload an unlimited amount of songs for a fixed annual fee and lets you keep 100% of the royalties that it receives. The store selling the music takes a cut of the royalties, but that's before it gets to DistroKid. If you want, DistroKid allows you to split up the royalties it receives by percentage and send them to collaborators you worked with on your songs.

If you choose to use DistroKid, the following link provides you with a discount for your first year: https://distrokid.com/vip/seven/701180.

DistroKid walk-through

Let's take a tour of a digital distribution company service so you know what you're getting yourself into. In this demo, we'll use DistroKid. If you pick a different service than DistroKid, your layout will look different, but the same overall features will be present.

DistroKid allows you to upload your songs and release them on online stores and streaming services. You can upload your music, album art, song details, and song lyrics. It allows you to track earnings from each service and distribute earnings to song collaborators.

Chapter 14   411

So, let's take a look:

1. When you sign in to DistroKid, you'll see a list of all the albums and songs you've released:

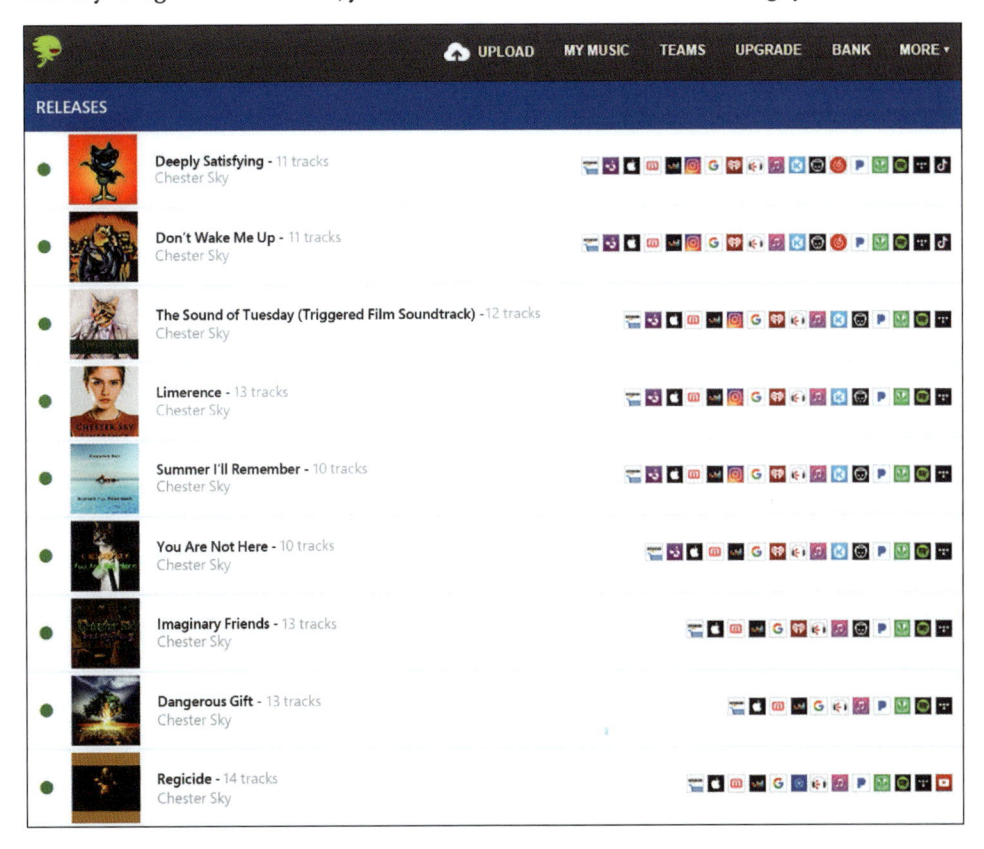

Figure 14.4 – DistroKid dashboard

2. If you go to the **UPLOAD** tab, you'll see a page allowing you to upload songs to online stores and streaming platforms:

Figure 14.5 – Uploading a song

3. DistroKid lets you enter information related to the song description, such as its name, whether it features any collaborators, and its genre, so online stores can categorize it.

Chapter 14

4. If you go to the **BANK** tab, you can see information related to how much money your songs are making. There's an option to view your royalties in excruciating detail and reveal your royalty earnings down to fractions of a cent:

REPORTING MONTH	SALE MONTH	STORE	ARTIST	TITLE	QUANTITY	SONG/ALBUM	CUSTOMER PAID	COUNTRY OF SALE	EARNINGS (USD)
Oct 2017	Aug 2017	Spotify	Chester Sky	Janitor Man	8	Song	n/a	CA	$0.029594675595 95% of team
Oct 2017	Aug 2017	Spotify	Chester Sky	Janitor Man	2	Song	n/a	GB	$0.013175711738 95% of team
Oct 2017	Aug 2017	Spotify	Chester Sky	Delicate Snowflake	8	Song	n/a	CA	$0.029594675595 95% of team
Oct 2017	Aug 2017	Spotify	Chester Sky	Delicate Snowflake	1	Song	n/a	FR	$0.005453949525 95% of team
Oct 2017	Aug 2017	Spotify	Chester Sky	I Hate Dubstep	6	Song	n/a	CA	$0.022195446743 95% of team
Oct 2017	Aug 2017	Spotify	Chester Sky	Eruption	7	Song	n/a	CA	$0.025894501215 95% of team
Oct 2017	Aug 2017	Spotify	Chester Sky	A Charming State of Confusion	12	Song	n/a	CA	$0.044390893485 95% of team
Oct 2017	Aug 2017	Spotify	Chester Sky	A Charming State of Confusion	2	Song	n/a	CA	$0.002875922460 95% of team

Figure 14.6 – Royalties earned

5. You can filter by date, artist, album, and type of store, and download the information to an Excel sheet.

You now know how to sell your songs through digital distribution companies.

Claiming revenue from songs on YouTube using AdRev

When someone plays a video on YouTube that uses your song without obtaining permission, you can claim revenue from the video. You don't have to do any of the work yourself. YouTube algorithms behind the scenes detect when your song is playing in a video and mark the video as using your song. Any ad revenue the video was generating then gets collected for you. If you're looking for more information about this, YouTube uses the terminology **ContentID** to refer to claiming revenue from videos.

ContentID monetizing is done using a service called AdRev. It's the official service for registering music on YouTube. Some digital distribution companies may include using YouTube AdRev in their features, but if not, you can do this yourself for free.

> If you signed up for Songtrust, it can claim revenue for you and you don't have to register your music on AdRev.
>
> AdRev is available at `https://adrev.net/`.

Contacting AdRev support is also how you notify YouTube to not claim the ad revenue from a video (for example, if someone paid you to use your music in a video and got your permission). On AdRev, you can whitelist your own YouTube channel so that it doesn't interfere with any YouTube channel revenue. Whitelisting means that AdRev won't claim monetization on a specific video or YouTube channel. If you want to submit your music to music promoter YouTube channels, they'll likely want you to whitelist their YouTube channels to play your songs.

Note that if you start claiming monetization whenever a YouTube video plays your song, it might dissuade YouTubers from using your song in their videos. So, there's a tradeoff you'll have to consider. If you want to be paid every time someone plays your song on YouTube, AdRev is the tool for you. If you don't mind people freely using your music and just want your song to get out there, maybe you don't need AdRev.

What's the risk? If you don't register your music on AdRev, there is always the risk that some unscrupulous person may register your song on AdRev and try to claim monetization even though they didn't create the song. This scenario happened with musician *TheFatRat*. People registered his songs and claimed YouTube monetization on them. If this is something you want to avoid, then you should register your songs with AdRev before releasing them. You can always whitelist an individual YouTube channel through AdRev.

On AdRev, you will come across the option to upload songs to YouTube Premium. Be aware that your digital distribution company may already have uploaded songs to YouTube Premium. If so, you don't need to do it here. In addition, if you upload to YouTube Premium using AdRev and also through your digital distribution company, you will see duplicates of your songs on YouTube.

When you log in to AdRev, you'll see a screen like the following where you can upload your songs:

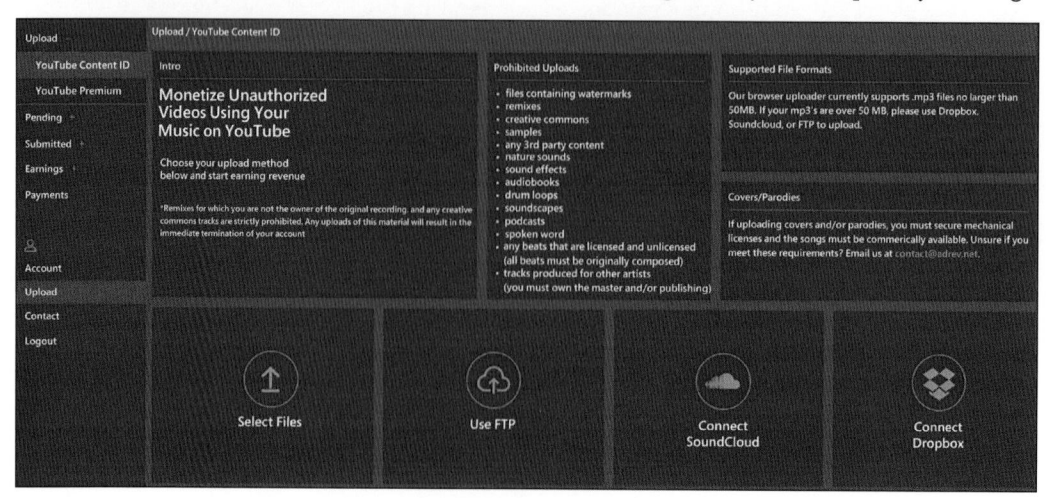

Figure 14.7 – AdRev

Once you've uploaded your songs, you'll need to enter information about them, such as the following:

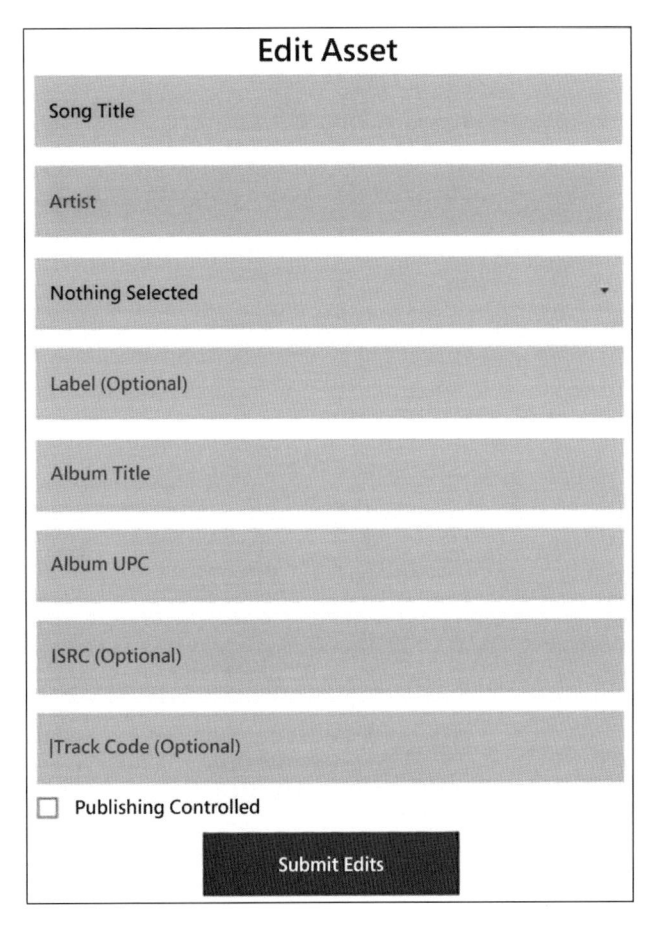

Figure 14.8 – Editing song information

On the form, two of the form boxes are for **Album UPC** and **ISRC**. You can find this information on your digital distribution company's (such as DistroKid's) website. Your digital distribution company automatically assigns ISRC numbers and UPC numbers to your songs and albums when you upload the songs.

What are ISRC, ISWC, and UPC codes?

ISRC, ISWC, and UPC numbers help PROs and music distributors identify songs to trace song usage. You can think of them as your song barcode numbers.

ISRC stands for **International Standard Recording Code**. Every song receives a unique ISRC number. If you have a label or publisher, they handle getting the code. If you use an online distribution company service such as DistroKid, they provide the ISRC code. Here's an example of one of my song's ISRC codes: `QZ-K6H-20-73696`.

The first two characters stand for the country code. The next three characters are issued by the ISRC agency and may reflect the record label/distributor or release number. The next two digits refer to the issue date; in this case, it was released in the year 2020. The last five digits are a unique identifier for the person or company.

ISWC stands for **International Standard Musical Work Code**. It's assigned by a collection society such as ASCAP in North America. It refers to a collection of musical works. It's used to identify a song title, songwriters, music publishers, and song splits. If you need to figure out what your ISWC number is, contact your country's collection society.

UPC stands for **Universal Product Code**. It's the code printed on products to identify them and is used to scan at the checkout counter at stores. Your digital distribution company website usually assigns your released album a UPC code. Here's an example of one of my albums' UPC values: `195596 62921 3`.

The first six digits identify the manufacturer of the product. The next five digits are the item's unique identifier. The last digit is called the check digit and is used in calculations to confirm to the checkout scanner that the UPC is valid.

You now know how to sell your music online and claim revenue.

Summary

In this chapter, you learned about publishing and selling music online. You learned how to register your music to collect royalties from live performances. You learned how to tag music to prepare it for distribution. You learned how to sell your music on online stores and streaming services. Finally, you learned how to claim revenue from YouTube videos using your music.

Share your music

If you'd like to share your music with other readers and students and ask for feedback, feel free to post your music in the following Facebook group: `https://www.facebook.com/groups/musicproducerandcomposercommunity`.

Conclusion

Our book has come to an end... but your music journey has just begun. You can now produce songs like an FL Studio pro and kick off your music career.

I hope you had a fascinating time learning about music production throughout this book. You're now up to date with the latest and greatest cutting-edge tools on the market. A few decades ago, people couldn't even imagine doing what you're now capable of.

A few final thoughts:

Music is meant to be shared. You can take influences from lots of sources and combine them to make something original. If you need ideas, try combining genres.

When you make something, be proud of it. Having a little ego at stake makes you strive to be better. Make something that you care about.

If your music isn't connecting, try changing the context the music is delivered in. For example, consider experimenting with different names and visuals. Often the presentation of your music shapes how it gets received.

Create lots of music; it's the only way to get good. If you make something that you or others don't like, don't dwell on it. It's okay, just learn from it and start thinking about what you want to make next. Remember, making music should be fun. If it doesn't feel like fun, you're doing it wrong. Good luck.

More from the author

Feel free to get in touch and check out the rest of my courses and products:

- **Website:** https://www.chestersky.com/
- **Facebook:** https://www.facebook.com/realchestersky
- **Instagram:** https://www.instagram.com/iamchestersky
- **Twitter:** https://twitter.com/realchestersky

Courses I offer:

- Music production: https://www.chestersky.com/music-producer-masterclass/
- Soundtrack composing: https://www.chestersky.com/soundtrack-composer-masterclass/
- Generating art using artificial intelligence: https://www.chestersky.com/stable-diffusion-masterclass/

If you liked this book, you'll like my book *Music for Film and Game Soundtracks with FL Studio*: https://www.amazon.com/dp/180323329X.

Figure 14.9 – Music for Film and Game Soundtracks with FL Studio

In the book, you'll learn the business of composing and how to communicate, score, market your services, land gigs, and deliver music projects for clients like a professional. Next, you'll set up your studio environment, navigate key tools, such as the channel rack, piano roll, playlist, mixer, and browser, and export songs. The book then advances to show you how to compose orchestral music using MIDI programming, with a dedicated section on string instruments. You'll create sheet music using MuseScore for live musicians to play your compositions. Later, you'll learn about the art of Foley for recording realistic sound effects, creating adaptive music that changes throughout video games, and designing music to trigger specific emotions, for example, scary music to terrify your listener. Finally, you'll work on a sample project that will help you prepare for your composing career.

By the end of this book, you'll be able to create professional soundtrack scores for your films and video games.

Further reading

If you want to go further and learn more about the business side of a music career, I highly recommend the book *How to Make It in the New Music Business: Practical Tips on Building a Loyal Following and Making a Living as a Musician,* by Ari Herstand (ISBN-10: 1631491504). This book is hands down the best book I've read on the music business. I cannot recommend it enough.

You may be wondering, how exactly do royalties get collected and what share of royalties do you get? On the surface, this sounds like a simple question. It turns out the legal details are really complex. If you want to learn how royalties are collected, read the book *All You Need to Know about the Music Business,* by Donald Passman (ISBN-10: 1501122185).

‹packt›

packt.com

Subscribe to our online digital library for full access to over 7,000 books and videos, as well as industry leading tools to help you plan your personal development and advance your career. For more information, please visit our website.

Why subscribe?

- Spend less time learning and more time coding with practical eBooks and Videos from over 4,000 industry professionals
- Improve your learning with Skill Plans built especially for you
- Get a free eBook or video every month
- Fully searchable for easy access to vital information
- Copy and paste, print, and bookmark content

At www.packt.com, you can also read a collection of free technical articles, sign up for a range of free newsletters, and receive exclusive discounts and offers on Packt books and eBooks.

Other Books You May Enjoy

If you enjoyed this book, you may be interested in these other books by Packt:

Music for Film and Game Soundtracks with FL Studio

Joshua Au-Yeung

ISBN: 9781803233291

- Compose production-ready music for films and video games
- Plan and deliver a soundtrack music score for clients like a professional
- Apply practical music theory using themes, leitmotifs, scales, and modes
- Compose orchestral music with MIDI programming
- Design music for specific emotions
- Create sheet music with MuseScore, score music for films with Fruity Video Player, and make diegetic music
- Design interactive music by leveraging horizontal resequencing and vertical remixing

The Music Producer's Creative Guide to Ableton Live 11

Anna Lakatos

ISBN: 9781801817639

- Understand the concept of Live, the workflow of recording and editing audio and MIDI, and warping
- Use Groove, MIDI effects, and Live 11's new workflow enhancements to create innovative music
- Use audio to MIDI conversion tools to translate and generate ideas quickly
- Employ Live's automation and modulation capabilities and project organization techniques to speed up your workflow
- Utilize MIDI Polyphonic Expression to create evolving sounds and textures
- Adopt advanced techniques for production and discover the capabilities of live performance

Packt is searching for authors like you

If you're interested in becoming an author for Packt, please visit `authors.packtpub.com` and apply today. We have worked with thousands of developers and tech professionals, just like you, to help them share their insight with the global tech community. You can make a general application, apply for a specific hot topic that we are recruiting an author for, or submit your own idea.

Share your thoughts

Now you've finished *The Music Producer's Ultimate Guide to FL Studio 21, Second Edition*, we'd love to hear your thoughts! Scan the QR code below to go straight to the Amazon review page for this book and share your feedback or leave a review on the site that you purchased it from.

`https://packt.link/r/1837631654`

Your review is important to us and the tech community and will help us make sure we're delivering excellent quality content.

Index

A

AdRev
  URL 413
  used, for claiming revenue from songs on YouTube 413-415
Aeropad 312
algorithmic digital reverb plugins 193
All Plugins Bundle 7
American Society of Composers, Authors and Publishers (ASCAP)
  URL 404
amplitude 144
antinode 148
Arpeggios 52
attack, sustain, decay, and release (ASDR) 151
audio
  exporting, for third-party mixing and mastering 380, 381
  formats 378, 379
  listening, in different environments 378
  panning 191
  routing, to mixer 102-108
audio clips
  freezing 132-139
audio samples
  retiming, with Newtime 247-254
Audio Stream Input/Output (ASIO) 65, 66
automation
  applying 114-118
  applying to external third-party plugins 124
  clips, editing 118-124
  Mod X and Mod Y, using 154-160
automation, to external third-party plugins
  editor thumbnail, creating to add 128-132
  MultiLink to controllers, using to add 124-127
Autotune 243
  reference link 243

B

backing vocals effects
  best practices 256
band filter 361
bandwidth (Q) 183
Bass pattern 175
beat 91
Beats Per Minute (BPM) 92
BooBass instrument 96
brand
  artist name, selecting for 384
  creating 384
  website, creating for 385
Broadcast Music, Inc. (BMI)
  URL 404
browser
  obtaining, most out of sample packs 38, 39
  samples, adding to 40-42
  sample's file location, locating 34-36
  samples, swapping 42

searching in 36-38
using 30-34
Bucket Brigade Delay (BBD) Chorus effect 208

C

carrier 260
channel rack
  color option 47-49
  icon option 47-49
  instrument, adding to 11-15
  instrument options 50-53
  layers, using 57-59
  new instruments, installing 55, 57
  options 44, 45
  Rename option 47-49
  used, for creating drum beat 9-11
  using 42-44
  windows, detaching 53-55
channel rack layers 261
channel rack, options
  Graph editor option 45, 46
  Piano roll option 45
channels
  routing, to mixer 17-19
chord 81
chord progressions
  composing 81-90
chorus effect
  applying, to instrument 206, 207
  best practices 207
  using 206
chorus plugins 206
compression 164, 165
  applying, with Fruity Limiter 165-170
  parallel compression 170

compressor 254
condenser microphones 233
constructive interference 146
ContentID 413
Control creator 305
convolution reverb 195
  applying, with Fruity Convolver 195, 196

D

Decibels (dB) 146
de-esser plugin 255
delay 202, 256
  doubling delay 203
  ping-pong delay 203
  slapback delay 202
  stereo-widening delay 203
  straight delay 202
delay effects 347
  applying, with Fruity Delay 3 203
  best practices 205
  creating, with Multiband Delay 347-349
destructive interference 146
Detached feature 53
diaphragm 232
Digital Audio Workstations (DAWs) 2
digital reverb
  applying, with Fruity Reeverb 2 193, 194
DirectWave 39, 79
  used, for creating instruments 297-301
distortion 217
  best practices 225
  bit crushing 217
  clipping 217
  effect, applying to instrument 218-220
  harmonic distortion 217

overdrive/fuzz 217
saturation 217
tube distortion 217

DistroKid 410-413

Distructor 217-225

Doppler effect 147

doubling delay 203

drum beat
creating, with channel rack 9-11

drum kits
recording 235, 236

ducking 172

dynamic microphone 232

dynamic range 365

E

Edison
recording with 240-242
used, for loop recording 242, 243

editor thumbnail
creating, to controllers to
add automation 128-132

Effectrix 288

effects rack 111-113

Electronic Dance Music (EDM) 38

equalization (EQ) 255
applying 181-184
best practices 184
general rules 185, 186

equalization, in mastering 361, 362
dynamics, adjusting 365
frequency problems, diagnosing 363
spectrograms 363, 364

event editor
used, for editing note articulations 94, 95

expanders 254
applying 170-172

external third-party plugins
automation, applying to 124

F

Fine Black 305

first harmonic 149

FLAC 23

flangers 210
effects, applying to instrument 211

FL Studio 5
audio, recording into 237-240
editions 6
workbench 26-29
workspace, exploring 7-9

FL Studio, editions
All Plugins Bundle 7
Fruity Edition 6
Producer Edition 6
Signature Bundle 6

FL Studio, workspace
buttons 9

formant 247

freezing 132

Frequency Shifter 338
controls 339
reference link, for video tutorial 341
ring mod settings 339, 340
sidechaining 340, 341
using 338

Frequency Splitter 349
multiband processing, with 349-353
use cases 349
used, for mastering 353-355
using 350

Index

Fruity Chorus 207
Fruity Convolver
   convolution reverb, applying with 195, 196
   reference link 197
Fruity Delay 3 203-205
   delay effects, applying with 203
Fruity Edition 6
Fruity Flanger 211
Fruity Granulizer 341
   controls 346, 347
   granular synthesis, creating with 341-345
   using 341
Fruity Limiter
   compression, applying with 165-170
Fruity parametric EQ 2 182
Fruity Phaser 212-213
Fruity Reeverb 2
   digital reverb, applying with 193, 194

G

gates 254
   applying 170-172
Glitch 2 288
glitch effects 287
   creating, with Gross Beat 288-292
Global Music Rights (GMR)
   URL 404
granular synthesis 341
   creating, with Fruity Granulizer 341-347
Graph editor option 45, 46
Gross Beat 288
   mapping time and volume effects 294, 295
   presets 292-294
   sequencer 296, 297
   time-travel envelope effect 289
   used, for creating glitch effects 288-292
   volume envelope effect 289

H

Harmless 173, 174, 314
harmonic exciters 374
Harmor 161
Harmor Classic preset 221
Hz 145

I

Imager 377
independent artist
   music, selling as 409, 410
infrasonic 145
insert mixer track 110, 111
instrument melodies
   comparing, with ghost notes 96, 97
instruments
   adding, to channel rack 11-15
   creating, sound with different pitches 147-151
   creating, with DirectWave 297-301
   playing, same pitch sound different 151
   recording 234, 235
   selecting 70-72
International Standard Musical Work Code (ISWC) 416
International Standard Recording Code (ISRC) 416
IONOS 385
   URL 385
iZotope
   URL 260

Index

iZotope's Ozone
  URL 361

J

Juno 6 Chorus I effect 208
Juno 6 Chorus II effect 208

K

Kick pattern 175
KNEE 167

L

LabelRadar
  reference link 409
  using, for get signed to labels 408, 409
limiters 374, 375
  using 179-181
list of music promoters, with LabelRadar
  reference link 409
live performances 385, 386
  gigs, booking 386
  shows, filming 387
  streaming, online 387
Local
  URL 385
longitudinal waves 145
Low Frequency Oscillator (LFO) 94, 120, 206, 281
LuxeVerb 197-202
  using 197, 198

M

main header toolbar features
  Audio Stream Input/Output (ASIO) 65, 66
  project info, viewing 66, 67
  purge unused audio clips 66
  Revert to last backup 64, 65
  undo and redo 66
  using 63
  version control 64
marketing
  essentials 383, 384
master channel 111
mastering 359, 360
  audio, listening in different environments 378
  criteria 360
  equalization 361
  music 360
  plugins 361
  practicing 360
master track 102
Maximus 366
  multiband compression, applying with 366-372
melody
  creating, with piano roll 15-17
Melodyne 243
metadata 406
microphone preamp 233
microphones 232
  condenser microphones 233
  dynamic microphone 232
  ribbon microphones 233
MID format 23
MIDI information
  passing, between instrument plugins 260, 261
MIDI notes 52
MIDI scores
  exporting 98, 99
  using 98, 99

Index

Midjourney 391
Midvore patcher 313
mix bus 225
  best practices 228, 229
  setting up 225-228
mixer
  audio, routing to 102-108
  channels, routing to 17-19
  components 108
  effect, applying 113
  effects rack 111-113
  insert mixer track 110, 111
  master channel 111
  navigating 108, 109
mixer control panel 102
mixer track 102
mixing 17, 102
Modular synthesis 301
modulator 260
Mod X and Mod Y
  points 160, 161
  using, for automation 154-160
monophonic sound 190, 191
MP3 bitrate 23
MP3 format 23
multiband compressors 366
  Maximus 366
  release time 372, 373
  usage examples 373
  using 366
Multiband Delay 347
  controls 348
  delay effects, creating with 347, 348
  using 347
multiband processing
  with Frequency Splitter 349-353
MultiLink to controllers
  using, to add automation 124-127
MultiLink to controllers feature 124
multiple notes
  selecting 72
MuseScore
  URL 98
music
  registering 403-405
  selling, as independent artist 409, 410
  selling, on online stores 408
  selling, on streaming services 408
  tagging, in preparation for distribution 406, 407
Musical Instrument Digital Interface (MIDI) 70, 260
music bars 82
musician
  career path 3, 4
music production landscape
  exploring 2, 3
music scales
  stamp tool, using to obtain assistance with 79-81
music scales, list
  reference link 81
music visuals
  creating, with ZGameEditor Visualizer 394-400

N

Native Instruments
  URL 260
Newtime
  audio samples, retiming with 247-254

Index   433

Newtone 330
   pitch correction, using with 243-246
node 148
noise gating
   need for 172
note articulations
   editing, with event editor 94, 95
notes
   adding, in piano roll 72
   deleting 73
   muting and unmuting 73, 74
   quantizing 93, 94
   slicing 74
   sliding 74-79
note's pitch
   reasons 145

O

octave 88
OGG format 23
online services
   examples 409, 410

P

panning 190
   audio 191
   best practices 192
parallel compression 170
parametric equalizer
   example 362
pass 184
Patcher 161, 354
   custom dashboards, creating 304-307
   effects, creating 301-304
   instrument, sending 308-310

Patcher presets
   exploring 310-315
Patreon 387
   URL 387
Performance Rights Organizations (PROs) 403
phantom center 190
phantom power 233
phaser effects 212
   applying, to instrument 212
piano roll
   instrument, selecting 70-72
   multiple notes, selecting 72
   notes, adding 72
   notes, deleting 73
   notes, muting and unmuting 73, 74
   notes, slicing 74
   notes, sliding 74-79
   stamp tool, using to get assistance with scales 79-81
   used, for creating melody 15-17
   using 69, 70
piano roll, with MIDI instruments
   instrument melodies, comparing with ghost notes 96, 97
   note articulations, editing with event editor 94, 95
   notes, quantizing 93, 94
   recording into 90, 91
   snap-to-grid (magnet) tool 91, 92
   velocity, using 95
ping-pong delay 203
pitch 145
pitch correction
   best practices 246, 247
   using, with Newtone 243-246

Pitcher
used, for harmonizing vocals 261-268

Pitch Shifter 330
controls 331
pitch effect, controlling with controller 333-337
using 330
voice tab controls 332, 333

playlist
element pattern options 62, 63
toolbar 61, 62
using 59-61

Plucker patcher 313

pop filter
using 237

postproduction activities 359, 360

Producer Edition 6

purge unused audio clips 66

Q

quantizing 93

R

Randomless patcher 314

RAZOR 260

recording environment
drum kits, recording 235, 236
instruments, recording 234, 235
setting up 234
vocals, preparing to record 236

Reezor patcher 314

reference tracks
using 373

resonance 210

reverb 256
using 192

reverb controls 194, 195

ribbon microphones 233

ring modulation 340

S

sample packs 38, 39

SAT (saturation) 167

saturators 374

second harmonic 150

second overtone 150

self-promotion
collaboration, with content creators 387-389
TikTok, for musicians 390-391
views, obtaining on YouTube 389-390
YouTube video titles, and thumbnails 390

sheet music
exporting 97, 98

shelf 184

sidechaining
applying 172-179

Signature Bundle 6

slapback delay 202

Slicex 94, 161, 275
using, to create vocal chops 276-285

snap-to-grid (magnet) tool 91, 92

Society of Composers, Authors and Music Publishers of Canada (SOCAN)
URL 405

song
composing, steps 4, 5

song, FL Studio
channels, routing to mixer 17-19

Index

creating 9
drum beat, creating with channel rack 9-11
exporting 19-22
exporting, options 23, 24
instrument, adding to channel rack 11-15
melody, creating with piano roll 15-17

songs, on YouTube
revenue, claiming with AdRev from 413-415

Songtrust 405

sound 143-145
creating, with different pitches using instruments 147-151
hearing, considerations 146, 147

sound envelopes
controls 154
modifying 151-154

SoundExchange 405

sound waves 143
longitudinal waves 145
transverse waves 145

spectrograms 363, 364
iZotope's Insight spectogram 365

Spectrum preset 364

SplitKit patcher 313

Stable Diffusion 391
album artwork, creating 392, 393
URL 391

stamp tool
using, to obtain assistance with scales 79-81

standing waves 147

Stereo 23

stereo imaging 376
best practices 377, 378
with vectorscopes 376, 377

stereophonic sound 190

stereo-widening delay 203
stereo width 189
stop 184
store in spare state 169
straight delay 202
Stutter Edit 288
SynthMaster 310
Sytrus 161

T

tags 406
Tail option
choices 23
tape 102
third harmonic 150
threshold 167
time-travel envelope effect 289
transients 154, 373
transverse waves 145
traveling waves 147
Twitch 387
URL 387

U

ultrasonic 145
Universal Product Code (UPC) 416
USB microphones 233

V

vectorscope 376
iZotope vectorscope 377
types 377
used, for stereo imaging 376

velocity
  using 95
VFX Sequencer 317
  advanced controls 325-327
  using 318-325
Vintage Chorus 207-210
Vintage Phaser 213-217
Virtual Studio Technology (VST) 37, 124
vocal chops
  creating 274, 275
  creating, considerations 285
  creating, with Slicex 276-285
vocal effects 255
  processing, best practices 254, 255
vocals 231
  harmonizing, with Pitcher 261-268
vocals, recording 236
  pop filters, using 237
Vocatcher patcher 314
vocoders 259, 260
  best practices 273
  using 261
Vocodex 269
  using 269-273
volume envelope effect 289

W

Wave Candy 364
WAV files 23, 380
Wobbler patcher 315, 316

Y

YottaSaw patcher 316, 317

Z

ZGameEditor Visualizer 394
  music visuals, creating with 394-400

Download a free PDF copy of this book

Thanks for purchasing this book!

Do you like to read on the go but are unable to carry your print books everywhere?

Is your eBook purchase not compatible with the device of your choice?

Don't worry, now with every Packt book you get a DRM-free PDF version of that book at no cost.

Read anywhere, any place, on any device. Search, copy, and paste code from your favorite technical books directly into your application.

The perks don't stop there, you can get exclusive access to discounts, newsletters, and great free content in your inbox daily

Follow these simple steps to get the benefits:

1. Scan the QR code or visit the link below

   https://packt.link/free-ebook/9781837631650

2. Submit your proof of purchase
3. That's it! We'll send your free PDF and other benefits to your email directly

Printed in Great Britain
by Amazon